W9-BWR-312

Spring 81

THE PSYCHOLOGY OF VIOLENCE

A JOURNAL OF
ARCHETYPE
AND
CULTURE

Spring 2009

SPRING JOURNAL
New Orleans, Louisiana

CONTENTS

CURRENT EVENTS

FILM REVIEWS

BOOK REVIEWS

CAPTAIN AMERICA AND HIS
ZEALOUS BLAST

RON SCHENK

Sigmund Freud, at some point in the mid-1920s, found himself depressed. He had cancer of the jaw, was in Berlin for a small operation, didn't think he had long to live, and was convinced that his death would be unimportant. He had written everything he wished to write, his mind carried no more, and he would be forgotten. In this state he was called upon by an acquaintance, a young American government official, William C. Bullitt (significantly named in light of the theme of this paper). Bullitt told Freud he was working on a book about the creation of the Treaty of Versailles, the culminating document of World War I, in which he, himself, had been involved. The book would contain studies of the major players including Bullitt's former boss, the American President, Woodrow Wilson. Bullitt later wrote, "Freud's eyes brightened and he became very much alive. Rapidly he asked a number of questions, which I answered. Then he astonished me by saying he would like to collaborate with me in writing the Wilson chapter of my book."[1]

Ronald Schenk, Ph.D., is a Jungian analyst practicing, teaching, and writing in Dallas and Houston. He has written three books: *The Soul of Beauty: A Psychological Investigation of Appearance,* regarding psychology as an aesthetic enterprise; *Dark Light: the Appearance of Death in Everyday Life*, a series of essays on culture and imagination; and, *The Sunken Quest, the Wasted Fisher, the Pregnant Fish: Essays in Postmodern Depth Psychology.*

Freud already had come to "detest" Wilson and had a general disgust for anything *ganz amerikanisch*.[2] Wilson had come to Europe casting himself as a messianic hero promising equitable status for all nations and everlasting peace, a task which he later framed as America's destiny. Ultimately Wilson caved in to the interests of the other Allied nations with disastrous results for world peace. What now stirred the master detective, Freud, about Wilson was the discrepancy between Wilson's arrogance and the results of his actions. Freud wrote,

> When, like Wilson, a man achieves almost the exact opposite of that which he wished to accomplish, when he has shown himself to be the true antithesis of the power which "always desires (to confront) evil and always creates good," when a pretension to free the world from evil ends only in a new proof of the danger of a fanatic to the commonweal, then it is not to be marveled at that a distrust is aroused in the observer.[3]

Freud was particularly taken by Wilson's statement to William F. McCombs, Chairman of the Democratic National Committee, after his election, "God ordained that I should be the next President of the United States. Neither you nor any other mortal or mortals could have prevented it."[4] Freud, who would soon embark on his essay, *The Future of An Illusion*, ever the ironist, could only remark,

> I do not know how to avoid the conclusion that a man who is capable of taking the illusions of religion so literally and is so sure of a special personal intimacy with the Almighty is unfitted for relations with ordinary children of men. As everyone knows, the hostile camp during the war also sheltered a chosen darling of Providence: the German Kaiser.[5]

Over several years Freud collaborated with Bullitt on the work, which became a book in itself and was finally finished in 1938, one year before Freud's death. In this study of Wilson, we can see Freud and Bullitt taking an approach consistent with Freud's view of the personality at that time, combining the Oedipus complex with Freud's newly formed sense of life and death instincts in conjunction with his formulations of defenses at work to protect the ego. At the same time, Freud took an unwittingly Jungian turn in designating an archetype, represented alternatively by Christ and God the Father ...

 Then the Lord rained upon Sodom and upon Gomorrah brimstone and fire from the Lord out of heaven. (Gen. 19:24)

The Lord is a man of war ... thy right hand O Lord, hath dashed in pieces the enemy ... thou sentest forth thy wrath, which consumed them as stubble ... all the inhabitants of Canaan shall melt away. (Ex. 15:3, 7, 15)

 For the Lord thy God is a consuming fire. (Deut. 4:24)

We are experiencing temporary disruption—fire from the heavens. These deliberate attempts at deconstructing the text are disconcerting but unfortunately unavoidable. Please try to keep your focus on the text before you ... but the explosions from above do bring to mind a fact not known by many: starting in 1964 and throughout the Vietnam War, America was secretly bombing the country of Laos, a small nation with a largely impoverished, agrarian population of about 3 million people. In 1971 alone 440,000 tons of bombs were dropped by the U.S. on Laos, twenty-five times the power of the atomic bomb dropped on Hiroshima. In all, a total of 2 million tons of bombs were dropped, more than all of the bombs dropped by all countries during World War II and equivalent to almost 2 tons of bombs for every three people in Laos, killing 10-20% of the population and leaving 2 million homeless. However, only two-thirds of the bombs actually exploded, making the entire country a veritable minefield for years to come. Now where were we? ... Oh yes, Freud and Woodrow Wilson and God the Father ...

... as the identification at the root of Wilson's neurosis.

Freud and Bullitt saw Wilson's career as an enactment of his identification with the super-ego through a chain of identifications from his father through Jesus to God the Father. As a Jesus figure, Wilson appealed to the masses but lost track of the actualities of the political situation at hand. Instead, he saw himself as a political Messiah, an agent of God, bringing peace to the world using language which primarily alluded to Biblical themes. The result of this psychological drama was the catastrophic psychophysical/political martyrdom of Wilson and the set up of a world political structure which ensured an ensuing cataclysmic world war.[6]

At the same time Freud and Bullitt noted the psychosomatic symptomatology that plagued Wilson throughout his life. At frequent times of crisis, he suffered from bouts of severe indigestion and dyspepsia, nervousness and neurasthenia, headaches and strokes, all of which resulted in frequent "breakdowns." These anatomical explosions culminated in the permanently debilitating stroke Wilson suffered in the final months of his Presidency prior to the vote of the Senate on the treaty which included his cherished proposal for a League of Nations.

To summarize Freud and Bullitt's assessment: Wilson, the son of a powerful Presbyterian minister, raised in the post-Civil War South, unconsciously was in love with the man whom he referred to as "my incomparable father,"[7] and identified completely with his father's Presbyterian values, especially the idea of the Covenant between the brotherhood of mankind and God which lay at the foundation of his fantasy of a League of Nations. Repressing both his hostility toward his father and his secret sense of inferiority, Wilson developed the higher defense of sublimation through his skill in language and oratory which he used throughout his life to express his Christian values in his conflicts with authorities. He longed for paternal recognition, but his accomplishments were never satisfactory to him. As a young man he wrote in a letter to his future wife Ellen Axson, that he had a "terrible ambition, a longing to do immortal work," and complained of his feeling "that I am carrying a *volcano* (italics mine) about with me."[8] It was Freud and Bullitt's opinion that Wilson's defenses of repression, identification, and sublimation, engaged to protect a fragile ego from the demands of a severe super-ego, resulted in an idealizing perception of himself and a naïve perception of the world. He was led to "ignore the facts of the real outer world, even to deny they existed if they conflicted with his hopes and wishes."[9] The result was tragic implosion.

In a larger sense, the depiction of Woodrow Wilson as self-interested, arrogant, entitled, and out of touch with the reality of his surroundings could be seen as representative of the character of American people. To put the issue into the form of a question, why do the people of the United States historically, regardless of party, place in power and support leadership whose political presence is grandiose, but which deprives the majority of the basic necessities which good government traditionally provides—freedom from influence by single interests, trustworthy infrastructure, readily at hand energy supplies, general access to physical and mental health care, sensitivity for the natural environment in which life is lived, quality in public education, adequate measures against teenage pregnancy, suicide, and violence, the opportunity for meaningful work and an equitable distribution of work privilege and profit, not to mention "defense" or "security" against the forces that are actually threatening the lives of the majority of its people—disease, pollution, urban decay, waste, both ordinary and toxic, crime related to drug use, underemployment, and the dissolution of fundamental civil rights? As the floods in New Orleans of 2007 indicated, all of these services would benefit the general population on a purely cost-effective basis alone, putting aside the moral question of making the country a better place for the majority to live in. Ultimately, a penetrating look at the political consciousness of the American people brings to mind the old adage, a nation always has the government it deserves. It would seem that a vacuum in statesmanship in America has to be seen as reflecting a flattened imagination of what it is to be a citizen.[10]

It is tempting to follow Freud in assessing national leadership through the lens of pathology, but following Jung's sense of soul as essence, I would like to put forth an alternative response. Jung saw the unconscious in terms of both singularity or essence and multiplicity. The unconscious holds many archetypal possibilities and exists on several levels personally, collectively, and in the world. One aspect of the collective unconscious is that of an element or image at the core of a nation's psyche, a national character or essential nature of a people. In a 1930 essay eventually entitled "The Complications of American Psychology," Jung wrote,

> Almost every great country has its collective attitude, which one might call its genius or *spiritus loci*. Sometimes you can catch it in a formula, sometimes it is more elusive, yet nonetheless it is indescribably present as a sort of atmosphere that permeates everything ....[11]

Following Jung, who believed that the psyche best expressed itself in metaphorical images, we might say that every country has its myth or underlying narrative as the fundament from which the thought, consciousness, images, and action patterns of that nation emerge.

A study of the discourse in American history reveals that one of its ongoing central narratives follows a model similar to that described in the Bible, particularly the first five Books of the Old Testament and the Book of Revelation in the New Testament.[12] From the time of the Puritans through the Founding Fathers, through Manifest Destiny, through the World Wars to contemporary political rhetoric, America's leaders in business, religion, and politics have founded their dialogue on a variety of Biblical themes which come together in a mythic image. The following is a survey of these themes, their Biblical antecedents, and historic American expressions:

(1) One well-known character trait of America is its entitlement and exceptionalism as a nation. "America is solidly organized egoism; it is evil made systematic and regular," wrote the French socialist, Pierre Buchez, in the 1840s.[13] However, what else would we expect from a people following an underlying narrative of a *chosen people* in the footsteps of the Old Testament Children of Israel? Yahweh said to Abram, "I will make of thee a great nation, and I will bless thee, and make thy name great and thou shalt be a blessing" (Gen. 12:2-3), and the vicissitudes of the dialogue regarding the covenant between God and his children continues throughout the Old Testament. It is from this model that Americans— from the Puritans who bestowed upon themselves the role of "God's covenant children,"[14] through the Founding Fathers who thought of their experiment in the imagery of the Children of Israel,[15] through the 19th century of Manifest Destiny, and the 20th century of Wilsonian, Reaganesque, and Bushite rhetoric referencing Americans as God's latter-day children—it is from this model that the American Father "Knows Best."

So the people shouted when the priests blew with the trumpets; and it came to pass, when the people heard the sound of the trumpet, and the people shouted with a great shout, the wall fell down flat, so that the people went up into the city, every man straight before him, and they took the city. (Josh. 6: 20-21)

And he rode upon a cherub, and did fly: and he was seen upon the wings of the wind. And he made darkness pavilions round about him, dark waters, and thick clouds of the skies. Through the brightness before him were coals of fire kindled. The Lord thundered from heaven and the most High uttered his voice. ... And the channels of the sea appeared, the foundations of the world were discovered, at the rebuking of the Lord, at the blast of the breath of his nostrils. (II Sam. 22: 11-14, 16)

And the angel took the censer, and filled it with fire of the altar, and cast it into the earth …. And the seven angels which had the seven trumpets prepared themselves to sound. The first angel sounded, and there followed hail and fire mingled with blood, and they were cast upon the earth: and the third part of trees was burnt up, and all green grass was burnt up. (Rev. 8: 5-7)

It seems the text is being terrorized. Those are the voices of God, and God has God's ways …. Free associating, however … the American bombing of North Vietnam does come to mind. The United States conducted three main bombing campaigns under two Presidents of different parties over the course of eight years. Close to 8 million tons of bombs, the equivalent of 640 atomic bombs, were dropped on a country of 18 million people, to no avail militarily.

(2) For Americans, as "chosen" by God and maintaining their innocence, anything *"other" is evil*—at best, not considered, or at worst, to be conquered or obliterated, a consciousness currently symbolized in the fence on the border of Mexico and made manifest in America's prison population, 1 out of every 100 people, proportionately the largest of any Western industrialized nation. Significantly, "heart dis-ease" ranks as one of America's most deadly afflictions.

But again, could there be any different attitude toward the "other" on the part of a people whose underlying myth has their Father/God proclaiming over and over, "I will bless them that bless thee, and curse him that curseth thee (Gen. 12:3), who practiced genocide at Jericho, or for whom the "other" is a "beast" to be vanquished (Isa. 30:6; Dan. 7:11,17, 19; Acts 10:12; Rev. 4:6-9; 5:6-14; 6:1-7; 7:11; 11:7, 13; 14:3, 9, 11; 15:2; 16:2, 10-13; 17; 19:4, 11-16, 19,20; 20:3, 4, 10).

(3) Following the dynamic of the wanderings of the children of Israel, American consciousness is one of constant movement or *journey*. Historically, the journey for Americans has been across the Atlantic to build the "new heaven," "Westward Ho" to conquer the frontier,[16] across the Pacific to civilize the Eastern world, to the Middle East to secure oil resources, to every country that America has occupied militarily in the 20th and 21st centuries in the name of "making the world safe for

democracy," and on to outer space. The image of the "journey home," sentimentalized, is a staple of Hollywood movies, and the themes of "move on," "picking up roots," "don't look back," "on the road," "back on the trail," "let's roll," etc. are predominant in a consciousness with its eye always on the horizon neglectful of what is at hand—infrastructure, health needs, environment. For America in the fast lane, "drive through" is a way of life in the procuring of everything from "fast food" to marriage and funeral services conducted from the car seat. America relocates home and job more than any other industrialized nation. A country—obsessed with "development," all optimism, all future, "upward mobility," for whom "progress is the most important product," and mortgages are given out without discrimination and lending institutions are backed several times over, all in the name of unlimited expansion—inevitably becomes an Alzheimer's Nation afflicted with cancer, the dis-eases of a "don't look back" mentality taken with "growth."

The myth blazes the trail. In the Old Testament, the journey is undertaken by Abraham from his home, by Noah and his family, by Lot whose wife is turned into a pillar of salt for looking back, by Moses and his people through the wilderness to Canaan, and by the Israelites returning from Babylon—home ever on the horizon. In the New Testament, the homeless Jesus deconstructs the journey in his person, "I am the Way" (John 14:6).

(4) The journey is toward the *Promised Land*—the New Jerusalem, the Puritan "city on the hill," "out west," the house behind the white picket fence, the New Eden, Paradise regained, utopia, the New Deal, the New Frontier, the Great Society, "I have a dream," Reagan's Star Wars shield of defense for the America of his New Federalism, globalization, reality as virtual, Disneyland, Disneyworld, disneyfication of the world. Americans are taken with change itself; youth in itself a value, the new, a necessity. America, where the spin of images by corporate media creates a fabric which Baudrillard calls "models of a real without origin … a hyperreal … the map that precedes the territory [which is] … the desert of the real itself."[17]

The imagination of America as Fantasyland is derived from a myth wherein Yahweh tells Abram to leave the home of his father for a new land (Gen. 12:1, 7, 18), a promise continually renewed with Abram's descendents until Jesus declares the Kingdom at hand, and finally Revelation's Holy City descends, rebirth attained.

(5) The Promised Land will be taken by conquest. At the 2008 Republican Convention John McCain testified as to his personal redemption through his experience as a prisoner of the Vietnamese in the form of a renewed love for his country, and his intention to take Washington by storm—the latest reincarnation of William Bradford as "Nehemius Americanus" fighting against the New England wilderness, George Washington against the British, George Custer against the Sioux, Theodore Roosevelt against the Spanish, Woodrow Wilson against war itself, George W. Bush's "Mission Accomplished," the March of Dimes, the War on Poverty—Captain America ever trampling out the vintage. Whereas Dante places Empire in the Inferno, Americans need *domination* (the word itself is associated with the root of the word "god"), dominate and are dominated within their own political and business structures. The models for America and domination are the Children of Israel led by a conquering god into Canaan and the anonymous messianic hero of Revelations riding his white horse into town subjugating the evil beast.

(6) The New Land is achieved through *suffering*, a sojourn in the wilderness, a time of travail. The bodily suffering of John McCain as a POW was described in detail at the Republican Convention that nominated him. Every Sunday *Parade Magazine* is full of stories of movie stars fallen on bad times, inevitably John Wayne falls off his horse, Brando is beaten up, and the cult of the victim flourishes for Oprah. All are children of Adam and Eve expelled, Abram in the unknown land, Noah flooded out, the Israelites and forty years of wilderness wandering, the persecuted prophets, Job and his boils, Jesus with his sojourn in the desert, temptations by the devil, Golgotha, and final cross up. "For as soon as Zion travailed, she brought forth her children" (Isa. 66:8).

(7) Just as Adam Smith's *The Wealth of Nations* and the Declaration of Independence emerged in the same year, so capitalism and America's brand of freedom go hand-in-hand. For the Puritans, *material well-being* was a sign of God's beneficence. Faith in God is reflected through work on earth, which is, in turn, rewarded materially by God. The Puritans turned this idea around so that one's wealth was a sign of one's virtue—if wealthy, then pure. The Yankees and the plantation owners who founded the nation furthered the idea into a political right to

wealth—for the individual, but more, for the individual Hamiltonian corporation. The American mantra of 19th century, "manifest destiny" was not only the conquest of land, but the acquisition of riches, wealth makes right, and profit was Christianized by evangelists. America, as consumer nation, now ingests about a third of the natural resources used worldwide. And why not, when the Lord "will rain bread from heaven for you," (Ex. 16:4), promises "a land that floweth with milk and honey" (Deut. 11:9), and "you may ask what you will, and it will be done for you?" (John 15:7)

(8) America talks democracy but acts aristocratically. *Elitism* is a bad word when applied to Barack Obama, but from the time of the Puritan circle of governing elite elders, to the upper crust of society that founded America's government, to the merchants who pushed for westward movement, to the industrial barons of the "Guilded Age," to the upper-class families and their associates that ran government before during and after the world wars, to the upper level management of contemporary corporations, an *elite circle* holds privilege in American consciousness.[18] Just as America sees itself at the pinnacle of a hegemonic international structure, so Americans also willingly subject themselves to the diminished benefits of the lower hierarchal scale in favor of the elite. The political structure of patriarchal elitism to which Americans, mollified by the language of democracy, subscribe is established in the Old Testament in the covenant between God and his people—God takes care of his children, the children are faithful to God. God commands Moses to set up a ruling council of elders to be given the spirit of God's laws, Jesus gathers a circle of disciples, and the body of saints govern the thousand-year millennial period.

(9) American psyche holds an *ambivalence toward the law*. Paradoxically, all problems are seen as soluble by making more laws, but each new law only invites more imagination in getting around it. Americans think of legislation as solving problems, but revere those who go above, around, and through the law. John McCain presented himself as the Maverick outside the establishment. Individuals find ways of avoiding taxes while corporations find loopholes as a way of passing through the "eye of the needle" into the capitalistic kingdom. Sixty percent of the top 400 corporations don't pay income tax. The ethical atmosphere of American business and individual finances is one

of "winking" at the transcribed letters in a perpetual Enron shell game of "How Much Can I Get Away With." And why not? Moses broke the laws ... literally, and the Israelites came up with books of laws just like the tomes of laws for contemporary American accountants with God and the SEC constantly trying to get the Children to obey. Finally, Jesus becomes sick of the game of earthly rules; he is in a different world, so that only God's law counts.

> The day of the Lord will come as a thief in the night; in the which the heavens shall pass away with a great noise, and the elements shall melt with fervent heat, the earth also and the works that are therein shall be burned up. (II Pet. 3:10)

... The Lord will roar from Zion, and utter his voice from Jerusalem .... (Amos 1:2)

... I will send a fire into the house of Hazael .... (v. 4)

... I will send a fire on the wall of Gaza .... (v. 7)

... I will send a fire on the wall of Tyrus .... (v. 10)

... I will send a fire upon Teman .... (v. 12)

... I will kindle a fire in the wall of Rabbah .... (v. 14)

... I will send a fire upon Moab .... (Amos 2:2)

...I will send a fire upon Judah .... (v. 5).

> And the fourth angel poured out his vial upon the sun; and power was given unto him to scorch men with fire. And men were scorched with great heat .... (Rev. 16:8-9)

... [F]ire came down from God out of heaven; and devoured them. (Rev. 20: 9)

> It seems Explosion is calling upon us to address it in relation to America,
> but first … though we think of Japan in World War II as the site of atomic
> bomb explosions, more destruction was actually brought about in Japan by
> the fire bombing of civilian populations. The American approach was
> formulated by Major General Curtis LeMay, that is, that industrial areas within
> cities would be targeted and then any "stray bombs" would bring about "bonus
> damage," namely the incineration of civilians. LeMay described the results of
> the bombing of Tokyo and over 60 other cities as over 200,000 people being
> "scorched and boiled and baked to death"[19] while 8 million were made
> homeless. The Japanese fire bombings had been preceded by the firebombing
> of German cities in which over 300,00 civilians were killed and almost 2
> million made homeless. None of the incendiary bombing in World War II
> produced military advantage and General Bonner Fellers described the
> bombing in Japan as "one of the most ruthless and barbaric killings of non-
> combatants in all of history."[20]

Now, America, its myth and its bomb …

As a nation, America has a particular affinity for the bomb as a
form of super-weapon reserved for its use to maintain its purity and
superiority in the name of peace. It was an American, Robert Fulton,
a pioneer in the invention of the first bomb-carrying submarine, who
imagined he would "secure perpetual peace between nations."[21]
Secretary of War, Henry Stinson, justified the use of the atomic bomb
as "the only way to awaken the world to the necessity of abolishing
war altogether."[22] Among the first usages of explosions from bombs as
such in warfare took place in the Civil War, and one of the first terrorist
bombs was exploded in the Haymarket Square of Chicago during the
late 19th century labor disputes. The United States conducted the first
multi-city aerial firestorm raids, invented the first atomic bomb, the
first intercontinental bomber, the first thermonuclear bomb, the first
laser-guided bomb, and the first automated system for launching
thermonuclear warheads. Even the delivery of food to Afghanistan after
9/11 was accomplished in the form of pallets dropped from the air,
causing destruction underneath.

America glorifies the bomb in its national anthem, "the bombs'
bursting in air," as well as in its literature. Captain Ahab, as America
personified, "piled upon the whale's white hump the sum of all the

general rage and hate felt by his whole race from Adam down; and then, as if his chest had been a mortar, he burst his hot heart's shell upon it."[23] America's shadow harbors the cult of the "mad bomber." In the film, *Speed,* a bus in Los Angeles is wired with a bomb so that if it goes under 50 m.p.h., the bomb will go off—an image of American character, slow down and you explode. The bomber, played by Dennis Hopper, justifies his actions in a particularly Jungian way, "The being of the bomb is unfulfilled unless it goes off." The bomber is simply helping the bomb to "individuate." One of the most exciting plays in football, America's most popular game, is called "the bomb," and bombing is a casual staple of American entertainment media except when an ill-received production bombs.

America created its god image in the atomic bomb, prefigured in the incredible description in II Peter (cited above) of the "melting" of the world. At the time of the bomb's explosion, Harry Truman framed its existence in American hands in a particularly messianic American way, "We thank God that it has come to us instead of to our enemies, and we pray that He may guide us to use it in His ways and for His purpose"[24]—the bomb as God's gift to his children for their use on earth in His name. The conventional rationalization for the bomb's use, that it was necessary to bring the war to an end, is questionable. Several times before the attacks on Hiroshima and Nagasaki the Japanese had expressed a desire to negotiate terms of surrender. Their only condition was that they be allowed to retain the Emperor in their political structure. There was no military need to drop the bombs. Most Japanese cities were already devastated, and Russia's army was ready for an assault on Japanese forces. The U.S. Strategic Bombing Survey subsequently stated unequivocally, "Japan would have surrendered if the atomic bombs had not been dropped."[25] Chief of Staff to President Truman, Fleet Admiral William Leahy, declared, "... the use of this barbarous weapon at Hiroshima and Nagasaki was of no material assistance in our war against Japan. The Japanese were already defeated and ready to surrender."[26] Weeks before the atomic explosions Truman had discussed in his diary a "telegram from Jap emperor asking for peace," and he regularly received reports on the terms of Japanese peace inquiries.[27] Recent scholarship points to the idea that President Truman, Secretary of State Byrnes, and Secretary of War Stinson felt it was necessary to use the atomic bomb in Japan as a way of keeping an advantage over Russia in the postwar world.[28] In fact, the atomic bomb did not bring about the end of World War II but was the first act in the ensuing Cold War between America and the Soviet Union.

After the war, America embarked on a 40-year nuclear arms buildup justified both as a necessity and means of progress for the defense of America and *de facto* of civilization, despite the warnings of its inventors. Enrico Fermi and I. I. Rabi, two Nobel laureate physicists on the scientific advisory committee to the Atomic Energy Commission, noted in 1949 that the hydrogen bomb

> goes far beyond any military objective and enters the range of very great natural catastrophes. By its very nature it cannot be confined to a military objective but becomes a weapon which in practical effect is almost one of genocide. … It is necessarily an evil thing considered in any light.[29]

Robert Oppenheimer, Chair of the Committee, admonished, "The notion that the thermonuclear arms race was something that was in the interests of the country to avoid if it could was very clear to us."[30] These scientists were proclaiming, in effect, that nuclear arms went beyond the category of military weapon, and the term "nuclear war" was a contradiction in terms. Niels Bohr said flatly, "We are in an entirely new situation that cannot be resolved by war."[31]

Nor was there need on the part of the United States to regard the Soviet Union as an immanent threat. It had just lost 25 million people and half its industry in World War II. Former Secretary of Defense, James Schlessinger, described the Soviet forces as "paltry … hardly enough to stage an attack on the United States."[32] Jerome Wiesner, President of MIT, suggested that 50 nuclear bombs were enough to put a society out of commission and 300 would destroy an entire civilization, but at the height of the nuclear arms race in 1966 America had 32,200 bombs. Robert McNamara, former Secretary of Defense explained, "each of the decisions taken by itself, appeared rational or inescapable. But the fact is that they were made without reference to any overall master plan or long-term objective."[33] In fact, the effort and expense of the United States in the nuclear arms race was based on wildly exaggerated reports of the armaments and delivery capacity of the Soviet Union, perpetrated by American officials deliberately playing on the fears of the public, reports which turned out to be completely false.[34] Reduction in armaments finally was brought about by the Reagan administration, but not before five trillion dollars had been spent for involvement in an effort that turned out to be morally reprehensible and militarily unnecessary. In 1946, at the dawning of what he saw as the insanity of the nuclear age, Louis Mumford wrote in a piece called, "Gentlemen : You Are Mad," "We are madmen, too. We view the madness of our leaders as if it expressed a traditional wisdom and a common sense."[35]

We are left with a mind-numbing realization regarding American bombing. The extensive bombing of civilians resulting in the deaths of almost a million people in various wars from WW II to the present, while intricately tied to an ethic of dominance and to American economic interests, did not produce ultimate military advantage. The fact is that since the months after Franklin Roosevelt's 1939 call to the world to cease the bombing of civilians, America has made the bombing of civilians an integral part of its aggressive tactics. This state of affairs has culminated in the bizarre imagery of the most technologically advanced American bombers attacking people who dwell in huts and caves in Afghanistan. Currently, thousands of civilians have been killed by American bombs in Afghanistan, as well as 100,000 in Iraq, and yet military advantage remains elusive. How can the continuation of this seemingly irrational behavior be explained?

Robert Jewett and John Shelton Lawrence, in their book *Captain America and the Crusade Against Evil*, make note of the affinity of the American character for bombing and trace its roots to America's identification with the Old Testament Israelites and the quality of "zeal" which God demands from his children and which corresponds to the Islamic notion of *jihad*. The authors focus on the story of Phinehas as told in Numbers 25:10-13. The Lord holds Phinehas up to Moses as an example of a worthy son in that he boldly broke into the tent of an Israeli man and his Midianite wife and killed them with a spear protecting the purity of the Israelite people. The Lord said, "He was zealous for my sake" (Num. 25:11). Jewett and Lawrence note that the word "zeal" has its roots in the Hebrew *gana* which in turn is derived from its Semitic root which means "to be dyed dark-red or black," the color of rage. In several passages in the Old Testament, a "consuming" zeal on the part of individual Israelites mirrors that of the Lord (Josh. 7:26, Ps. 69:9, 119:139), or the Lord is depicted with the "burning heat" of zeal (Ps.

18: 13-15, 79:5, Isa. 66:15, Eze. 36:5, 38:19, 39:6, Zeph. 1:18). To show zeal indicates a willingness to go beyond the law in identification with God's righteousness. Zeal makes the division of good and evil absolute, enabling behavior beyond the confines of the law.

The purity of the Israelite nation was upheld in the practice of *herem*, or in English, "the ban." After every battle the priests would order the booty and prisoners be destroyed or dedicated to God such as after the battle of Jericho when the entire city was destroyed (Joshua 6: 17-21). Bombing then accomplishes the utter destruction of the "other," through a fiery form that indicates the zeal required by God to stay in His grace, as well as maintains a sensibility of purity and innocence central to the psyche of Americans as the "chosen ones." After the Pequod Massacre of 1637 in which an entire community was slaughtered, Captain John Underhill declared,

> It may be demanded, Why should you be so furious? But I would refer you to David's War. When a people is grown to such a height of blood, and sin against God and man ... then he hath no respect to persons ... sometimes the Scriptures declareth women and children must perish with their parents. ... We had sufficient light from the word of god for our proceedings.[36]

Almost 330 years later, Richard Nixon would say, "Our beliefs must be combined with a crusading zeal, not just to hold our own but to change the world ... and to win the battle for freedom."[37]

We can see that the "bomb" fits in well with America's underlying identification with Biblical narrative and imagery. Ezekiel envisions that with a "noise" and a "shaking" the Lord will "open your graves ... and bring you into the land of Israel" (Eze. 37:7, 12). The Greek root for the word "apocalypse" means an "unveiling of that which is hidden," so that the bomb serves the Lord's revelatory purpose. In its fundamental aspect, the bomb would be, as its first use in ancient China would indicate, an event in the service of fertility. When asked about the recent explosive hostilities between Hezbollah and Israel, Condoleezza Rice responded "What we're seeing here ... is the growing—the birth pangs of a new Middle East, and ... we have to be certain that we're pushing forward to the new Middle East."[38] In the American imagination, the bomb, whose etymology has to do with a loud popping sound, is a form of birth, a loosening, an opening up for "opportunity," to use George W. Bush's word in the aftermath of 9/11.

Through the bomb, America both identifies with God hurling fire from the heavens and acts as His agent of purification so as to "march toward the clean world our hands can make" in the words of FDR.[39] America can kill in God's name and retain its innocence, dissociated from the bombs' effects. Joseph Biden, Chair of the Senate Foreign Relations Committee at the time of 9/11 and a framer of the resolution to allow the President unlimited force in retaliation as well as an initial supporter of the invasion of Iraq, said, "There is zero need for declaration of war," and "No one should think that what we did here was less than a declaration of war,"[40]—innocence and aggression at once. Explosion cleanses with its radiance. As the sons of Levi are purified in the refiner's fire of the Lord and God's servants, Shadrach, Meshach, and Abednego, emerge as pure from the fire, so America makes the world pure with the terrorizing "shock and awe" of its bombs, explosion ridding the world of evil. 9/11 was a time to "go massive," as Donald Rumsfeld proclaimed, "Sweep it all up, things related and not."[41]

Finally, explosion is the occasion for the Rapture, the final ascension into the sky and meeting with Christ. "Top of the world, Ma," cries James Cagney in the final scene of "White Heat" on top of a refinery tank which is about to explode. Paul writes to the Thessalonians, "Then we which are alive and remain shall be caught up together with them in the clouds, to meet the Lord in the air: and so shall we ever be with the Lord" (I Thess. 4:17). Redemptive and regenerative as we see every Fourth of July, explosion becomes the ritual of America's myth *par excellence*.

In conclusion, we have heard the narrative and seen the images which make up the container for what Jung would call the *genius loci* of American psyche. This is not the Jung of conceptualizations, but the aesthetic Jung of *esse in anima*, the Jung of image. This Jung allows us to address ourselves not by addressing particular parts of the collective psyche as pathology nor selected parts of the society as pathological, but by seeing how the individual parts fit into a singular form. The myths of other peoples enact similar archetypes, there are many nations that consider themselves as chosen, for example, but the particular gathers itself in a unique way for each nation. The form which we have been exploring reveals to us the fundament or rhizome from which America cannot escape, the limits of its national psychological structuring, what it is, not what we would like it to be.

We might well ask, is real change possible within any mythic structure? Might not a new myth, a new tradition, be created out of crisis?[42] From Freud and Jung, we know that the unconscious has us, that myths have us. We can only look into myth for its multiple sensibilities as Lincoln did in his Second Inaugural Address when he suggested that the Civil War might have been God's punishment to the people for the sin of slavery, (although he was prudent enough not to use this as a campaign theme!) and through myth to the imagination that underlies.

As psychologists of culture, with what are we left as ground to address a core image that is so repugnant? Dante's underworld wanderers are greeted by the sign "Abandon hope ye who enter here," and Eliot tells us that hope is always for the wrong thing. So without conceptual tools for understanding: sans "transcendent function", sans "integration," sans "individuation," sans "creation out of destruction," sans "ego-self axis," sans "wholeness," sans "union of opposites," without pathological orientation: no "pathology," no "cultural complex," no "psychological defenses," no "healing;" and without humanistic concepts: no "homeland," no "security," no "freedom," no "liberty," no "democracy"... no hope, no meaning, not even meaning in the image ... just image, just imagination to see through what will always be there, or paraphrasing Blake, helping Jesus as Imagination itself, homeless and barefoot, making Its way through the sands of the world ... allowing vision itself to have its effect.

NOTES

1. Sigmund Freud and William C. Bullitt, *Thomas Woodrow Wilson: A Psychological Study* (Boston: Houghton Mifflin, 1967), pp. v–vi.

2. Peter Gay, *Freud: A Life for Our Time* (New York: W. W. Norton and Company, 1988), p. 554.

3. Freud and Bullitt, p. xiii.

4. *Ibid.*, p. xi.

5. *Ibid.*, p. xi. Freud's insight foretells a classic in the history of American psychiatry, *The Three Christs of Ypsilanti,* about the unsuccessful attempt of a psychiatric hospital in Michigan to cure three patients who thought of themselves as Christ by putting them all in the same ward.

6. The psychoanalytic drama of father/son was further enacted by Bullitt who had worked closely with Wilson during the Paris Peace

Conference, but then felt betrayed by Wilson's concessions to the Allied powers and subsequently resigned, and, when called to testify before a Senate Committee, revealed that Wilson's own Secretary of State, Robert Lansing, did not support the treaty that Wilson was pushing.

7. Freud and Bullitt, p. 58.

8. *Ibid.*, p. 28.

9. *Ibid.*, p. xii.

10. There are exceptions to this pattern as evidenced in the elections of Franklin Roosevelt and Barack Obama, which came about, however, in the midst of financial catastrophe. Disappointed liberals point out that Obama followed a fundamentally centrist course in his first 100 days as President: choosing two people who voted for the invasion of Iraq as his Vice President and Secretary of State, picking a Secretary of the Treasury who was allied with the banks whose mismanagement caused the financial crisis, organizing the bailout of Wall Street institutions without significant change in regulation, instituting the government's purchase of toxic assets at great risk to taxpayers, not making significant changes in the handling of prisoners in Guantanamo, increasing America's military presence in Afghanistan, and bombing in both Afghanistan and Pakistan. The point here is that no matter who is in power, the American people acquiesce to being governed by a system that is not democratic, but rather aristocratic in nature. I am suggesting that this is reflective of an essential mythic element in American character.

11. C. G. Jung "The Complications of American Psychology," in *Civilization in Transition, The Collected Works of C. G. Jung,* Vol.10, trans. R. F. C. Hull (New York: Bollingen Foundation, 1964), p. 511.

12. See Ernest Lee Tuveson, *Redeemer Nation: The Idea of America's Millennial Role* (Chicago, IL: University of Chicago Press, 1968); Robert Bellah, "Civil Religion in America," in *Religion in America,* ed. William C. McLoughlin and Robert Bellah (Boston, MA: Houghton Mifflin, 1968); *God's New Israel: Religious Interpretations of American Destiny* (Englewood Cliffs, N.J.: Prentice Hall, 1971); Robert Jewett and John Shelton Lawrence, *Captain America and the Crusade Against Evil: The Dilemma of Zealous Nationalism* (Grand Rapids, MI: William B. Eerdmans, 2003); Christopher Collins, *Homeland Mythology: Biblical Narrative in American Culture* (University Park, PA: Pennsylvania State University Press, 2007).

13. Tony Judt, "America and the War," *The New York Review of Books*, November 15, 2001, p .4.

14. Sacvan Bercovitch, *The Puritan Origin of the American Self* (New Haven, CT: Yale University Press, 1973), p. 61.

15. John Adams wrote that the new nation was an "opening of a grand scene and design in Providence." See Ernest Lee Tuveson, *Redeemer Nation: The Idea of America: Millennial Role* (Chicago, IL: University of Chicago Press, 1968), p. 25. Jefferson thought of farmers as "God's chosen people," and wanted the Great Seal to portray the Children of Israel led by a pillar of light.

16. Whereas Dante placed "Empire" in the Inferno, Thomas Singer brings our attention to the American attitude toward empire in the 1872 painting of John Gast entitled "American Progress" in which the "Star of Empire" leads the migration west conquering everything in its path. See "A Personal Meditation on Politics and the American Soul," *Spring 78—Politics and the American Soul* (Fall 2007): 142.

17. Jean Baudrillard, *Simulations*, trans. Paul Foss, Paul Patton and Philip Beitchman (New York: Semiotext(e), 1983), p. 2.

18. See *Ruling America: A History of Wealth and Power in a Democracy*, ed. Steve Fraser and Gary Gerstle (Cambridge, MA: Harvard University Press, 2005).

19. John W. Dower, *War Without Mercy: Race and Power in the Pacific War* (New York: Pantheon Books, 1986), pp. 40–41.

20. *Ibid.*, p. 41.

21. H. Bruce Franklin, *War Stars: The Superweapon and the American Imagination* (New York: Oxford University Press, 1988), p. 15.

22. *Ibid.*, p. 153.

23. Herman Melville, *Moby Dick or The White Whale* (New York: New American Library, 1980), p. 186.

24. Jewett and Lawrence, p. 259.

25. Franklin, p. 150.

26. *Ibid.*

27. *Ibid.*, p. 151.

28. See *Ibid.*, p. 223, n. 5 and Gus Alperovitz, *Atomic Diplomacy: Hiroshima and Potsdam* (New York: Penguin, 1985).

29. Richard Rhodes, *Arsenals of Folly: The Making of the Nuclear Arms Race* (New York: Alfred A. Knopf, 2007), p. 76.

30. *Ibid.*, p. 76.

31. *Ibid.*, p. 101.

32. *Ibid.*, p. 86.

33. *Ibid.*, p. 99.

34. Dick Cheney and Donald Rumsfeld were involved in one of these reports in 1976 foretelling their role in the deceit perpetrated to justify the invasion of Iraq.

35. Franklin, p. 4.

36. Jewett and Lawrence, p. 253.

37. David Bromwich, "Euphemism and American Violence," *The New York Review of Books*, April 3, 2008, p. 28.

38. Jewett and Lawrence, p. 256.

39. *Ibid.*, p. 16.

40. Bromwich, p. 28.

41. See Gary Hart, "Toward a New American Myth," *Spring 62* (Fall and Winter 1997): 1- 9.

A MYTHOLOGY OF BULLETS

GLEN SLATER

There's a phrase you often encounter concerning gun violence in America—"an addiction to guns." The term addiction captures the national obsession and inability to disarm in the face of destructive and deadly consequences. It is evident first in the prevalence of guns (two out of five households[1]), second in their manufacture (3.85 million new firearms in 2007, 95% of which remained in the country[2]), and third, most of all, in the results (30,000 annual deaths and 70,000 non-fatal injuries[3]). Talk of an addiction to guns is heard most often in the aftermath of shooting sprees and always implies an armchair diagnosis and treatment plan: "If only we were less fixated on guns and their availability was limited, we'd not see so much bloodshed." There is certainly something to this initial hit on the matter. Yet addictions and fixations are immune to rational argument and indicate enduring patterns of fantasy and behavior. And whereas the availability of firearms is problematic and must be continually taken up in social and political arenas, focus on this aspect can deflect our attention away from the issue's deeper roots. We need

Glen Slater, Ph.D., is on the faculty of Pacifica Graduate Institute where he teaches in the Mythological Studies and Depth Psychology programs. This essay is based on a paper presented at the 2008 Foundation for Mythological Studies Conference on "The Mythology of Violence." It also contains excerpted material from a previously published paper, "The Psychology of Bullets," in *The Salt Journal,* March /April 2000.

to understand the need for guns, and we need to put our finger on what makes us so inclined to pull the trigger when we get them.

The idea of an addiction may both reveal and conceal the extent of the problem. What addiction reveals relates to addiction psychology: the intractability, the fabrications, the rituals, the denials and dissociations. It conveys the resistance to admitting the extent of the problem and the lack of will to do anything about it. Fitting associations abound: When guns are your drug of choice, highs at the firing range increase along with the caliber, but hitting bottom means certain death and may lead to innocent bystanders memorialized on the cover of *Newsweek*. Yet declaration of war on this substance remains a distant prospect. Imagine the irony of a war on firearms in a country that is the world's chief supplier—though the government does put alcohol, tobacco, and firearms together in one bureau. As with other substances, when the addiction becomes normative, the neurotic pattern is cloaked—a phenomenon well conveyed in the oft-quoted statement by the former senator Phil Gramm of Texas: "I have more guns than I need, but fewer than I want."[4]

The idealization of guns and the rationalizations for their accessibility are part of the syndrome. Shooting sprees lead to short periods of critical attention, but after the fleeting analysis the patient regresses back to a defended state. Like a complex that's thrashing about after exposure to the light, spectacles of gun violence just motivate the gun barons to reinforce the supply lines, while their lobbyists double their efforts and crazies start arguing how much safer we'd all be carrying concealed weapons. But we would be missing something to simply address the problem at this level. Addictions and their defense mechanisms conceal deeper problems. Their self-medicating function prevents a more conscious suffering and provides a boilerplate for more enduring and harder to address concerns, concerns that are apt to confront the whole of the personality (in the case of an individual) or the entire collective character (in the case of a nation). Let's cut to the chase: There's a vested interest in maintaining the status quo on guns; gun violence keeps the national psyche in a holding pattern, preventing it from a more conscious encounter with more soul-wrenching issues. The obsessive need for guns, the paranoid fear of having guns taken away, the lack of will to effectively legislate or litigate, and even the violence itself are bonded in a conspiracy of collective defense and denial against a deeper darkness and pathology. Cracking open the neurotic dynamics means going in search of mythic and archetypal roots. The first step is to take a few theories off the table and cut through the most convenient but ultimately insubstantial understandings of the gun violence problem.

THE USUAL SUSPECTS

Of the 30,000 people killed by guns each year in the United States, about half are suicides, but more than a third are homicides. On average, for a quarter century now, between ten and fifteen thousand people per year are deliberately targeted and killed by someone else with a gun. These raw numbers are startling enough, but they are shocking when placed in global perspective. A study published in 1998 in the *International Journal of Epidemiology* indicated that in the United States the likelihood of being deliberately shot and killed by someone else is more than 10 times that of Canada, 17 times that of Australia, 35 times that of Germany, 89 times that of England and Wales, and 355 times that of Japan.[5] Even with these comparisons, the nationwide view can dilute the impact of the problem in particular communities. For example, during the first half of the 2007-2008 school year, the Chicago public school system had already seen 20 students killed by other students with guns.[6]

A theory we immediately turn to for answers is *access* to firearms, which, while it has some bearing on the overall rate of violence, doesn't account for many aspects of the issue. It's important to be differentiated on this matter: On the one hand, we need to unhook the availability and the use of guns so that the availability factor doesn't prevent us from digging deeper. On the other hand, as we will see in the American context, the accessibility of firearms *in combination with* the proclivity to point them at others is a volatile mix.

Let's take the first side of the question: Whereas some studies have shown a worldwide correlation between the availability of guns and their homicidal use, others have shown little correlation. Switzerland and Finland have high rates of gun ownership but very low firearm homicide rates.[7] The gun lobby loves to hear this, thinking it supports their cause. "Guns don't kill; people kill" is their motto. Yet while these numbers support the idea there may be no *necessary* link between having a gun and using it to kill someone, it only provides a vivid backdrop to the American *tendency* to use guns in deadly ways: International surveys indicate that Americans use guns in homicides between 60 and 75% of the time, compared to 30-40% of the time in Canada and about 30% of the time in other comparable nations.[8] In other words, murderous impulses are more hardwired to gun use in America. Which simply underscores the question: what is it that makes this nation more inclined to kill others with guns?

Is it a function of overall crime? Well, no, the overall number of reported crimes *per capita* is similar to that of Australia and less than that of Britain.[9] Besides, the prison population here is about six times higher than these countries, which might lead one to assume that all the dangerous folks must already be behind bars.[10] Not so, apparently. Is it about the influence of media violence? This favorite argument is unloaded each time someone who grew up in the information age shoots a bunch of fellow citizens. So are *Grand Theft Auto, Marilyn Manson*, and the offspring of *Dirty Harry* to blame? Although there's some evidence that violent imagery leads to more aggressive behavior in children, especially in those with a predisposition to aggression (!), there's little to suggest direct links to criminal behavior.[11] More compelling is the fact that many European countries with low rates of crime in general and of gun violence in particular consume violent imagery with similar gusto as Americans. Japan provides another point of comparison: Violent anime films, manga comics, and video games are pervasive. They are also on a steady diet of Hollywood movies. Businessmen read pornography on trains. Alcohol may be found in vending machines on street corners. Japan has higher rates of suicide than the United States and mental illness is on the increase; it's not a perfect culture. But violent crime is almost non-existent, the population accepts the highly restrictive gun laws, and people aren't going around shooting each other. So the almost universal diet of violent imagery is hardly an explanation for rates of gun violence, either here or abroad. Images of gratuitous violence may add to the pervasive desensitization and numbness of modern culture, but it's worth keeping in mind that the association of violence and the dramatic arts is archetypal—as any reading of Shakespeare or *The Bible* will attest. The media is implicated in other ways, but we will get to that in a moment.

Mental illness is another suspicious culprit, dragged out for shadowy treatment whenever gun violence is in the spot light. Sometimes the evidence seems compelling, as in the case of Seung-Hui Cho, the Virginia Tech shooter.[12] But as psychologists well know, being depressed or anxious or schizophrenic even is not in itself a predictor of violence. A more compelling idea is that the mad concretize the fault lines of society, living the pathological aspects of our myths in literal ways, which still brings us back to the basic question: What makes the gun the American drug of choice?

While the above survey is only a thumbnail sketch of some common arguments, the resulting picture is fairly clear: The usual suspects produce no smoking gun. Neither availability, nor criminality, nor media influence, nor general states of psychological distress offer decent paths of understanding.

A PSYCHOLOGY OF BULLETS

Shortly after Klebold and Harris shot 12 students, a teacher, and themselves at Columbine High School, I started to consider the gun violence problem. Beyond the polarized glibness of the blame game, I was struck and continue to be struck by one thing: So often in these mass shootings the shooter appears to walk straight out of the fabric of everyday life. As I wrote in an article at that time: Inevitably there'll be an interview "with a benign-looking elderly woman whose lawn the shooter once mowed. In a chillingly honest statement, she will say . . . 'He seemed like an ordinary American boy to me . . .'"[13] Alongside such impressions, the search for motives and causes in these most dramatic and deadly incidents of gun violence often produces meager results. It all begs the question: what *is* ordinary and American about gun violence?

It didn't take long to discover that "beneath the cloak of normative goals and aspirations . . . [lies] . . . a cluster of social values that can be identified as precursors to gun violence."[14] A book by two sociologists, Steven Messner and Richard Rosefield, *Crime and the American Dream*,[15] came closest to articulating my sense that the decision to pick up a gun, take aim, and pull the trigger has to be traced back to cultural pathology. They describe the American Dream as "entail(ing) a commitment to the goal of material success, to be pursued by everyone in society, under conditions of open, individual competition," but also note that this ethos produces a shadow effect: "an environment in which people are encouraged to adopt an 'anything goes' mentality in the pursuit of personal goals." They reach the conclusion that the high rate of gun violence in particular "result(s) in part from a cultural ethos that encourages the rapid deployment of technically efficient methods to solve interpersonal problems."[16]

As it turns out, sociology has a name for this collective backdrop to overt violence; it's called "structural violence." When you look hard enough, you come to see that the ethos of the American Dream has a built-in but well camouflaged structural violence, a series of dynamics that promote opportunity but create disenfranchisement. Both the shock and awe over shooting rampages as well as the pressured rhetoric about pursuing the Dream work to keep this built-in violence under wraps. But once your eyes adjust to the dark, gun violence can be seen growing in the backwoods of the country's highest aspirations.

For one thing, there's a blurry line between legitimate and illegitimate ways of being successful in America. If you think there's no connection between what happened on the trading floor of Enron, or in the offices of Bernie Madoff, and what happens in South Central Los Angeles, think again. In his book *The Cry for Myth*, Rollo May, meditating on that archetypal self-made man, Jay Gatsby, writes:

> There has been in America no clear-cut differentiation between right and wrong ways to get rich. Playing the stock market? Finding oil under your shack in Texas? Deforesting vast areas of Douglas fir in the state of Washington? Amassing piles of money for lectures after getting out of prison as a Watergate crook? The important thing in the American Dream has been to get rich, and then those very riches give a sanction to your situation.[17]

For another thing, whereas the ethos of the American Dream suggests that you can become whoever or whatever you want—that everyone can be a winner—it's just not so. Few are willing to see this. People in low-income brackets often vote for candidates and policies that support the wealthy because they believe that one day they too will be wealthy. They don't see the bind they are in, a phenomenon that's been carefully described by Thomas Frank in *What's the Matter with Kansas?*[18] The conditions within which both idealized goals and significant but largely unrecognized obstacles to those goals are fostered are continually reinforced. Gaps between aspiration and reality are the result, gaps that are far larger in this country than anywhere else in the developed world, gaps that appear on whatever rung of the ladder you happen to be standing.

Whether it's in the high school cafeteria, the college lecture hall, the streets of Detroit, in a Wendy's restaurant, or between the Crips and the Bloods, gun violence grows out of these gaps. As I wrote previously:

> The gun appears when the gap between actual life and the idealized American Dream opens too wide; the gun is fired when there is no thing left to satisfy the belief that we make our own destiny. . . . As a distorted realization of willful accomplishment, the gun becomes the final solution, the way out, (and often) a ticket to immortality, even in the face of suicidal intent. The gun is a pure expression of controlling one's life. As such, it is the dark epitome of the self-made way of life.[19]

Neither the danger involved, nor the prospect of life in prison, nor in some instances the idea of taking one's own life can compete with the shame and belittlement that occurs with not "making it." These deterrents can't compete with the need to eliminate feelings of failure and social alienation. As James Gilligan writes:

> The death of the self is of far greater concern than the death of the body. People will willingly sacrifice their bodies if they perceive it as the only way to avoid "losing their souls," "losing their minds," or "losing face."[20]

When "soul," "mind," and "face" are all aligned with climbing a narrowly defined socio-economic ladder and you lose your footing, violence becomes an attractive option. The narrowness starts early. To compensate for their outsider status in high school, Klebold and Harris imagined shooting their way to the cover of *Time* magazine. The prospect of notoriety on the heels of being alienated from the adolescent version of American Dream surpassed the significance of life itself. This is quite an inversion of values. No doubt today's blurry line between fame and notoriety parallels that between legitimate and illegitimate paths to success.

What I'm getting at is this: There's an idea or fantasy behind the gun that animates its role in this society long before anyone picks the thing up. It's the fantasy of ultimate individualism and willfulness, which can be engaged when all else fails, to compensate for the lost Dream. When you can't live like the Bradys or the Huxtables, the Corleones and the Sopranos are offering an alternate lifestyle on other side of town. In this alternate American Dreamscape, one pull of the trigger and you can instantly and permanently alter the world and whoever or whatever is standing in your way.

The power of this fantasy is at the root of the addictive attraction of guns. When you hear from childhood on that you live in "the land of opportunity," that you are "special," that you can "be all you can be," or you simply see this self aggrandizement all around, then someone or something comes along and clips your wings, the ability to reach for a gun is like having a god-like sense of agency in your back pocket.

A MYTHOLOGY OF BULLETS

The psychology of bullets, which stands behind the addiction to guns, derives from a deeper mythos. One of the earliest images of humans assimilating god-like powers has to do with the fashioning of projectiles by smith-gods or divine-smiths. As Eliade points out, myths in which smith-gods make weapons for divinities indicate the movement into the Metal Age. He writes: "The smith of the gods forges weapons similar to lightning and the thunderbolt . . . In their turn, human smiths imitate the work of their super-human patrons."[21] A Finnish myth amplifies the same theme—the story of a world-tree, a Giant Oak, being felled by a hero from the sea, whereupon the chips are taken to a sorcerer who crafts the first arrows. At the moment of dissolution of original unity the first projectiles fall into human hands. In the words of the story: "So as the Cosmos is created with light, earth and the conscious man, the arrows of evil are also made simultaneously."[22]

So myth tells us that the original projectiles belonged to the gods and only secondarily did they fall into human hands. Thousands of years of weaponry have yet to dilute this root metaphor, this original transmission of god-likeness. It backgrounds the grandiosity, the inflation that comes from having your finger on the trigger. As Caroline Burnham says in the iconic film *American Beauty*, "All I know is that I LOVE shooting this gun." And she drives home from the firing range singing along to Bobby Darin: "Nobody, I said nobody, had better rain on my parade." The more one is swept up by the idea of pulling a trigger here and instantly, profoundly, altering someone's reality over there, the more you transcend the normal limits and boundaries of human interaction. The ability to launch a cruise missile a few hundred miles from its target, or aim a few hundred nuclear warheads at Russia has the same feeling—the feeling of omnipotence.

At a certain point you can't help but see the connections between projectiles at home and projectiles abroad. Lying on the couch watching laser-guided bombs going through doorways in Baghdad reinforces the idea that you can deal with everything by firing from a distance. It's a distance that no number of "imbedded" reporters on the network newscasts can overcome. It goes too deep. It's a mirror of the distance between the upper and underworld of the American character. It's the distance between the rhetoric of Operation Iraqi Freedom and the faces of dead Iraqis that the imbedded reporters never seem to come across. Seeing this pattern in 1970, in the aptly titled *The Pursuit of Loneliness: American Culture at the Breaking Point*, Philip Slater wrote, "America has developed more elaborate, complex, and grotesque techniques for exterminating people at a distance than any nation in the history of the world." He suggested that, "perhaps the distance itself carries special meaning."[23]

Projectiles are fired when the imagination can see no option but continued forward movement, when the only way out of a predicament is to move ahead by targeting, then removing the objects in your way. "Objects" being the operative word, because by the time someone pulls the trigger that's what their targets have become. In Klebold and Harris' case it was the jocks and the Christians, at Virginia Tech it was the "rich kids." It may just be "the cashier," standing between you and what you want. By the time you pull the trigger, the human face has already gone and some projection has stepped in to beckon its projectile twin. Objectification and distancing, projection and projectiles go together. Your victims are the disagreeable parts of your inner pantheon, in need of a lightning bolt or two.

If we can for a moment deliteralize the gun, keeping in mind its psychic firepower and its mythic background, we see that working on the problem means working on the cultural values and imaginings that give weight and energy to the *idea* of needing and using a gun. What it comes down to is this: Can a way of life be cultivated in which there isn't such exclusive emphasis on willful accomplishment and material success, where it isn't as easy to objectify and stereotype others, where instant gratification is a sickness not a right? If the playing field in each of these areas were altered, the need for guns and the motivation to use them would significantly decline. Which brings us back to the question of media influences.

Can the media open up the imagination with complex, multifaceted characters with strengths and shadows rather than express formulaic American success stories? Media images of *structural* violence, including objectification, stereotyping, character assassination, and polarizing commentary may well be doing more damage than depictions of overt, literal violence. Graphic violence imbedded in an underworld narrative and aura of psychopathology should not be confused with the constant stream of gun-toting bright, shiny heroes who swagger through the world and shoot from the hip. Television shows like *American Idol*, with its endless parade of winners and losers, may promote more violence than *The Sopranos*, with its anxiety-ridden and deeply flawed protagonist. The former is full of structural violence but hides it; the latter puts the violence in your face but places it in context. Here's the point: Half an hour of Nancy Grace or Rush Limbaugh with their rapid-fire opinions and inability to sustain dialogue is effectively more violent, more sustaining of a bullet psychology and mythology than an afternoon of Spaghetti Westerns.

Looking Back

What I hinted at the start can now be stated more directly: The obsession with guns, with projectiles and with their devastating effects, whether in the world or in media depictions, keeps us from seeing a deeper more pervasive cultural violence. Both the incessant drive forward that goes with the gun and the utter blindness to what's going on beneath the surface indicates where the missing and corrective mythos resides: namely, backward, down and in.

Gun violence is the most acute expression of the American propensity to act rather than think or reflect. The actual gun translates this tendency into bloodshed, but the real culprit is the constant movement and the rugged individualism that's welded to it: The going West in the Western; the sense of rights in the right to bear arms; the hip's swagger not what it's wearing. Gun violence is a perverted, mindless attempt to maintain progress in a world that values assertion and getting ahead above all else. When you hit a wall there are too few images for turning around, looking back, retracing steps, or simply stopping for a while. What's missing on the Juggernaut that moves the American psyche is a rear-view mirror—something, *anything*, that helps us engage the underworld, that aspect of the imagination that holds the weight of death and cultivates a relation to loss, mourning, and sacrifice. An underworld imagination gives us options and alternate routes when the way ahead is blocked. It would make meaning from failure. It would give us a real understanding of being stuck. It would slow the *Titanic* down. It would provide a counterweight to the trigger-happy mania of this collective. Beyond individual psychopathology, failed background checks, assault rifles, and video games, open up any incidence of American gun violence and you'll find a distorted idea of achievement and an incapacity to imagine well being when the movement stops.

James Hillman, in his recent work, *A Terrible Love of War*, emphasizes this downward direction in trying to understand the pull of warfare. He considers the American Civil War by "attempting to imagine it from below."[24] He writes:

> To visit the dead for knowledge repeats a long tradition. The great teachers of culture entered the underworld to gain understanding, sometimes to rescue or repent. Ulysses, Orpheus, Aeneas, Ianna, Dionysos, Psyche, Persephone, even Hercules.[25]

Hillman links this underworld style of understanding to the very nature of understanding, reminding us that Hans-Georg Gadamer said "understanding involves a 'loss of self'." He goes on: "It is an unconditional surrender, a falling from mental superiority to a falling in with, going along with, the peculiarly devious paths of Hermes *chthonious*, the earthly aspect of the god of hermeneutics."[26] This idea echoes Keats' notion of "negative capability" and is present to Paul

Ricoeur's idea of "second naivety." It points to the ability to value mystery. Put another way, what deep insight often requires is "a willing renunciation of willing."[27] In other words, to gain any real understanding, we need to stop simply going forward.

FINALLY

If you've tracked the meandering path I've taken here, it's not too difficult to see that actual guns and their use are extensions of a whole series of cultural conditions, psychological patterns, and ultimately mythic images. Episodic acts of gun violence literalize an everyday mythology. Guns express the compulsive need for individual agency, for expedient, black and white solutions to complex problems, and for the exercise of power at a distance. They carry the feeling of connection to something essentially American, running through the Wild West, the second amendment, the citizen militia and reach back into an entire mythos of projectiles. "God and Guns" is the bumper sticker version, conveying just how much guns carry an archetypal power in the national psyche.

With few exceptions—think of Melville, the Gothic vision of the South, the subterranean power of the Vietnam memorial, and the Coen brothers' films—America has little imagination for loss and failure. It knows only how to move forward. Perhaps both the recent economic downturn and the prospect of leadership with an eye for what we've turned our backs on will begin to loosen the collective blinders. But I wouldn't hold my breath. For the most part, America remains identified with *Butch Cassidy and the Sundance Kid* running to their deaths with guns blazing, with Caroline Burnham in *American Beauty* at the shooting range, with Dirty Harry's law unto himself, and with the psychopath, Anton Chigurh, in *No Country for Old Men.*

There's no surgical solution to gun violence because the tumor is growing on too many vital organs of the collective body. The symptoms, which might be curtailed or managed, will ultimately resist treatment because they're imbedded in the national character, whose great strengths—perseverance against the odds, innovative spirit, and determination—are also its weaknesses—a lack of introspection and an inability to digest its transgressions. Transfixed by "the rocket's red glare" and "the bombs bursting in air," the night goes unseen.

The consistent aim of projectiles is to distance the shooter and an experience of the underworld. The corrective move—the therapeutic intervention—would be to validate and cultivate ways in and down rather than up and out: mindful reflection instead of mindless action, negative capability instead of the power of positive thinking, imagination instead of concretization. Perhaps then the eagle eye of American consciousness, which is always scanning the horizon, always searching, might start soul-searching too.

NOTES

1. According to a survey conducted in 2004 by L. Hepburn, M. Miller, D. Azrael, and D. Hemenway at the Department of Health Policy and Management, Harvard School of Medicine, 38% of households in the United States have firearms.

2. http://www.atf.gov/firearms/stats/index.htm. Retrieved 2/19/09.

3. See the Centers for Disease Control and Prevention website for up-to-date and comparative statistics on firearms related deaths and injuries: http://www.cdc.gov/. In 1993, according to another survey, 39,595 were killed by firearms. (E. G. Krug, K. E. Powell and L. L. Dahlberg, "Firearm-Related Deaths in the United States and 35 other High- and Upper-Middle-Income Countries," *International Journal of Epidemiology*, [1998], 27, 214-221).

4. Bob Herbert, *The New York Times*, January 1, 2001.

5. Krug, *et al., op. cit.*

6. National Public Radio. "All Things Considered." Broadcast 4/3/08.

7. Switzerland and Finland have household gun ownership rates of 27% and 23% respectively (http://www.allcountries.org/gun_ownership_rates.html). However, the homicide by firearm rate in the United States is 8 to 10 times higher than these countries. Retrieved 2/19/09.

8. Krug, *et al., op. cit.*

9. Gordon Barclay & Cynthia Tavares, "International Comparisons of Criminal Justice Statistics 2001," Issue 12/03, http://www.crimereduction.homeoffice.gov.uk/statistics/statistics30.htm. Retrieved 2/19/09.

10. *Ibid.*

11. Kevin D. Browne and Catherine Hamilton-Giachritsis, "The Influence of Violent Media on Children and Adolescents: A Public Health Approach," *The Lancet*, Volume 365, Issue 9460, 2005, 702-710.

12. See the Virginia Tech Review Panel Report, available online: http://www.vtreviewpanel.org/report/report/11_CHAPTER_IV.pdf.

13. Glen Slater, "A Psychology of Bullets," *The Salt Journal*, Volume 2, Number 3, 19.

14. Steven Messner and Richard Rosefield, cited in Slater, *op. cit.*, p. 20.

15. Steven Messner and Richard Rosefield, *Crime and the American Dream* (Belmont CA: Wadsworth Publishing, 1997).

16. Slater, *op. cit.*, p. 21.

17. Cited in Slater, *op. cit.*, p. 21.

18. Thomas Frank, *What's the Matter with Kansas?* (New York: Henry Holt and Company, 2004).

19. Slater, *op. cit.*, p. 21.

20. James Gilligan, *Violence: Reflections on a National Epidemic* (New York: Knopf, 1997), p. 96.

21. Mircea Eliade, *The Forge and the Crucible: The Origins and Structures of Alchemy* (Chicago: University of Chicago Press, 1978), p. 101.

22. http://www.finnishmyth.org/p11projectiles1.html. Retrieved 2/19/09.

23. Philip Slater, *The Pursuit of Loneliness: American Culture at the Breaking Point* (Toronto: Beacon Press, 1970), p. 42.

24. James Hillman, *A Terrible Love of War* (New York: Penguin Press, 2004), p. 102.

25. *Ibid.*

26. *Ibid.*, p. 103.

27. Roberts Avens, *The New Gnosis: Heidegger, Hillman and Angels* (Putnam, CT: Spring Publications, 2003), p. 99.

IS PEACE THE CAUSE OF VIOLENCE?

ALLAN GUGGENBÜHL

The land is full of bloody crimes and the city full of violence.
—Ezek. 7:23

More than 5,000 applicants registered during the first two days. The organizers were overwhelmed by the response. They had called for a human peace chain, linking the German cities of Osnabrück and Münster. Their intention was to take a firm stand against violence. *Nie mehr Krieg!* was written on their posters. All the local newspapers and even some national television channels covered the event. Everyone was full of praise for the courageous act.

A sign of change? Does a demonstration like the one in Osnabrück indicate that humans are finally putting an end to violence? Gradually, we might conclude, it is dawning on us that violence is *not* the answer. Peace movements are often hailed as vanguards, on the forefront of a new development. Change is possible and peace in our hands, if we

Allan Guggenbühl is a psychologist and Jungian psychotherapist in Zürich, Switzerland, Professor at the University of Education of the State of Zürich (www.phzh.ch), Director of the Department for Group Psychotherapy for Children and Adolescents at the Educational Counselling Center of the State of Bern, and Director of the Institute of Conflict Management and Mythodrama in Zürich (www.ikm.ch). He specializes in violence among adolescents, men's issues, and conflicts in public transport organizations. He has published various books on violence, school culture, and gender issues. His books in English include *Men, Myth, Power* (New York: Continuum, 1997) and *The Incredible Fascination of Violence* (Putnam, CT: Spring Publications, 1996).

try hard enough. According to Ashley Montagu's UNESCO resolution, violence is non-human, universal brotherhood more natural.[1]

Historically, our longing for peace is not unique. The abhorrence for violence is as old as humanity itself. Apparently, humans have always expressed disgust for wars and killings, and looked down on warriors. The condemnation of violence can be traced back to ancient times.[2] If we look at history we see, though, that the attitude towards violence remained ambivalent. Soldiers were both admired and looked upon with contempt. War heroes receive victory parades and are then neglected and marginalized. To be consciously violent was, and is, considered *insane,* permitted only under special circumstances—as an act of defense or in retaliation. Our wish for peace is genuine, deep-rooted, and mutual.

There is a problem, however: declarations, statements, and conscious attitudes do not reflect our actual motives. Pledges against violence are outcomes of conscious reflections about life. We contemplate our existence, analyze the experiences we have, and then try to understand what we see. We try to make sense of our *Dasein* and obtain an orientation in our life. But formulating rules and devising concepts has its dangers. Focused thinking can lead us astray. Instead of being touched, inspired, or repulsed by the phenomenon of violence, we operate with categories, definitions, and logical assumptions so as to avoid confronting the issue. We retreat into abstractions in order to gloss over the paradoxes, irrationality, and obscenities with which we are presented. We draw lines, act intelligent, and talk of the good, but actually we are distancing ourselves from the messiness of the world around us. We lose contact with the phenomena themselves. This danger is especially pronounced when we are dealing with violence. Unconscious preconceptions may limit our view. When we condemn dreadful events, when we call them an insult to humanity or consider them pathological, we run the risk of failing to recognize the true significance of violence, for we have left the realm of psychology. We may become acclaimed do-gooders, but we are unable to recognize the essence of violence. Taking a moral stand against violence might be courageous under certain conditions (if, for instance, you were member of a Nazi firing squad during the uprisings in the Warsaw Ghetto), but often it is no more than an act of avoidance. From a psychological point of view, the affirmation of non-violence is risky. Morality can blind us to the intricacies of our shadow. A consciousness of impurity is a prerequisite for dealing with the contents of our shadow. Without it we are unable to appreciate the dynamics and motives behind darker issues.[3]

They had been planning the crime for some time. They had chosen one of their classmates as their target. They were not against him; he just seemed like the appropriate victim. They had their reasons: he often behaved strangely and was a bit stuck up. The two youngsters were convinced: he had to be dealt with. One Friday afternoon they were ready. They invited their unsuspecting victim to play hide and seek. When it was his turn to be the seeker, they crept up on him while he was counting and stabbed him with a kitchen knife. He died on the spot.

The murder caused bewilderment and a major upheaval in the small town of Dägerswil in the state of St. Gallen, Switzerland. The townsfolk were stunned; they could not think of any possible reason why these two amiable youngsters had killed their friend. As part of the crisis intervention initiated at the school, we were commissioned to take care of the students in the victim's class and provide assistance to the teachers. We talked to the classmates of the perpetrators. Shock, horror, and fear prevailed. A lot of tears were shed and many candles were lit. Every other student confessed to being a friend of the murdered boy. What surprised us, though, was that a considerable number of the female classmates of the perpetrators did not react with disgust, but with open admiration. Of course, they followed the prevailing moral code and made token condemnations of the brutal act, but at the same time they clandestinely wrote long, passionate love letters to the two juvenile murderers, confessing their "true love" for them and promising to wait for them until they were released from the juvenile delinquent detention center. Some of the girls explicitly offered themselves to the two boys.

How shall we understand this reaction? The phenomenon is widespread. Serials killers who manage to make it into the news and get their face in the tabloids are often flooded with marriage proposals! Being a killer obviously increases one's chances with the opposite sex. Media exposure alone does not have the same effect. Appearing on TV *and* being described as a killer apparently makes men sexy to a lot of women. Of course, we cannot generalize. We are convinced that our own daughters, wives, sisters, and female neighbors would certainly never get involved in a liaison with a killer. The phenomenon is an indication, though, that our attitude towards violence is more complex than we are aware of. When it comes to violence, our reactions are unpredictable and uncanny. Brutal, evil men and women evoke strange emotions and eerie fantasies. Our morals vanish in a haze when these unconscious urges take over. We have to realize that our condemnations of violence and our demonstrations for peace are only skin deep.

Viewed in historical perspective, it is obvious. As soon as moral barriers are torn down or the *Zeitgeist* permits it, our ambivalent attitude towards violence emerges.[4] Violent, aggressive individuals are praised when the political circumstances allow it and it is socially acceptable. In times of national crisis or war we cheer the heroes who defend our country or fight for a noble cause. "Well done, boys!" the crowd enthusiastically cheers. Many—including me—had tears in their eyes when members of the brave Falklands War forces paraded past us down the streets of London. They had just returned from the South Atlantic, where they had been attacking and shooting the ill-fated and abused young Argentine conscripts. The emotions of the bystanders were palpable. A challenge to the nation's sovereignty had legitimized this adoration of men and women who excelled in the use of violence. Killers had turned into heroes, just like the defenders of the turf among the Crips and Bloods in Los Angeles, or the pirates off the coast of Somalia, who tout themselves as protectors of the fishing grounds. The enthusiasm for violent individuals has many historical antecedents. Crowds of enthusiastic people applauded the German soldiers as they marched to their deaths in the trenches of the First World War. The *kamikaze* pilots in Japan, who were considered demi-gods, lived a life of abundance and were afforded any pleasure that struck their fancy before they were called up for duty. When a society sanctions the use violence, this is usually welcomed with praise, joy, and even relief. One finally has official sanction to glory in acts of violence.[5]

When the official doctrine forbids the praise of violence, the situation becomes a bit more complicated. We are confronted with a moral dilemma. In order to avoid moral condemnation or the odd look, mental tricks are devised and loopholes exploited. We cover up our admiration by using plausible excuses or constructing a rationale for it. We need a subterfuge so our fascination with violence is not obvious. Women who propose to killers claim that their objects of adoration are victims of society or childhood abuse, or are lost souls. They are convinced that these men are not evil because their eyes tell a different story. Some of them are certain that they will be able to vindicate these poor souls through their relationship. They offer their empathy and love as a remedy.

Confessions by ex-convicts or terrorists invite adulation. If they admit having been a sinner, then they are worth our forgiveness. We admire the gang leader who has turned peaceful and writes children's books about peace, or the terrorist who regrets that people have suffered because of him. The daughter of Ulrike Meinhof, the adored and famed leader of the RAF, a terrorist group active in Germany in the 70s, told me she was absolutely appalled by the adoration her mother received. The public praised her mother as a strong-willed, ingenious leader and idealist led astray. In the eyes of her daughter, she was just pathetic— a psychopath and a mental case.

The media feeds our desire for violent issues. Day after day, we are presented with scenes that allow us to express at the same time both our contempt and our fascination with violence. We shake our heads when we see horrid pictures of a car bombing in Kabul, but stay glued to the screen. Violence knows many cunning ways to reach us. When we finally see the images, we are transformed, shocked, energized, and alerted. Although we consciously condemn violence, we are attracted to acts of brutality. It seems we continuously need to be fed with stories and images of the dreadful.

VIOLENCE HAS DIFFERENT MEANINGS

Violence is energy which aims to destroy, eliminate, or harm an object or person. Violence deconstructs or alters a given situation. In most cases, to be violent means to violate boundaries, social codes, or gradually developed conditions. We are violent when we live in aggression without any restraint, disrespecting codes. When I slap someone I disagree with during a debate about gardening, then my behavior is not appropriate. I violate the code that disputes should be carried out civilly. When I cut down the trees in front of my house because I believe I am entitled to have a full view of Lake Zürich, in the eyes of the town council I have acted violently, ignoring the Preservation Act. When I shoot a fellow car driver because he refused to give me the right of way, my behavior exceeds the standard reaction to an insolent car driver; an angry face, a honk, or maybe a gesture would have been a more proper response. Violence is aggression gone haywire.

In European countries, violence is delegated to the State, which is allowed to use it to enforce law and order. If we rely on violence for personal goals or deeds, this is considered not normal—a pathology, or at least a mistake. We call for sanctions. When a man beats up his wife to settle a dispute once and forever, he needs to be detained. When an adolescent robs a liquor store because he wants to impress his friends, he will be placed in a corrections center. Violence on a large scale is even more condemned. We are appalled by the genocide that took place between the Tutsis and the Hutu in 1994, and in the killing fields of Cambodia. We value such events as something out of the normal, not human. People engaged in such acts must certainly be over the edge.

As violence is considered an anomaly, we search for causes. We try to explain the outlandish behavior by identifying an event that can be blamed for the obscene or deviant incident. As psychologists, we search for clues in childhood. Why can't he or she adapt? Something must have gone wrong between the infant and the parents; an abusive or toxic environment, or severe mistreatment must be the cause of the violent behavior. We search for past sexual abuse or pathetic relations when we work with deranged men or women. The family situation comes under close scrutiny. We search for clues among the kin of the perpetrators. Violence calls for explanations. Pundits appear and share their background knowledge about the origins of violence. A bigoted social environment and a problematic relation to an older brother were proposed as the main factors that turned the friendly, gregarious Urs Hans von Asch into the brutal rapist and murderer who killed the five-year-old Ylenia. In public, his vile deed was interpreted as an unconscious act of revenge.[6] Often, we search for answers on a more general level. We turn to social, political, or religious systems to comprehend violence. The dire economic situation is identified as one of the reasons for the violence in Somalia and in the Northwestern Provinces of Pakistan. Violence is perceived as a sign of a desperate or dissolving society. Unjust political agreements or situations are also seen as causes of violence. The reparation payments imposed on Germany by the Treaty of Versailles are said to have led to the outbreak of the Second World War. Sociologists are always quick to present answers: the exploitation of the Békés[7] is seen as one of the main reasons for the outbreak of violence in the French Caribbean islands of Guadeloupe and Martinique in February 2009.

The pattern repeats itself: when confronted with violence, we link the horrendous or irritating incident with a theoretically manageable situation. The economic situation in Somalia or the Northwestern Provinces could be improved by economic aid. Peace treaties can be negotiated in a just and fair way and children can be given love and understanding. "Violence would not occur if we had behaved sanely and sensibly" is the underlying message. If we had all done our homework, things would be better. We just did not try hard enough.

It is interesting to observe, though, on what lines we argue. When trying to identify the causes of violence, we quote the ideologies, values, and professional points of view we adhere to anyway. Violence is used as a subterfuge to expound our personal, national, and professional beliefs. "The killing happened because the school was built on a site where the water streams radiate bad energy!" a young woman declared at the town hall meeting in Degersheim after we tried to soothe the locals by giving some explanation for the stabbing of a youth there: it was a freak accident. Our efforts were in vain. Everyone already knew the answer as to why the murder had taken place; no explanations from experts were required. "Those beastly foreigners are to blame!" asserted an elderly gentleman, ignoring the fact that the victim was himself a foreigner. A stylishly dressed lady held up the Bible and blamed the lack of religious organization as the cause of the killing. The major finally stopped her ranting.

The town hall meeting draws our attention to a common phenomenon: we take advantage of violence incidents to propound our well-established positions and religious beliefs. We reveal ourselves as Protestant, Catholic, Jew, a member of the Green Party, a socialist, a conservative, or a follower of the Buddha. This happens on a personal as well as on a professional level. The only difference is that as professionals we insist on the *objectivity* of our position. We recite the core arguments of our profession and argue along those lines: if we belong to the teachers' guild, we declare that violence can be eliminated if children undergo violence prevention training and are better informed about the consequences of violence; as feminists, we are convinced that the solution lies in rooting out unconscious male chauvinism. We identify the causes in terms of our own ideology in an attempt to locate the violent incident in an appropriate realm. In retrospect, at least, we want to gain control over the disturbing event. The key message is that the likelihood of violence and conflicts would diminish if others would adhere to our values and norms and rely on our competencies. Confronted with violence, we react by offering our belief system as a remedy. We psychologists are no exception. Psychologists are convinced that a happy childhood, analysis, motherly love, and empathic relations can alleviate the problem of violence.[8] If only our unconscious fellow citizens would listen!

In trying to understand violence, we also often invoke scientific explanations. If we belong to academia our answers might even carry some weight. What comes out of the mouth of a university professor or an acclaimed scholar is considered more intelligent and is consequently less likely to be criticized. Statements by experts relieve ordinary folk of the necessity to think for themselves. The assumption is that the explanation of experts is based upon knowledge that has been cleansed of subjectivity and bias, that it is based on sound, objective methodology. Answers from academia are prone to be influenced by the *Zeitgeist*, just like explanations offered by any other body. Adverse stimuli, social learning, genetic factors, race, cognitive dissonances, repressed sexuality, instrumental conditioning, a dysfunctional brain, and overpopulation are some of the explanations that have been given over the course of time.[9] Currently, neurological and Darwinian explanations are in vogue. Violence is seen as a result of an underdeveloped frontal cortex[10] or the malfunctioning of the limbic system.[11] Brain metaphors insinuate materialistic correspondences—proofs. The danger lies in thinking that we are certain we know the hard facts and are therefore exempt from taking into account the debates taking place within neuroscience and the fuzziness of many of the results of neurobiological research. Brain metaphors feed our illusion that we can pin down violence once and for all.

Violence can be placed within a historical context. It can be seen as a residue of a prehistoric, primitive society, in which continuous fights and attacks were a prerequisite for survival,[12] or perhaps just the opposite, the result of the emergence of cognition.[13] Often violence is linked to injustice or political events of the past. The violent humans of today bear the brunt of the missteps of their forebears. We deride the endeavors of our ancestors. Africa would be a peaceful continent today if the British and French colonists had respected ethnic boundaries instead of creating fictitious nation states. The Paris riots of 1968 could have been avoided if government officials had been more flexible and offered an open dialogue.

THE PLATONIC ATTITUDE

Under closer scrutiny it becomes obvious that this type of reasoning reflects a Platonic attitude. To understand or account for the phenomenon, it invokes conditions that are beyond the actual situation. A domain is assumed that transcends current circumstances. A stable system is offered as a reference point, be it the equilibrium of nature, a psychological condition, or a model society. Violence is seen as a deviation from this hypothetically perfect system. Everything would have been fine if an unforeseen flaw had not disrupted an otherwise perfect system. When we argue along these lines, we are implying that there is still hope that we can do things perfectly. Let's get it right the next time! Also, by citing a supreme standard we maintain our innocence. Faced with violence, we theorize about an ideal economic system, demand equal rights, dream of effective communication skills, call for a socialistic or a free-market economy. "Violence need not be" is the gist of the message. Jungians refer to wholeness, a successful individuation; or they start talking about the gods. By choosing a reference point beyond our realm, we of course distance ourselves from the empirical reality of life. The sublime role model influences our thinking and perception. Violence is a sad, undisputable reality of life. Africa might have been bellicose anyway and the French students perhaps rioted because it was their way of partying. We cling to our ideals even when they hardly ever materialize. When we consult history books, we detect a blood trail up to the present. Things keep going wrong. Repeatedly, societies were convinced that they had found the key to peace and that wars would no longer happen. When trains were introduced in Europe connecting the major cities and clocks consequently had to be synchronized, both experts and laymen were convinced that the increased possibilities of cross-cultural contact would make war impossible or at least less likely! This was shortly before the outbreak of the First World War. Today the European Union is praised as a vanguard against conflicts between European states; let's hope and pray that this expectation will be fulfilled. Judging from the past, we would have to conclude that only *one* premonition is certain: violence and armed conflicts will not leave us! Although we know the answers *theoretically* and continually convince ourselves that we are right, we fail; violence remains a great scandal. The results of our endeavors and noble intentions have been disastrous.

Consciousness of Failure

A possible explanation for this phenomenon is our lack of consciousness of failure. We have difficulty acknowledging that every society or system has its flaws, just as we, personally, constantly make mistakes and create disasters. Romantic relationships end up unintentionally in a nasty divorce; CEOs' ambitious plans for turning a company around often lead to bankruptcy, just as a long-planned hiking trip up the Rigi may perhaps turn into a nightmare. Fiascoes belong to our lives. They are an integral part of our existences; let's stop believing we can control our future.

We have difficulty accepting that our grand plans, concepts, and solutions are rarely foolproof. Even though they might be scientifically proven or represent the mainstream, they are often more akin to dreams than to the hard-edged reality of life. For instance, it has not yet been proven that economic well-being renders people more peaceful.[14] Rich people are not happier or more civilized than poor people; wealth might, in fact, spoil us. Also, communication does not necessarily lead to better mutual understanding. When we talk to each other, we might become aware of the disdain we feel for the other person. And, nowhere has it been proven that honesty, altruism, and love pay off. Perhaps crooks are indeed more successful; they might run our society. The smartest ones conceal their evil deeds behind soothing phraseology.[15] It is even possible that more psychology is a problem rather than a solution. Instead of becoming more sensitive, we turn tricky and false. Psychology may actually increase our skills at deception.

Although the counter-evidence around us is manifold, we still believe in our solutions and draw up nice models. We don't want to relinquish "*das Prinzip Hoffnung*" when we try to comprehend and prevent violence. We refer to idealistic situations, quote ideologies, or appeal to religious beliefs when the great irritant, violence, crosses our path. We react to violence by promoting solutions that are in accord with an idealistic *Weltanschauung*.

It is highly improbable that our models provide a sufficient explanation for violence. Violence is by definition largely an unexpected event. Because of the vast number of variables that influence the occurrence of a specific event, violence is unpredictable. We observe patterns and draw conclusions only in retrospect. When we overestimate past experience, we become victims of linear thinking. The idea that we can learn from the past is something of a delusion, since future events are often influenced by variables that we have not even begun to identify. Nobody could have foreseen the attacks of 9/11 or imagined the atrocities of Nazi Germany. Because we can hardly ever program violence, it is scientifically impossible to identify definitive causes for it. The rioting by adolescent immigrants in the *beaulieus* of France could not have been predicted and cannot be replicated under "controlled conditions" to arrive at "evidence-based" knowledge. Since violence comes as a surprise, our explanations remain speculative. The immigrant youth in France may have started looting stores and torching cars because of alienation from society or a lack of job opportunities, or because they came from deprived families, but it is equally possible that they turned violent because they were not beaten up by their peers or they were not allowed to participate in orgies. There are thousands of plausible explanations that can be offered in retrospect—some politically correct and some outlandish. What we consider credible depends on our ideology, the norms and values of our peers, and our general attitude towards life. When we try to explain violence, we tend to recite fantasies. We interpret the past according to our belief system in order to promote our ideas. Our explanations are always belated. If a school turns out peaceful and knowledgeable students, we of course attribute this to school discipline, good morale, a friendly atmosphere. If the very same school is ravaged by a violent incident, we immediately have other interpretations at hand: lack of discipline, uncommunicative surroundings, poor leadership. Unexpected events generate explanations that we project onto the past.

To identify causes in retrospect is perfectly sane, and even necessary. In order to gain control over our lives, keep our cool, and remain active, we need plausible explanations of what is happening around us. They are the basis of our undertakings. We need *Handlungstheorien* in order not to lose faith in life and ourselves. Simple ideas make the world go round. We need theories that clarify our challenges and problems so we can become active. We are not in need of philosophical or psychological deliberations. We gain confidence in ourselves because of simplified answers. When we realize that we are oblivious to the backgrounds, then we might stop abating violence and be motivated to fight for a better world. To remain doers, we need a theory that legitimizes actions and points in a specific direction, even though it might be the wrong one. If we are aware that we are advancing in a foggy terrain, then maybe we turn into cynics, aloof philosophers, or hurdy-gurdy men. We would lack the courage to become engaged citizens. Restricted views enable us to become involved and fight violence.[16]

VIOLENCE AS A SOUL MATTER

"Everything was calm. The passengers of the first two second-class carriages willingly presented me their tickets and IDs. I was expecting no difficulties as I advanced into first class. A brief look at the toilet door made me suspicious. Someone was rattling the unlocked door from the inside. I knocked and said hello, but did not receive an answer. When I carefully pushed the door open, it happened. The toilet door burst open and a well-dressed woman planted herself squarely before me, disgust in her eyes. "You asshole, how dare you!" she yelled, punching me in the stomach, and spitting in my face. I felt her saliva sliding down between my eyes. I shivered and was stunned. Before I had a chance to answer, the lady got off the train, having given me the finger as a goodbye!"

A minor incident—violence between passengers and train personnel is widespread in parts of Europe. At the Institute of Conflict Management and Mythodrama,[17] of which I am head, we try to help and train personnel of the Swiss Federal Railways to handle conflicts and gain competence in diffusing potentially violent situations. Part of our job is to analyze violent incidents and propose remedies. The incident narrated above was one of the cases we had to deal with. At first glance it is a quite trivial event with not much violence involved. Passengers regularly try to avoid paying the fare by hiding in the toilet and leaving the door unlocked, so the train conductor does not get suspicious—an old trick. Sure, this fare dodger was unusually aggressive; spitting does not belong in the basic repertory of fare dodgers, and it is not proper for women to hit railway staff! What I want to concentrate on here is the trauma the incident caused in the young female train conductor. The psychological repercussions were manifold and paradoxical. She was unable to shrug off the event as easily as she had wiped off the salvia of the bellicose passenger. She felt deeply humiliated and discontinued working for a while. She kept thinking of the aggressive woman's demeanor; the hatred she detected in the woman's eyes was burned into her mind and the spitting offended her deeply. Other images kept coming up. Memories of a nasty schoolteacher were suddenly very present. Paradoxically, at the same time her relationship with her boyfriend improved and she started to act more assertive.

What does this example tell us about violence? The conductor reacted according to her personal profile. You and I might have responded differently: we might have stayed cool, jumped off the train, or spat back. The impact of violence cannot be anticipated. Violence unfolds its meaning during the actual event. It is not a question of stimulus and response, but rather, a simultaneous, multilayered process. Provided that we don't deal with violence professionally on a regular basis and therefore manage to shield ourselves from its effects, violent incidents trigger various dynamics in a number of directions. Basically, when we experience violence, we are thrust back upon ourselves. Our emotions run amok and our conventional thinking patterns are dismantled. Our inner life turns into an outer experience and outer experiences are re-enacted internally. The boundary between inner and outer becomes porous and permeable. Violence can weaken our internal structures and defenses. Everything is in turmoil. The cards are flung into the air and we don't know in what order they will land. Complexes are reactivated, old fears and desires awakened. Our personality experiences a major shake up. Violence launches us into existence, *das Dasein*; simultaneously we are confronted with our inner self.

Violence makes our psychological functions go out of control; our perception changes. Often we lose confidence in familiar procedures and well-accustomed codes. Following the spitting incident, the railway employee felt she was working in a fiendish environment. Under the influence of violence, a hitherto comfortable situation can become *intolerable.* Suddenly we feel unsafe, angry, revved up, and ready to strike. He insulted me! I need to beat him up! We see the world through different eyes. When we interview young men at my institute who have been sent to us by the courts because of their involvement in violence, we are astonished at the picture they draw of the violent acts in which they were involved. In most cases their descriptions of the events have little resemblance to the police reports. What strikes us, though, is that unlike the dry accounts by the police or the court officials, their version of the events often has narrative qualities. They talk of vile provocations and threats; they report feeling that their values were being endangered. They were fighting for the honor of their country, avenging a despicable act by a rival, or retaliating against a degenerate Albanian gang from Bümplitz; in the police reports we read merely of a group of bored youngsters looking for trouble. In the midst of violence, we are forced to re-interpret our surroundings and the behavior of our fellow human beings. The world of the moment becomes aggrandized and deepened. People trapped in scenes of violence often assign significance to behavior patterns, words, and objects that they were hitherto unaware of. They become acutely conscious of the emotional loading of the situation and the in-depth meaning of minor details. A gesture, a stern look, a trifling movement become major events. The scene is enlarged. The hatred in the eyes of the spitting woman on the train is transmuted into a gorgonic stare and the obscene gesture becomes an act of deliberate shaming. A banal event becomes part of a grand drama. An aggressive juvenile is no longer arguing with Officer Hugentobler, who is trying to convince him not to smoke pot on the train; in the juvenile's eyes the police officer is a representative of an oppressive capitalistic society, a society that seeks to deprive him of his natural rights and to press him into a little box. Police officers are not human; they are pigs! Grand stories, tales of horror emerge and myths are being told.

The turmoil we are thrown into through violence is the product of a fusion of inner and outer issues. Our personal stories, complexes, bottled-up angers or frustrations are re-activated by the repulsive, uncomfortable, or uncanny situation or physical pain we are experiencing.[18] The train conductor saw her teacher in the attacking woman: she loaded the situation with a childhood memory. When engaged in a violent situation, we often re-define our mode of being; a new story emerges in order to protect,[19] traumatize,[20] or irritate us.

Violence leads to a re-shuffling of the different components of personality. As defenses break down and taboos are violated, decompensations are common. Hot issues, personal injuries, or anger, which under normal conditions remain hidden, appear on the scene. Violence releases us from the obligation to abide by social norms. We can't hide behind our persona any more; we now have license to become raw, primitive, or visionary. This re-shuffling might bring sensitive issues to the surface. A potentially dangerous image or memory re-emerges and irritates us, causing us trauma. The image does not have to originate in an actual historical event. It can be a powerful fantasy, locked away in us as a result of circumstance or political correctness. The violent incident destabilizes us and brings forward a destructive or creative element that had hitherto been neutralized. The traumatized train conductor was confronted with the image of a nasty teacher. It is possible that this raving and ranting schoolmistress never existed. The image may well have had not personal, but archetypal roots. The incident on the train brought forward a tendency in her of which she had not been aware. She abided by rules and regulations willingly, but at the same time may have created a nasty authoritarian figure in order to justify her suffering and perhaps initiate a rebellion. Her psyche took advantage of the general turmoil the incident caused to re-enact a part of her life that had been repressed. She constructed a vile authoritarian figure and exaggerated the humiliation done to her in order to gain some autonomy and perhaps even have a better sex life. Unconsciously, the re-shuffling caused by the irritating violence was used as a pretext. An opportunity knocked at the door!

Our ambivalence towards violence is caused by an existential dilemma, which is expressed in the case of the young train conductor. We condemn violence in our personal life because we know it is a horrible, even devastating, experience. At the same time, we love the psychological impact violence has on us. We are excited about violence on TV, enjoy gossiping about the evil deeds of other people, and even pay to see violence in the movies, because violence for us is psychologically significant. The repercussions of a violent act or image are opportunities. We hope that violence will re-set us. When we are shaken up, we might be able to free ourselves from inhibitions and social obligations, and reconnect to unattended inner or outer resources. Violence frees us from the restraints that society and education thrust upon us. Through violence we might re-enact a primordial event. We distance ourselves from our embeddedness with nature and become individuals in our own right. Television killers are admired because they promise deliverance from existential drudgery: the adaptation trap. The assumption is that a violent male has the strength to break the chains that bind us in a peaceful society with its orderly surroundings. The otherness in me, my shadow, can finally live and I can disregard moral and social codes.

VIOLENCE HAPPENS MAINLY IN OUR HEADS

Violence in real life is dreadful, and often marks the end of a civilization. In real life, we should do our best to prevent violence. The problem is that the psyche is not interested in reality. It understands violence symbolically and concentrates on its meaning. This is why a society in which violence is not represented is unthinkable. Our psyche needs violence in order to be disturbed from time to time. It sees in violence an antidote to an ordered, structured, and over-managed society. Societies therefore need vessels in which images of violence can be transmitted and experienced, and debates in which violence can be discussed. Violence should be integrated into our lives as story, image, fantasy, or part of a ritual so it can keep on irritating us.

VIOLENCE MUST BE OBSERVED, NOT UNDERSTOOD

The great danger with violence is that we want to reduce it to an epiphenomenon. However, identifying possible causes does not relieve us from violence. Trying to understand violence is natural and important, as long as we don't overestimate our conclusions and overvalue our belief in our forecasts. We need to identify causes because they legitimize our actions, but we will never be able to eliminate violence as an issue from our lives. If we start censoring films depicting brutality, ban bloody video games and toy guns, and stop giving expression to our fascination with violence, we become psychologically naïve. This approach only increases our attraction to violence. Violence cannot be comprehended in a linear fashion. We cannot detect causes and come up with plausible explanations. Primarily violence has to be observed, not understood. Violence is a chthonic energy; it will never be completely civilized. We need to observe violence to perceive its psychological significance.

FOCUS ON THE IMAGERY; NEGLECT REALITY

Violence is transmitted to us through imagery. The fantasies, accusations, and explanations of a violent incident contain psychological information. As psychologists or psychotherapists, our prime interest should be the imagery the client presents. It is difficult for us to distinguish between actually experienced events and fantasies when we are working with someone traumatized, shocked, or revved up by a violent incident. We are not experts in distinguishing fact from fiction, but we are specialists in understanding fabrications. It can get rather embarrassing when psychologists construe the conclusions they draw from their therapeutic work as facts and start engaging themselves politically, knowing for sure that "abuse is on the increase," or that patients suffer because of "gender issues."[21] The stories we hear should be valued from a psychological viewpoint and not abused and used as the basis for political work. Violence re-activates memories, complexes, personal histories, dreams, and ambitions and re-interprets what we have experienced. From the point of view of psychology, it is therefore important to concentrate on these mental amplifications. We are not criminal investigators; reality is the subject. Violence itself, as an act of destruction or intrusion, might be an intriguing topic for a physicist, but as psychologists we concentrate on what humans make out of it and try to read the images. Maybe we can connect them to the myths, social codes, and personal history of the individual.

BE SKEPTICAL TOWARDS STORIES; BELIEVING LEADS YOU ASTRAY

Fortunately, the vast majority of people living in the West do not encounter violence on a regular basis. Men do not return home in the evening and casually tell their wives that they had to beat up the taxi driver because he shortchanged them, or that they had a brawl at the local bar over an insult. Actual violence is banned from public and professional life and punishable in our private lives. In Western cultures the most common encounter with violence is through stories. We read of the slapping of patients in hospitals, are appalled by reports about a gang rape by students, are grieved by a suicide attack in Baghdad. Unlike the members of a drug gang in the Favelas of Rio de Janeiro, a bouncer working at a bar in Kreuzberg in Berlin, or maybe a slumdog in Mumbai, we are rarely confronted with real violence. According to young male immigrants from Somalia or Albania, Swiss adolescents have lost their capacity to defend themselves physically. We are presented with violence through the media, the tabloids, or gossip; there, violence is omnipresent. We are permanently confronted with second-hand accounts of violent events, which supposedly happened in the dark alleys of our towns, while we were sitting at home in our cozy chairs. Shocking incidents attract our attention, become major conversation pieces, and mobilize experts and pundits, who inform us that they knew it all along.

The "true" stories we are confronted with are, of course, not hard facts, but narratives. Just as Christian monks exaggerated the lootings and rapings of the Vikings, these stories do not portray what actually happened. They were created to feed our lust for horror, abase an alien, or make us excited. This is what we also experience in our consulting rooms. Patients refer to violence in order to develop a good narrative and personal myth.[22] The middle-aged man who describes his heroic engagements during the Globus riots in Zürich in 1968 might want to impress himself and his therapist. The woman who is convinced that her husband mistreats her and is undoubtedly the vilest person in the Western hemisphere might be relating a good story to achieve victim status. As therapist, friend, colleague, and even professional police investigator, it is nearly impossible to distinguish between truth and fiction. Empathy leads us astray. We stop questioning a biased view because we understand the story teller. What is presented to us as the truth and nothing but the truth might be an urban legend, a myth, a fabrication, a lie, or an actual incident. From the psychological point of view, this is irrelevant. Psychologically, *all* stories are true, but they might not depict what actually happened. They might be a product of the imagination, a personal myth, or a hysterical symptom—a hystory.[23] As psychologists, we read the stories presented to us as narratives. They tell us a lot about the respective individual, but maybe not about the world out there.

IS TOO MUCH IDEALISM A SIGN OF IRRESPONSIBILITY?

Another trap we have to beware of is too much idealism. To believe in a better world, fight for change, and identify with "*das Prinzip Hoffnung*" is certainly not a bad thing, but there is a snag: idealism can blind us to the intricacies, dynamics, and symbolism of violence. We believe in the good and fail to reflect on violence itself. We distance ourselves from the murkiness, pain, and hideousness of violence and instead start chanting peace slogans, participating in peace chains, or promoting training programs against violence. We are all against violence, but holding hands, signing pledges, and handing out leaflets will not chase "naughty" violence away. Peace demonstrations, pins, or happenings can be a means of avoidance. We choose to remain infantile and refuse to assume our responsibility to alleviate violence in society, often a nasty business.

THE ART OF VIOLENCE PREVENTION: SPECULATE, DREAM, AND FANTASIZE

What scene, topic, or face violence will choose for its next strike we do not know. Violence nearly always takes us by surprise. Neither is there *one* sound theory that can predict violent incidents or explain all the causes behind violence. In order to reduce violence and help perpetrators and victims, we need to have *an open mind*. Too much knowledge might hinder us from detecting possible dangers. We have to analyze incidents and *fantasize* about further developments and possible worst-case scenarios. It is essential that we allow and reflect on the stories, allegations, emotions, and fantasies about violence *in* and *around* us. Violence does not disappear by banning toy guns, organizing peace chains, or finding culprits in the past; we have to face the ugliness of violence *per se*, look the beast in the eye. If we are ready to accept our ambiguity, our fascination, and failures, we have the right attitude to get to the core of the issue. By studying the incidents, repercussions, and psychological implications, we might neutralize violence and the dangers of the next assault. We have to study the fascinations, the expectations, the hopes, and dreams we associate with violence and speculate about possible worst cases to find a way out of violence.

NOTES

1. See Steven Pinker, *The Blank Slate* (New York: Penguin, 2002), p. 307.

2. Lawrence Keeley, *War before Civilization: The Myth of the Noble Savage* (New York and Oxford: Oxford University Press, 1996), p. 147.

3. Paul Ricoeur, *The Symbolism of Evil* (Boston: Beacon Press, 1967), p. 30.

4. Ervin Staub, *The Roots of Evil: The Origins of Genocide and Other Group Violence* (New York: Cambridge University Press, 1992), p. 67.

5. James Hillman, *A Terrible Love of War* (New York: Penguin Press, 2004), p. 114ff.

6. Weltwoche, Nummer 8, 19, February 2009. pp. 32-37.

7. The descendants of the white settlers in Guadeloupe.

8. Alice Miller, *For Your Own Good: Hidden Cruelty in Child-Rearing and the Roots of Violence* (London: Faber, 1983).

9. For an overview, see John F. Knutson (ed.), *The Control of Aggression* (London: Transaction Publishers, 2007).

10. Barbara Strauch, *The Primal Teen* (New York: Doubleday, 2003).

11. Hans Markowitsch & Werner Siefer, *Tatort Gehirn* (Frankfurt: Campus, 2007).

12. Keeley.

13. Richard Wrangham & Dale Petereson, *Demonic Males* (Boston: Mariner, 1996).

14. Gunnar Heinsohn, *Söhne und Weltmacht* (Zürich: Orell Füssli, 2003).

15. See Allan Guggenbühl, *Anleitung zum Mobbing* (Oberhofen: Zytglogge, 2008).

16. David Livingstone Smith, *Why We Lie: The Evolutionary Roots of Deception and the Unconscious Mind* (New York: St. Martin's Press, 2004).

17. www.ikm.ch.

18. C. G. Jung, *Das Grundproblem der gegenwärtigen Psychologie.* GW Bd. 8, § 680 / p. 386.

19. "Myths and Symbols serve such protective purposes for the vulnerable human psyche, they buffer and deflect the devastating impact of radical evil." Stephen A. Diamond, *Anger, Madness, and the Daimonic: The Psychological Genesis of Violence, Evil, and Creativity* (New York: State University Press. 1996), p. 81.

20. Donald Kalsched, *The Inner World of Trauma*: *Archetypal Defenses of the Personal Spirit* (London: Routledge, 1996), p. 71.

21. See Reinder Van Til, *Lost Daughters: Recovered Memory Therapy & the People it Hurts* (Grand Rapids, MI: Eerdmanns Publishing, 1999).

22. Elisabeth Loftus & Katherine Ketchum, *The Myth of the Repressed Memory: False Momories and Allegations of Sexual Abuse* (New York: St. Martin's Press, 1994).

23. Elaine Showalter, *Hystories: Hysterical Epidemics and Modern Media* (New York: Columbia University Press, 1997).

FANATICISM:
A PSYCHOPOLITICAL ANALYSIS

LAWRENCE R. ALSCHULER

INTRODUCTION

What is fanaticism? *Wikipedia* states: "Fanaticism is an emotion of being filled with excessive, uncritical zeal, particularly for an extreme religious or political cause, or with an obsessive enthusiasm for a pastime or hobby."[1]

Why attempt to understand fanaticism? Fanaticism may contribute to a number of social evils: terrorism, racism, religious intolerance, oppression, and inter-ethnic and sectarian strife.

According to some specialists, fanaticism belongs to the personality profile of terrorists, who, in recent years, have given "globalization" a new meaning. A noted authority on terrorism, Louise Richardson, describes the psychology of the terrorist in a way that strongly suggests fanaticism:

> From the vast literature on psychology a few points can be extracted. Three in particular stand out. Terrorists *see the world in Manichean terms, that is in black and white*; they identify with others; and they desire revenge. *They have a highly oversimplified view of the world in which good is pitted against evil and in which their adversaries are to blame for all their woes.*[2] (my italics)

Lawrence R. Alschuler, Ph.D., is a retired Professor of Political Science. He has taught political economy of the Third World at the Universities of Hawaii, Zürich, Ottawa, and the Catholic University of Argentina. He studied at the C. G. Jung Institute-Zürich for four years in the 1980s. His latest book is *The Psychopolitics of Liberation: Political Consciousness from a Jungian Perspective* (New York: Palgrave Macmillan, 2007).

Why approach fanaticism from a Jungian perspective? In two recent critical reviews of research on the psychology of the terrorist, not one Jungian study was mentioned, nor was fanaticism, for that matter.[3] In my own book, *The Psychopolitics of Liberation,* relying on Jungian psychology and Third World social theories, I found fanaticism to be a stage in the development of political consciousness among the oppressed. In this article I extend my Jungian psychopolitical approach.[4]

How do I explore fanaticism? This article proceeds in four steps: (1) C. G. Jung's thoughts on fanaticism; (2) "fanaticized consciousness" as articulated by Paulo Freire and Albert Memmi; (3) a linkage of the first two steps; and (4) the psychopolitical healing of fanatics, based on case studies of three oppressed persons.

1. FANATICISM FROM THE PERSPECTIVE OF JUNGIAN PSYCHOLOGY

Jung associates fanaticism with repressed doubt. Several Jungians embellish this idea: Marie-Louise von Franz, V. Walter Odajnyk, and Mario Jacoby.[5] After presenting these views, I shall weave them into a coherent whole. Since these Jungian ideas are ordered chronologically, the reader can trace their development.

C. G. Jung

A new insight or understanding, such as that revealed to a patient about himself, may give him the feeling that "...he possesses a key that opens many, perhaps even all, doors." This arrogance, reflecting an uncertainty over one's boundaries, is a "psychic inflation." And, according to the principle of "psychic compensation," one's arrogance hides an "anxious sense of inferiority."[6]

> In fact we shall see clearly how his uncertainty forces the enthusiast to puff up his truths, of which he feels none too sure, and to win proselytes to his side in order that his followers may prove to himself the value and trustworthiness of his own convictions. ... Only when convincing someone else does he feel safe from gnawing doubts.[7]

Here, Jung brings together the concepts of psychic inflation and psychic compensation to explain fanaticism and doubt ("his truths, of which he feels none too sure"), as yet unnamed. Jung then refers to

> … the fanatical one-sidedness and sectarian exclusiveness of
> certain psychoanalytical groups. Everyone knows that this
> attitude is a symptom of over-compensated doubt.[8]

Jung does not elaborate further, leaving the reader with the impression
that "everyone knows."

In the compensatory relationship between consciousness and the
unconscious, Jung points out that sometimes the counteraction of the
unconscious is suppressed, allowing the conscious beliefs, attitudes,
or intentions to remain "unchecked" or to become even more one-sided.
He concludes:

> For instance, when someone makes a rather bold assertion and
> suppresses the counteraction, namely a well-placed doubt, he
> will insist on it all the more, to his own detriment.[9]

Once again, Jung joins the notions of one-sidedness in ego-consciousness,
suppressed doubt, and an exaggerated insistence on being in the right.
For him, doubt acts as a helper, as a natural compensatory signal from
the unconscious that is meant to guide the ego away from one-sidedness
toward a more balanced position. Jung states:

> People who merely believe and don't think always forget that
> they continually expose themselves to their own worst enemy:
> doubt. Wherever belief reigns doubt lurks in the background.
> But thinking people welcome doubt: it serves them as a valuable
> stepping-stone to better knowledge.[10]

Jung theorizes that complexes structure the personality. He defines
the complex as a group of images in the unconscious held together by
a common feeling tone.[11] According to this theory, the ego is also a
complex, the center of personal identity and body awareness. When
associated with the ego, a complex may become partly conscious. But
there are also autonomous complexes that may never become conscious.
As an example, Jung describes fanaticism in the conversion of St. Paul.

> Saul, as he was then called, had unconsciously been a Christian
> for a long time, and this would explain his fanatical hatred of the
> Christians, because fanaticism is always found in those who have
> to stifle a secret doubt. That is why converts are always the worst
> fanatics. The vision of Christ on the road to Damascus merely
> marks the moment when the unconscious Christ-complex
> associated itself with Paul's ego.[12]

Although Jung makes no reference here to one-sidedness, we can infer that Paul's ego is one-sided, in the sense that the autonomous Christ-complex remains in the unconscious, divided from consciousness (as if split off). The unconscious projects this complex onto Christians who bear the brunt of Paul's fanatical hatred.

The principle of opposites has a long history, from the *I Ching* through Heraclitus to Freud, according to Jung.

> I formulated it as a heuristic principle always to seek for the opposite of every given trend, and all along the line the principle worked. Extreme fanaticism I found to rest on a concealed doubt. Torquemado, as the father of the Inquisition, was as he was because of the insecurity of his faith; that is, he was unconsciously as full of doubt as he was consciously full of faith.[13]

Jung continues to examine the fanaticism of religious belief:

> Fanaticism is always a sign of repressed doubt. You can study that in the history of the Church. Always in those times when the Church begins to waver the style becomes fanatical, or fanatical sects spring up, because the secret doubt has to be quenched. When one is really convinced, one is perfectly calm and can discuss one's belief as a personal point of view without any particular resentment.[14]

Jung, for the first time, applies his ideas about fanaticism to the political beliefs of "mass man, the ever-ready victim of some wretched 'ism.'" Jung refers to such an "ism" as a "one-sided 'truth.'"

> If the subjective consciousness prefers the ideas and opinions of collective consciousness and identifies with them, then the contents of the collective unconscious are repressed. The repression has typical consequences: the energy-charge of the repressed contents adds itself, in some measure, to that of the repressing factor, whose effectiveness is increased accordingly. The higher its charge mounts, the more the repressive attitude acquires a fanatical character and the nearer it comes to conversion into its opposite, i.e., an enantiodromia.[15]

Jung elaborates the notion of enantiodromia:

> I use the term enantiodromia for the emergence of the unconscious opposite in the course of time. This characteristic

phenomenon practically always occurs when an extreme, one-sided tendency dominates conscious life; in time an equally powerful counter-position is built up, which first inhibits the conscious performance and subsequently breaks through the conscious control.[16]

In Jung's political thought, often politics and religion are linked:

> The dictator State has one great advantage over bourgeois reason: along with the individual it swallows up his religious forces. The State takes the place of God; that is why, seen from this angle, the socialist dictatorships are religions and State slavery is a form of worship. But the religious function cannot be dislocated and falsified in this way without giving rise to secret doubts, which are immediately repressed so as to avoid conflict with the prevailing trend towards mass-mindedness. The result, as always in such cases, is overcompensation in the form of *fanaticism*, which in its turn is used as a weapon for stamping out the least flicker of opposition.[17]

Jung goes on to say that the dictatorial State allows "only one truth" and believes "... anyone who thinks differently is a heretic."

Marie-Louise von Franz

Von Franz[18] extends Jung's thoughts on fanaticism by including the concept of projection, which she defines as "...an involuntary transposition of something unconscious in ourselves into an outer object." She continues:

> The need for the withdrawal of a projection is always constellated at that moment when conscious or semi-conscious doubts about the rightness of one's own way of looking at things arise and when on the conscious level this view is fanatically defended. Doubt therefore indicates that the time is ripe for the withdrawal of some projection.[19]

Walter Odajnyk

Odajnyk[20] treats both religious and political fanaticism:

> Of course, doubt, heresy, and fanaticism are not new, nor are they confined to secular ideologies. But the dislocation of the religious function into the secular realm, its serious distortion, as

well as the absolute state's insistence on unquestioning adherence to the official ideology all work to produce greater doubt and resistance than is normally the case with a religious movement. The greater doubt and resistance then lead to a more intense propaganda, fanaticism, and so on.[21]

Odajnyk mentions the compensatory relationship between fanaticism and skepticism (doubt) as a pair of opposites: the projection ("externalization") of repressed doubt compensates for fanaticism.

> Underlying many of Jung's arguments, including his treatment of surplus psychic energy, of consciousness and the unconscious, of positive and negative psychic inflation, of individualism and collectivism, of fanaticism and scepticism, of power and rebellion, it is possible to discern basic principles involving the interplay of opposites in complex relationships. Opposites "strive" to attain a balance, or homeostasis: there is the possibility of the synthesis or union of opposites. There is the concept of the conversion of an extreme element into its opposite, a process that Jung calls *enantiodromia*. And frequently there is a compensatory relationship between opposites, as in the case of external compensation for neglected inner psychic needs through the 'externalization' of repressed psychic contents.[22]

Summary of Step 1

Jung associates fanaticism with repressed doubt drawing on his theories of opposites and complexes, and on the processes of dissociation (splitting), repression, projection, and compensation. The wealth of concepts found in the Jungian views on fanaticism form a coherent whole as follows.

Extreme beliefs, strongly held and defended, characterize fanaticism. One believes, for example, that one possesses some political or religious "truth." Identifying with such beliefs, one falls victim to psychic inflation, a puffing up of the ego, often resulting in the dissociation (splitting-off) and repression of any thought or self-image that is incompatible with these beliefs. The resulting one-sidedness of the inflated ego activates a compensatory counteraction. The unconscious attempts to moderate the ego's one-sidedness by confronting it with an opposite image, a doubt (disbelief). Were the doubt to become conscious, the ego would have to reconsider its one-sided adherence to some "truth." When the ego dimly senses such a doubt, in order to protect the ego's inflated self-image, the doubt is split off and repressed. The fanatic encounters these repressed doubts in projections onto a non-believer. This "heretic" must be eliminated or else converted into a believer, whose support will then confirm the beliefs of the fanatic.

I reformulate the Jungian views as a vicious circle in which fanaticism increases as repressed doubt is projected. First, one holds absolutely to some extreme belief; second, doubts arise about the belief; third, these doubts are repressed; fourth, the repressed doubts are projected onto a non-believer who must disappear or show unquestioning adherence; and, finally, in the absence of the moderating influence of doubt, the extreme belief strengthens. A compensatory process, however, can break the vicious circle: when the extreme one-sidedness of the fanatic reaches a limit it converts into its opposite, an enantiodromia. The result, unfortunately, is a *new* one-sidedness where only others possess some incontrovertible "truth."

2. Fanaticized Consciousness (Freire and Memmi)

Paulo Freire, a Brazilian educator, developed programs of conscientization in order to raise the political consciousness of the oppressed. He locates "fanaticized consciousness" just before "critical consciousness," the final stage of conscientization. Albert Memmi is a Tunisian sociologist who, in the 1950s, foretold the inevitable demise of colonialism. Memmi situates fanaticism at the "stage of revolt," preceding the "stage of revolution" in the development of the political consciousness of the colonized.

Paulo Freire

Smith reformulates Freire's ideas on fanaticism:[23]

> Fanaticized consciousness is *not* one of the three principal developmental stages of conscientizacao, but rather a distortion which Freire discussed as being somewhere between naïve and critical consciousness. ... The emphasis in fanaticized consciousness is on massification; not the transformation of an oppressive situation into a liberating one, but rather the exchange of one oppressive situation for another.[24]

The extreme one-sidedness of the fanatic as "all-good" contrasts sharply with the oppressor as the "incarnation of evil":

> For the fanatic, the most crucial problem is the oppressor, the incarnation of evil, *the enemy* to be destroyed. Nothing good can be said about the oppressor. They are seen not as individuals equally victimized by the system, but as rather the demonic cause of oppression. Opposing the evil oppressor is the all-good "*super-ethnic.*"[25]

Freire examines the fanaticism of those oppressor elites he calls "sectarians." In Freire's thinking, sectarianism contributes to fanaticized consciousness:[26] "Sectarianism is predominantly emotional and uncritical. It is arrogant, antidialogical and thus anticommunicative." The sectarian's beliefs are extreme: "… herein his taste for sloganizing, which generally remains at the level of myth and half-truths and attributes absolute value to the purely relative."[27] With reference to a sectarian elite, Freire notes:

> Rightist and leftist sectarians do differ in that one desires to stop the course of history, the other to anticipate it. On the other hand, they are similar in imposing their own convictions on the people, whom they thereby reduce to mere masses.[28]

A sectarian elite conveniently labels as "criminals and subversives" those who challenge its "truths." Fanaticism, supported by sectarian irrationality, is characteristic of "massification," and the "mass man" in the way that Jung uses the term, "the masses." "They follow general formulas and prescriptions as if by their own choice. They are directed; they do not direct themselves …."[29]

In a comment on sectarians of the left and right, Freire approximates Jung's observation about fanaticism and repressed doubt.

> Each, however, as he revolves about "his" truth, feels threatened if that truth is questioned. Thus, each considers anything that is not "his" truth a lie. As the journalist Marcio Moreira Alves once told me: "They both suffer from an absence of doubt."[30]

A tendency toward an "activism that takes the naïve and highly emotional form of rebellion" also characterizes fanaticized consciousness. Freire recognizes the need to move from "naïve rebellion to critical intervention,"[31] just as Memmi endorses the transition from "revolt" to "revolution."

Albert Memmi

Memmi deals with fanaticism both of the colonized oppressed and the colonizer oppressor. He identifies two phases in the process of liberation from colonialism: revolt and revolution. The latter entails the colonized's recovery of their true personality, enabling them to be whole and free.[32] Memmi devotes considerable attention to the phase of revolt, because it must be surpassed by revolution, leading to the complete disappearance of colonialism. Revolt, a negative phase, serves as a prelude to a positive one. During revolt fanaticized consciousness produces "a reactive drive of profound protest." It is negative in that the colonized define themselves with reference to what they are *not,* how they differ from the colonizers.[33] Fanaticized consciousness may even appear as xenophobia and racism of the colonized.[34] For Memmi, this racism has three components: asserting the differences between the colonizer and the colonized, evaluating the differences in favor of the colonized, and declaring the differences to be absolute and unchangeable.[35]

Memmi considers revolt to be a "reversal of terms."[36]

1. Prior to revolt the colonizers reject the colonized, even blocking assimilation on a large scale; during revolt the colonized reject the colonizers, their culture, life, and motherland.
2. Prior to revolt the colonizers endorse colonial racism, believing the inferiority of all the colonized to be inborn; during revolt the colonized reject the "irremediable noxious nature of the colonizers" as a whole.
3. Prior to revolt the colonized admire the colonizers and seek to adopt their language, culture, religion, and customs; during revolt the colonized value exclusively their own culture, language, religions, and customs.
4. Prior to revolt the colonizers disparage anything belonging to the colonized; during revolt "Suddenly, exactly to the reverse of the colonialist accusation, the colonized, his culture, his country, everything that belongs to him, everything he represents, become perfectly positive elements."
5. Prior to revolt the colonizers develop a negative myth of the colonized; during revolt the colonized promote a positive counter-myth of themselves.

The suddenness of this reversal as well as the absoluteness of the images (of self and other) announce the presence of fanaticism: extreme and incontrovertible attitudes. During revolt, Memmi notes, such attitudes may be accompanied by violence and relentless attempts to quell self-doubts by demanding approval from others.

> Realizing that these attitudes are essentially reactions, he suffers from the pangs of bad faith. Uncertain of himself, he gives in to the intoxication of fury and violence. In fact, he asserts himself vigorously. Uncertain of being able to convince others, he provokes them... He demands endless approval from his best friends, of even that which he doubts and himself condemns.[37]

According to Memmi, it is the colonizer who engenders fanaticized consciousness among the colonized, who participate in "a reactive drive of profound protest." Memmi's explanation reminds us of Jung's on self-doubt and fanaticism:

> (1) the colonial relation imposes on the colonizers certain privileges at the expense of the colonized; (2) neither colonizers nor colonized can escape this situation of advantage and disadvantage as long as colonialism continues; (3) it is not possible for the colonizers to be unaware of the fact of their privilege. On these facts Memmi founds his diagnosis of the personality of the colonizers. The colonizers suffer from guilt: the colonizers "plead guilty" to the misery they cause the colonized. They suffer from *self-doubt*: the colonizers doubt their self-worth and wonder whether they truly deserve the privileges they enjoy.[38]

The colonizers cope with their guilt and self-doubt by adopting an ideology of self-justification, an expression of fanaticized consciousness: the colonizers exaggerate their own merits and the demerits of the colonized.[39] This readily becomes an ideology of colonial racism.[40] Considering how the colonizers tend to polarize the two "mythical portraits," it is now more understandable that the colonized will *react* eventually, passing through the stage of revolt (fanaticized consciousness).

Summary of Step 2

The idea of "fanaticized consciousness" belongs to Paulo Freire and Albert Memmi. Political consciousness, what Freire terms "conscientization," develops in three stages: magical, naïve, and critical. At the "naïve" stage, the oppressed believe in their own inferiority and in the superiority of the oppressors. On the way to the "critical" stage a distortion may take place, called "fanaticized consciousness," when the oppressed believe in their own superiority and in the inferiority of the oppressors, a radical reversal of polarities. Although this marks progress over the previous stage, the oppressed now have fallen into a new one-sidedness. They fail to develop either a balanced or a realistic self-image and image of the oppressors. In the absence of doubt, one-sidedness prevails whether the beliefs are about political, religious, racial, or ethnic traits.

Memmi concludes in a similar fashion about the political consciousness of the colonized at the "stage of revolt" against the colonizers. The racism and xenophobia of the colonized, both fanatical beliefs, develop as reactions to the racist ideology of the colonizers. During colonial rule the privileges of the colonizers derive from the exploitation of the colonized. The colonizers try to justify their privileges by asserting their racial superiority over the colonized whom it is their mission to "civilize."

3. A Linkage between Steps 1 and 2

In this step, I link Jung's views on fanaticism to Freire's and Memmi's on fanaticized consciousness.

One-Sidedness and Fanaticized Consciousness

Knowledge of complexes contributes to an understanding of the one-sidedness of fanaticized consciousness.

> In more clinical terms, dissociation is a normal unconscious process of splitting the psyche into complexes, each personified and carrying an image and an emotion. Splitting occurs because the image and emotion are incompatible with habitual attitudes of consciousness. Jung believes that feeling-toned complexes are "living units of the unconscious psyche" that give the psyche its structure. The ego shapes its identity by aligning itself with what is compatible with habitual attitudes, and by splitting off and repressing that which is incompatible.[41]

Perry's modification of Jung's theory of complexes offers insights into fanaticized consciousness. Perry believes that all complexes are found in bipolar pairs, one of which aligns with the ego and the other is found in projection onto another person.[42] By aligning with the ego, a complex provides the ego with a self-image, certain attitudes, and a sense of identity. According to Perry's formulation, the ego of an oppressed person with fanaticized consciousness aligns with a complex having only positive qualities (e.g., superiority, righteousness, in possession of some truth). A second complex in the pair, with only negative qualities, including self-doubts, appears in projections onto an oppressor, a colonizer, or a non-believer. Jung tells us that the unconscious produces self-doubts to compensate extreme beliefs. However, the repression of self-doubts renders them powerless to mitigate these beliefs, confirming the one-sidedness of fanaticized consciousness.

Enantiodromia and the Emergence of Fanaticized Consciousness

Fanaticized consciousness may appear suddenly, following a stable stage of "naive consciousness" during which the oppressed reject themselves in order to assimilate, to resemble the "superior" oppressors. In the stage of fanaticized consciousness, a positive self-image replaces a negative one; also the oppressed's positive image of the oppressor becomes negative. In Jungian terms, an *enantiodromia* takes place: an extreme is converted into its opposite. Expressed in terms of Perry's model of complexes, the ego-projected member of a bipolar pair of complexes and the ego-aligned member trade places.[43] We can imagine the two complexes of a bipolar pair to be on opposite ends of an axis: at first, the complex at one end aligns with the ego; when the axis rotates, the complex at the other end that was formerly projected becomes aligned with the ego.

4. CASES OF FANATICIZED CONSCIOUSNESS AND THE PSYCHPOLITICAL HEALING OF FANATICS

In my recent book, *The Psychopolitics of Liberation,* three of my four cases of Native people in Canada and Guatemala, living under conditions of oppression, pass through a stage of "fanaticized consciousness" to another stage in which their fanaticism is healed.[44] What are their experiences of fanaticism? What enables them to heal their fanaticism? Their personal testimonies, on which the case studies are based, teach us about fanatics. In what follows, I present each of the three cases in two parts: (a.) fanaticized consciousness, and (b.) self-healing and liberated consciousness.

Before analyzing the cases we need to understand the process of psychopolitical healing. The case studies show a succession of stages. At the stage of fanaticized consciousness, as I have already mentioned, there is one-sidedness: the oppressed believe absolutely in their own ethnic superiority. In the next stage, called "liberated consciousness," this one-sidedness yields to "holding the tension of psychic opposites, where the opposites are images of ethnic groups in conflict."[45] Now both complexes in a bipolar pair become integrated into ego consciousness: the ego-aligned complex (positive qualities) and the ego-projected complex (negative qualities).[46] If we consider the splits and resulting one-sidedness to be "wounds" in the psyche of fanatics, it is fitting to view the attainment of liberated consciousness as psychopolitical healing. Despite speaking of "healing," I do consider fanaticism to be one of the normal conditions of the oppressed, not a pathology.

Two key conditions foster the healing process, ego strength and a rootedness in the ancestral soul. Ego strength means the ability to assert one's own will power in the face of opposition and resistance, resulting in a sense of freedom of choice.[47] A maturation crisis challenges one's ego with dilemmas such as rival life choices concerning marriage, career, education, and work; a confrontation with the death of someone close; or a conflict between personal goals and family obligations. A crisis may create emotional depression, confusion, anger, and frustration. The successful resolution of this crisis, rather than its postponement or "taking the easy way out," strengthens one's ego.

Rootedness in the ancestral soul, in Jungian terms, corresponds to a connected ego-Self axis. For a Native person, rootedness depends on a positive identity as an Indian, a sense of community as an Indian, and pride in the Indian heritage.[48] More specifically, the Indian heritage includes: language, music, spirituality, history, legends, tradition, and relationship to nature. In contrast,

> "Loss of ancestral soul" refers to a condition of rootlessness that one experiences as a loss of identity, a loss of meaning, and a sense of inferiority accompanied by fervent attempts to live and imitate an alien persona.[49]

Atanasio: A Quiché Maya Man, a Factory Worker in Guatemala

a. Fanaticized Consciousness

In childhood Atanasio developed a positive Indian identity, thanks to lessons of his grandfather, a Mayan priest, and learned respect for the village elders. As an adult he remains proud of his Indian heritage, including his relationship to the land, community, spirituality, language, and music.[50] Atanasio's fanaticized consciousness first appears at the age of eight when he experienced humiliation as an Indian in Guatemala City, far away from his native village. His rootedness in the "ancestral soul" enabled him to resist the *Ladinos'*(non-Indians) view that Indians are inferior.[51] "At this early age, Atanasio's reaction was not to feel inferior, but rather to reject all *Ladinos* whom he began to view negatively."[52]

Years of oppression reinforced Atanasio's fanaticized consciousness, his one-sidedness. As a perceptive adult he was able to describe four aspects of oppression in general.[53]

Economic exploitation. Ladino bosses violate the labor code, deny humane working conditions and adequate wages for the Indian garment workers where Atanasio is employed.

Social discrimination. The unfair treatment of Indian laborers extends to Indians throughout Guatemalan society. In the justice system, trials are conducted only in Spanish and favor the *Ladinos* even when they are in the wrong.

Military domination. The threat of communist subversion by guerrillas serves as a pretext for *Ladino* landowners to eliminate Indians and take possession of their land. Forced recruitment of Indians into the military, who engage in this repression, accentuates the enormity of this injustice.

Cultural invasion. Foreign Christian missionaries undermine indigenous religions, replacing them with competing sects that divide Indians among themselves. Schools promote foreign cultural values to the detriment of indigenous ones, including their history and language. The mass media reinforce this tendency, even among those unable to attend school.

In his own words, Atanasio expresses his fanatical one-sidedness:

> We, Indians, have been reduced to being a country within
> another country. We are like spirits, we have names, but we do

not exist. Since we are nothing to *Ladinos*, they are completely
indifferent to the way we live: alone, isolated, sick, illiterate,
without the opportunity to progress. They want to immobilize
us, to annihilate us.[54]

b. Self-Healing and Liberated Consciousness

Atanasio's self-healing begins at age eighteen as he successfully
resolves a maturation crisis. The burden of his family's poverty, worsened
by his father's drinking, falls upon Atanasio when his father dies
suddenly. This event plunges him into despair because he must
abandon his own ambitions for higher education in order to provide
for the family.

Insisting that his father is not entirely to blame for his family's
poverty, Atanasio searches fervently for another explanation. He resolves
part of his crisis through an ideological innovation: he understands his
family's poverty and his father's alcoholism both as consequences of
the oppression of Indians on a societal scale.[55] He resolves the conflict
between his educational ambitions and his family obligations as well.
While working in the garment industry to provide for his family, he
reads, on his own, the classics in Spanish translation.

Emerging from a successful resolution of his maturation crisis,
Atanasio's ego is strengthened, enabling him to overcome his one-
sidedness. In place of his one-sided, absolute (fanatical) convictions
about the superiority of Indians over *Ladinos*, Atanasio opens himself
to nuances and ambiguities. He discovers that not all *Ladinos* are rich
and that some are no better off than Indians. He learns that not all
Ladinos are bad and that not all Indians are good. In fact, Indian bosses
can be as oppressive as *Ladino* bosses. He distinguishes between the
good and bad works of the Catholic Church, their social work with
Indians, for example, in contrast with their support of the *Ladino*
elites.[56] He empathizes with Indians and *Ladinos*, both of whom may
suffer from identity problems. Knowing that they are neither Indian
nor Spanish, the *Ladino*'s identity problem underlies much of the
ethnic conflict in Guatemalan society. Indians, seeking assimilation,
enter a state of identity confusion, hindering their adaptation and
mental health. Atanasio further perceives ethnic conflict, whether in
his factory or in the army's repression of Indians, as a clash between
modernism and traditionalism.[57]

Atanasio is rooted in Indian culture and takes pride in his Indian identity. The ego strength resulting from his maturation crisis enables him to make distinctions in the poles of the psychic opposites, finding "good" and "bad" in both the Indian and *Ladino*. His self-education furthers his understanding of ethnic conflict in psychological and cultural terms. He recognizes the harm as well as the potential benefits of modernism, mourns the losses in Indian culture, yet reaffirms its potential benefit for all Guatemalans. In this sense, Atanasio endures the tension of opposites and attains liberated consciousness.[58]

Lee Maracle: A Coastal Salish and Métis Woman, a Writer in British Columbia, Canada

a. Fanaticized Consciousness

Unlike Atanasio, whose political consciousness appears to begin at the fanaticized stage, Lee Maracle starts from a prior stage, what Freire calls "naïve consciousness." In her adolescence she identifies one-sidedly with the positive image of the oppressor. Having internalized a self-image of Indian inferiority and dependence, Lee desires to assimilate into White society. She recalls this period:

> As a ragged, battle-worn teenager—the only "injun" in my class— I did try to deny my own heritage. I donned the sacred mantle of self-centered individualism, the heart and spirit of Canadian achievement, and stumbled through my studies. I dressed in blue serge skirts and painted my face with Maybeline and I even cut my hair.[59]

Here, Lee splits off her dark side in order to identify only with the light. In terms of Perry's bipolar model of the complexes, we could say that Lee's ego is aligned with the White pole while her Indian pole is repressed and encountered in projection onto "inferior" Indians, those she deplores. However extreme this situation might appear, it often characterizes those oppressed who reject their ethnic identity in favor of acquiring a new persona modeled on the oppressor.

Such extreme one-sidedness is susceptible to a sudden reversal into its opposite, an enantiodromia. This happens to Lee when her ego changes its alignment to the Indian pole in place of the White pole, resulting in fanaticized consciousness. She tells of this reversal just before reaching sixteen, when she experiences ethnic humiliation as an Indian. She is asked to read a text in her history class about a hero of her mother's Native people.

> "Louis Riel was a madman who was hanged ...." I could not buy that any more than I could the cannibalism fairytale of fifth grade. I could not forsake my ancestors for all your students to see.[60]

From the age of sixteen, when Lee rejects assimilation, until reaching twenty-five, she lives this reversal of her one-sidedness, fanaticized consciousness. While reconnecting with her ancestral roots, she overvalues her rediscovered Indian culture: its history, customs, and teachings. She values White culture only negatively: its parenting, legal code, philosophy, education, relation to nature, racism, capitalism, and sexism.[61]

b. Self-Healing and Liberated Consciousness

Lee's self-healing begins after a maturation crisis lasting through a grueling period of seven years to age twenty-five. She experiences drug abuse, violence toward her children, divorce, emotional depression, and ideological confusion. The shocking news that her mother has cancer precipitates the crisis. Lee realizes that she will have to accept adult responsibilities: to finish school, face a difficult home life, raise her younger siblings, have a steady job, marry, and start a family. Though her mother survives, Lee's ego strengthens by facing her new responsibilities and abandoning her "misguided youth."

At this time Lee discovers her need to write: political pamphlets for Native rights, stories, poetry, and a diary. By writing she ceases being "invisible." "The colonizers erase you, not easily, but with shame and brutality. ... Being a writer is getting up there and writing yourself onto everyone's blackboard."[62] Largely through her activity as a writer, she emerges from her stage of fanaticized consciousness and heals her psychic wounds of oppression. As is characteristic of liberated consciousness, Lee turns a critical eye toward her own people and Whites, finding fault both with Native subservience and White racism. Her ego strength and rootedness in the ancestral soul enable her to endure the tension of opposites, images of ethnic groups in conflict.

Recalling Jungian thought on the association of fanaticism with repressed doubt, it is noteworthy that Lee's doubt increases as her fanaticism decreases. Lee's states: "To be critical of all and doubt everything is the first step to the creation of new thought."[63]

> A reconnection with her ancestral soul, especially through writing, slowly and painfully dispelled her depression, enabling her to love her children, her husband, and her people. Her keen intelligence, confounded by drug-taking, emotional depression, and limited schooling, had kept her probing for a clear ideological understanding of oppression. Many experiences, apparently unconnected, marked her life and called for clarification: experiences of racism, of violence among Indians, and a weak sense of identity.[64]

Rigoberta Menchú, a Quiché Maya Woman, a Labor Organizer and Later, a Human Rights Activist, in Guatemala

a. Fanaticized Consciousness

Rigoberta Menchú's upbringing in a rural Indian community, where she learns her people's customs, religion, traditions, and language, all combine to root her firmly in the Mayan ancestral soul. This rootedness in the ancestral soul enables her to deny Indian inferiority in a nation dominated by *Ladinos,* who view Indians as inferior. An experience at the age of eight triggers her phase of fanaticized consciousness during which she identifies one-sidedly with the positive image of her ethnicity while rejecting *Ladinos.* At this time her little brother dies of malnutrition while the family is working on a cotton *finca* (plantation) owned by *Ladino* landlords. Rigoberta believes this tragedy to result from their impoverishment at the hands of *Ladino* oppressors.[65]

> For her, being Indian, even a poor Indian, meant being all good and superior to a *Ladino.* As in the cases of Atanasio and Maracle, this resembles the one-sided identification of the colonized in the stage of revolt, reversing the previous evaluations. Certain of Rigoberta's commentaries confirm the one-sidedness of her political consciousness. She knows that *Ladino* "society rejects us." In return she completely rejects *Ladino* society, elevating Indian culture in her mind to a plane of natural wholesomeness. She holds the attitude that Indians must protect themselves from learning the ways of the White Man and prevent them from learning Indian ways. She contrasts the Indians' respect for life with the *Ladinos'* willingness to kill. Her respect for Indian

ancestors is mitigated neither by their defeat during the Spanish Conquest nor by the apparent advantages of modern ways. Indian ways, both wholesome and natural, must not be mixed with the modern ways of the White Man, even in the preparation of food. Only in the realm of religious belief does Rigoberta seem less one-sided.[66]

After violent confrontations over the land, Rigoberta summed up her total rejection of the *Ladinos*: "I saw why we said *Ladinos* were thieves, criminals and liars." After the imprisonment, kidnapping, and beating of her father because of the land dispute, Rigoberta reaffirmed her rejection of *Ladinos* as a group: "we hated all those people. We weren't only angry with the landowners, but with all the *Ladinos*. To us, all *Ladinos* in that region were evil."[67]

b. Self-Healing and Liberated Consciousness

At age 13, Rigoberta successfully traverses a maturation crisis, which strengthens her ego, enabling her to withstand the tension of opposites. The death of a close friend, Maria, precipitates an emotional depression. Maria dies of poison sprayed on cotton plants by agents of the *finca* landowners. The flood of emotions, her grief, despair, anger, and hatred, accompany the emergence of new ideas. In opposition to her father's wishes and Indian ways, she decides to learn Spanish, attend school, and postpone marriage. This decisiveness strengthens her ego and marks the turning point that ends her depression and begins her self-healing.

At age 18, Rigoberta increases both her political understanding of oppression and her confusion.[68] She is unclear about who are the enemies of her people in the overlapping pairs of adversaries: landowner-peasant, *Ladino*-Indian, rich-poor, and government-people. This confusion begins to weaken her fanaticized consciousness that insists on absolutes and leaves no room for doubt.

Rigoberta makes new distinctions: she discovers that there are both good and bad *Ladinos* as well as good and bad *Ladino* institutions; she moderates her once absolute adherence to Indian ways. By the age of twenty-one she crosses a threshold in her progress toward liberated consciousness: she learns to love *Ladinos*.[69] In sum, Rigoberta transcends the one-sidedness that characterized her fanaticized consciousness, bringing about self-healing. She is able to hold the tension of opposites and attain liberated consciousness.

CONCLUSION

Fanaticism can be healed. By holding the tension of opposites between images of ethnic groups in conflict, all three Native persons effectively transcend the one-sidedness of fanaticized consciousness, allowing for the development of liberated consciousness and self-healing. The emergence of conscious doubt, distinctions, and ambivalence mitigate the absoluteness of fanatical beliefs and attitudes. The preconditions for this are first, a rootedness in the ancestral soul, and second, an ego strengthened by the successful resolution of a maturation crisis.

The healed fanatics, those with liberated consciousness, continue to confront oppression, though their new style of confrontation corresponds to newly formed attitudes. The oppressed now view their adversaries as human beings, also caught within the socio-historical context of oppression. Freed from many projections, the former fanatics develop realistic perceptions of themselves and the oppressors, of the strengths and weaknesses of both their own and the oppressors' ethnic community.[70]

My three case studies of oppressed Native people reveal how they healed their fanaticism as they developed liberated consciousness. Further, I discern a pattern of causes and effects. The two conditions for healing are linked to the ways in which a Native person reacts to a significant experience of ethnic humiliation[71], that is, being treated as inferior by an oppressor or a dominant ethnic group member.

1. If one is neither rooted in the ancestral soul nor has a strong ego, one attempts assimilation into the oppressors' society. Collective consciousness overwhelms the Native person's ego, motivating him or her to conform.
2. If one is rooted in the ancestral soul but has not a strong ego, one develops "fanaticized consciousness." In the absence of the moderating influence of a strong ego, capable of managing doubt, the Native person becomes inflated and identifies with an idealized ethnic self-image.
3. If one is both rooted in the ancestral soul and has a strong ego, one develops "liberated consciousness" by holding the tension of

opposites. The fanaticism is healed. A connected ego-Self axis counterbalances a strong ego, allowing the Native person to avoid the one-sidedness either of assimilation or fanaticized consciousness.

In conclusion, I believe that this causal pattern, whether generating or healing fanaticism, offers new insights into the political consciousness of the oppressed.[72]

NOTES

1. "Fanaticism," *Wikipedia*, <http://en.wikipedia.org/wiki/fanaticism>, accessed April 4, 2007.

2. Louise Richardson, *What Terrorists Want: Understanding the Terrorist Threat* (London: John Murray, 2006), p. 62. See also Walter Laqueur, *The New Terrorism: Fanaticism and the Arms of Mass Destruction* (New York: Oxford University Press, 1999), p. 99, 274.

3. Jeff Victoroff, "The Mind of the Terrorist: A Review and Critique of Psychological Approaches," *Journal of Conflict Resolution* 49, no. 1 (2005): 3-42; Randy Borum, "Psychology of Terrorism," (Tampa, FL: University of South Florida, 2004), <www.ncjrs.gov/pdffiles1/nij/grants/208552.pdf>.

4. Lawrence Alschuler, *The Psychopolitics of Liberation: Political Consciousness from a Jungian Perspective* (New York: Palgrave Macmillan, 2007).

5. Jacoby comments on Jung's quote from *Two Essays on Analytical Psychology* (1916/1972), p. 142: "Put in terms of the theories of narcissism, Jung is talking about the fact that a grandiose self really craves for narcissistic gratification, that is, for admiration. Followers are needed in order to prove the value and the trustworthiness of convictions. Yet, the ego is identified with these convictions to such an extent that transpersonal 'truths' are experienced as being part of one's personal worth. At the same time, the individual's craving for affirmation of his own greatness serves as a defence, as a protection against 'gnawing doubts'—as Jung puts it." See Mario Jacoby, *Individuation and Narcissism: The Psychology of Self in Jung and Kohut* (London: Routledge, 1990), p. 86. The fanaticism of the grandiose self, a form of inflation, seeks protection from self-doubt through the admiration of others, which serves as confirmation. The theory of

narcissism incorporates Jung's reasoning. Memmi's analysis of the colonized has much in common with Jacoby. See Alschuler, chap. 3. For an early view on the relationship of narcissism to fanaticism, see Erich Fromm, *The Heart of Man* (New York: Harper and Row, 1964), pp. 62-94.

6. C. G. Jung, *Two Essays on Analytical Psychology,* vol. 7 of *The Collected Works of C. G. Jung*, ed. Herbert Read, Michael Fordham, Gerhard Adler, William McGuire, trans. R. F. C. Hull (Princeton, NJ: Princeton University Press, 1972), pp. 141-143. (Hereafter referred to as *CW* followed by volume number and page or paragraph number.)

7. *Ibid.*, p. 142.

8. C. G. Jung, "General Aspects of Dream Psychology," in *Dreams* (Princeton, NJ: Princeton University Press, 1974), p. 63.

9. C. G. Jung, "The Transcendent Function," in *Jung on Active Imagination*, ed. Joan Chodorow (London: Routledge, 1997), p. 51.

10. Jung, *CW* 11, § 285.

11. Jung, *CW* 8, p. 96.

12. Jung, "The Psychological Foundations of Belief in Spirits," in *Psychology and the Occult* (Princeton, NJ: Princeton University Press 1977), p. 114-115.

13. Jung, *Analytical Psychology: Notes of the Seminar Given in 1925 by C. G. Jung,* ed. William McGuire (Princeton, NJ: Princeton University Press, 1989), p. 77.

14. Jung, *Analytical Psychology: Its Theory and Practice* (New York: Vintage Books, 1970), p. 172.

15. Jung, *On the Nature of the Psyche* (Princeton, NJ: Princeton University Press, 1969), p. 117, 129.

16. Jung, CW 8, p. 426.

17. Jung, *The Undiscovered Self* (Princeton, NJ: Princeton University Press, 1990), p. 15.

18. Von Franz refers to being possessed (a form of psychic inflation) and fascinated by the numinosum "...when an archetype comes to the threshold of consciousness"—Marie-Louise von Franz, *Psychotherapy* (Boston, MA: Shambhala, 1993), p. 186. "Possession also means fanaticism. One has and represents the only truth and feels justified in beating down everything else" (p. 187). "Only a person who doubts himself feels compelled to win over as many admirers as possible so as to drown out his own doubt" (p. 188). Here, von Franz gives the

impression that doubt becomes conscious and that the compulsion to win over admirers is also a conscious effort to reduce one's own doubt.

19. Marie-Louise von Franz, *C. G. Jung: His Myth in Our Time* (Boston, MA: Little, Brown & Co., 1975), p. 78.

20. Odajnyk reformulates Jung's views on fanaticism, found in *The Undiscovered Self.* "Still, in the end, Jung believes, the religious function cannot be perverted in this manner permanently. In time, doubts arise in the individual. In most cases these are immediately repressed because of the fear of opposing the general trend and the official doctrine. The doubts then lead to overcompensation in the form of fanaticism with the repression of the doubts supplying the psychic energy. The fanaticism, in turn, is used to stamp out any opposition or divergence of opinion, both in the fanatic and in others ..."—V. Walter Odajnyk, *Jung and Politics: The Poltical and Social Ideas of C. G. Jung* (New York: New York University Press, 1976), p. 56. Once again, repression seems to be a conscious act and the mechanism of projection is not mentioned.

21. *Ibid.*, p. 56.

22. *Ibid.*, p. 64.

23. Oppression refers to unjust relationships between people in a society: exploitation, discrimination, repression, and denial of human rights.

24. William A. Smith, *The Meaning of Conscientizacao: The Goal of Paulo Freire's Pedagogy* (Amherst, MA: Center for International Education, University of Massachusetts, 1976), p. 68.

25. *Ibid.*, p. 69.

26. Paulo Freire, *Pedagogy of the Oppressed* (New York: Herder and Herder, 1972), p. 21; Paulo Freire, *Education for Critical Consciousness* (New York: Seabury Press, 1974), pp. 18-19.

27. Freire, *Education*, p. 11.

28. *Ibid.*, p. 11.

29. *Ibid.*, p. 14, 20.

30. Freire, *Pedagogy*, p. 23.

31. Freire, *Education*, pp. 35-36.

32. Albert Memmi, *The Colonizer and the Colonized* (Boston, MA: Beacon Press, 1967), p. 153.

33. *Ibid.*, p. 138, 140.

34. *Ibid.*, pp. 129-130.

35. *Ibid.*, p. 71. When the differences are evaluated in favor of the *colonizer*, it is called colonial racism.

36. Source for the following list: Memmi, p. 128, 130, 132-34, 138, 139.

37. *Ibid.*, pp. 139-140.

38. Alschuler, p. 44.

39. Memmi, p. 52-53.

40. *Ibid.*, p. 71.

41. Alschuler, p. 15.

42. John W. Perry, "Emotions and Object Relations," *Journal of Analytical Psychology* 15, no. 1 (1970): 9.

43. Perry gives an example of this. See Perry, p. 4.

44. Alschuler.

45. *Ibid.*, p. 80; see also Alschuler, pp. 65-70, on the tension of opposites in Jungian psychology.

46. In my book I focus on the bipolar pair of complexes, paternalism and dependence. See Alschuler, pp. 24-28.

47. Edward Whitmont, *The Symbolic Quest: Basic Concepts of Analytical Psychology* (Princeton, NJ: Princeton University Press, 1978), pp. 247-248.

48. *Ibid.*, p. 95.

49. *Ibid.*, pp. 71-72. For the origin of the concept, "loss of ancestral soul," see Roberto Gambini, "The Soul of Underdevelopment: The Case of Brazil," in *Zurich 95: Open Questions in Analytical Psychology,* ed. Mary Ann Matoon (Einsiedeln, Switzerland: Daimon Verlag, 1997), pp. 145-147.

50. *Ibid.*, p. 95.

51. The distinction between a *Ladino* and an Indian is cultural rather than biological. "*Indigenas* can redefine themselves or their children as *Ladinos* by some combination of moving away from home, getting a good education, disclaiming their natal language, marrying into the *Ladino raza*, or acquiring wealth." See David Stoll, *Rigoberta Menchú and the Story of All Poor Guatemalans* (Boulder, CO: Westview, 1999), p. 17.

52. Alschuler, p. 94.

53. These four conditions are in Alschuler, pp. 96-97.

54. *Ibid.*, p. 98.

55. *Ibid.*, p. 99.

56. *Ibid.*, p. 100.
57. *Ibid.*, p. 102.
58. *Ibid.*, p. 103.
59. *Ibid.*, p. 118.
60. *Ibid.*, p. 118.
61. *Ibid.*, p. 125.
62. *Ibid.*, p. 122.
63. *Ibid.*, p. 125.
64. *Ibid.*, p. 122.
65. *Ibid.*, p. 129.
66. *Ibid.*, p. 130.
67. *Ibid.*, p. 132.
68. *Ibid.*, p. 132.
69. *Ibid.*, p. 135.
70. *Ibid.*, p. 146.

71. This experience is said to "constellate" a complex, that is, to activate an existing complex in the unconscious.

72. I invite anyone to explore further the validity of my findings by analyzing new cases. In a recently published personal testimony from a context far removed from that of indigenous people in North and Central America, I found additional confirmation of the conditions favoring the transition from fanaticized to liberated consciousness. See Ed Husain, *The Islamist: Why I Joined Radical Islam in Britain, What I Saw Inside and Why I Left* (London: Penguin Books, 2007).

War: Some Psychological and Spiritual Underpinnings

Lionel Corbett

I would like to make three points in this paper. The first is that war is driven by unconscious motivations as well by as its obvious political aspects. The second is that for many people war has important spiritual, archetypal, and mythic dimensions, and the third is that war is a form of emotional disorder.

Theories of the Origin of War

Freud[1] believed that war arose as part of our instinct for aggression, and sociobiologists have described war as the result of male sexual selection, resulting in accelerated cultural evolution.[2] However, the idea that human aggression is biologically programmed[3] and therefore inevitable has been discredited.[4] To say that war is a biologically inherited instinct ignores the fact that violence is also learned. Since many people go to great lengths to avoid war, do we also inherit the need for peace? Surely, the preparation and training for war are too complex to be purely instinctual, and this attitude risks making the idea of innate aggression a self-fulfilling prophecy, so that we become resigned to violence. Non-violence is a powerful alternative. (Think of Gandhi's insistence on *Satyagraha*, soul-force, or the insistence on

Lionel Corbett, M.D., is a Jungian analyst who teaches depth psychology at Pacifica Graduate Institute. He is the author of *Psyche and the Sacred: Spirituality Beyond Religion* and *The Religious Function of the Psyche.*

truth.[5]) Neither is it enough to say that war and peace are archetypal; the archetype is pure potential, so we still have to explain why this potential incarnates into actual behavior.

A further reason we cannot rely on purely instinctual forces to explain war is that normal human beings have a natural resistance to killing other humans, so that the military has to program soldiers to be able to kill.[6] Hunting societies even felt guilty about killing animals and needed ritual atonement for killing. Because of this reluctance, we have to train people to kill other people; tribal cultures use elaborate initiation ceremonies to make someone into a warrior, and have often used drugs to help them kill. In our culture, the rituals of boot camp, with its intensive social pressures, uniforms, and facial paint transform ordinary young people into killers by turning them into automatons who are not allowed individuality. Young soldiers are conditioned to do as they are told using military discipline, which insists on conformity and identity with the group. Repeated often enough, marching, drilling, and belonging to a tight-knit group seem to be gratifying. At the extreme, these lead to a loss of personal boundaries, primitive bonding, and even a kind of ecstatic state or trance.[7] At the very least, recruits experience either a sense of unity with others or an alter-ego or twinship transference[8]—the sense that one is the same as others. Both of these reinforce one's sense of self. However, after the killing is over, it can be extremely difficult for soldiers to re-adapt to normal society. Many new soldiers are not prepared for the reality of killing other people, not to mention the effects of seeing one's friends killed. There is a serious price to pay for these events in terms of guilt, emotional pain, and Post Traumatic Stress Disorder ("PTSD.") Consequently, Native American tribes used to purify warriors when they returned from battle so they could be restored to a peaceful state and not cause trouble in the community.

The argument that war is part of our evolution does not take into account that peace would be at least as conducive to our evolution as war. Neither is there any value in invoking explanations such as the "culture of militarism" found in some countries, since this culture itself begs for an explanation.[9] Can the reason for war be simply utilitarian, a fight over territory? Was territory really the reason that 60 million people died in World War II, and millions have died since then? It is also suggested that war is the result of the cynical manipulation of a powerful élite for its own benefit, or just something to do with the Y chromosome or testosterone.[10] Because wars are usually begun by high status males and fought by low status males, it is also suggested that older men in authority are envious of the sexual energy and strength of the young, and so do not mind young men being killed. These sound like simplistic explanations. Wars are usually more destructive than utilitarian; they cost the winners a great deal, usually more than they gain,[11] so that wars are often self-destructive. Neither are wars simply the result of bad economic times; in fact, some wars, such as World War I and World War II, occur during periods of economic recovery.[12]

Another theory of war suggests that war may have persisted because it is prestigious and exciting.[13] According to some anthropologists, as the number of game animals and the danger from them decreased, and as agriculture replaced hunting, men had less to do, so they replaced their hunting associations with war. War gives them something to do, something uniquely manly. That is, as Eherenreich[14] puts it, men make war because war makes them men; it has an initiatory function in some cultures.

It has also been suggested that one of the causes of war is war itself—war is a kind of epidemic. That is, we go to war in response to war, to retaliate because we were attacked or because our national pride was offended. Our mythology tells us that we must go to war in response or be lost. Atrocities and the need for revenge inevitably escalate. What happened after September 11 is typical; national grief and rage, exploited by politicians, resulted in the justification of misdirected aggression. The problem however is that, once we kill others, we increase our fear of being killed in return; we become afraid of retribution, so we resort to more violence, producing more danger, leading to a vicious circle. Retaliation—not to mention preemption—ignores two facts: violence often produces a cycle of increasing destruction, and the effects of violence are unpredictable.

War and Transcendence

At the beginning of World War I, there was great excitement in Europe and the U.S.A. The idea of war was intoxicating, and evidently met a need for national unity. Toynbee[15] likened the glorification of war to a kind of religion that provides spiritual sustenance as traditional religion fades. This hints at the profound psychological and spiritual process that war involves. When we are joined in a common purpose with millions of other people, we feel strong, no longer isolated and insignificant but part of the totality. Loyalty to the country is a way of belonging to a larger whole and a noble cause, producing an emotional intensity that gives a taste of transcendence. Being part of a common purpose allows people to deal with anxiety, restore a sense of self-importance, and feel powerful in the face of threat. We project this sense of power into flag waving, patriotism, and the passions of nationalism, which lead to a state of identification with the larger group, which allows us to deny our vulnerability. Media and government propaganda foster this process of unification and contribute to crowd psychology. Individual differences no longer seem important, and people are swept away with intense nationalistic sentiment.

The problem, of course, is that the tribe we are fighting feels the same way. War glues together each of the nations involved, as if the nation were a kind of organism that is not interested in the individual, who is only one cell in the body. War is also used by politicians to produce a rebirth of national purpose and values. The glorification of our military prowess, and the stress on our power, magically restore the national potency when we are attacked. This restoration is easier to achieve if the enemy is much weaker than we are, as we saw, for example, when the U.S. attacked Iraq, Panama, and Granada.

SPIRITUALITY AND WAR

Killing seems righteous when war is felt to have spiritual underpinnings. Normal morality does not seem to apply in wartime. The leader is able to invoke religious language by suggesting that dying and suffering are to be accepted as part of the great archetypal battle of good against evil. Killing is then a sacred task. It is not surprising that some historians see nationalism as a kind of religion, and it is no wonder our cemeteries and monuments to war become so important; they are in fact shrines to the divisive religion of nationalism. In the U.S.A. these feelings are referred to as "patriotism," but there is no psychological difference—the sociologist Robert Bellah[16] called American nationalism our "civil religion." Our rituals on days like the Fourth of July, Flag Day, or Veterans' Day are occasions for parades, commemoration of wars, laying wreaths, and political speeches about duty and sacrifice. The historian George Mosse[17] has suggested that these observances *make* war sacred, although it may be that we perform these ceremonies *because* we feel war to be sacred. For some, the flag has become a quasi-religious symbol, which is why people speak of "desecrating" the flag. I hardly need mention other aspects of our fusion of nationalism and religion, such as the frequent invocations of God by our politicians, the emphasis on God in the pledge of allegiance and on coins, and so on. Bellah points out that this God is the Old Testament God, mostly concerned with law and order rather than love. People feel better when they think that God blesses America, and when they can identify with a strong military, despite the fact that the military-industrial complex has no interest in ordinary people except as cannon fodder.

When these religious passions are stirred up, the enemy becomes the heretic or heathen and we revert to the behavior of our atavistic tribal ancestry. The extreme example is the Nazi phenomenon, which at its spiritual level was hostile to Christianity. Nazism had its own faith, its prophet, a canon of literature, a hierarchy, its own mythological images that invoked ancient Germanic pagan imagery, and ritual on a large scale. Some Nazis took the crosses and Bibles off church altars and replaced them with swastikas and copies of *Mein Kampf*. People were encouraged to pray to Hitler; the League of German Girls had its own version of the Lord's Prayer that invoked Hitler: "thy Third Reich come, thy will alone is law upon earth." People professed the "religion of the blood." Hitler compared himself to Jesus or the Messiah. There were holy days such as January 30, the anniversary of the day Hitler came to power, and April 20, his birthday.[18] Hitler's unconscious spirituality was a spirituality of war. According to Toland, war filled him with "rapturous enthusiasm,"[19] and he described the trenches of World War I as "a monastery with walls of flame."[20] These are religious sentiments. (Even the date of Hitler's death on April 30, which coincided with the pagan celebration of *Walpurgisnacht*, was said to be no coincidence.)

PREDATOR ANXIETY

Predator anxiety is an important source of human aggression. Although humans are now effective predators, for a long time in our evolutionary history we were the prey of carnivorous animals that hunted and killed our early hominid ancestors. Accordingly, predator anxiety evolved, the fear that we may become prey, an anxiety that obviously had value for the survival of the species. It may be that these behaviors are hardwired into our brains; Darwin noticed that his 2-year-old son was afraid of large animals at the zoo, even though he had never seen them before. Our terror of predators may contribute to the fear of strangers that babies develop around nine months of age. Predator anxiety adds to our intolerance of people different from us, and increases paranoia and abandonment terrors.

Blood sports, such as fox hunting, act out our fear of being prey by making us the hunter instead of the hunted, the predator rather than the prey—this defensive reversal turns passive into active. This psychological mechanism for dealing with predator anxiety also operates when we make pre-emptive war, or whenever we make others feel terror rather than ourselves. Since we prefer to identify with predators rather than prey, it is not surprising that predatory creatures feature on the flags of many countries. (The eagle for the U.S., Germany, Mexico, Poland, and Spain; the lion for Britain, Finland, Kenya, Norway; the hawk for Egypt, the bear for Russia, and so on).

Many of our movies foster predator anxiety by depicting people being eaten by animals (*Jurassic Park*). Some of the stories we tell children are about being eaten by wild beasts ("Red Riding Hood.") Such fears are implanted in childhood and are culturally transmitted from generation to generation. These stories allow us to experience predator anxiety vicariously, and may be an attempt to master it, but they also perpetuate this anxiety. When a terrorist attack happens out of the blue, such atavistic predator anxiety surfaces; we have become prey.

The Problem of Sacrifice

War can seem legitimate if one declares the necessary sacrifice to be for a good cause, such as fighting for one's religion or country—a favorite theme of politicians. Sacrifice may unconsciously feel acceptable if one had to sacrifice oneself to a parent; one then expects oneself or others to die for the motherland or the fatherland. Various psychodynamic factors allow us to sacrifice our children in wars, such as parental envy of children because of their innocence and beauty and because the child has its life ahead of it. As well, children are given roles in families, such as the hero, the pariah, the scapegoat, or the savior of the family. It is also important that the notion of necessary sacrifice is a shadow aspect of the Christian story, which is so much a part of western mythology—if God can sacrifice his son, we can sacrifice our sons for the right reason.

War then becomes a modern equivalent of the ritual human sacrifice that was common in antiquity, when human sacrifices were carried out to ensure the growth of crops, success in war, or to appease the gods. We sacrifice our youth in war for the values that are most important to us, just as children used to be sacrificed to the local pagan gods. The underlying assumption is that the gods need blood, an obvious projection of our own violence onto our god-images.

Ritual sacrifice has always been bound up with religion, a fact that illustrates an archetypal connection between violence and the sacred. The root of the word "sacrifice" means to make sacred, and everywhere in the world the gods were fed with sacrificial animals or human beings, whether in India, China, South America, Africa, ancient Greece, Egypt, Rome, or the temple at Jerusalem. The gods of Olympus enjoyed the smell of the meat; the Aztec and Incan gods needed blood; and, the Hebrew deity sends down his fire to consume the flesh on the altar.[21] Sacrifice is therefore very much a part of our cultural mythology.

Apparently there is something very powerful about causing death and watching blood flow—in some sacrificial rituals the victim's blood is sprinkled about to "purify" the participants. War is often seen as having a "purifying" effect on the nation; this is a common image during wars, because the enemy becomes the container into which we can project our own poison and the bad parts of ourselves. The extreme example is ethnic cleansing; the Nazis sometimes spoke of their murders as a necessary purification, but images of "national purification" are actually fairly commonly used about war.[22] The blood that soldiers shed is seen as a kind of purging. For example, in 1914, there was a general feeling that the world had become degenerate because of material progress, and a bloody purging would be good for the country.[23] One military leader of that time wrote that war cures people of their softness and worship of comfort.[24] Thomas Jefferson thought that war was necessary to "refresh the tree of liberty" with the blood of patriots.[25] After the American civil war, Howe wrote that America had been regenerated by a second birth.[26] Note that the purity crusaders—today they are against any kind of sexuality or marriage not allowed by the Bible—are usually in favor of war. The conscious fantasy of purity may actually conceal an unconscious fantasy of getting rid of the bad parts of the self.

THE SCAPEGOAT ARCHETYPE

Freud thought that violent ritual sacrifice just vents aggression. Taking this further, Girard[27] suggested that war and ritual sacrifice both serve the purpose of channeling outwards aggression that might otherwise cause conflict within society. Instead, aggression is directed to an external focus, the sacrificial victim or the foreign enemy. That is, we need socially acceptable targets of our aggression instead of killing each other or killing the king. The victim is a scapegoat, according to Girard, and sacrificing the scapegoat preserves social cohesion. War also has this effect, partly by promoting acquiescence with the status quo. Wars bring us together and our internal differences are temporarily forgotten.

The need to scapegoat is archetypal. In ancient Jerusalem, the sins of the people were loaded onto a goat, which carried the sins of the people into the wilderness, where the demons lived. This ritual act purified the people by symbolically projecting their sins onto the goat as substitute, which was cast out into the "other side." That is, the goat was punished for the sins of the people; instead of feeling guilty, we can find someone else to blame. Of course our guilt then remains unconscious. The same phenomenon was seen in bronze age Greece, where a pauper was designated as the *pharmakos*, or cure, and driven out of the city to ward off a plague or invasion or other social problem. The scapegoat pacifies the angry god and thus gets rid of pollution.

THE PSYCHOLOGY OF POLITICIANS MAY CONTRIBUTE TO WAR

DeMause[28] has suggested that politicians who are emotionally damaged because of child abuse are prone to start wars in an unconscious attempt to re-stage and re-work early trauma. One of the dynamics involved in the human need for war is an unconscious need for revenge against early bad objects; the enemy is not only the bad child part of the individual, the part that is destructive, but also the bad mother. As evidence for this idea, deMause notes that war is often depicted in cartoons as a battle with a mother figure.[29] For example, in the western media Saddam Hussein was depicted in cartoons as a dangerous pregnant woman with a nuclear bomb in her womb. The soldier is therefore simultaneously attacking bad parts of himself in projection and he is also intent on revenge for early trauma.[30] An event such as the attacks of September 11 could easily stimulate memories of such abuse, producing significant terror in the mind of the politician who was abused as a child.

These psychodynamic factors are important because the emotional difficulties of politicians may become incorporated into their public policy. Here we have to be careful to acknowledge that we can only suggest a psychodynamic perspective on a politician's historical record, combined with whatever biographical material is available. We also face the problem that, not only are leaders idealized, we may also project our own negative material into them. Given these limitations, it is important that, as deMause[31] points out, the biographies of most American presidents reveal abusive or neglectful childhoods—Carter and Eisenhower being the exceptions. Reagan's mother was obsessively religious, while his father was a violent alcoholic. As a child, Reagan was phobic and fearful, with a great deal of rage and anxiety—his autobiography was titled *Where's the Rest of Me?* As an adult he often carried a pistol and is known to have considered suicide. Instead he became an anti-Communist crusader. George H. Bush's childhood was also characterized by fear and physical punishment.[32] His father is described as aloof and frightening, and often beat his son. Not surprisingly, George H. became a depressive personality.

Frank[33] tells us that, as a child, George W. Bush would shoot and blow up frogs. It is well established that torturing animals is a sign of significant emotional disturbance in children—we torture others because we were tortured. It may not be an accident that Bush approved so many executions while governor of Texas. A preference for violent, authoritarian politics is associated with punitive parenting. In her memoir,[34] Barbara Bush says that she grew up in a home without much emotional nurturing and with stern discipline. Her mother was emotionally cool and depressed, and hit Barbara a great deal. In turn, Barbara Bush herself is reported to have been quite violent with her children: she was known as a taskmaster who would slap the children and "instill fear" into them. George W.'s mother was therefore cold, stern, and emotionally unavailable, while his father was mostly absent, either physically or emotionally.[35] Children whose parents dominated them excessively chose totalitarian leaders; the evidence of history suggests that the more punitive the child-rearing style of a culture, the more punitive are its political behaviors.[36] Our internal fantasies are projected into the culture.

It is important to stress that war may not only be an attempt at revenge on our current enemies. When confronted with the images from Abu Ghraib, it is useful to remember Miller's[37] suggestion that cruelty to others is revenge for cruelty done to oneself in childhood. Revenge is a way of re-working childhood persecution by inflicting it on others. Revenge is therefore a primitive response to being hurt, an attempt to restore self-esteem and one's sense of self, redress the wrong, and balance things according to the principle of an "eye for an eye." Rather than use the word "revenge," which sounds undignified and immature, politicians often claim that they go to war to seek justice. Given the abuse that some politicians suffered in childhood, it is important that, in his study of violent men, Gilligan[38] found that their violence is an attempt to achieve justice, compensation, or retribution for what happened to them in childhood. Since early abuse is often accompanied by massive shame, the adult's violent reaction to injury is also an attempt to prevent further shame. Gilligan suggests that such shame can lead to mass violence, for example when Hitler promised to "undo the shame of Versailles," a theme that resonated with the German people. Unfortunately, as current events confirm, revenge and retaliation usually escalate a cycle of violence.

A childhood level of terror and rage is stirred up when we are attacked as adults—the terror that we feel inside, from persecutory internal objects, is projected onto our outer enemies, adding to the threat from them, so that the world is seen as very dangerous. There is then a war on terror, but it is the inner world that is dangerous. Preemptive action against the enemy is necessary partly because of a fear of the envy of our enemies, as in "they hate our freedom," combined with the projection of the politician's own hostility onto them. Primitive splitting defenses lead to the notion that people are either on our side or on the side of the terrorists, and our own evil is projected onto other countries. If one is burdened by childhood abuse, violence towards others may produce a degree of relief. If one's sense of self is fragile, if one is narcissistically vulnerable because of a traumatic childhood, it helps to feel chosen by God, and hence very special, part of a very special country.

Such defenses allow the politician to commit war crimes, such as the deliberate Gulf war destruction of civilian infrastructure such as water purification plants, irrigation and sewage systems, and electrical systems. According to a UNICEF report in 1999, 500,000 children under the age of 5 died of preventable disease and malnutrition as a result of sanctions between 1991-1998. In Iraq, the incidence of childhood cancer has increased threefold because of the use of depleted uranium, which ended up in the food chain. The unwillingness to admit guilt and responsibility for these crimes against humanity is a manic defense that obliterates our perception of human suffering. During the war, no such images were shown on television. Instead, as part of the media marketing of the war, high-tech images of "precision" weapons were shown that made it all look like a video game, which reinforced denial of civilian casualties.

Politicians are not just leaders; they sense and act out the unconscious wishes of the nation, just as Hitler articulated the unconscious of the German people. Sometimes we need a foreign enemy on which to project our fears. After the fall of the Soviet Union in 1989, there was no obvious enemy, and the mood of the nation was depressed;[39] it was as if the nation could not tolerate peace and prosperity because of its Puritanism. We had to be punished, because for the Puritans pleasure is sinful and requires expiation. A long period of peace and prosperity can be intolerable; it produces guilt at being happy, especially if we feel too greedy. When the nation is depressed, war is sometimes a solution that allows us to feel better. War produces a temporary high. War is then an anti-depressant, which is why we have to periodically find enemies.

Events like 9/11 produce shared cultural fantasies and images of monsters in our minds that stir up memories of early traumas. These monsters are then projected onto real monsters such as Saddam Hussein. When we go to war against such people, war acts as a mechanism that relieves stress and anxiety related to our early trauma. The task of the leader is partly to find an appropriate enemy for this to happen. When bin Laden could not be found, Saddam Hussein was the obvious solution. The fact that the U.S. had supported him in the past was now ignored, and we focused on his evil. In any conflict, both sides see war as a trial of good vs. evil—we sometimes need to externalize an internal conflict between the good and bad parts of ourselves. The job of the politician is to help people to project evil and fight it out there.

THE RELIGIOUS JUSTIFICATION FOR WAR

The support of some of avowedly Christian politicians for war raises the issue of its religious justification. The Hebrew Bible raised the huge problem of why God would allow his chosen people to be defeated by idolatrous and wicked nations. The rabbis assumed that this occurred because of disobedience to God's teaching—clearly a projection of human psychology onto the divine. Early Christianity solved the problem of the oppression of the faithful by renouncing military might and by glorifying those who are poor, downtrodden, and defeated, who will eventually triumph. Christ himself suffered torture and humiliation and seemed to be defeated until he was resurrected. Christianity therefore initially spiritualized suffering and martyrdom, but by the 5th century Augustine was able to propose a "just war" doctrine in response to the many invasions of Europe that threatened to destroy the Church. Gradually, Jesus became the leader of the Church Militant, the Lord of the Last Judgment. Christian wars were often led by warrior saints such as St. Michael (patron of various orders of knights during the Middle Ages) or St. George. The bloodthirsty nature of some Christians since then needs no comment. Unfortunately, as the Church became militarized, war itself took on overtly religious significance, for example in the Crusades against the infidel Saracens, which cleansed the soldier from sin and guaranteed his entrance to heaven. In Christian mythology, Constantine conquered under the sign of the cross, which became a battle symbol, and gradually war became a sacred activity. At the same time, there is a long and noble history of Christian nonviolence, based on Jesus' actual teachings, exemplified by Dr. Martin Luther King, Jr., but somehow this doctrine never took hold among western politicians, presumably because a platform of nonviolence does not win elections.

The association of war and human god-images is nothing new, and is not confined to Christianity. People have long been devoted to war gods such as the biblical Yahweh, Ares, Hercules, Jupiter, or Mithras. Athena supported the Greeks, Hera supported the Trojans. The Dioscuri, the heavenly twins Castor and Pollux, were seen fighting alongside the Roman soldiers at Lake Regillus in 496 B.C.E. as they fought the Etruscans. The Angel of Mons appeared to Allied soldiers in 1914, saving them from disaster.

THE RELATIONSHIP OF LEADERSHIP AND WAR

Leadership has various problems attached to it. In times of crisis, fearful people need charismatic leaders who can be idealized. Either people project onto the leader their need for strength, in order to deal with their feelings of helplessness, or they project their own grandiosity onto him and he becomes wonderful. The idealized leader is supposed to calm people's anxieties and solve problems; he is a kind of savior figure. When we are threatened, we can merge psychologically with a phallic leader who will make us feel strong. Accordingly, when there is a national crisis such as September 11, the leader produces tough talk such as "dead or alive" or "bring it on," dresses up in a costume such as a flight suit to act the part, and looks very confident. However, a period of disillusionment gradually sets in as it becomes clear that war is not solving all our problems and is actually creating more of them. Then the leader gradually looks weaker, his flaws start to show, and a process of de-idealization sets in.

Narcissistically vulnerable people may cope with their shame and fear by developing a sense of rightness and grandiosity. Their rage makes them wish to use violence to deal with feelings of humiliation such as that produced by September 11. It is difficult for such people to admit faults, so for them it was possible to deny the fact that the foreign policy of the western powers has long contributed to turmoil in the Middle East because of western meddling in that area. Instead of a balanced approach to September 11, which would have acknowledged the historical roots of the attacks at the same time as their heinous nature was condemned, the president had to find a scapegoat for this behavior that absolved him and this country from all responsibility. An enemy had to be found; if bin Laden was too elusive, Hussein was a useful substitute. An attack on the enemy displaces anger away from the leader's own failings. Had there been no obvious enemy, we could have removed the leader in the next election, but, because there was an obvious enemy after September 11, the leader was kept in office so he could carry out the nation's agenda of ritual cleansing by warfare. War was sold as a battle between our goodness and their evil.

Part of the power of the leader lies in his acting out the national psychology; otherwise people do not take him seriously. This is why people who don't have these particular psychological difficulties find Bush hard to understand. The leader embodies and acts out the emotional problems of people who can identify with him, so Bush acted out attitudes that are part of the emotional make up of particular segments of the country. The leader is the people's emotional delegate; not only does he act out his own emotional problems, he also expresses the emotional demands of the people, or the popular group fantasy. By doing so he tries to resolve the shared emotional problems of the country as well as his own. Because of an idealizing transference to the leader, he is also expected to help defend people against the repetition of early trauma and abandonment. That is why Bush is constantly talking about strength. Bush's advice after September 11 that we should "go shopping" was a typical manic defense against feelings of depression and helplessness. The current surge of troops to Iraq prevents acknowledging the shame of defeat, which would be enormously difficult for someone with narcissistic character difficulties.

THE LARGER VISION

In our list of the psychological origins of war, we also have to add the obvious desire for power, prestige, and dominance, belief in ideology, and the sickness of organized religions with their competing God-images and theologies. Because society is made up of individuals, to the extent that we participate in these problems we are all responsible for war. Unfortunately, rather than look at our own responsibility, we want to blame politicians. However, political ideals and social revolutions have failed to stop wars. In the long run, it is pointless to think that a particular leader will give us peace. We cannot have peace unless we are peaceful internally.

External threat brings us together and produces group solidarity. This mechanism was once necessary when we were faced with predatory attack. It is now time for a larger vision than violence in response to violence. Either we continue to be driven by fear, perpetuating the illusion that we are separate individuals, or we realize that human beings are a deeply connected spiritual unity. The real solution to the problem of war is the transformation of consciousness. As Krishnamurti[40] puts it: "But if you really loved the family, the children, if you really loved with your heart, do you think you would have a single day of war?"

NOTES

1. Sigmund Freud, "Why War?" (1932), *Standard Edition of the Complete Psychological Works of Sigmund Freud*, ed. James Strachey, (London: Hogarth Press and the Institute of Psycho-Analysis, 1953-57), vol. 22, p. 21.

2. Irenaus Eibl-Eibesfeldt, *The Biology of Peace and War: Men, Animals, and Aggression* (London: Thames and Hudson, 1979), p. 123; Michael P. Ghiglieri, *The Dark Side of Man: Tracing the Origins of Male Violence* (New York: Perseus Books, 1999), p. 10.

3. Robert Ardrey, *The Territorial Imperative: A Personal Inquiry into the Animal Origins of Property and Nations* (New York: Kodansha America, 1966).

4. J. R. Davitz, "The Effects of Previous Training on Postfrustration Behavior," *Journal of Abnormal Social Psychology* 47 (1952): 309-315. See also the UNESCO declaration of Seville, 1986.

5. Non-violence does not work by coercion but by persuasion, so it does not produce a backlash the way violence does. The difficulty is that non-violence requires empathy rather than retaliation, and empathy is difficult when one is narcissistically wounded by an attack.

6. Jonathan Shay, *Achilles in Vietnam: Combat Trauma and the Undoing of Character* (New York: Scribner Touchstone edition, 1995); *Odysseus in America: Combat Trauma and the Trials of Homecoming* (New York: Scribner, 2003).

7. William H. McNeill, *Keeping Together in Time: Dance and Drill in Human History* (Cambridge, MA: Harvard University Press, 1995), p. 8.

8. Heinz Kohut, *How Does Analysis Cure?*, ed. Arnold Goldberg (Chicago, IL: University of Chicago Press, 1984).

9. Niall Ferguson, *The Pity of War: Explaining World War I* (New York: Basic Books, 1999).

10. Testosterone is often blamed for causing the greater level of violence in boys than girls, but testosterone levels are actually lower in aggressive boys than in non-violent boys. All boys experience a surge in testosterone levels at puberty but only some become violent. Before puberty, testosterone levels are the same in boys and girls. It is the differential treatment of boys and girls that causes more violence in boys—more violent punishment, more frequently; they are less nurtured than girls and are often coached to be violent.

11. Richard Hobbs, *The Myth of Victory: What is Victory in War?* (Boulder, CO: Westview Press, 1979); John V. Denson, ed., *The Costs of War: America's Pyrrhic Victories*, 2nd ed. (New Brunswick, NJ: Transaction Publishers, 1997).

12. Joshua S. Goldstein, *Long Cycles: Prosperity and War in the Modern Age* (New Haven, CT: Yale University Press, 1988).

13. Clifton B. Kroeber and Bernard L. Fontana, *Massacre on the Gila: An Account of the Last Major Battle between American Indians, with Reflections on the Origin of War* (Tucson, AZ: University of Arizona Press, 1986).

14. Barbara Eherenreich, *Blood Rites: Origins and History of the Passions of War* (New York: Metropolitan Books, 1997), p. 13.

15. Arnold Toynbee, *A Study of History* (New York: Oxford University Press, 1987).

16. Robert N. Bellah, "Civil Religion in America," in *Nationalism and Religion in America: Concepts of American Identity and Mission,* ed. Winthrop S. Hudson (New York: Harper Forum Books, 1970), pp. 146-152.

17. George L. Mosse, *Fallen Soldiers: Reshaping the Memory of the World Wars* (New York: Oxford University Press, 1990), p. 33.

18. Robert G. L. Waite, *The Psychopathic God: Adolf Hitler* (Cambridge, MA: Da Capo Press, 1993), pp. 30-31.

19. John Toland, *Adolf Hitler: The Definitive Biography* (New York: Doubleday, 1976).

20. *Ibid.*, p. 103.

21. Among early humans, the ritual sacrifice of animals may have been partly an attempt to master or regulate our terror of being hunted by them. Animal sacrifice deals with our physical vulnerability by making it a spiritual problem. We ritualize our vulnerability in an appeal to the gods to save us—we bargain with them for protection or favors, and we offer the animal as a scapegoat for our sins. As well, by giving the animal to the gods (even though humans usually ate its flesh) we can assuage our guilt at the killing which seems necessary—W. Burkert, *Homo Necans: The Anthropology of Ancient Greek Sacrificial Ritual and Myth* (Berkeley, CA: University of California Press, 1997). Divine beings were often imagined to take the form of beasts of prey such as lions and leopards, jaguars or crocodiles. The beast is a deity who likes meat; that is, an anthropomorphic projection occurs. Ehrenreich therefore suggests in *Blood Rites* that religious rituals of sacrifice arose as a face-saving device that softens the harsh reality of being prey. The loss of one's child to a wild animal is more bearable when understood as a sacrifice to a god that will ward off further losses. The loss then does not seem random.

22. Lloyd deMause, *The Emotional Life of Nations* (New York: Karnac Books, 2002).

23. Michael C. Adams, *The Great Adventure: Male Desire and the Coming of World War I* (Bloomington, IN: Indiana University Press, 1990), p. 57.

24. *Ibid.*, p. 61.

25. *Ibid.*, p. 51.

26. Quoted in Adams, p. 55. See also James A. Aho, *Religious Mythology and the Art of War: Comparative Religious Symbolisms of Military Violence* (Westport, CT: Greenwood Press, 1981).

27. René Girard, *Violence and the Sacred*, trans. Patrick Gregory (Baltimore, MD: Johns Hopkins University Press, 1997).

28. DeMause.

29. *Ibid.*, p. 56.

30. Sidney Halpern, "The Mother Killer," *Psychoanalytic Review* 52, no. 2 (1965): 73.

31. DeMause, p. 13.

32. Suzy T. Kane, "What the Gulf War Reveals about George Bush's Childhood," *The Journal of Psychohistory* 20, no. 2 (1992): 149-166.

33. Justin A. Frank, *Bush on the Couch: Inside the Mind of the President* (New York: Regan Books, 2004).

34. Barbara Bush, *Barbara Bush, a Memoir* (New York: Charles Scribner's Sons, 1994).

35. Bill Minutaglio, *First Son: George W. Bush and the Bush Family Dynasty* (New York: Three Rivers Press, 1999).

36. Michael A. Milburn and S. D. Conrad, "The Politics of Denial," *The Journal of Psychohistory* 23, no. 3 (1996): 238-251.

37. Alice Miller, *For Your Own Good: Hidden Cruelty in Child-Rearing and the Roots of Violence*, trans. Hildegarde and Hunter Hannum (New York: Farrar, Straus and Giroux, 1990).

38. James Gilligan, *Violence: Reflections on a National Epidemic* (New York: Vintage Books, 1997).

39. DeMause.

40. J. Krishnamurti, *You Are the World* (Chennai, India: Krishnamurti Foundation of India, 1972).

"AND DEATH WAS A MIST ABOUT HIM": NOTES TOWARD A HOMERIC POETICS OF VIOLENCE

BRIAN NOWLIN

Despite the agitations of some contemporary cultural pluralists, to construe the Homeric poems as the root of the Western intellectual tradition is not to work against the postmodern, Rushdian notion that imaginative hybridity constitutes the ever-shifting ground of cultural identity. After all, just as the Greek and Trojan armies on the battlefields of Troy each consisted of innumerable kings and citizens from diverse geographical locales, so the *Iliad* and the *Odyssey* as a whole borrowed from Near Eastern, Hittite, Mediterranean, and other fluid cultural sources to create, in a kind of poetic bricolage, the mythological moorings of the Western mind. To read Homer deeply is to recognize that, far from undergirding the by-now endlessly criticized and deconstructed (as logocentric, phallocentric, or just plain centric) rational fantasy of what constitutes the Western tradition, the Homeric poems gave birth to a Western culture that, at its innermost core, has always been polemically

Brian Nowlin, Ph.D. (ABD), is currently completing a dissertation on Wallace Stevens and the *mundus imaginalis* at the University of Dallas, where he has worked as an adjunct professor of English (teaching both poetic epic and rhetoric) and as the director of the writing center. Brian's scholarly areas of interest especially center upon the intersection of poetic metaphor, desire, memory, and the *anima mundi*.

polytheistic and polymorphously perverse. What today remains legitimately controversial about Homer's poems is not, then, their foundational importance to Western culture, nor is it the "Homer Question," that tired debate about the compositional status of the poems; rather, what should continue to give readers pause as they engage Homer is the extraordinary violence that characterizes these two poems, the *Iliad* in particular. When the poems, rather than being read in their entirety, are selectively mined for psychologically rich mythologems, nascent philosophical and political formulations, and/or moralistic models of heroic virtue—in other words, when a New Age enthusiast follows his or her bliss into the mythology section of a bookstore so as to thumb through an excerpted compendium of mythological tales—it becomes too easy to forget that, taken in their original literary context, the tales of the gods and goddesses are soaked in blood: poetic insight apparently flourishes in a context of violence. The Western imagination, in all of its rational sophistication and psychological perspicuity, is born out of incredibly bloody books.

What, then, do the Homeric poems teach us about the precise connection between imagination and violence? The current essay proposes that the violent scenes in Homer's *Iliad*, far from being gratuitous or sadistic, are essential to the poem's ability to embody and indeed inaugurate *psychological* reality, what Jung termed *esse in anima*, that dimension of depth within everyday life that connects the soul to the reality of death, to Hades, in other words, to the imaginative blood[1] in and through which the psyche creates reality every day by means of fantasy.[2] Homeric violence figuratively inscribes the inherent violence of the imagination, a quality that paradoxically may enable the soul to maintain its reflective vigor when confronted with literal, outward violence. Further, the essay seeks to show that Homer's poetics of violence violently shocks all imaginations numbed by reductive sociological, psychoanalytic, and political explanations of violence, thereby initiating a ritualized engagement with and accommodation of Ares, that god responsible for the terrible love of war (in Hillman's phrase) that is an ineradicable quality of the soul. In making the above arguments, this essay pursues the secondary, broader aim of returning the mythological imagination to its literary context, a move *not* to reduce "myth" merely to the "literary," but rather to bring a mythological eye to literature and a literary eye to myth: literature, which both engages and creates multifaceted structures of the imagination, is indeed more truly "mythological" than is "myth" dislocated from literature.

Even though roughly half of the *Iliad* consists of often-gruesome battle scenes, the immense industry of Homer criticism has, by and large, avoided directly confronting the poem's violence. When scholars do comment on Homeric violence, they often dismiss it out of hand as excessive, a distraction from dramatic highpoints like the encounter between Hector and his wife and child, or the unforgettable communing of Achilles and Priam. Ferber's comment is fairly representative:

> While it may be interesting to learn how many ways a man may be done in by different weapons, such an interest is of a minute and morbid sort and no answer to the cumulative weight of death upon death. Perhaps Homer's original audience took delight in all the names and details, but it is hard to believe that they too did not feel the tedious burden of it all.[3]

Interestingly enough, if scholars have avoided fully dealing with the violence in Homer, they have certainly not avoided wielding the most violent of interpretive strategies, dismembering the Homeric corpus in the name of an anatomical and anti-poetic "higher criticism"— "minute and morbid" indeed—that would rip the poems into a thousand bits and pieces of rote memorization, as if scholars willy-nilly transmute their scholarly journals into Homeric battlefields so as to practice indirectly the kind of violence they refuse to deal with directly in Homer's text. Psychoanalytic critics such as Eli Sagan are more self-reflective than 19th-century higher critics, but Sagan's thesis that Homeric violence reveals the fundamental ambivalence of a Greek culture caught between barbarism and sublimation[4] fails to account for the connection between the beautiful horror of Homeric violence and the overarching meaning(s) at work in the *Iliad* as a whole. Plus, the optimistic teleology grounding Sagan's work—the idea that violence can be utterly sublimated—seems increasingly naïve: psychoanalysis has failed to eradicate violence, both in the world at large and in the world of texts.

Several critics have confronted Homeric violence directly and have drawn remarkable conclusions—Simon Weil comes to mind,[5] as does

Jonathan Shay, who uncovers astounding parallels between the combat trauma suffered by Vietnam veterans and Homeric warriors, respectively[6]—but I will not recount their work here. While I prefer to give my interpretive foils some space, I honor my interpretive friends primarily in between the lines of this unapologetically hermetic essay that delights in Odyssean borrowings, twistings, and recombinations.

To the battlefield, then. Listen:

> But now Poseidon beat him down at the hands of Idomeneus, / for he bewitched his shining eyes, made moveless his bright limbs, / so that he could not run backward... but stood like a statue or a tree with leaves towering / motionless, while fighting Idomeneus stabbed at the middle / of his chest with the spear, and broke the bronze armour about him / which in time before had guarded his body from destruction. / He cried out then, a great cry, broken, the spear in him, / and fell, thunderously, and the spear in his heart was stuck fast / but the heart was panting still and beating to shake the butt end / of the spear. Then and there Ares the huge took his life away from him. (XIII. 434-444)[7]

Notice here the exquisitely precise physical details—"the heart was panting still and beating to shake the butt end / of the spear."[8] To imagine violence with such specificity requires a form of imaginative violence that fatally wounds all the simplifications, generalizations, and euphemisms that would clean violence up and reduce its horror to a PG version in which the stark reality of death is not present. The butt end of the deadly spear takes on a horrible kind of life in this Homeric scene, shaking to the rhythmic beat of the heart its cold steel is in the process of silencing forever. Also note the rich poetic simile describing Idomeneus' victim as a statue or a tree, a simile that both objectifies and ennobles this casualty of war, suggesting in the process that Homeric warfare is simultaneously an outgrowth of natural energies and a humanly constructed form of behavior: the life force that issues in the towering leaves of a tree is inseparable from the psychic energy that figures itself forth in human artistic creations, and Homeric warfare is most deeply an expression of this at once natural and figurative *prima materia*. Paradoxically, in the natural art of war that animates Homer's battlefield, the primary energies of the psyche express their living reality in deadly destruction, an *opus contra naturam* that, as will be seen further in the next example, infuses death and destruction with the vibrant beauty of imaginative particularity that is the *sine qua non* of psychological reality. As to the precise nature of the psychic energy animating the Homeric battlefield, notice, finally, the role of the gods in this scene: Poseidon paralyzes the soon-to-fall soldier, and Ideomeneus' spear is ultimately an instrument of Ares, that more-than-human force inseparable from the gruesome rage of battlefield slaughter. As will be seen below, perhaps Ares is the mythological figure who best "figures" the lively destruction of life at the heart of war's terrible beauty. Regardless, the fundamental point here is that the basic psychic energies that visibly and invisibly animate Homeric violence were known to the Greeks as gods, immortal forces which, called or uncalled, continue to characterize the *mundus imaginalis* and thereby fundamentally shape human life-in-the-world.

Another example:

> He then stabbed with the spear Ilioneus / the son of Phorbas the rich in sheepflocks, whom beyond all men / of the Trojans Hermes loved, and gave him possessions. Ilioneus was the only child his mother had borne him. / This man Peneleos caught underneath the brow, at the bases / of the eye, and pushed the eyeball out, and the spear went clean through / the eye-socket and tendon of the neck, so that he went down / backward, reaching out both hands, but Peneleos drawing / his sharp sword hewed at the neck in the middle, and so dashed downward / the head, with helm upon it, while still on the point of the big spear / the eyeball stuck. He, lifting it high like the head of a poppy, / displayed it to the Trojans and spoke vaunting over it. (XIV. 489-500)[9]

Here Homer's simile, by comparing a speared eyeball to the head of a poppy, overtly dares readers to see something beautiful in this violent scene, or rather to see the violence itself as a gruesome kind of beauty. If beauty is understood not as what is pleasing to the eye (quite literally the eyeball is not pleased in this scene) but as what is precisely and exquisitely imagined, then this violence is indeed beautiful—and, *nota bene*, all the more graphically disturbing. The beauty largely results because the particularity of the wounding is matched by the particularity of the victim: this is not an anonymous, bloodless enemy mowed down in a video game, but Ilioneus "the son of Phorbas the rich in sheepflocks," beloved by Hermes, a mother's only son. As critics have pointed out, Homer's killing scenes function also as mini-obituaries, memorializing and particularizing fallen soldiers.[10] Victorious warriors may vaunt over the fallen, but casualties of war—both Greek and Trojan—share in the poetic glory and immortality that Homer's verse bestows. Homeric memorializing succeeds because the agonies of violent death imprint themselves in the memory so that the poignant particularity of an individual life is felt in all its fleeting ineffability. As Margo Kitts puts it, "The *Iliad* has its own share of vengeful boasting and gory slaughter, of course, but even the most unsophisticated listener will notice that death tends to be focalized with an ear for the victim's last breath."[11] With all this in mind, Ferber's above comment seems unwittingly partly right: The innumerable violent scenes in Homer indeed function to force readers to feel the "tedious burden" of war, but this does not betray a gratuitous Homeric celebration of blood and guts but rather an unflinching engagement with the horrors of war. Even if George Steiner is correct, then, in claiming that Homer "revels in the gusto of physical action and in the stylish ferocity of personal combat,"[12] Homer does not blindly celebrate war as a human good. In fact, it bears noting that innumerable characters in the *Iliad*, including the major warriors, unambiguously refer to war as an evil. Seeing the evil of war with open eyes, however, requires seeing war itself as a fierce expression of the fundamental physical and imaginative energies of life. Homeric war is both horrible and beautiful, inscribing within the poetic representation of violence both the reality of human pain and loss *and* the heightened imaginative awareness that comes with seeing death's particularity and war's numinousness.

One last little point to catch your eye (pardon the pun): when Ilioneus reaches out both hands just before being wounded, his gesture of supplication subtly evokes the code of guest-friendship central to Greek life, a code broken by Paris when he whisked away Helen, which eventually led to the Trojan war. And speaking of Paris, might not our first example, in which divine intervention brings about the paralyzed limbs, bewitched eyes, and still-beating heart of Idomeneus' opponent, call to mind the typical effects of the divine being—Aphrodite—intimately wrapped up in Paris' seduction of Helen and indeed in the overarching mythological backstory that undergirds Homer's poem? Regardless, violence in Homer is never *just* violence, for in its very literalness it transports one into the ritualistic, mythical realm where the literal and the figurative meet. As Margo Kitts has persuasively demonstrated, many of the violent battlefield scenes in Homer contain images of wounding and suffering that remarkably parallel the sacrificial, ritual wounding and suffering of victims in the poem's several oath-sacrifice scenes, thereby tying battlefield violence to the overriding topos of oath-making and oath-breaking at the heart of the poem's action.[13] Thus, even as Homeric violence brings to the fore the deadly horrors of war, it mythologically transmutes these horrors into a larger ritual of communal transformation.

In sum, the above two battle scenes demonstrate that there is undeniably more going on in Homeric violence than meets the horrified scholarly eye determined to see only tedious bodily carnage, and perhaps the speared-eyeball, disembodied and raised high, looks out at readers primarily to challenge them to see beyond bodily violence into the subtle body of myth and imagination at the center of the poem's energies. Homeric violence, in large ways and in small, in the red raging of Ares and the subtle plotting of Zeus, involves the terribly beautiful slaughter of particular human beings by more-than-human forces that can never be fully understood because they themselves, as not only cosmic forces but also the archetypal figures at the base of the mind, are the very means of human understanding. The Homeric battlefield reveals *in extremis* a general psychological truth: in Auden's phrase, we are lived by forces we scarcely understand. The resistance of scholars to Homeric violence is therefore ultimately a resistance to the kind of direct confrontation with the reality of death that touches the soul's depths and makes visible the invisible reality of the polytheistic, transpersonal psyche. Scholars seem habitually prone to resist the reality of the gods, so they find it much easier to dismiss Homeric violence as excessive rather than to acknowledge what Homer so powerfully sees and conveys: the presence of the gods in death's sting.

Speaking of the gods: Homeric violence, indicative of neither a univocally pro-war nor a naively anti-war stance, achieves a complex accommodation of Ares, a monumentalizing of the god of violent warfare that goes beyond sublimation as psychoanalytically understood. Homer undoubtedly realizes that one cannot pacify Ares by running into the peaceful arms of a different, less-violent god, so he honors

Ares by portraying war in a poetic and rhetorical style that is Ares-like: close, direct, bloody, intense, unyielding. Readers, by imagining poetic violence violently described, are forced to exercise the inherent violence of the imagination—the faculty that, according to Bachelard, relishes de-forming and dis-membering images, transmuting the old so as to imagine the new, draining the blood from the dayworld so as to create psychological reality.[14] Homer's poetics of violence thus provokes in readers what Wallace Stevens refers to as the imaginative violence from within that counteracts the violence from without that would block psychological reflection.[15] Such imaginative violence does *not* merely sublimate violent urges into creative expressions of culture; rather, it honors Ares by basking in his desire for destruction, utilizing this desire as a mode of reflecting upon Ares himself and his role in the processes of the imagination. As such, Homeric violence memorializes the fragile preciousness of life at the same time that it celebrates the violent proclivities of the poetic imagination that are responsible for acutely apprehending life's poignant reverberations. Only a violently alive imagination such as Homer's could craft a multi-dimensional simile that utilizes the shock of discontinuity simultaneously to evoke the odd stillness and horrified peace that comes with literal physical woundedness, and to figure the artistic process itself by which the poetic imagination precisely imagines the horrible beauty of violence. Listen:

> As when some Maionian woman or Karian with purple / colours ivory, to make it a cheek piece for horses; / it lies away in an inner room, and many a rider / longs to have it, / but it is laid up to be a king's treasure, / two things, to be the beauty of the horse, the pride of the horseman: / so, Menelaos, your shapely thighs were stained with the colour / of blood, and your legs also and the ankles beneath them. (IV. 141-147)[16]

One cannot discuss violence in the *Iliad* without speaking about the poem's most violent figure of all, the half-human, half-divine Achilles, whose divine wrath (*menis*), the stated subject of the poet's song, "hurled in their multitudes to the house of Hades strong souls / of heroes" (I. 3-4).[17] Achilles not only sends the souls of innumerable warriors down into the realm of Hades, but also moves the entire poem, and readers with it, into an underworld context, the realm of soul. Especially after the death of his beloved friend Patroclus, Achilles violently transforms himself into a living embodiment of Death, both taking the lives of others and descending into the imminent reality of his own death in such a way as to make visible within the poem the invisible realm of Hades. In a brilliant essay, Glenn Arbery associates the arc of Achilles' development in the *Iliad* with the Jungian, psychic ontology elaborated most fully by James Hillman. Arbery writes:

> The unconscious, which Freud describes as timeless, amoral, and capable of sustaining contradictions, Hillman refigures as the realm of the "dead," with death understood as the metaphor of that locus of images that constitutes psyche or soul. Psyche is above all poetic—that is, the work of making or fashioning images, as in dreams, and reworking them in interpretation. Hillman's thesis enables one to see Achilles' movement in the *Iliad* as a poetic initiation into the vertical dimension of depth that characterizes psyche as opposed to the more horizontal dimension of *thymos* in its relation to honor.[18]

For Arbery, the raging, violent rampage of Achilles poetically enacts a thymotic, homeopathic burning away of the thymos—that part of the soul that, for the Greeks, was the seat of both courage and wrath, and thus the source of achievement vis-à-vis the external honor code that Achilles philosophically struggles with throughout the poem. By burning away his thymos, and by recognizing the insufficiency of the Greek notion of honor when viewed from the ontological perspective of death, Achilles both discovers and incarnates psychological reality: thymos becomes psyche, and courage and wrath therefore transmute into forms of imaginative energy that make and remake the stuff of the world into soulful images. Upon awakening from a dream in which the vaporous, insubstantial soul of Patroclus appears to him, Achilles exclaims, "'Oh, wonder! Even in the house of Hades there is left something, / a soul and an image'" (XXIII. 103-104).[19] Achilles' discovery of this ineffable reality of the psyche—the realm of Hades where images become the subtle body of the individual and world soul—is inseparable from his own vertical descent into and horizontal provocation of the exquisitely violent agonies of mortality.

    I cannot here summarize all the provocative insights that Arbery develops in his treatment of Achilles, but of crucial importance is his elucidation of the background myth that intertwines Achilles' fate with that of his divine mother, Thetis, an intertwining inseparable from the root mythological causes of the entire Trojan War. As Arbery points out, Achilles is quite explicitly born to die, his parents' forced marriage being a means of Zeus to maintain the existing Olympian order. As Pindar tells the story, both Zeus and Poseidon lusted after the sea-goddess Thetis, but, since a prophecy indicated that Thetis' son was destined to be vastly more powerful than his father, Zeus decided it was wise to force Thetis to marry a mortal, Peleus, and thereby give birth to a mortal son. At the marriage feast of Thetis and Peleus, Eris introduced the Golden Apple that Paris eventually awarded to Aphrodite, an act that earned Paris the favors of the goddess of love and, with them, the semi-divine Helen whose abduction led to the Trojan War. Keeping in mind this background myth adds immense gravitas to Achilles' grappling with his mortal fate, since, more than any other Greek hero, Achilles is a figure whose full immortal glory is expressly denied through the plotting of Zeus. Homer, in granting Achilles the supreme poetic honor of placing him at the center of an epic poem, thus celebrates the inescapable poignancy of human mortality. At the end of the poem, Achilles works through the debilitating suffering that ensues from his newfound closeness to death, discovering the transformational propensities of human communion in his encounter with Priam. All of this occurs, it seems, because of Achilles' related discovery of the wondrous reality of the psyche, a discovery readers make along with Achilles by deeply engaging the problematic violence of the poem.

Taking to heart Achilles as a figure whose actions and very being evoke the imagistic realm of psyche transforms the way one encounters the immense violence in the *Iliad*. As we have seen, Homeric violence is not gratuitous, a pointless celebration of blood and guts meant merely to titillate or nauseate the reader; rather, the violent scenes in Homer honor human suffering and mortality at the same time that they pay tribute to the immortals, especially Ares whose divine wrath delights in war—a delight that, despite the squeamishness of most scholars, may figure the imaginative vigor inherent in a lively engagement with the world. Homer's poetics of violence—and Achilles serves as a fitting emblem of the violent wisdom contained in Homer's poem—initiates the Western tradition into an open-eyed confrontation with death and the concomitant imagining of a soulful existence in the world. Much further work deserves to be done on this topic, but drawing together all of our insights here at the close, we can claim that the cumulative violence in the *Iliad*—the innumerable pierced and bloodied bladders and buttocks and chests and eyeballs that cause a dark mist to rise from the pages of Homer's epic—this cumulative violence serves as one giant sacrificial offering at the alter of psyche, that imaginative terrain the contours of which the archaic Greek mind was just beginning to explore.

NOTES

1. Note that I specify imaginative blood. If I were to enter into the famous Hillman-Giegerich debate of a number of years ago concerning the role of sacrificial violence in establishing the reality of the psyche, I would side with Hillman—not the literal act of violence, but the imagining, the metaphorical shaping of this act is the ground of psychic reality. The Hillman-Giegerich debate can be read in *Spring 54* (Giegerich's essay "Killings") and *Spring 56* (Hillman's response, "Once More into the Fray").

2. My notion of "psychological reality" explicitly follows Jung's ontology of psychic reality. *Collected Works* 6, § 78: "This autonomous activity of the psyche, which can be explained neither as a reflex action to sensory stimuli nor as the executive organ of eternal ideas, is, like every vital process, a continually creative act. The psyche creates reality every day. The only expression I can use for this activity is fantasy. Fantasy is just as much feeling as thinking; as much intuition as sensation."

3. Cited by James Holoka, editor. In Simon Weil's *The Iliad or the Poem of Force* (New York: Peter Lang, 2003), p. 16.

4. Eli Sagan, *The Lust to Annihilate* (New York: Psychohistory Press, 1979).

5. Simon Weil, *The Iliad or the Poem of Force.*

6. Jonathan Shay, *Achilles in Vietnam* (New York : Touchstone, 1994).

7. Homer, *Iliad*, trans. Richard Lattimore (Chicago, IL: University of Chicago Press, 1951).

8. Another example of the almost joyful precision with which Homer describes violent wounding occurs in Book Five of the poem: "This man Meriones pursued and overtaking him / struck in the right buttock, and the spearhead drove straight / on and passing under the bone went into the bladder. / He dropped, screaming, to his knees, and death was a mist about him" (V. 65-68).

9. Homer, *Iliad*.

10. See Shay, *Achilles in Vietnam*, p. 130.

11. Margo Kitts, *Sanctified Violence in Homeric Society* (New York: Cambridge University Press, 2005), p. 12.

12. George Steiner, "Homer and the Scholars," *Homer: A Collection of Critical Essays* (Englewood Cliffs, NJ: Prentice-Hall, 1962), p. 8.

13. See Kitts, *Sanctified Violence*, p. 115-116.

14. Gaston Bachelard, *On Poetic Imagination and Reverie*, trans. Colette Gaudin (Indianapolis, Ind.: Bobbs-Merrill, 1971), p. 19.

15. Wallace Stevens, *The Necessary Angel* (New York: Vintage, 1951), p. 20.

16. Homer, *Iliad*.

17. *Ibid.*

18. Glenn Arbery, "Soul and Image: The Single Honor of Achilles," *The Epic Cosmos* (Dallas: Dallas Institute Publications, 1992), p. 32.

Cultural Rupture: A Call to Poetic Insurgency

GEORGE MCGRATH CALLAN

In the life of an individual, the work of soul making is often revealed in the presence of rupture. Latent symptoms stalk the unconscious and roam the landscape of the ego like sleepwalkers. A soul crisis calls for an insurgency, a "rising up" out of a solitary and particular suffering to become the source material from which an alchemical transformation is made. Destruction, dismemberment, and annihilation take place in the crucible of individuation. The old vessel is shattered and familiar notions of identity, relationship, security, containment, self, and other must be abandoned. Solidified notions of good and evil, right and wrong, just and unjust must break open. And so it is with nations.

A psychology of the soul is one that addresses the hidden, invisible aspects of the individual and the collective psyche. A psychology of the soul cultivates an attention to the unconscious and is as fascinated with the nightmare as the erotic reverie, as devoted to the chthonic depths as to the cosmic heights, to war as to diplomacy, to the oeneric as to the factual, to violence as to beauty. A psychology of the soul is devoted to what has been forgotten, what lies behind the screen of

George McGrath Callan, Ph.D., is a depth psychologist in private practice in Seattle, Washington. She is an adjunct faculty member at Pacifica Graduate Institute in Santa Barbara, California and Antioch University in Seattle, Washington.

remembrance. In our profound forgetfulness, the crucible of war, ecological destruction, and other forms of human and planetary suffering is overflowing. We find ourselves in a *nepenthian* relationship to our world. *Nepenthe* is derived from the word *ne*, not, and *penthos*, grief.[1] Its definition includes anything that induces oblivion of sorrow or eases pain. If we wake from our forgetfulness, we might be overcome with terror and grief for what we are losing, what we have lost, and what we have yet to lose. This induction to oblivion is at the very core of the problem of individual and cultural rupture. The word rupture is derived from the Latin, *rumpere*, "to break."[2]

In *Violence,* professor of philosophy and social critic, Slavoj Žižek, exposes the violence that is inherent in the most potent socio-political systems of our day: capitalism, fundamentalism, and globalization. He addresses these powers as subversive purveyors of violence. Žižek distinguishes the subjective or visible forms of violence from the invisible objective forms, both symbolic and systemic. Symbolic violence can be found embedded in our language. It veils a socio-political ideology that promotes a culture of exploitation and domination. Systemic violence excludes all that does not serve capitalism and pits market participants against those unable to take part. By delineating objective forms of violence, Žižek's theory allows for a conception of a violence of non-action: not-seeing, not-hearing, not-knowing, not-storying— a violence of neglect and distortion—ultimately, a violence of systemic forgetfulness, like an unchecked melanoma spreading its tentacles in unsuspected places.

> Is there not something suspicious, indeed symptomatic, about this focus on subjective violence—that violence which is enacted by social agents, evil individuals, disciplined repressive apparatuses, fanatical crowds? Doesn't it desperately try to distract our attention from the true locus of trouble, by obliterating from view other forms of violence and thus actively participating in them?[3]

In the United States of America we live in a culture that promotes knowledge as a form of materialism, sells information as a commodity, and uses the word as a form of trance induction. We live with the language of violence that fills out newspapers and the images of brutality that flash across our screens, sandwiched between ads for commodities manufactured at a human and planetary price we cannot repay. Beyond that, we live every day with the silent accumulated effects of hundreds of years of terror in our own homeland and in lands afar. The United States of America was born out of two powerful and opposing impulses: violence, as enacted in the unconscionable slaughter of indigenous peoples—and the highest expression of our mythic consciousness, articulated most poignantly in the Declaration of Independence. The circumstances of our birth are not mere historical events, but living, breathing forces in the American psyche.

In the Pacific Northwest where I live, we walk on the bones of our massacred native peoples every day: baby girl bones and 10-year-old boy bones, mother and father bones, grandmother and grandfather bones. The pavement between those bones and the bones of our own feet provides a kind of nepenthian forgetfulness, a false security against the visceral truth of our collective violations. We all walk on bones in one way or another. It is of value to know whose bones we walk upon and whose blood our particular soil bears. War making and peacemaking, memory and imagination are rooted in the body, encoded in the earth and carried on the winds of the long-ago breath of those who proceed us. Attention to particularity is a way of meeting violence psychologically. In a version of the 1854 treaty, Chief Seattle is known to have said:

> The sable braves, and fond mothers, and glad-hearted maidens, and the little children who lived and rejoiced here, and whose very names are now forgotten, still love these solitudes, and their deep fastnesses at eventide grow shadowy with the presence of dusky spirits. And when the last red man shall have perished from the earth and his memory among white men shall have become a myth, these shores shall swarm with the invisible dead of my tribe, and when your children's children shall think themselves alone in the field, the shop, upon the highway or in the silence of the woods they will not be alone. In all the earth there is no place dedicated to solitude. At night when the streets of your cities and villages shall be silent, and you think them deserted, they will throng with the returning hosts that once filled and still love this beautiful land. The white man will never be alone. Let him be just and deal kindly with my people, for the dead are not altogether powerless.[4]

I make a distinction here between remembering and *unforgetting*. Remembering is a re-assembling of the images that have faded from consciousness. We can be re-minded. Our memory can be re-freshed. We reminisce, re-collecting shards and fragments from the past. What I call "unforgetting" might be understood to mean to re-member what has never made its way to our personal consciousness: what the land knows, what others have known before us, what has been in our presence and has been concealed from us, that which is hovering or ghostly. In reverie, visionary and dream states, and in moments of creation we practice unforgetting for the earth and for ourselves, our ancestors and our descendents. This aspect of consciousness I am calling unforgetting is akin to Heidegger's description of *poiesis*. In his reflections on responsibility Heidegger uses this Greek word *poiesis*: "bringing forth." The Greek understanding of responsibility, as he describes it, is not associated with moral liability or indebtedness. He closely associates *poiesis* with *aita*, which means "starting something on its way to arrival." Embroidered into these companion words is the notion of bringing something out of concealment.[5] It is the essential work of the artist, the craftsperson, and the psychologist in all of us. In her work as social artist and mythmaker, Jean Houston calls psychology "the work of the gods." It is the work of soul making, and it is in this sense of responsibility to the world that I use the word "poet, poetic, poiesis" throughout this paper.

Violence is local and particular, and its presence requires confrontation, either subjective or objective with an Other. When we are distanced from the reality of violence by time, space, intent, or manipulation we lose our connection to the personal and the particular so essential for a visceral and phenomenological knowledge of suffering. Violence is our collective inheritance. The history of our ancestors and their deeds, for good and for ill, hides in the background like a geological map, charting unseen patterns in our current personal and collective stories. When I listen to the history of my ancestral America, the hidden narratives, the untold details reveal something particular about our beginnings in bravery and brutality. If we hear them in the spirit of conscious *unforgetting*, listening carefully to the ghosts of our history— to the nuances and the unspeakable sorrows—we will not be tempted to translate them into heroic ballads or utilize them as opportunities for further moralization and polarization. If we enter the story with a mytho-poetic consciousness we may find occasion to dialogue with our humanity in all its courage, generosity, greed, and hubris.

From an archetypal perspective, pathologies that roam the dark realm of the individual and cultural psyche are not to be eliminated. They are to be illuminated. A personal or societal rupture creates a necessary aperture through which we may gaze into the disturbing domain of our human and earthly condition. A movement from the literal to the mythic, from the informational to the poetic is an archetypal trajectory in violation of the discourses that predominate in the information-laden and unexamined psyche of western society. Spanish poet, Antonio Machado, invites us, by way of oeneric consciousness, into the landscape of remembering:

> Last night, as I was sleeping,
> I dreamt—marvelous error!—
> That I had a beehive
> Here in my heart.
> And the golden bees were making white combs
> and sweet honey
> from my old failures ....[6]

When we turn our faces from our old failures, we forget how to listen to the lament of the fish and sea mammals as their kin are dying and washing to shore. When we turn our faces from our old failures, we forget how to mourn the loss of the most ancient agricultural knowledges held by agrarian cultures in sacred trust from one generation to the next. We can no longer imagine the grief of the bombed-out land for its blossoms, the thirst of contaminated water for its own vitality and usefulness, the agony of the village for the loss of its homes and libraries and museums and shops, its inhabitants— animals, birds, bugs, reptiles, humans. We forget the rhythms of community that give village and city its song, and hence its meaning. When we forsake our failings, we cannot hear the howling and keening of a mother for her lost children, the cries of hundreds of orphaned children for their mothers and fathers, sisters and brothers, neighbors and friends; the lover for her spouse, the refugee for her home, the soldier for her limb. The poet is free to speak of old failures, the politician— not so likely.

Violence lives psychoactively in language. Among the most pervasive of cultural practices of forgetting is the ever-streaming dissemination of propaganda that hides behind the free press veneer.

As a purveyor of violence, propaganda arrives in subjective and objective, visible and invisible, symbolic and systemic forms. It speaks in an encoded language. It operates as a pervasive presence in the public experience in much the same way that a complex functions in the personal psyche. In the context of the media we are moved from headline to breaking news, from crisis to scandal. Our human capacity for tender attention to detail is disrupted by this insidious and speedy trajectory. We are given massive amounts of fact, laden with subliminal and unexamined corporate and cultural values. Particularly in times of social and economic rupture, repressive governments and their media minions obsess on two primary questions: "What are the facts?" and "Who is to blame?" "The facts," says Miguel de Cerventes in *The Man of La Mancha,* "are the enemy of truth."[7]

In the context of public media we are offered no invitation to reflect upon the voice of the speaker who may be many times removed from the researcher or writer who actually saw the event in question or developed the text. We are expected to hear data as the voice of truth. By its very nature, propaganda has no breath, no diversity, fluidity, or spirit. If we allow ourselves to be entranced by the drumbeat of propaganda, we will find ourselves disenfranchised from our own imagination, wandering in an airless and barren land of information. The suppression or distortion of communication and the theft of imagination are predominant signs of oppression. Oppression is at the heart of violence.

Disassociation, addiction, distraction, fundamentalism, narcissism, consumerism, and other multiple forms of materialism are among the many ways that the unconscious collective psyche can maneuver to keep us circling the cauldron of a suffering world—balancing on the periphery of human angst.

Enter the poet. The poet is known for her long and lingering gaze. She hovers over the crevices, lingers in the nuances, rides on the aura of the most minute gesture. This is the watchfulness that despotic governments are most fearful of. The censoring of imagination is the first sign of the violent oppression of the mind. The anti-image is a form of propaganda because its purpose is to diminish plurality and establish a single unmovable voice. It validates the supremacy of slogans over images, freezes ideas as material objects, and sacrifices the sonorous nature of our human endeavors for a monotonous and redundant note.

In the process it eliminates a host of symphonic possibilities. Political speeches, for example, can be excellent sources of research as we seek to understand the impact of dead language on the citizenry.

Both poet and propagandist are devoted to the careful and intentional use of language and to the utilization of cadence and rhythm. Poetry distills the action and stirs the imagination. The poet calls forth the animate quality of matter, wooing us toward revelation by way of the pathos of embodied language. The propagandist defines the meaning in an event, labels it in the context of his own value or dogma, extracts imagination, and approaches matter, even human matter as dead object. It could be seen poetically as a kind of murder by word. The relational and erotic nature of things is hidden in the capsule of a culture of concealment. The dominant patriarchal paradigm will gladly relieve us of our innate knowing and our subjective experience, seating us in the bleachers as cool spectators of its global blood sport. The poet, on the other hand, will show no mercy, throwing us into the center of the human arena to be ripped apart with the others. In the hands of the poet we cannot forget our common corporality.

Neither poet nor propagandist turns his face from violence. The propagandist reports it from a remote location. He sometimes presents it as an insidious form of drama or entertainment. The poet embodies it and thus imagines it in all its intricate detail. Propaganda, like fundamentalism, privileges nouns while poetic reverie seeks nuanced expression in adjectives, adverbs, and verbs. In the United States, President George W. Bush established himself as a maker of confrontational nouns and sound bites with idioms like "axis of evil," "war on terror," and "enemy combatant." He replaced the word "torture" with "alternate procedures" and practiced, with religious fervor, the ritual repetition of "the terrorists," a phrase that was marked by its absence of particularity—leaving the impression that *they* are everywhere. Hence, any action to eliminate them trumps moral discernment.

As we stand on the edge of civilization, teetering between destruction and creation, we witness the changing of the guard. President Barack Obama arrives as a consummate orator, referencing in his political speeches Lincoln, Emerson, Faulkner, and Shakespeare. In his inaugural address, he spoke, not only *of* enemies, but *to* them— and in sentences laden with images...."We will extend a hand if you are willing to unclench your fist." He spoke of our "patchwork heritage" and named us "keepers of this legacy." While we do not know if the poet in this president will prevail over the instinct toward symbolic and systemic violence so deeply embedded in our personal, national, and global history and in our economic and political systems, we cannot help but be moved by this invocation to rise up and bring forth.

The view of matter as dead object and the consequent and deliberate depletion of language are at the very heart and soul of violence. Even the word *violence* has been victimized by this kind of reductionism. The word violence, like the words depression, abuse, dysfunction, and terror, when confined to the cubical of the noun, loses its texture and particularity and becomes generic and meaningless, covering a range from "rude gesture" to "murder or rape." When we hear powerful words like violence and terror with a politicized or clinical ear, we are not moved. Like Orwellian Newspeak, words and phrases serve as manila envelopes, concealing volumes of voluptuous correspondence. Violence lives in our language, in its absences, distortions, and generalities. It originates in the mind as a kind of hollow vernacular. The primary intention of this phantom oppression is severance. Divided from our own deeper instincts, from one another, and from the world soul, we begin to experience ourselves as powerless. The tension between the powerful and the powerless drives the twin engines of symbolic and systemic violence.

In his reflections on Auschwitz, Žižek states "it is not poetry that is impossible after Auschwitz, but rather prose. Realistic prose fails, where the poetic evocation of the unbearable atmosphere of a camp succeeds."[8] His illustration of this assertion is drawn from the memoirs of the Russian poet Anna Akhmatova. After the Stalinist purges she stood in a crowd at the Leningrad prison where she awaited news of her son.

> One day somebody in the crowd identified me. Standing behind me was a young woman, with lips blue from the cold, who had of course never heard me called by name before. Now she started out of the torpor common to us all and asked me in a whisper (everyone whispered there), "Can you describe this?" And I said, "I can." Then something like a smile passed fleetingly over what had once been her face.[9]

There is a powerful distinction in this conversation between the literal and political description of violence and the lived, poetic, and archetypal experience of human violation. Žižek reflects:

> This is not a description which locates its content in historical space and time, but a description which creates, as the background of the phenomena it describes, an insistent (virtual) space of its own, so that what appears in it is not an appearance sustained by the depth of reality behind it, but a decontextualised appearance, an appearance which fully coincides with real being.[10]

In times of extreme social injustice, devastation, and war we have an urgent need for the voices and the mentorship of our poets, our fiction writers, playwrights, screenwriters, and mythmakers, our artists and filmmakers and musicians, choreographers, dancers, and puppeteers. Traditionally it has been these makers who have touched the conscience, the very soul of their nations in such times. In her 1986 Bryn Mawr commencement address American novelist Ursula Le Guin exhorts her young audience to attend to the distinction between embodied and disembodied language, which she refers to as the mother tongue and the father tongue.

> People can't contradict each other, only words can: words separated from experience for use as weapons, words that make the wound, the split between subject and object, exposing and exploiting the object but disguising and defending the subject....So what am I talking about with this "unlearned language"—poetry, literature? Yes, but it can be speeches and science, any use of language when it is spoken, written, read, heard as art, the way dancing is the body moving as art.[11]

The dominant cultural/political forces engage in violence by dulling our senses, seducing us into dualistic battles, distancing us from our own experience, luring us into a state of forgetfulness by way of the materialistic accumulation of goods and information. The poet is, by profession, preoccupied. It is her vocation. She becomes a reflective occupied territory. *Occupare*: to seize.[12] She is seized by the world. Seized by the wilderness. The poet revives our archetypal memory and brings us back to our senses. Le Guin continues:

> The father tongue is spoken from above. It goes one way. No answer is expected, or heard. In our constitution and the works

> of law, philosophy, social thought, and science, in its everyday
> uses in the service of justice and clarity, what I call the father
> tongue is immensely noble and indispensably useful. When it
> claims a privileged relationship to reality, it becomes dangerous
> and potentially destructive. …The mother tongue, spoken or
> written, expects an answer. It is conversation, a word the root of
> which means "turning together."[13]

Every day in the early morning, I sit at my kitchen table with a
cup of hot tea, relishing my morning rituals. In my imagination, I visit
the shattered homes of Iraqi and Afghani women of my own age. I
ponder what it would be like to be separated from the simple, familiar
rhythms and gestures of a life—not to hear music playing in the
background, sounds of grandchildren bantering freely with playmates
in the yard, a casual chat with a neighbor, a bouquet of peonies or lilies
from the garden, the smell of fresh vegetable soup cooking on the stove,
a candle flickering on the table. In solidarity, I feel the grief of a life
separated from friends and family and stalked by the constant presence
of fear and death. The alchemist and the poet know this place, each in
his own language. The poet may call it the wilderness, the underworld,
the abyss—the alchemist, the *nigredo*. Both will linger there, practicing
their intentional preoccupation with the *prima materia*—the stuff of
their unique crafts. Seized by necessity and love of the world they
become the habitat of the wilderness.

Symptom is the unruly child of the undiscovered complex. It is
the envoy of the soul trying to remember something. In the absence of
the heartfelt image, a collective symbolic violence is forged. Might it
then be our poetic duty to our humanity to practice with one another
the invocation of images of violence? In the interior tribune of our
collective memory and imagination we know what occupied body bags
look like. We see lines of flag-draped coffins arriving home, Afghani
and Iraqi mothers grieving, children screaming, emotionally and
spiritually shattered soldiers returning, women and children kept in
physical, emotional, and sexual bondage, and hungry and illiterate
people foraging in lands afar and in on our own "civilized" domain.
From a psychological perspective we ask not to be rescued from these
dark dreams for they are the fragile threads that tie us to those whose
lives we impact by our participation in the economic/political system—
those who we will never know. There is no question that events of our

day call us to social, political, and humanitarian action. Yet to act without fully engaging the imagination is to act from an old paradigm that is riddled with unconscious forms of violence. If we recognize the archetypal forces with which we are wrestling, we may be less likely to respond from vindictive or moral impulses. Action and non-action are shadow reflections of one another. We sever them at our own peril.

As violence is embedded inextricably in our language and in our gestures, so is it forged in our economies. A society that manifests its currency predominantly by way of investment and debt inducement is a violating society, many times removed from the earthly harvest and the experience of the exchange of goods and services—the human touch, the handshake, the satisfaction of trade, the smell of the earth as it is turned, the sound of the coin as it drops in the cash register—removed from the great exchange of nature and community, from the seed, the crop, the impact of weather, the gestures of nature. Even though we are touched daily by the work of people of many nations, they are invisible to us. The consumption of the object has become more alluring than the human exchange. Most of us do not know where our "things" come from, who touched them, and how we might be complicit in the exploitation of people, other living creatures, and the planet herself. Žižek reflects:

> Therein resides the fundamental systemic violence of capitalism, much more uncanny than any direct pre-capitalist socio-ideological violence: this violence is no longer attributable to concrete individuals and their "evil" intentions, but is purely "objective," systemic, anonymous. Here we encounter the Lacanian difference between reality and the Real: "reality" is the social reality of the actual people involved in interaction and in the productive processes, while the Real is the inexorable "abstract."[14]

The web is tightly woven. The ordinary citizen buying a pair of running shoes, fueling and driving a car, drinking a cup of coffee, paying a bill, investing in a retirement fund, or cooking a chicken, is never far removed from some form of violence and suffering. Embedded as we are in modernity's existential complexity, and caught in the grips of mercenary globalism, it seems impossible to avoid complicity. Through the lens of poiesis the knowledge of our complicity is a movement toward revelation.

Consider the indigenous hunter who, in reverie, dream, or in prayer engaged with intention and consciousness the particular animal he pursued. He understood the encounter between species as a profound conversation in the context of the mysteries of life and death. From a psychological/poetic perspective, we have some essential questions to ask. If we eat meat that has been procured by means of the torture of animals, what makes us think we are not ingesting terror? If we eat produce that has been treated with pesticides, what makes us think we are not poisoning ourselves—physically, socially, and spiritually— nor complicit in the skin infections, illnesses, and death of those who harvest that food? Can we feel the suffering of a sweatshop child touching our skin in the clothing we wear? These examples are not given to induce guilt, incite moral outrage, or evoke a call to action. Guilt too often serves as a narcissistic distraction; moral outrage keeps us detached from the truth of our invisible consent. Action devoid of *poiesis* may serve to relieve us of the disturbing and complex dilemmas and paradoxes that lie just below the surface of our consciousness, and define the agonizing impossibilities of our modern existence.

Might we sacrifice our search for a disembodied and morality-based cure of violence on the altar of poetic consciousness? When our attention is turned to personal and particular anguish our hearts are stirred. It is in this deep recognition that psyche is awakened to its true calling. By way of an embodied imagination we seek to become poetic insurgents, to unveil the story underneath the story, and so to rise up to our humanity in its darkness and its luminosity. We awaken from the spell of propaganda, and in the rampage of our inescapable complicity turn together in the direction of the world.

NOTES

1. *The American Heritage Dictionary* (New York: American Heritage Publishing Co., Inc. & Houghton Mifflin Company, 1969), p. 881.

2. *Ibid.,* p. 1136.

3. Slavoj Žižek, *Violence* (New York: Picador, 2008), pp. 1-12.

4. "Excerpt from Chief Seattle's Speech 1854," <http://www.jowsey. com/pix/house/ChiefSeattle/index.html> (accessed October 31, 2008).

5. Martin Heidegger, *Basic Writings* (San Francisco, CA: Harper Collins, 1977), pp. 292-293.

6. Antonio Machado, *Times Alone: Selected Poems of Antonio Machado*, trans. Robert Bly (Middletown: Wesleyan University Press, 1983), p. 43.

7. *The Man of La Mancha*, Film, dir. Arthur Hill (1972: United Artists [US], Produzioni Europee Association).

8. Žižek, pp. 4-5.

9. *Ibid.*, p. 5.

10. *Ibid.*, pp. 5-6.

11. Ursula Le Guin, "Ursula K. Le Guin Bryn Mawr Commencement Address (1986)," <http://serendip.brynmawr.edu/sci_cult/leguin/> (accessed October 31, 2008).

12. *The American Heritage Dictionary*, p. 908.

13. Le Guin.

14. Žižek, pp. 12-13.

Titanic Violence:
Vaclav Havel and the Dangers of
Ideological Thinking

DAVID BARTON

I

Violence is sometimes understood as opening a connection to the sacred. From this point of view, violence fascinates us because of its creative potency, which is one reason why creation myths are so bloody. The creative aspect of violence is further suggested by the etymology: *violentia*, meaning vehemence, was itself probably formed from the Latin *vis,* meaning power, as in *vis major* (higher power), *vis medicatrix naturae* (the healing power of nature), *and vis divina* (divine power). The first of these terms, still used in law, refers to an overwhelming force of nature (sometimes also called an "Act of God") that can exempt one from a legal contract; the last term is common usage among early classical writers, such as Cicero, who uses the phrase to refer to the power of the gods that manifests itself in the world, where it can be experienced or felt by humans. This etymology suggests violence and religion are interwoven, a situation that helps explain the awe that many, including myself, have felt when witnessing natural catastrophes. So much terrible destruction seems, quite surprisingly, to carry a terrible beauty as well.

David Barton is the former editor-in-chief of *The Salt Journal.* He is currently Assistant Professor at Northern New Mexico College, where he teaches mythology and religion.

Not all violence, however, is full of terrible wonder. There is a far more sinister form of violence that can be recognized by its lack of potency; while the generative violence of creation myths uncovers the mythic imagination, breaking down and breaking through the surface of appearances, the second form of violence seals up and seals out, making imagination difficult if not impossible. This violence relates to what the Central European philosophers, including Tomas Garrigue Masaryk and Jan Patocka, describe as "Titanic," a term used to refer to the rapaciousness with which modern, industrialized society destroys both the spiritual inwardness and the organic beauty of the world.[1] In a psychological context, the same term has been used by Rafael Lopez-Pedraza to describe a primal force within the psyche that works against the imagination.

The basic outlines of psychological Titanism are presented in a collection of essays in Lopez-Pedraza's book *Cultural Anxieties*. In his well-known essay "Moon Madness—Titanic Love," Lopez-Pedraza makes it clear that just as the Titans of Greek mythology were characterized by massive, undifferentiated force, so the Titanic level of the psyche represents excess, lawlessness, and a lack of form and order.[2] The implications of his ideas, however, remain curiously unexplored, at least in print, perhaps because Titanism refers not to "archetypal configurations" but rather to what is "formless in human nature."[3] Archetypal psychology may be unable to incorporate the ideas of Lopez-Pedraza precisely because the Titanic level of the psyche is not archetypal. The Titanic consists not of a constellation of bright stars in the night sky of the imagination but of black holes that escape the optical telescopes normally used to observe the psyche.

According to Lopez-Pedraza, some individuals, although highly cultured, lack the ability to form images (presumably as the result a trauma). When images do enter their psyche, then "something coming from nowhere comes along and destroys any such possibility." Such individuals have a corresponding lack of "psychical feelings" and "creativity" and are only able to experience the life of the imagination as a stereotype or abstract idea. The psychological makeup of such people "makes sense only if one can detect the Titanic element" of their psyche—an element which can not be "reflected" because it has no image but can be detected "through its Titanic rhetoric."

Titanism, Lopez-Pedraza explains further, is thus understood not as an archetypal experience but as *lacunae* whose presence block the archetypal image. These empty spaces can be found not only in individuals but in cultural excesses. The Titanic lurks wherever there are no "laws, no order, no limits" and where the natural or sacred order of life has been eclipsed by mere mimicry. A taste of how each of us experiences these empty spaces can be found in the following passage:

> We are all inhabited by these abstractions, these empty names; we are flooded in our daily lives by empty names—our daily 'blah-blah-blah'—not to mention our psychotherapy, in which, if we are unaware of our Titanism, we can fall into empty jargon, even when using the most beautiful words. ... There are areas in our psyches, in our lives, in which we have no reflection because there are no images and so no feelings to judge.[4]

Any further investigation into the nature of Titanism is fraught with difficulties. How do we reflect upon an object that repels reflection? There is a danger, for instance, in investigating the image of the Titanic, since the term "Titanic" is itself nothing more than an abstraction. For this reason I will forgo an examination of Titans of Greek mythology (including the standard symbolic interpretations: the Titans as an archaic force of nature or as the primordial infant self) and turn towards the work of individuals who have written about the affect of Titanism on individual life.[5]

II

One person who has written a great deal about Titanism (without using the term) is the former Czech playwright and dissident Vaclav Havel.[6] Havel was the country's most successful playwright in the fall of 1968 when the Soviet invasion ended the political and cultural liberalization known as the Prague Spring. During the so-called period of normalization, Havel's plays and other writings were banned from publication, and by the late 1970s he was one of the leading dissidents in Eastern Europe, both becoming a founding member of Charter 77 (the human rights organization that documented abuses under the communist government) and writing many of the essays (they were circulated in *samizdat*, the underground press) that provided the intellectual foundation for dissent. Not altogether incidentally, Havel also served several prison sentences on political charges before the regime fell in 1989, after which, quite famously, he was elected as the first post-communist president of what was then Czechoslovakia.

Havel's writing is astonishingly broad. As a playwright, he is a major influence in what Martin Esslin has called the "theater of the absurd,"[7] but he has much wider readership as a cultural essayist; in the U.S. he is known for the highly literary speeches he gave as president (they were often reprinted by such publications as the *New York Review of Books*), but his original influence came from the political and philosophical critiques of communism.

The genres may be eclectic, but his work is tied together by a focus on the absurdity of modern life. Here is one typical example, taken from a letter written to his wife from the Hermanice prison in Ostrava, a coal mining town in Northern Moravia:

> Not long ago, while watching a report on cows on the television news, I realized that the cow is no longer an animal: it is a machine that has an 'input' (grain feeds) and an 'output' (milk). It has its own production plans and its own operator whose job is the same as the job of the entire economy today: to increase output while decreasing input. The cow serves us quite efficiently, really, but at the cost of no longer being a cow ….

The letter, of course, is about a crisis of meaning—both personal and cultural—that Havel relates to the increasingly mechanized world. Humanity, Havel suggests, has "grasped the world in a way that has caused him, de facto, to lose it." Part of what we have lost, he says further, is our sensitivity towards the mystery of "Being."[8]

This theme—the mechanization of the world and the destruction of the "authentic" and the "natural"—is an underlying element in most, if not all, of Havel's plays and much of his political writing, including his many critiques of what he called "post-Totalitarian" systems, a term that refers to the fact that, although the Party exercised total control, its power was much more subtle than crude dictatorships of the past.[9]

Perhaps the most profound development of this theme can be found in *Temptation*, the absurdist re-telling of the Faust myth Havel first conceived while serving his time in the Ostrava prison.[10] *Temptation* takes place within a nebulous scientific institute (a "lighthouse of knowledge and science") that exists to root out the irrational elements of society. Dr. Henry Faustka, the central character, is a sophisticated but overbearing scientist—what Havel has elsewhere called a careerist, or someone who fails to subordinate his own ambition to matters of greater spiritual significance. *Temptation* presents a Kafkaesque world of empty-headed bureaucrats who specialize in nonsense and jargon (the first sign that the Titanic is present); ironically enough, the crisis that begins the play is that the youth are reading the works of C. G. Jung, leading to certain vague mysticism that The Institute is expected to exterminate.

Like Faust from Medieval folklore, Havel's Faustka secretly dabbles in the occult himself, evidently caught between an attraction to dark mysteries and a rationalistic desire to destroy them. He is, in fact, in the middle of performing a ritual in his living room to contact the spirit world when he receives a knock at the door from an agent of the dark forces (his name, Fistula, reminds us that *faust* is the German word for fist). Fistula offers to "initiate" Faustka into necromancy; by way of demonstrating the power of the irrational, he further suggests that he arrange for a young secretary at The Institute, Marketa, to briefly fall in love with him.

Faustka moralistically refuses to play this game, but later that evening, in a moment of synchronicity, Marketa listens to Faustka hold forth about the nature of the cosmos, suggesting that something more than chance was involved when the universe came into being. Of all possible forms, Faustka tells her, the universe "chose" one "having sufficient time and other requirements needed for the formation of solid bodies." Marketa is struck by Faustka's rather mystical idea. She listens as he suggests that all lives are built on such "unbelievable coincidences that it exceeds the bounds of all probability." Revealing the effect that dabbling in the occult has already begun to have on his thinking, he suggests that these "coincidences" must "conceal some deeper design of existence." It is, he says, as if nature willed life to exist and desired to create a human psyche "capable of fathoming it all!"[11]

Marketa—a naive, starry-eyed young woman—falls in love with his talk of cosmic mysteries, not understanding the discord between the mystic and the dominant, dried-up careerist whose job consists in policing the world of such unscientific thinking. Eventually Faustka betrays Marketa, just as he betrays his own high-minded ideals. When his interest in the occult is uncovered, he claims he is studying mysticism only to serve as a double agent, and in order to save his career he volunteers to become an informer on those who practice the "dark arts."

Like many Havel characters, Faustka inhabits an absurdist world where
Being and action remain unreconciled. Pontuso puts it this way: "Faustka
sells his soul but not for the same reason as Faust."[12] While Faust makes
the choice so common since the Enlightenment, choosing mastery over
the natural world over spiritual care, Faustka lives in a world where the
idea of soul is no longer possible to take seriously. All that's left for
Faustka to do is to try and salvage his career. Faust sells his soul to the
devil but Faustka is a lost soul, unaware of the bargain he's made or the
consequences the bargain will bring.

III

In a roundabout way, we have come back to the theme of violence.
We normally think of violence as a form of vehemence (the meaning of
the Latin root "*violentia*") directed at people or things. The world of
Temptation, however, gives us a more convoluted picture of a softer but
more insidious form of violence that attempts to eliminate interior
experience so that depth is no longer possible.

As the agent of this "post-totalitarian" violence, The Institute (in all
of its existential vagueness) is an image of that inner police state that has
the power to totalize our lives, reducing all things to a simple
mathematical formula. What does this mean? Wendell Berry has written
that he can imagine a time when humans will split between those who
wish to live as machines and those who wish to live as creatures. The
situation exposed in *Temptation* is about a world where living as creatures
is no longer possible. The post-Totalitarian world of *Temptation* is both
out there, where the characters are dominated by a police state, and *in
here*, where their inner police state dominates the life of the soul. The
tragedy of Faust—which is often understood as the desire for
knowledge—is thus reimagined in Havel's play as a conflict between
different kinds of knowledge (the calculating intellect on the one hand
and the "dark arts" on the other). The Faustian nature of the bargain is
that the rationalism advanced by The Institute not only destroys other
kinds of knowing but kills the creature in us. Faustka is a lost soul whose
tragedy is partly that he no longer feels the loss of soul as tragic.

As an archetypal motif, the loss of soul is usually understood in
psychological terms as an absence of feeling and imagination that is
replaced by anxiety, destruction, and stereotypical behavior, since one

can only act in such ways when one has lost personal meaning. In contradistinction to the classic tale of Psyche and Eros, which gives us an image of psychological development, these stories reveal a destruction that occurs in Titanic moments. It is no coincidence that Havel's play revolves around the mechanization of life, since in our own times the machine has become a natural symbol for the loss of soul (the unconscious association: losing our soul we become nothing more than a machine).[13] This is a common theme in contemporary science fiction in which borgs, cyborgs, or cybernetics become powerful and frightening symbols of an increasingly Titanic world.

As for Havel's intentions, he imagined *Temptation* as a commentary on overly rational forms of thinking and the ways they tempt us into leaving behind our life as creatures. In letters to his wife from his prison cell, Havel called *Temptation* a "Beckettian comedy about life" and "an authentically absurd experience, one that every careful reader of Kafka should recognize." Using the language of phenomenology that was so common among Eastern European intellectuals, he went on to suggest the play would be about "the state of thrownness" in the world, and thus about the great existential crises of humanity.

Thrownness, of course, is Heidegger's term to describe the experience of Being in the world. Havel himself uses the term to describe the panic of feeling separated from a whole we can intuit but never fully experience. He is reminded of the experience of "thrownness" one day in prison while watching a weather report on television. Due to a technical problem, the sound was cut and the confused weather announcer began staring into the screen, unsure how to respond. Suddenly "the mantle of routine" was stripped from her and she was "exposed to the view of millions, yet desperately alone," having been "thrown into an unfamiliar, unexpected and unresolvable situation" where she was forced to stand "face-to-face" with "all the primordial nakedness of human helplessness."[14] This Kafkaeque situation, Havel suggests, mirrors our own state of "throwness", and it is only the routine of everyday life that numbs us to what has been lost by being "thrown" into the world.

The topic of how to respond to our "thrownness" is central to the last section of sixteen letters he sent from prison. The first of these letters begins with a central metaphor that explains how he sees the human condition. The letter begins this way:

> Birth from the maternal womb—as the moment one sets out on
> one's journey throughout life presents a telling image of the initial
> condition of humanity: a state of separation. Of release. Of
> breaking away. ... The idea that the human spirit and reason are
> constituted by a severing of something from the hidden spirit ...
> is one that is constantly occurring to us in one form or another,
> and at the very least, it suggests that 'separation' is a fundamental
> experience that man has of himself and his existence in the world.

The crisis, Havel says further, is that as humans we are both "bound
up in Being" and "alienated from Being", creating a double
inheritance.[15] Havel had seen the effect on men who replaced this
existential crisis with a bulwark of Party dogma. As Havel wrote,
"Fanaticism may make life simpler—but at the cost of hopelessly
destroying it."[16] His insight is similar to that of Erich Fromm, who
wrote that ideologues, sensing an original oneness that they can no
longer experience, find themselves caught in a paradoxical tension
between an unbearable sense of freedom and feelings of worthlessness,
a situation they resolve by reducing the complexity of life into an
ideology that makes thinking no longer necessary.[17] Sadly, the problem
of ideology remains as serious as ever, not only in the growing tide of
fundamentalism but in our diminished capacity to have reasoned
dialogue about the great issues of the day.

To return to Havel's play, it is important to note that Faustka
himself is not a fanatic, but he works for one, and The Institute itself
is clearly fanatical. Faustka's downfall is thus partly that he is willing
to work in a corrupt system. He tries to play "both ends against the
middle," as he puts it in the play. He remains at The Institute,
convincing the director that he is studying the occult in order to
understand how the dark forces might be undermined; on the other
hand, he tells Fistula that he is remaining at The Institute "to serve
our cause [the occult] by being our own man hidden in the heart of
the enemy."[18] This life as a double-agent is the real devilry that takes
place in the play, and Havel's central insight is that the calculating
intellect can destroy the soul of everything it touches.

How should we behave in such a problematic world? How avoid
living a lie, being a double agent in our own lives? Surely this is the
question that makes Havel feel so relevant in our own culture. There
isn't much of an answer in *Temptation*, but Havel's political writings

give us a window on a creative mind that worked on this problem constantly from the end of the Prague Spring, in 1968, to the beginning of the Velvet Revolution, in 1989. In the late 1970s, for instance, he coined the term "living in truth" to describe the purpose of Eastern European dissidence. Living in the truth is the not-so-simple matter of remaining connected to the "authentic existence" of ourselves that is all too often hidden by the "orderly sphere of the life of lies."[19] Dissidence, as Havel understood it, was not a new ideology (anticommunism, for instance), but the act of openly living in the truth of Being. In theory at least, living in truth removes one from Machiavellian ideas of power, just as it removes one from acting through the machinery of ideology, with its limited and one-sided way of seeing the world.

Although Havel doesn't use the term, living in truth resembles the idea of the "care of the soul" that so preoccupied Havel's friend and fellow dissident, the Czech philosopher Jan Patocka. Patocka was a grand synthesizer who claimed that the care of the soul was "the fulcrum of all great thinkers of antiquity."[20] The West, Patocka believed, was fundamentally formed by this idea, especially as developed in the Socratic dialogues, and yet we are also in danger of losing this inheritance (the last presidential election, for instance, seems to have been at least partly about trying to reclaim and recapture the care of the soul in our politics).

In the tradition represented by Tomas Masaryk, the Czech philosopher who served as president from 1920-1935, Patocka was deeply committed to rational thinking even while being attracted to romantic elements in Heidegger, Husserl, and Nietzsche. These twin influences are represented in his philosophical attempt to reconcile Enlightenment and the Romantic tendencies in Western thought—defining rationality, for example, as "the ability to grasp the *ratio*, the meaning of the whole" and thus as something deeper and more mysterious than intellectual understanding.[21]

Rather than oppose the rational and the irrational, Patocka opposes two forms of reason—one limited and positivistic, the other capable of grasping ideas in all of their negation. The second form is exemplified by Socrates who rarely, if ever, gives us a positive answer in the dialogues (he knows only that he does not know). Ideas are never treated as something positive for Socrates, and Patocka repeatedly encourages us to return to "negative Platonism" as a way of seeing through the way we literalize ideas in a positivistic culture.[22] From Patocka's point of view, all ideologies (including archetypal psychology) have a totalitarian tendency that results in alienating the spontaneous images of the psyche through the replacement of genuine reflection with the violence of calculating structures.

Some have argued that Patocka's return to "negative Platonism" deeply influenced Havel as a playwright and politician. Whether or not that is true, the care of the soul must have been on Havel's mind as he wrote about Faustka. A parallel idea can also be found in Havel's understanding of the crises facing humanity. The post-communist police state, Havel wrote in a speech given in 1982, was "a convex mirror" of the modern condition. Why a convex mirror? Totalitarianism was simply an exaggeration of the Titanism that Patocka saw as a defining trait of the 20th century. Eight years of the Bush administration ought to have convinced us that Titanism might be the defining characteristic of the 21st century as well.

IV

Any discussion of the Titanic seems to bring us to an increasing level of abstraction. As a term, the Titanic does not seem to refer to a thing or to an archetypal image but to situations and influences in which one experiences the absence of a connection to both the organic world and the world of Being. The Titanic is experienced as a loss of soul.

One way to think about the Titanic is by thinking of what it is not. We might find a hint of this by returning to Lopez-Pedraza, who asks us to remember those ineffable moments when the heart is flush with feeling and enthusiasm. Among *afficionados* of the bullfight, for instance, such moments are understood according to what *tauromachy* calls *temple*. *Temple* is presented in the "enormously animated slowness" when the bullfighter and bull are harmonized so that the bull always has the cape within reach without ever reaching it.[23] In ordinary life, we have many similar moments, including the brief exchange that penetrates us to the quick and whose value far outweighs the thousands of words and actions that fill up the majority of the day. Such moments have a soul to them.

In the bullring, Lopez-Pedraza stresses that such moments (*temple*) can be characterized by a slowing down of time, a fact he understands as entering into a state of timelessness and eternity. We all have such moments. Childhood, for instance, has its endless summers, its moments when the clock stands still.

It is a far more common in our culture, however, to experience the tyranny of time—the sense that time is a stopwatch and we're continually running out of it, that we are whirled about by time's demands. When time is experienced as a whirlwind of chaos and speed (the gyre of Yeats' poem "The Second Coming"), a mythic sense of the world is no longer possible.

It is traditionally assumed, especially in theology, that a relationship to the past (time as *chronos*) can open us into the eternal (time as *kairos*). The crucifixion of Jesus, for instance, allows Christians to experience the eternal image of Christ. It is, however, a characteristic of both Titanism and the totalitarian world that such movement is no longer possible. The Titanic effect of time may partly explain the modern sensation that time is speeding up and marching on. It is sometimes said that we experience the quickening of time as we age because the elderly have traveled through more time than a child; having experienced more of time, each second feels shorter. It might be more accurate, however, to say that time is slow for the child because she still lives in a world where the mythic is possible. Childhood, for instance, has its endless summers when the clock stands still.

We might ask ourselves whether there will be space for the mythic in the world now being created. Perhaps. We live in times of great change, and one possible change is a renaissance of Being. I myself am more of a skeptic. Although there is a great hunger in the culture for what Patocka called "care of the soul," the Titanic is as threatening as ever. Not only does technology threaten to re-define what it means to be human, but our factories now have the potential to destroy the earth itself. Much will depend on the ability of each of us to become Havel's brand of dissident.

NOTES

1. See Jan Patocka, "Titanism," *Jan Patocka: Philosophy and Selected Writings*, trans. Erazim Kohak (Chicago, IL: University of Chicago Press, 1989), pp. 139-143.

2. The essay originally appeared in *Images of the Untouched*, ed. Joanne Stroud and Gail Thomas (Dallas, TX: Spring Publications, 1982). A later version of the essay appears in Rafael Lopez-Pedraza's book *Cultural Anxiety* (Einsiedeln, Switzerland: Daimon Verlag, 1990), pp. 9-27.

3. Lopez-Pedraza, p. 14.

4. *Ibid.,* pp. 13-15.

5. A thorough background on the Titans of mythology can be found in "Moon Madness." For further context see Carl Kerenyi, "The Titanic and the Eternity of the Human Race," *Prometheus: Archetypal Image of Human Existence* (Princeton, NJ: Princeton University Press, 1991), pp. 19-32. Also see Joanne Stroud, "The Prometheus Paradox," lecture at the Dallas Institute of the Humanities and Culture, Spring 2002.

6. Although Havel does not speak of "Titanism," it is nevertheless central to his work. He was influenced by both Masaryk and Patocka who wrote extensively about the spiritual crises of modernity. His most important essay, "The Power and the Powerless," which is dedicated to Patocka, is a meditation on cultural Titanism that he refers to as "post-totalitarian." The prefix does not imply that the system was no longer totalitarian but that, in its attempt to totally divorce individuals from their experience, it was fundamentally different from classical dictatorships or even from earlier "totalitarian" regimes that relied on brute force to exercise power.

7. See Martin Esslin, *The Theater of the Absurd* (New York: Random House, 2001). Esslin coined the term "theater of the absurd" in 1961 to describe the emergence of a new type of theater represented by Beckett, Ionesco, and Pinter. Havel's plays are discussed on pp. 324-326.

8. Vaclav Havel, *Letters to Olga* (New York: Henry Holt, 1989), p. 293.

9. The fullest explanation of this idea is found in Vaclav Havel, "The Power of the Powerless," *Open Letters: Selected Writings 1965-1990*, trans. Paul Wilson (New York: Vintage, 1992), pp. 125-214.

10. Vaclav Havel, *Temptation*, trans. Marie Winn (New York: Grove Press, 1989).

11. *Ibid.*, pp. 28-29.

12. James F. Pontuso, *Vaclav Havel: Civic Responsibility in the Postmodern Age* (New York: Rowman and Littlefield, 2004), p. 103.

13. Another word for human-like machine is a robot, a Czech word that entered worldwide usage after it was introduced in Karel Apek's *R.U.R. (Rossum's Universal Robot)*, a play first performed in 1921. Robot is a play on *robota*, meaning a peasant worker—in other words, someone who can be treated by the same sort of will that one applies to a machine.

14. Havel, *Letters to Olga*, p. 322.

15. *Ibid.*, pp. 319-321.

16. *Ibid.*, p. 364.

17. Erich Fromm, *Escape from Freedom* (New York: Henry Holt, 1965), pp. 32-38.

18. Havel, *Temptation*, p. 87.

19. Havel, "Power of the Powerless," p. 148.

20. Peter Lom, "Foreword," in Jan Patocka, *Plato and Europe*, trans. Peter Lom (Stanford, CA: Stanford University Press, 2002), p. xv. Patocka's essay "The Transformation of the Ontological Project in Aristotle—The Return to the Cave" summarizes his ideas on the "care of the soul" as the fundamental theme in European history—see pp. 180-194.

21. Erazim Kohak, *Philosophy and Selected Writings of Jan Patocka* (Chicago, IL: University of Chicago Press, 1989), pp. 35-38.

22. *Ibid.*, pp. 54-60.

23. Lopez-Pedraza, p. 65.

A Depth Psychological, "Polytheistic" Reading of Pedophilia through Greek Myth

HOWARD G. KAPLAN

Pedophilia from the Perspective of Depth Psychology

Pedophilia is such an alarming, provocative, and divisive form of sexuality that depth psychology, notwithstanding its fundamental concerns with irrational and unconscious factors, has paid relatively scant attention to it in the literature. Perhaps part of the reason is that pedophiles rarely seek analysis.[1] Moreover, the highly-charged taboos, stigmas, and ethical/legal ramifications associated with this issue deter not only clients, but theoreticians and clinicians from overcoming their resistances to addressing it. Although research and theory regarding pedophilia and child molestation have been weighted heavily towards epidemiological and cognitive-behavioral studies of recidivism rates, risk factors, and relapse prevention techniques, depth psychology has made some important contributions to the understanding of these phenomena.[2] Furthermore, classical Greek mythology—one of the primary sources of depth psychological paradigms—can provide an illuminating and humanizing lens through

Howard G. Kaplan, LMFT/Ph.D. (Theatre & Drama) is a psychotherapist in Irvine, California. Currently, he is a clinical psychology doctoral candidate at Pacifica Graduate Institute, conducting dissertation research on dreams of pedophilic adult males.

which the dynamics of these prohibited forms of sexual behavior and
desire can be seen more clearly.

The broad spectrum of depth psychological perspectives encompass
psychoanalysis, analytical psychology, attachment theory, and to some
extent evolutionary psychology. Post-Jungian psychology provides a
particularly salient framework for apperceiving archetypal motifs and
dynamics. Indeed, James Hillman, the "father" of archetypal
psychology—a postmodern approach to psychology that shares Jung's
concern with archetypes, but in a more relativistic, individualistic
framework that eschews transcendental teleologies—argues for what
he (extrapolating from Jung) calls a polytheistic psychology:

> Jung wrote of the *lumen naturae* as a multiplicity of partial
> consciousness[es], like stars or sparks or luminous fishes' eyes. A
> polytheistic psychology corresponds with this description and
> provides its imagistic formulation in the major traditional
> language of our civilization, i.e., classical mythology. By providing
> a divine background of personages and powers for each complex,
> polytheistic psychology would find place for each spark. It would
> aim less at gathering them into a unity and more at integrating
> each fragment according to its own principle, giving each god its
> due over that portion of consciousness, that symptom, complex,
> fantasy, which calls for an archetypal background.[3]

A comparable approach, I believe, may be very helpful in opening new
perspectives on pedophilia, including the possibility of deepening,
nuancing, and humanizing our understanding of it, even if we cannot
eliminate its moral reprehensibility.

Before going on to examine pedophilia and child molestation
(incestuous or extra-familial) in Greek myth, it will be helpful to look
at the contemporary cultural context that informs our understanding
of and relationship to these phenomena. In America, at the beginning
of the new millennium, it is very hard to be a child, and very hard to
be an adult. Collectively, adults feel stressed out, irritable, and under
continual pressure to produce and perform. It is hard for them to accept
fundamental existential limits, such as aging and death, as well as the
limits that increasingly seem to be undermining many of the premises
on which we have based our national faith (such as boundless growth
and opportunity, adequate leisure time in which to develop and nurture
a healthy family and a personal social life, trust that the exercise of

authority in our democratic political institutions and in our organized religions will be fundamentally ethical, and a preponderance of respect and goodwill towards America from the rest of the world). Furthermore, in this environment, children are also under tremendous collective pressure to perform, to get ahead, and to fulfill their parents' high expectations. If they don't, they may have to endure parental disappointment and anger; if they do, they may evoke conscious or unconscious envy.[4] As a consequence of these and other factors, it is often difficult for adults (not only parents, but educators and other adults in positions of leadership or mentorship) to model, maintain, and protect secure boundaries with and around our children.

In the sphere of sexuality, a similar crisis of expectations and a blurring or dissolution of boundaries can be seen. In his book *Observing the Erotic Imagination,* Robert Stoller makes a provocative statement: "… [T]he desire to humiliate… [is] an essential theme in erotics."[5] While there is clearly far more to sexuality (and even to sexual perversion, which was Stoller's focus) than humiliation, his observation seems especially pertinent in the current socio-historical climate. In our postmodern society, television talk shows and the tabloids provide a steady supply of sensational disclosures of the dirty laundry of "real people," and even the mainstream news media serve up a more-or-less daily diet of lurid and sensationalized stories about sex offenders. In many cases, regardless of the extent and severity of their crimes, sex offenders are now subjected to public humiliation, followed by incarceration, probation, "registration" of their photograph and address on public websites, and greater or lesser degrees of ongoing banishment from mainstream society.[6] A particular irony of this state of affairs is that it has arisen within the context of a society and (in particular) a media culture pervaded by provocative and tantalizing images of all forms of sexuality and sexual behavior, including a disturbing trend towards the sexual objectification of children.[7]

The past several decades have seen the insidious proliferation of what various authors have referred to as the "culture of narcissism,"[8] "psychic numbing" and the "protean self,"[9] the "saturated self,"[10] and the "era of rage."[11] In various ways, all of these concepts speak to a chronic sense of passivity and voyeuristic spectatorship towards our lives and those of others, vague feelings of emptiness, lack, and boredom, and chronic stresses that smolder within the inner fabric of our technology-driven,

media-saturated, profoundly materialistic culture—all of which
intermittently and unpredictably ignite into anger. Witness the epidemic
of shooting sprees we have witnessed in schools and workplaces across
the country; or since 9/11, the threats to our civil rights, the increase in
religious intolerance, and the overall climate of finger-pointing, paranoia,
and backlash we have seen, in various forms, towards those who diverge,
or appear to diverge, from mainstream norms.[12]

Adult ambivalence towards children is not new; it derives from
deep-seated memories, wishes, hopes, and fears.[13] Our current obsession
with the "child molesters lurking in our midst," however, emerges out
of a matrix of pervasive anomie. Moreover, deep ambivalence about
sexuality in American culture and the pervasive sexual objectification
of children reflect our denial and repudiation of aging as well as the
enormously high expectations placed upon children in our society.

Child molestation and rape are the core archetypes with which all
forms of sexual misconduct are equated in the collective imagination.
In some ways, this makes intuitive sense, because these are glaringly
obvious and egregious forms of boundary violation at the physical,
sexual, emotional, and spiritual level. Unfortunately, however, as a
society, we are increasingly coming to treat sexual misconduct as if it
were a unitary phenomenon, i.e., that any and all sexually offensive or
deviant acts are equally reprehensible, and that the proper approach
to any and all sex offenders is punishment and isolation from society
primarily, treatment and rehabilitation (if attempted at all) only
secondarily. Given that we, with our modern values, may not consider
it acceptable that pedophilia (within certain clearly defined limits) was
a part of ordinary life in Ancient Greece, our first impulse might be to
deny the relevance of classical Greek mythology for pedophilia in the
world today. However, there are several considerations that point to
its pertinence and indicate that the humanistic insights of Greek myth
can help us to gain a better understanding of adult sexuality directed
towards youth.

Finally, before going on to consider some of the ways in which classical
Greek mythology is illustrative of the dynamics of pedophilia, it will be
helpful to look at what depth psychology has had to say about this
disorder. From the perspective of depth psychology, it appears that seven
core factors define male pedophilia, broadly understood: (1) regression
(generally in the face of trauma or unbearable conflict) to childhood forms

of sexuality, or fixation (as a result of developmental deficits or arrest) upon the child as sex object (often to the age at which the pedophile or incest perpetrator himself was traumatized); (2) identification with a particular child or children, especially insofar as they embody or can contain projections of the role of victim and/or aggressor; (3) identification with children and nostalgia for childhood as resistance to change, growth, and the maturing process; (4) narcissistic disturbances, most notably absence of or significant gaps in empathy, dysregulation of self-image and self-esteem, and intense susceptibility to feelings of shame, which the pedophilic male attempts to compensate for by way of implicit or explicit strategies for exercising power and control over children as erotic objects; (5) impoverished or problematic relationships with other adults, resulting from insecure attachment styles, inadequate social and intimacy skills, underlying oppositionalism, and pervasive distrust; (6) difficulties with establishing and maintaining functional interpersonal boundaries, often beginning in the relationship between the son and his mother, with whom he is often emotionally enmeshed and in relation to whom he feels emasculated; (7) a fundamental sense of lack of vitality, adequacy, or potency resulting in a sense of inner deadness.[14]

While all seven factors are not present in every case, in most cases several can be found in combination. In depth psychological theory, aspects of all these factors would be seen as symptoms of underlying sexual deviance in general, but the factors and sub-factors that focus on regression, fixation, over-enmeshment, or insecure attachment with either or both parents (especially the mother), identification with children and nostalgia for childhood, and a highly concretized form of narcissism are the hallmarks of pedophilia specifically. Pedophilic desire involves a combination—in differing strengths and at different levels of awareness—of fantasies of mastery and power, fantasies of revenge, and fantasies of fusion and/or repair that are misguided psychic attempts at compensating for childhood trauma and deficits in attachment. Underlying the sexual desire for the child or adolescent is an identification with, and/or use and abuse of the child as a kind of talisman or amplified mirror of the self at a critical age or stage when the perpetrator sustained, whether acutely or chronically, traumatic disillusionment or loss, traumatic vulnerability, dependency, rage, and shame.

The Relevance of Greek Mythology

Ancient Greek mythology—which has so frequently provided paradigms for depth psychology—can help us to illuminate and humanize the dynamics of pedophilia. Throughout Greek mythology, powerfully-charged alliances and misalliances between parents and offspring, siblings, and gods and mortals result in destinies blessed or ruined by intense love, jealousy, envy, and the use (actually *ab*use) of individuals—especially children—as narcissistic objects by others. Ancient Greek gods and goddesses, heroes and heroines appear in the most admirable and enviable light in one mythic event, but venal and monstrous in another.

In Greek mythology, both idealization of youth and sexual abuse of children are perpetually and inextricably interwoven with love and aggression; *eros*, *hubris*, and *Thanatos*. The blurring or transgression of physical, emotional, or sexual boundaries between adults and children harks back to the theogonic myth in which the Titan Kronos devours his own offspring. Refusing to be annihilated, Kronos's children are emetically regurgitated through the cunning of the quintessential pre-Oedipal couple in crime, Zeus and his mother Rhea, and spring forth to become the Olympian Gods.[15]

Orestes and Electra's entire lives are eviscerated by the curse of Atreus, which spans back over a history of adultery and murder to an act of parental infanticide and subsequent cannibalism, as recounted in the myth of Tantalus. In an fit of obscene *hubris*, Tantalus serves up his son Pelops as part of a banquet he hosts in "honor" of the gods. Most ironically, the goddess Demeter—the bountiful, loving Earth mother, preoccupied by her grief over the loss of her daughter Persephone—alone among the Olympians fails to recognize the ingredients of the sacrificial meal, and unwittingly partakes of it.[16] Through divine intervention, Pelops is quickly restored to life, albeit with a prosthetic ivory shoulder, which bears the sign of the cannibalistic act. What befalls Pelops next is one of the many instances of pedophilic desire that can be found throughout classical Greek myth: Poseidon becomes enamored of the divinely reconstituted youth, and the two, for a brief period, become lovers.[17]

Highly illuminating traces of the core etiological factors for pedophilia (that I enumerated earlier) can, in fact, be found in Ancient Greek myths directly or indirectly related to a number of the Greek gods and goddesses, including Zeus and Apollo, Dionysus, Demeter, Persephone and Hades, Hera and Aphrodite, Hepahistos, and Hermes, Priapus, and Pan.

MODELS OF THE *PUER/SENEX* AND *EROMENOS/ERASTES* RELATIONSHIP: ZEUS AND APOLLO

Myths associated with Zeus and Apollo are the best illustrations of identification with the Child archetype. Regression or fixation of the adult (god) in relation to the child (mortal) that he selects as an erotic object is implicit in these myths, as are the power dynamics of *eros,* whereby these gods function primarily as victimizers although secondarily as victims (of their own longings). The abject and perverse nature that we associate with pedophilic desire, however, is defended against in these myths by a powerful tendency towards idealization, which is rooted in part in the ancient Greek institution of *paiderastia.*[18] In our own time, this tendency finds a parallel in the discourse of those pedophiles or ephebophiles who, when not consciously repressing themselves because of the danger involved in expressing their feelings openly, speak of "man-boy love" as an aesthetic ideal, or at least, as natural and inevitable.

To understand Zeus and Apollo psychologically in those myths in which they appear as lovers of male youths, it is helpful to refer to the Jungian theory of the *senex* and *puer* archetypes. Marie-Louise von Franz and Hillman[19] have both developed the concept of the *puer aeternus* ("the child god in the Eleusinian mysteries"[20]) as a psychological type characterized by hypersensitivity, restlessness, flightiness, and a resistance to committing oneself to the fixed identity and relationships of the "mature" adult. A blend of the ever-innocent child and the eternal adolescent, the *puer* is characterized by infectious charm but also various forms and degrees of carelessness ranging from endearing absent-mindedness and haplessness to reckless, self-aggrandizing, and/ or self-destructive acting-out of impulses. In addition, the *puer* typically is narcissistically captivated by youth and beauty (both his own and that of others), while repulsed by and unable to deal with ugliness, aging, or death. (Michael Jackson and his "Neverland" is an example that comes readily to mind.[21])

The *puer* often finds himself in relationship (sometimes fleeting) with one or more *senex figures,* i.e., more pragmatic, usually older, men who serve as mentors, initiators, and gatekeepers for those with less age and authority. The *senex*, Hillman explains, is associated with Kronos/Saturn, the father of Zeus and several of his Olympian siblings, whose practice is to devour his offspring: an attempt to nip his children's (particularly his sons') competitive and individuation strivings in the bud. The *senex*'s coercive aggression, rigidity, suspiciousness, and cynicism are the reverse image (shadow) of the *puer*'s seductiveness, vulnerability, and naïveté (puerility). "The negative *senex* is the *senex* split from its own *puer* aspect. *He has lost his 'child.'*"[22]

Suggesting a linkage between the dynamics of pedophilia and the *puer/senex* archetype does not necessarily imply that real-life individuals who present either *puer* or *senex* personality dynamics will inevitably display signs or symptoms of pedophilia or pedophilically-oriented desire. Rather, extrapolating from what von Franz and Hillman have synthesized about these personality styles as archetypes enables us to draw out one of the salient aspects of the phenomenology of pedophilic object relations, i.e., the subject of desire finds in its object—the beautiful *youth*—either an idealized mirror (the *puer*) or the photographic image of an earlier, encapsulated aspect of the self that is forever lost, and consequently, forever drenched in nostalgia (the *senex*).

The composite set of myths associated with Zeus and Apollo abounds in *puer/senex* dynamics in general, and instances of erotic love between adult males and male youths in particular.

Zeus displays many *puer* characteristics in his love life (a kind of perennial search for greener pastures, which leads him from one marriage or liaison to another, reminiscent of the Don Juan complex which, according to von Franz[23] is one major subtype of the *puer* personality). Nevertheless, he identifies primarily with the *senex* role (in particular the aspect of the role that embodies the powerful patriarchal lover who brooks no refusal). His relationship with Ganymede, the only male with whom he has a relationship that is described in any detail in the myths, is in some senses a special case. Robert Graves, for example, notes that

> [t]he Zeus-Ganymedes myth gained immense popularity in Greece and Rome because it afforded religious justification for a grown man's passionate love of a boy. ... It turned Greek philosophy into an intellectual game that men could play without the assistance of women.[24]

Above and beyond the idealized, "Platonic" aspects of this form of love, there clearly seem to be concrete linkages between it and the institutionalized practice of *paiderastia* (pederasty). *Paiderastia* provided for the social and sexual initiation of pubescent boys (*eromenos*) by adult male citizens, whom the boys had "accepted" to be their lover (*erastes*).[25] This experience often afforded the *eromenos* an education, emotional support, and even economic advantages; however, the relationship could never avoid being inherently coercive, given the age and power differential upon which it was based.

Christine Downing captures the essence of the Zeus-Ganymede relationship as follows:

> The mythological traditions about Ganymede beautifully evoke the numinous dimension of same-sex love. The myth persuades that to love a youth with the passion, tenderness, and fidelity exhibited by Zeus is divine. It also expresses the sense in which the beloved is eternally young and beautiful. ... Of course, a darker truth may also be discovered in this tale. It can be seen as representing the obsession with youth and beauty that may lead a lover to turn from one beloved to another, wanting to stay "forever" at the beginning state of love. It can also be seen as depicting a love stuck in its beginning phase, with no opportunity for Ganymede (or Zeus) to move beyond the roles assumed in their initial encounter.[26]

It should also be noted that despite the great "honor" bestowed upon Ganymede by Zeus, it is unclear to what extent he himself has accepted and maintained this position in accordance with or against his will. These musings about the dark overtones of erotic involvement between men and male youths also shed light on the dynamics of aspects and subtypes of pedophilia, in particular its associations with fixation on the image of the self at a younger age, and differentials in experience of the world and the control over one's choices that these imply.

Venturing a couple of steps farther into Zeus's "dark side," Jean Bolen has identified the archetype of the incestuous father as an important component of his mythos:

> He [Zeus, in one version of the Persephone myth] was either an incestuous father who seduced his daughter Persephone, or the father who gave permission to Hades to abduct and rape her, and thus did not respond to her cries for help when she called out to him ....[27]

On the other hand, Apollo, the god of music, measure, and moderation in all things, the god of pure light and penetrating vision (his "arrows shot from afar"), is also the god of youthful masculine beauty and the "patron saint" of male youths. Interestingly, it is in his love life—primarily involving females but in some instances males, most notably Hyacinthus, who may in fact be the only love object with whom he was able to achieve a significant degree of mutuality—that Apollo shows an uncharacteristic immoderation. His relationships, both with males and females, tend to end quite unhappily (as in his amorous pursuit of the mortal Daphne, a nymph, who, in her terrified attempt to flee his advances, ends up being transformed into a tree, never able henceforth to satisfy his desires). Bolen succinctly recounts the tale of Apollo and Hyacinthus:

> Once he [Apollo] was taken with a young man, Hyacinth, son of the king of Sparta—so much so that he abandoned Delphi to spend all his time with him. One day, when the two competed in [a] discus-throwing contest, Apollo's discus ricocheted off a stone, struck Hyacinth, and killed him. In anguish at the death of the man he loved, Apollo vowed that Hyacinth would be remembered. From Hyacinth's blood sprang the flower that bears his name.[28]

Bolen's gloss on the myth emphasizes the predominantly therapeutic, self-actualizing (although ultimately limited) role of narcissism and "the mirrored self"[27] in this relationship, which she portrays as being one between equals (Hyacinthus clearly loves Apollo, as well, and he is a "young man"; thus, pedophilia is not an issue here, but ephebophilia might be, depending on how "young man" is interpreted, and the underlying psychological dynamics seem similar). In the myth, then, we can see some of the complex ambiguities surrounding how pedophilia is defined and understood, e.g., how are pedophilia and ephebophilia similar or different, and how is the age of consent construed in different socio-historical contexts?[30]

Downing characterizes Apollo as "the Immortal *Erastes*," that is, "the accomplished initiate who becomes the model initiator."[31] In the myths associated with him, and particularly with his same-sex love affairs, we can see: (1) Apollo's connection to rites of initiation, particularly for males negotiating the transition between boyhood and young manhood, and particularly by way of *paiderastia*; (2) Apollo's underlying misogyny (an important element in Zeus's make-up, as well), which is connected to the anthropological and historical context in which his mythos arose (the suppression of matriarchal societies),[32] reflecting deep-seated fears of women's "irrationality," "immoderation," and inability to be easily controlled. Downing characterizes Hyacinthus as a "paradigmatic ... *eromenos*."[33] Furthermore, the story of Apollo's love for him (which, she points out, is reciprocated and began with his freely choosing Apollo among a number of other suitors), is a tale "... about mortality and death, about the inescapable connection between love and transience, about how much in us resists that conjunction ...."[34] Her reading of this myth (and her work on Greek mythology and same-sex love in general) provides a basis, I think, for a more humane understanding of the pedophile's fixation on youth, and understanding that helps us to connect the perversity of that condition with concerns that all of us face.

An important difference between the mythos of Zeus and Apollo on the one hand and pedophilia or adult sexuality towards minors in modern society on the other, I think, is that childhood trauma, whether in the form of sexual abuse, physical abuse, neglect, or gross failures in attachment, is usually clearly evident in the case histories of pedophiles or sex offenders, whereas as it is difficult to think of Zeus and Apollo as being "traumatized as children." Difficult maybe, but maybe not so far-fetched. Zeus grew up in the shadow of his father's acts of cannibalism towards his own children, and Apollo's early years include a great deal of wandering, punctuated by struggles with serpentine monstrosities.

GODS AND GODDESSES BEYOND THE PALE: DIONYSUS, HADES, AND PERSEPHONE

While Dionysus—the god of wine and "unbridled" sensuality—has most typically been seen in juxtaposition with or as antithetical to Apollo, we have already noted that Apollo is also capable of being immoderate, at least in affairs of the heart; and others have noted that one element within Dionysus's "personality" is that he is, to a surprising extent "detached," "unconcerned," or "persistently ambivalent" in his relationship to sex, or downright "paradoxical" in this regard ("the effeminate god of the phallus, the phallic god of women").[35] Dionysus, like Zeus and Apollo, manifests both *puer* and *senex* qualities; depending on the situation, he may act in an iconoclastic and liberating, or a retaliatory and reactionary manner; he is sometimes portrayed as a man with a long beard, at other times as a beardless youth.[36] Dionysus's relevance to pedophilia is not primarily connected with *puer/senex* issues, however; rather, it is in the area of the blurring and transgression of boundaries, especially around age and sexuality, that his evocative power is constellated.

Dionysus's unnatural double birth (he was first born, prematurely, after he was conceived through his father, Zeus's impregnation of his mother, Semele, by a bolt of lightning; subsequently, he was born again after a period of incubation, sewn inside Zeus's thigh) already connects him to extraordinary and perverse experiences and behaviors. He is also associated with the underworld (by way of his search there for his lost mother), which in turn, closely connects him to two other gods who are even more fundamentally associated with the underworld.

Hades, Lord of the Underworld, and Persephone, the young maiden Hades abducts there to be his bride, are also key figures in the mythos of pedophilia (in this case, of a quasi-incestuous variety, since Hades is Persephone's uncle). Bolen notes how Hades functions as one of the "shadow aspects"[37] of Zeus, containing his split-off irrationality, mysticism, powerlessness, and unconscious. At another point, she refers him to as the "incestuous shadow of Zeus,"[38] noting, as stated earlier, that Zeus was complicit in Hades' rape of Persephone. She also paints a picture of Hades as a lonely, asocial (perhaps to the point of being schizoid), incommunicative god who "fathered no children"[39]—all typical traits of pedophiles. For her part, Persephone, who is fated to live in the underworld during the dark months of every year, forcibly separated from her beloved mother (Demeter), exhibits key characteristics of victims of sexual abuse. Most typically, female victims (although certainly awareness has grown in recent years of the pervasiveness of sexual abuse of males, as well) are capable of great empathy and compassion but are, at the same time, depressive, given to fused relationships, and potentially destructive towards others.[40] Significantly, what immediately precedes her abduction by Hades is Persephone's fascination with a narcissus flower. Moreover, Persephone plays a key role in Orpheus's tragic loss of his wife, Eurydice, when he attempts to reclaim her from the underworld (Persephone and Hades agree to allow Eurydice to leave provided that Orpheus not look back). The bitter aftereffects (and retreat into narcissism) entailed by the loss of his wife have frequently been associated with Orpheus's reputation as a "lover of boys" later in his life.[41]

INCARNATIONS OF THE MOTHER/LOVER: HERA, DEMETER,
APHRODITE ... AND HER WOUNDED SON, HEPHAISTOS

The third main player in the Hades/Persephone myth is Demeter, whose anguish over the loss of her daughter is so extreme that it bespeaks narcissistic enmeshment in addition to maternal grief.[42] Demeter, Hera, and Aphrodite are all essentially fertility-based Mother goddesses, and as such, they constellate various elements of the Mother complex,[43] which is frequently a key factor in pedophilia. That is to say, a failure to separate and individuate adequately from the mother may lead to an inability to love anyone other than her—with the possible exception of someone who mirrors (whether directly, or contrasexually) the little boy to whom she, often unconsciously, has remained suffocatingly over-attached from the moment of his birth onwards. In psychoanalytic theory, an analog to the negative mother archetype is the fantasy of the phallic mother. Possessed of "monstrous" (albeit erotic and hyper-arousing), "Sphinx-like" omnipotence, she threatens to overwhelm the young boy. At the same time, however, she functions as a magical, talismanic image that defends against the "reality" of the castrated (weak, subservient, wounded) mother that arises out of the perception that the mother (and other females) lacks a phallus.[44]

A beautiful illustration of the dynamics of the phallic/castrating/castrated mother and the negative mother complex can be found in the recent film, *Little Children*.[45] The character Ronald James McGorvey, a presumably rehabilitated pedophile (played by Jackie Earle Haley), hounded and scapegoated by his entire community, has only one friend and love object: his long-suffering mother (played by Phyllis Somerville). Her courageous attempts to help him maintain his rehabilitation and her determination to defend and protect him against his persecutors have the unwitting effect of reinforcing his morbid dependency on her and his inability to relate to others, with ultimately tragic consequences. These include his castration by his own hand—his attempt, in his unbearable grief over his mother's death and guilt over his pedophilic and unconsciously incestuous urges, to live out, irreversibly, the role of the obedient, subservient, and asexual son who remains fused with his mother in a state of pre-genital "innocence."

This tragic/pathetic narrative of a pedophile and his mother resounds with overtones of the mother archetype, which are played out, on a mythic scale, by Demeter, Aphrodite, and Hera. Most apparently, Mrs. McGorvey, the pedophile's mother, incarnates Demeter in her archetypal role as the long-suffering mother devoting her life to rescuing and reclaiming her child, Persephone (who is incarnated contrasexually in McGorvey, the emasculated and "shadowy" pedophile, but also in the form of an *anima* figure, the deeply abused and suffering woman he goes out with on a disastrous date). Unwittingly, Mrs. McGorvey-as-Demeter becomes guilty of enabling sexual abuse either by denying how prone her son remains to committing it, or by being so over-vigilant and over-protective towards him that he is hampered from moving forward in his arrested development.

Hera and Aphrodite, for their part, might be seen as shadow figures submerged far beneath this mother's persona (and to a considerable extent, those of her son, in his role of dangerous seducer, as well). These goddesses display a high degree of narcissism, manifested through vanity, manipulation, possessiveness, jealousy, or envy. Despite their positive aspects of maternal authority, pride, and loyalty (Hera) and warmth and gratification (Aphrodite), in their negative aspects these powerful deities are legendary for their wiles and their fury when crossed or spurned. These negative characteristics fuel fantasies and stereotypes that portray women as irrational, intemperate, and potentially emasculating seductresses or shrews. If the boy's experience of the mother is overly dominated by these imagos to the exclusion of other influences and attachments, the initial template upon which his experience of women is based remains highly threatening.

Aphrodite is a "polymorphous, perverse" goddess associated with unbridled, irrational passion, and amorality with respect to how, and between whom, erotic love is ignited or extinguished.[46] Her conception out of the blood spilled onto the foam of the sea when Uranus is castrated by his son Kronos, and her associations with the phallus-like mandrake plant and witchcraft resulting in male impotence and infertility are emblematic of her unconscious associations with the phallic mother.[47] Her potentially devastating effect—as well as a possible hint of female pedophilia—is inherent in the account of her love for the youth, Adonis. The progeny of an incestuous union (between his mother, Smyrna, and her father, Cinryas), this tremendously attractive but also possibly "effeminate" youth becomes, as a result of fate combined with his own choices, a continual consort to Aphrodite (for two-thirds of the year) and Persephone (for the remaining third). In the end, Persephone, driven by jealous rage at Aphrodite for prevailing over her as Adonis's preferred lover, ends up indirectly causing the youth's awful death. She instigates Ares, Aphrodite's lover, by igniting his jealousy towards Aphrodite over her love for the beautiful youth, and Ares, bent on revenge, "disguised as a wild boar, rushed at Adonis and gored him to death before Aphrodite's eyes."[48] When taken together with the other phallic associations already ascribed to Aphrodite, the image of her lover being gored to death by an enraged Oedipal father figure (Ares) wielding a phallic and castrating-type object (the boar's tusk) has a terrifying effect (much like that of the scene of McGorvey nearly bleeding to death from his self-inflicted wound).

Hera's particular significance may be seen in connection with one of her sons, the god Hephaistos. Murray Stein[49] portrays Hephaistos, Aphrodite's cuckolded husband, as a crippled, grotesque, and implicitly hermaphroditic god, whose misfortunes date back to his mother Hera's parthenogenic conception of him as an act of retaliation against Zeus for conceiving Athene out of his own head. Two different accounts of his crippling as a child both point to the role of the negative mother complex in deforming his body and implicitly wounding his masculinity, so that in his adult life, rather like his brother Apollo, his love affairs "tend to conclude in disappointment."[50] In one version, Hera was so disgusted by Hephaistos's deformities that she violently cast him out of heaven: "... [S]he had bred and borne him by herself to show Zeus what she could do without his help ... [but] instead, to her acute disappointment, this malformed cripple shows up her inferiority and embarrasses her."[51]

In the other version, Zeus is so angered by the circumstances of Hephaistos's birth that *he* casts him to the ground, which is what causes him to be crippled. In either case, Stein sees Hephaistos as "definitely having a phallic significance."[52] He also highlights an incident in Hephaistos's adult life, namely, the moment in which he "seeks impetuously and passionately to make love to Athene; at the moment of climax she pushes him aside, and his semen falls to the earth where it impregnates Gaia."[53] Here we see another example of regressive enmeshment with the mother archetype (in this case in the form of Mother Earth), fueled by rejection by a female peer (i.e., a peer who is "age appropriate," of the same generation). The pedophile in *Little Children*, I would suggest, in his social awkwardness and his symbolic and literal acts of self-castration, incarnates Hephaistos, and in an even more grotesque light, Pan, for reasons which I think will quickly become clear.

HERMES, PRIAPUS, AND PAN: MESSAGES AND IMPULSES;
THE GROTESQUE, THE DELINQUENT,
AND THE CRIMINAL

In this final section, I will draw on ideas and images explored by Lopez-Pedraza in his book *Hermes and his Children*.[54] Hermes, the messenger of the gods, god of the crossroads and the marketplace, of liminality and border crossings, god of thievery and trickery, god of inspired, incisive communication, and (at least in Lopez-Pedraza's thinking) one of the gods of psychotherapy, can be seen to relate to pedophilia at a number of different levels. For example, Lopez-Pedraza observes that Hermes' love for the nymph, Dryops, is the primary basis for his "classic image … [which] suggests the indirection of *falling in love with another man's fantasy*: the fantasy/erotica provided by the nymph."[55] Here it is easy to spot the link between pedophilia and pornography—an extremely lucrative and manipulative medium, which trades on any traces of perverse interests (including pedophilic ones) that might potentially lie suppressed, dormant, or latent within anyone's psyche. Other potential links between Hermes and pedophilia would include the crossing of legal and ethical boundaries, and the trickery and manipulation that go along with the "grooming" process that sets children up to become victims of sexual abuse.

In exploring the mythos of Hermes, Lopez-Pedraza pays considerable attention to two of his children, who are also gods (albeit more minor ones): Priapus and Pan. Priapus, the god of the phallus, relates to pedophilia as he does to all of the perversions (which, in my working definition, equate to distortions and displacements of emotional and attachment needs whereby an overemphasis on body parts, inanimate objects, aggression, transgression, and/or power results in immediate gratification but longer-term frustration, restriction, or exhaustion of those broader needs). Lopez-Pedraza emphasizes how ugly and grotesque Priapus appears: essentially, he is the archetype of the "dirty old man." Pan—another lecherous god, less off-putting than Pan but still a bit of a ne'er-do-well or buffoon—can be seen as relating particularly to the role of substance abuse as a disinhibitor that can open the floodgates to illicit sexual fantasies and behavior as well as to the sense of panic that the entire subject of pedophilia generates in society as a whole.

CONCLUSION

My hope is that this brief essay has provided food for thought (that ultimately will be digested) about a most unpalatable platter offered up by the moveable feast of human sexuality; also, that anger and hatred might yield somewhat to reflection and compassion, since all sexuality, however misguided, might be seen as another form of appetite. Appetite is not only predilection. It also embodies basic needs, for without appetite, the organism cannot cling to life. All forms of erotic desire weld the bonds of attachment and tend towards survival, even if perversion ultimately diverts them from these goals. Desire originates in hunger, and hunger at times is satisfied through aggression. The child is both the subject and object of our most primal love ... and destructiveness.

NOTES

1. Andre Green, "Notes on Paedeophilia," in *The Chains of Eros: The Sexual in Psychoanalysis,* ed. Andre Green, trans. L. Thurston (London: Rebus, 2000), pp. 173-175.

2. Howard G. Kaplan, "Dreams as Windows into the Lived Experience of Males with Pedophilia: A Depth-Psychological Study through Phenomenological Interviews" (Ph.D. dissertation, Pacifica Graduate Institute, in progress).

3. James Hillman, *A Blue Fire: Selected Writings by James Hillman,* ed. Thomas Moore (New York: Harper & Row, 1989), p. 39.

4. David Elkind, *The Hurried Child: Growing Up Too Fast, Too Soon* (Reading, MA: Addison-Wesley, 1988); Christopher Lasch, *The Culture of Narcissism: American Life in an Age of Diminishing Expectations* (New York: W. W. Norton, 1979).

5. Robert Stoller, *Observing the Erotic Imagination* (New Haven, CT: Yale University Press, 1985), p. 3.

6. M. M. Kleinhans, "Criminal Justice Approaches to Paedophilic Sex Offenders," *Social and Legal Studies* 11, no. 2 (2002): 233-255; M. Sykes-Wiley, "Secret Lives: Pedophilia and the Possibility of Forgiveness," *Family Therapy Networker* (November/December 1998):

39-59; D. West, "Paedophilia: Plague or Panic?" *Journal of Forensic Psychiatry* 11 (2000): 511-531.

7. James R. Kincaid, *Erotic Innocence: The Culture of Child Molesting* (Durham, NC: Duke University Press, 1998).

8. Lasch.

9. Robert Jay Lifton, *The Broken Connection: On Death and the Continuity of Life* (New York: Simon & Shuster, 1979); *The Life of the Self: Toward a New Psychology* (New York: Basic Books, 1983).

10. Kenneth J. Gergen, *The Saturated Self: Dilemmas of Identity in Contemporary Life* (New York: Basic Books, 2000).

11. Stephen A. Diamond, *Anger, Madness, and the Daimonic: The Psychological Genesis of Violence, Evil, and Creativity* (Albany, NY: State University of New York Press, 1996).

12. Norman J. Finkel, "Moral Monsters and Patriotic Acts: Rights and Duties in the Worst of Times," *Psychology, Public Policy, and Law* 12 (2006): 242-27; Marina Warner, "Angels and Engines: The Culture of Apocalypse," *Raritan* 25, no. 2 (2005): 12-41.

13. Paul Adams, "Childism as Vestiges of Infanticide," *Journal of the American Academy of Psychoanalysis* 28, no. 3 (2000): 541-556; E. Burman, "Appealing and Appalling Children," *Psychoanalytic Studies* 1, no. 3 (1999): 285-300.

14. F. De Masi, "The Paedophile and His Inner World: Theoretical and Clinical Considerations on the Analysis of a Patient," *International Journal of Psychoanalysis* 88 (2007): 147-165; David Finkelhor, *Child Sexual Abuse: New Theories and Research* (New York: Free Press, 1984); A. Nicholas Groth, "Patterns of Sexual Assault against Children and Adolescents," in *Sexual Assault of Children and Adolescents,* ed. A. W. Burgess *et al.* (Lexington, MA: Lexington Books, 1978), pp. 3-24; Nicholas Groth, *Men Who Rape* (New York: Plenum Press, 1979); John Money, "Pedophilia: A Specific Instance of New Phylism Theory as Applied to Paraphilic Lovemaps," in *Pedophilia: Biosocial Dimensions,* ed. J. R. Feierman (New York: Springer-Verlag, 1990), pp. 445-463; Lawrence Shengold, *Soul Murder: The Effects of Childhood Abuse and Deprivation* (New Haven, CT: Yale University Press, 1989); S. W. Smallbone and M. R. Dadds, "Attachment and Coercive Sexual Behavior," *Sexual Abuse* 12, no. 1 (2006): 3-16; Charles W. Socarides and Loretta R. Loeb, eds., *The Mind of the Paedophile: Psychoanalytic Perspectives* (London: Karnac Books, 2004); Stoller, *Observing the Erotic*

Imagination; Tony Ward *et al.*, "Attachment Style and Intimacy Deficits in Sexual Offenders: A Theoretical Framework," *Sexual Abuse: A Journal of Research and Treatment* 7 (1995): 317-334; Tony Ward, J. McCormack, and S. M. Hudson, "Sexual Offenders' Perceptions of their Intimate Relationships," *Sexual Abuse: A Journal of Research and Treatment* 9 (1997): 57-74.

15. Robert Graves, *The Greek Myths: Complete Edition* (London: Penguin Books, 1992).

16. J. Naiman, Review of *Mythologie Grecque et Psychanalyse*, by Graziela and Nicos Nicolaidis, *Canadian Journal of Psychoanalysis* 4, no. 2 (1996): 377-381.

17. Christine Downing, *Myths and Mysteries of Same-Sex Love* (New York: Continuum Publishing, 1989).

18. The reader is cautioned that applying the concept of pedophilia to male-male relationships in ancient Greece does not necessarily reference the same set of psychiatric and legal definitions that pedophilia entails in contemporary Western society. Rather, the relationship between contemporary pedophilia and classical Greek pederasty is a broad analogy. Although it appears that pederasty involved pubescent or verging-on-pubescent youths no younger than 12 years old (Eva Cantarella, *Bi-sexuality in the Ancient World* [New Haven: Yale University Press, 1992]), the concept of pederasty is intertwined with Greek ideals of masculine beauty, pedagogy, and Platonic as well as sexual love ("Pederasty," in *Readers' Guide to Gay and Lesbian Studies*, ed. Timothy Murphy [Chicago/London: Dearborn Fitzroy, 2000], pp. 441-442), which transcend the concrete parameters of age and secondary sexual characteristics. Furthermore, "it is unusual that an individual diagnosed as a pedophile or guilty of committing sexual offenses against minors is exclusively interested in a single age category," i.e., in some men, various combinations of primary or equal levels of sexual attraction can be manifested simultaneously, episodically, or situationally to adults, adolescents, and/or children of either or both genders (Wesley Maram, Ph.D., personal communication, May 7, 2009).

19. Marie-Louise von Franz, *Puer Aeternus: A Psychological Study of the Adult Struggle with the Paradise of Childhood,* 2nd ed. (Boston: Sligo Press, 1981); James Hillman, "*Senex* and *Puer*," in *Puer Papers* (Irving, TX: Spring Publications, 1979), pp. 3-5.

20. Von Franz, p. 1.

21. Kincaid.

22. Hillman, *"Senex* and *Puer,"* p. 20.

23. Von Franz.

24. Graves, p. 117.

25. Downing.

26. *Ibid.,* p. 152.

27. Jean S. Bolen, *Gods in Everyman: A New Psychology of Men's Lives and Loves* (New York: Harper Perennial, 1989), p. 50.

28. *Ibid.,* p. 133.

29. *Ibid.,* p. 148.

30. Vern L. Bullough, "History of Adult Human Sexual Behavior with Children and Adolescents in Western Societies," in *Pedophilia: Biosocial Dimensions,* ed. J. R. Feierman (New York: Springer-Verlag, 1990), pp. 69-90.

31. Downing, p. 154.

32. Anne Baring and Jules Cashford, *The Myth of the Goddess: Evolution of an Image* (London: Viking Arkana, 1991); Edward Whitmont, *The Return of the Goddess* (New York: Continuum International Publishing, 1982).

33. Downing, p. 157.

34. *Ibid.,* p. 159.

35. M. Jameson, "The Asexuality of Dionysus," in *The Masks of Dionysus,* eds. Thomas H. Carpenter and Christopher A. Faraone (Ithaca, NY: Cornell University Press, 1993), pp. 41-64.

36. Thomas H. Carpenter, "On the Beardless Dionysus," in *Masks of Dionysus,* pp. 18-26.

37. Bolen, p. 43.

38. *Ibid.,* p. 107.

39. *Ibid.,* p. 102.

40. Graves; Downing.

41. Downing.

42. *Ibid.*

43. C. G. Jung, "Psychological Aspects of the Mother Archetype," in *Four Archetypes: Mother, Rebirth, Spirit, Trickster,* trans. R. F. C. Hull (Princeton, NJ: Princeton University Press, 1969), pp. 7-44.

44. L. Balter, "The Mother as Source of Power: A Psychoanalytic Study of Three Greek Myths," *Psychoanalytic Quarterly* 38 (1969): 217-274; Ruth M. Brunswick, "The Pre-oedipal Phase of Libido

Development," *Psychoanalytic Quarterly* 9 (1940): 293-319; J. C. Flugel, "Polyphallic Symbolism and the Castration Complex," *International Journal of Psychoanalysis* 30 (1924): 108-123; Geza Roheim, "Aphrodite, or the Woman with a Penis," *Psychoanalytic Quarterly* 14 (1945): 351-390; Lawrence Shengold, *Soul Murder: The Effects of Childhood Abuse and Deprivation* (New Haven, CT: Yale University Press, 1989).

45. *Little Children*, directed by Tom Porratta, New Line Cinema, 2006.

46. Bolen; Downing.

47. Roheim.

48. Graves, p. 70.

49. Murray Stein, "Hephaistos: A Pattern of Introversion," in *Facing the Gods,* ed. James Hillman (Dallas, TX: Spring Publications, 1980), pp. 67-86.

50. *Ibid.*, p. 79.

51. *Ibid.*, p. 68.

52. *Ibid.*, p. 76.

53. *Ibid.*, p. 80.

54. Rafael Lopez-Pedraza, *Hermes and His Children*, 3rd ed. (Einsiedeln, Switzerland: Daimon-Verlag, 2003).

55. *Ibid.*, p. 136.

MEDEA AND MOTHERS WHO KILL

KATE SMITH-HANSSEN

As Euripides' Medea is in the palace killing her children, the Greek chorus chants:

> O your heart must have been made of rock or steel,
> You who can kill
> With your own hand the fruit of your womb ....
> What horror more can be?[1]

For most of us, the prospect of Medea or any mother killing her children is untenable, an intolerable image. We are shocked at this deviation from what most of us would consider normal behavior in a mother-child relationship, given our understanding of mothering behavior as nurturing, protective, and self-sacrificing. We simply do not understand this kind of mother or have any compassion for her actions. But we are also inexplicably drawn to the stories and, as with the Medea figure, we remember the names of the women involved. We remember that in 1994 Susan Smith, a mother of two young sons, 14-month-old Alex and 3-year-old Michael, drove her car into a lake in rural South

Kate Smith-Hanssen, Ph.D., has degrees in Art History, Counseling Psychology, and Mythological Studies and Depth Psychology. She was Adjunct Faculty at Pacifica Graduate Institute from 1994-2000. She presented this paper at the Foundation for Mythological Studies conference on "Mythology and Violence" held at Pacifica Graduate Institute in 2008. She now lives in Lake Tahoe, California.

Carolina, but got out at the last moment and watched her sons slowly drown as the car floated for six minutes and then sank with its headlights still on. We still discuss the tragedy of Andrea Yates, who in 2001 drowned her five young sons, one by one in the family bathtub.

Mothers who commit violence are universally condemned as either "mad" or "bad": *mad* because they must be mentally unstable, psychotic, suffering from postpartum depression; *bad* because they must be selfish, manipulative, or evil if they act out their murderous rage against their children. And yet it happens. It is precisely because of the extreme, heinous nature of these incomprehensible acts that we should try, as mytho-psychologists, to avoid judgment and condemnation, although there is much to be condemned ("What horror more can be?"—Euripides, *The Medea*). That is why understanding this pathology is so important, so vital. It is our task to try and shed some light on this most dark side of the psyche, its mother-violence, its mother-mystery.

According to the most recent U.S. government statistics, in 2005 an estimated 1,460 children in the United States died from abuse or neglect—at a rate of almost 2 deaths (1.96 deaths) per 100,000 children. More than three-quarters (76.6%) of children who were killed were younger than 4 years of age. Nearly half (44.3%) were White, one-quarter (26.0%) were African-American, and one-fifth (19.3 percent) were Hispanic. Three-quarters (76.6%) of these child fatalities were caused by one or both parents, but almost thirty percent (28.5%) were caused by the mother acting alone.[2] What is happening here? Are these statistics an aberration, or an indication of something gone terribly wrong in our society? Can a mother be nurturing one moment and murderous the next? What's the matter with mother?

WHAT'S THE MATTER WITH MOTHER?

In the 1970s, Adrienne Rich published her revolutionary book, *Of Woman Born*, which became a kind of manifesto for mothers in the early throes of what would eventually be called "the feminist movement." The book included the phrase "the myth and the reality of motherhood," which reflected the beginnings of a new discourse on motherhood. Rich declared, "The words are being spoken now, are being written down; the taboos are being broken, the masks of motherhood are cracking through."[3] Her book argued that the divide between a mother's lived experience and motherhood as an institution, its myth, was radically changing. Among other things, she called for a new paradigm of motherhood, one that would free it from the limitations of its institutional existence, while becoming a catalyst for a transformed world.

The book records a discussion that took place in one of the first "support groups" that Rich attended for mothers in the mid-70s. Talk centered on the case of a local mother of eight who had murdered and then decapitated her two youngest children on the front lawn of her home. Rich reflected:

> Every woman in that room who had children ... could identify with her. We spoke of the wells of anger that her story cleft open in us. We spoke of our own moments of murderous anger at our children, because there was no one and nothing else on which to discharge anger.[4]

The insight contained in Rich's book was a radical shift in the perception of the mother persona and the beginnings of a new paradigm for women—one that would not only give voice to the "murderous anger" of mothers but also treat with compassion those mothers who act it out, rightly or wrongly.

In "What's the Matter with Mother?" Jungian analyst Patricia Berry argues that in its mythic origins motherhood has a built-in dichotomy. In Latin and Greek, the word mother is a cognate of "matter," which is paradoxically both an abstraction (unknowable, invisible, and incorporeal) as well as physical (concrete, tangible, visible, bodily). So, in the very word-image itself there is a paradox, and contained within that paradoxical tension is a multiplicity of contradictory meanings. The word-images in "mother" point not only to an ambiguity of meaning, but to an ambivalent valuing of the mother: she is both the most necessary and the most lacking, the most something and the most nothing.[5]

Pat Berry writes:

> When we get closer to our "matter," ... our lower physical nature, our cruder emotions, it is not surprising that we feel something unsettling, something inferior, chaotic. ... [T]hese feelings are given with the very nature of mother's matter.[6]

Berry's argument is supported by Jungian psychology, which differentiates between the positive mother and the negative mother. Berry suggests that the appearance of the negative mother in the psyche might be an attempt to rebalance the way we concretize our psychic "children," returning us to soul. For the purposes of this article, the negative mother might be experienced as a "Medea complex" which metaphorically "kills" off the fragile, young parts of the psyche that

Medea (1862), by Eugène Ferdinand Victor Delacroix.

are trying to manifest through creativity, inspiration, idea-making, goals, dreams, etc. Or, the negative mother might appear to "kill" a woman's psychic children in order to return the woman's mother-identity back to the virgin or *puella* state. This might occur because of a woman's over-identification with the archetypal image of the mother and the need to rebalance the psyche.

However, as an expression of a soul crisis of the most extreme kind, this negative mother complex can also manifest in the killing of one's literal children, as in the story of Medea. In this case, mothers do not have a metaphorical appreciation of their psychological feelings and believe that the only solution for them is to kill their children in order to return to a pre-mother state of mind and heart. In this case, having children at all is viewed as an urgent problem to be solved so that they can rid themselves of whatever negative feelings are plaguing them. Or, as we shall see later, in the case of Medea, the children are sacrificed in order to appease feelings of betrayal and revenge. In the case of filicide, there is only one solution, however horrifying. The mother's narrow focus on getting rid of her children becomes her "final solution" with little thought or consideration given to the morality (or legality) of her actions.

THE MYTH OF MEDEA

Euripides' play *The Medea* was first performed in 431 B.C.E. It begins with Medea not only lamenting Jason's marriage to the daughter of Creon, but her outrage at having been told that Creon was soon going to banish her and her sons from Corinth. Medea came to Corinth with a legacy of murderous deeds. She was an outsider, a sorceress, half-human and half-divine (her father was a sorcerer and son of Helios, the Sun God). By the time the play begins, she has already murdered her own brother in order to escape from the land of her birth with her new husband, Jason (it was with her help he succeeded in gaining access to the Golden Fleece). After settling in Jason's homeland, Medea tricks the daughters of Jason's uncle, Pelias, into poisoning him because he had usurped his father's throne. Now exiled from both their ancestral lands, Medea and Jason have found refuge in Corinth, where Jason marries King Creon's daughter.

In revenge for Jason's betrayal of her and her sons, Mermeros and Phres, Medea murders his new wife by sending her a dress tainted with poison, which also accidentally kills her father, King Creon. Medea then goes on to kill her own two sons as a final gesture of her anguish and her punishment of Jason. Euripides' interpretation of Medea's story, which was well known throughout ancient Greece, was a radical one for its time, for it suggested that her actions resulted from jealousy and from seeking vengeance upon Jason rather than from insanity. This differentiation of motive and intention is the beginning of the recognition that mothers who kill have the capacity to plan such a murder and that, furthermore, these mothers can also escape the censure of society. Although the Chorus laments her actions, Medea lives on in the end. Euripides has aroused our interest in these mothers and left Medea untouched at the end of the play to become an eternal archetypal image in a mother's psyche.

Medea has become the figure against whom all mothers who kill are subsequently measured, compared, and analyzed.[7] But the criminal and psychological association of Medea with filicide points not to an actual person or historical event, but to a mythic figure—half-human, half-divine—a fictional character from a play. Thus, filicide is not only an act that involves the actual *personal* mother, according to her unique circumstances and mental health, and stands as a crime against the social order, one that is "larger than life," but also an act of the divine and the fictional, a mystery that bridges the mundane world with the sacred and the imaginal. James Hillman suggests that "[r]ather than looking at myths morally, archetypal psychology looks at moralities mythically."[8] This is important as we attempt to unravel the actions of Medea with the play.

The play tells us that Medea is an outsider, alone and without a supportive community. Her husband has just married another, and although Jason rationalizes his decision as being made to protect Medea and his children in this foreign land, Medea feels rejected and believes that she and her children have been slighted. She is suicidal.

> Oh, I wish
> That lightning from Heaven would split my head open.
> Oh, what use have I now for life?
> I would find my release in death
> And leave hateful existence behind me.[9]

In the contemporary case of Susan Smith, she was also separated from her husband, who had a girlfriend, and Susan's boyfriend had told her he was not interested in raising anyone else's children. Like Medea, Smith was extremely manipulative and, in addition to her infidelity during her marriage, she had told a series of lies, which were gradually coming to light. In her confession she spoke about

> the crushing isolation she had felt while driving her Mazda along Highway 49 on the night of October 25th and the consuming desire she had to commit suicide ... that her whole life had felt wrong and that she felt she could not escape the loneliness, isolation and failure that had ensnared her.[10]

Andrea Yates, the other filicidal mother, had come under the spell of Michael Peter Woroniecki, a self-styled itinerant fire-and-brimstone preacher, whose fundamentalist message of eternal doom and damnation was a contributing factor in the breakdown of her psyche and the subsequent murder of her children. In her case, the raging conviction and certainty of an archaic, fundamentalist belief drove her to kill her children in order to protect them from exile from this world and from the subsequent damnation she had come to believe in. Yates was convinced that Satan had taken over her children and that they must be killed in order to "save" them. Despair, isolation, and futility as well as a pathological sense of protecting the children by killing them emerges as some of the aspects of this Medea complex. But the question still remains: Why *do* mothers kill?

TYPOLOGIES OF MOTHERS WHO KILL

Even though filicide has been part of all societies throughout history, the first attempt at creating a scientific system of classification for it was undertaken only in the late 1960s by Philip Resnick, a forensic psychiatrist. His system provided the foundation for all those that followed. He identified five major motives of mothers who commit filicide: (1) altruistic filicide, in which the mother kills the child to prevent his or her suffering from present circumstances or if the mother is herself planning to commit suicide; (2) acute-psychosis, in which the mother is afflicted with severe mental illness; (3) unwanted children, in which the mother does not want to care for the child any longer or be a mother any longer; (4) accidental filicide from either neglect or abuse; (5) spousal revenge, in which the mother wants to inflict pain on her spouse by killing their children for reasons of marital betrayal or divorce.[11] Of course, in each of these categories, there can be multiple or overlapping motives as was the case with Medea.

Based on Euripides' play, it can be concluded that Medea's rationale for killing her children falls into the following categories in Resnick's system:

(1) Altruistic filicide: From Medea's point of view, she kills her children to spare them from exile, which for the Ancient Greeks meant facing great social prejudice and suffering. To the Chorus, Medea replies:

> Women my task is fixed: as quickly as I may
> To kill my children ... and not ... to suffer my children
> To be slain by another hand less kindly to them.
> Force every way will have it they must die, and since
> This must be so, then I, their mother, shall kill them.[12]

(2) Spousal revenge: For Medea, who had betrayed her own father and homeland in order to procure for Jason the Golden Fleece and who had gone into exile sacrificing her own status in Greek society, Jason's marriage to Creon's daughter was the ultimate betrayal. She wanted him to suffer. The Chorus asks:

> But can you have the heart to kill your flesh and blood?
> Medea answers:
> *Yes, for this is the best way to wound my husband.*[13]

Susan Smith's motives can be characterized under Resnick's typology as resulting from: (1) acute psychosis and (2) having unwanted children. An analysis of Yates might focus more on acute psychosis and, like Medea, altruistic motives, since she felt her children were doomed to evil in this world. However, although these scientific explanations and categories attempt to explain and understand the motives of these mothers, we are still left with the uncomfortable sense that this cannot be the whole story. For this reason, we must keep going and ask what is it about the mother psyche that might contribute to an unconscious drive towards murder and death?

MOTHER OF LIFE, MOTHER OF DEATH

For the ancient Greeks, creation began with Chaos. Then there appeared Gaia, the first form, the first matter, Mother Earth. From her comes the starry sky, the mountains, the depths, the sea. The Homeric Hymns begin with Gaia, "The mother of us all, the oldest of all ...."[14] With Gaia, the full range of motherhood had a place. She represented not only the created reality of the upper world—our conscious and ordered existence—but the shadowy depths of the underworld. However, eventually a differentiation of the mother archetype occurred as expressed in the myth of Demeter and Persephone. Demeter came to represent the upper world mother of created life and fertility, while Persephone, or Kore, as the myth tells us, came to be Queen of the Underworld, reigning over death. Eventually, Christianity continued this splitting of the mother by giving us a "first mother," Eve, who is rebellious, shamed, and exiled, and then a Virgin Mother, Mary, who eventually ascends to heaven becoming the eternally disembodied yet ever present, asexual, suffering, grieving, and enduring image of mother.

It is hard to say when women began to lose the full range of what it is to be mother, splitting off from soul and abandoning any conscious, psychological initiation into the underworld. Unconsciously, women mourn this loss and in their grief, like Demeter, they often cause great destruction to their families and to themselves. With only the concrete, visible mother to identify with, women are bereft and do not know how to allow the invisible mother, the mother of the depths, to "matter." This raises an important question. Is the mother who kills—who feels she cannot go on with the daily, mundane tasks of mothering— unconsciously seeking a psychological connection to the sacred realm of death that would make the invisible mother visible? In focusing only on the action and morality of mother-violence, have we lost what it is trying to communicate? Its psychic speech? Its longing?

Medea was a devotee of Hecate, one of the manifestations of the Triple Goddess ruling over Heaven (Selene), Earth (Artemis), and the Underworld (Persephone). Hecate presided over childbirth and was also the mother of Dionysus, who was regarded as the son of Persephone, so that her connection to Death as the Crone was well established.[15] Because of her association with fertility, Hecate was also closely connected to Demeter in ritual and was sometimes called Demeter's "daughter." It is through Hecate's intervention that Demeter locates Persephone after she is abducted by Hades. Hecate also ruled over the crossroads, those moments we might call "turning points," at which we must decide "which way to go."[16]

Feelings of depression, grief, loss, hopelessness, of being lost in our lives, of being at a crossroads bring us unwillingly to the depths of the underworld. For the Greeks, the gods required sacrifices, offerings to "make sacred" the divine order of things between the mundane world and the divine. Medea offered up her sons, Demeter lost her daughter to Hades, Eve's rebellious actions condemned the whole human race to exile from Paradise, and Mary's son was crucified for our sins. These myths tell us that in the archetypal image of mother, a connection to the invisible mother must be made through sacrifice, to make sacred. It is an integral part of the mother mystery. At the end of the play, Medea laments:

> I will bury them myself,
> Bearing them to Hera's temple on the promontory;
> ... In this land of Corinth
> I shall establish a holy feast and sacrifice
> Each year forever to atone for the blood guilt.[17]

CONCLUSION

At the end of the play, Medea does not die. The point of the mother's sacrifice is the killing of the children, not the mother herself. She lives on as a living reminder of the dark mother and her capacity to do harm when she experiences injustice and betrayal directed at her role in life. Yates has been confined to a mental institution and Smith is currently serving a life term in prison. But Euripides ends his play with a *deus ex machina*: Medea soars off in a golden chariot provided by Helios to Athens under the protection of King Aegeus. With this ending, he reminds us that the Medea figure is not wholly human, but will live on in the psyche. As the granddaughter of Helios, she shines a light for the dark mother and brings light to her murderous thoughts. Whether consciously or not, Medea lives on in every mother's psyche.

In "On Violence," Hannah Arendt states, "Violence can be justifiable, but it can never be legitimate."[18] She goes on to say, "Power and violence, though they are distinct phenomena, usually appear together."[19] And again, "... [E]very decrease in power is an open invitation to violence."[20] As the archetypal image of the mother has decreased in range and scope, her powerful connection to the "all" of creation undermined and subdued, the danger of literally acted-out mother violence has increased. When identifying mothers at risk, we are reminded by Euripides' Medea that we cannot assume that a mother will *not* kill. When mothers kill, it is often out of a sense of powerlessness in their lives, a sense of being trapped in a role that discounts, belittles, and devalues the mother's power over all created life and the divine order of things.

Psychology must re-imagine the mother in her wholeness, her power, and her sacred calling as containing the light and the dark, the living and the dead, the mundane and the divine, the spoken and the unspoken in order to assist a mother with her murderous feelings. In her book *The Sacrament of Abortion*, Ginette Paris states:

> There's no such thing as a good Goddess and a less good one. Each is an aspect of reality, and in every religion that recognizes a maternal deity that fosters life there's a complimentary figure standing for death, ending, rupture. Mother Nature is both the giver of life and the taker of life, for there is no life without death.[21]

Transforming a mother's impulse to kill her children from a literal action into a reflection on her soul is paramount. Then the depth and range of a mother's feelings can be enacted on a much larger stage, in a richer, more imaginative theater. The prospect of killing her children no longer needs to be the only hope for an unhappy mother and the solution to all her problems. Rather, a mother's emotions can be deepened through a connection to a psychology that recognizes the dangerous power of the mother's dark side. As she moves through motherhood, a mother can then have the opportunity to be continually reborn, half-human and half-divine, bringing her dark and murderous feelings to a mythological altar instead of the corpses of her literally sacrificed children.

NOTES

1. *The Medea*, in *The Complete Greek Tragedies, Euripides I*, ed. David Grene and Richard Lattimore, trans. Rex Warner (Chicago, IL: The University of Chicago Press, 1955), p. 102.

2. These statistics are from the website of the Administration of Children and Families/U.S. Dept of Health and Human Services, <http://www.acf.hhs.gov/programs/cb/pubs/cm05/chapterfour.htm>.

3. Adrienne Rich, *Of Woman Born: Motherhood as Experience and Institution* (New York: W. W. Norton & Company, Inc. 1981), p. 8.

4. *Ibid.*, p. 5.

5. Patricia Berry, "What's the Matter with Mother?" *Echo's Subtle Body: Contributions to an Archetypal Psychology* (Dallas, TX: Spring Publications, 1982), p. 3.

6. *Ibid.*

7. Belinda Morrissey, "The Medea Complex: 'Radical Evil' and Modern Motherhood," unpublished paper presented at the 8th Global Conference, "Perspectives on Evil and Human Wickedness," Salzburg, Austria, March 19-23, 2007, p. 1. Available online at <http://www.inter-disciplinary.net/ati/Evil/Evil 8/morrissey paper.pdf>.

8. James Hillman, *Re-Visioning Psychology* (New York: Harper & Row, 1975), p. 179.

9. *Medea*, p. 64.

10. http://www.crimelibrary.com/notorious_murders/famous/smith/bibli_11.html.

11. See Geoffrey R. McKee, *Why Mothers Kill* (New York: Oxford University Press, 2006), pp. 22-33.

12. *Medea*, p. 101.

13. *Ibid.*, p. 87.

14. *The Homeric Hymns,* trans. Charles Boer (Dallas, TX: Spring Publications, 1970).

15. Barbara Walker, *The Woman's Encyclopedia of Myths and Secrets* (San Francisco: Harper & Row, 1983), pp. 178-179.

16. Edward Tripp, *The Meridian Handbook of Classical Mythology* (New York: New American Library, 1974), p. 261.

17. *Medea*, p. 106.

18. Hannah Arendt, *On Violence* (New York: Harcourt Brace & Company, 1970), p. 52.

19. *Ibid.*

20. *Ibid.*, p. 87.

21. Ginette Paris, *The Sacrament of Abortion* (Dallas, TX: Spring Publications, 1992), p. 33.

CONFRONTING DEATH MOTHER:
AN INTERVIEW WITH MARION WOODMAN

DANIELA SIEFF

Marion Woodman, LLD, DHL, Ph.D., is a Jungian analyst, teacher, and author of numerous books, including *The Owl Was a Baker's Daughter; Addiction to Perfection; The Pregnant Virgin; The Ravaged Bridegroom; Leaving My Father's House; Conscious Femininity; Dancing in the Flames* (with Elinor Dickson); *Coming Home to Myself* (with Jill Mellick); *The Maiden King* (with Robert Bly); and *Bone: Dying Into Life.* She has been exploring the relationship between psyche and soma through her work and teaching for 30 years. A visionary in her own right, she has worked with the analytical psychology of C.G. Jung in original and creative ways. She is the Chair of the Marion Woodman Foundation and lives in London, Ontario, Canada.

———————

Daniela Sieff: Much of your recent work focuses on the "Death Mother" archetype. Could you describe this archetype?

Daniela Sieff has a Master's Degree in psychology and anthropology and a Ph.D. in biological anthropology. Her academic research, with the semi-nomadic cattle-herding Datoga of Tanzania, explored human behavior through the lens of evolutionary theory. She has produced documentaries, written articles, and completed the leadership training program with the Marion Woodman Foundation. She is currently working on a book of interviews which will explore emotional wounding and healing from the perspectives of depth psychology, neuropsychology, and evolutionary anthropology. This interview forms part of a more extensive interview with Marion Woodman, which will appear in that book. She lives on a farm in Hampshire, United Kingdom.

Marion Woodman: The Death Mother wields a cold, fierce, violent, and corrosive power. She is rampant in our society right now. When Death Mother's gaze is directed at us, it penetrates both psyche and body, turning us into stone. It kills hope. It cuts us dead. We collapse. Our life-energy drains from us and we sink into chthonic darkness. In this state we find ourselves yearning for the oblivion of death. Eventually this yearning for death permeates our cells, causing our body to turn against itself. We may become physically ill.

This energy is most destructive when it comes from somebody that we love and trust. It's the archetypal Death MOTHER, which means we are with somebody who is supposed to love us and all of a sudden —bang! It's what happened in the original trauma; we trusted our beloved mother and suddenly we were hit with the realization that we were not acceptable. We realized that our mother wished that we, or some part of us, was dead.

When Death Mother is released from someone's unconscious that person can say something which seems simple and innocuous, but the physical body is changed. I experienced it most dramatically when I was with somebody with whom I was feeling perfectly safe, but it was an extremely sad situation, and the woman turned to me and fired an arrow that was sheer poison. If I hadn't had such a strong heart, I'm sure it would have killed me—but I did experience arrhythmia, which has given me warnings ever since.

Daniela: You've said that if we experience Death Mother while growing up, we internalize the archetype and eventually it becomes written into our physical bodies. Can you expand on this dynamic?

Marion: If, while growing up, we sensed that we were unacceptable to our parents, if we were not wanted, or if we intuited that we threatened our parents, then our nervous system will have become hyper-vigilant. Our cells will have been imprinted with a profound fear of abandonment; as a consequence our body will numb-out the moment that we feel threatened. As soon as we realize that we are no longer pleasing somebody, we freeze; we are thrown back into our belief that we are unlovable, which then activates our ever-present, but unconscious, terror of annihilation. In such moments the autonomic nervous system says "NO" and the ego withdraws. I call this being catapulted into "possum mentality"; as soon as we sense a whiff of rejection we are paralyzed with fear, we close down and we stay absolutely still in order to survive. Eventually, that possum becomes a permanent feature in our body-psyche; then life is experienced as a minefield in which we are knocked down by explosions that are inaudible to others. If there is unconscious hostility in the environment, the inner body, acting autonomously, retreats and falls over "dead". At the same time we may develop defense mechanisms that manifest in an armor of fat, oedema, vomiting, anything to keep poison out. Ultimately, our body may turn against itself as it does with cancer or auto-immune diseases. Death Mother has been incorporated into the fabric of our cells.

Last summer, at the age of seventy-nine, following a cataract operation, I developed cellulitis which spread into my bloodstream and became life-threatening. While in intensive care, I had the following dream:

There are two immense lobsters in a huge, long concrete drain-pipe. The lobsters have blood-red heads, and are trying to kill each other. I am also in the drain and I am terrified. There is a black door in the wall of the drain, and I am trying to open it so I can escape. I can't get the door to open. I bang on it with all my might, hoping that someone will hear me and come to help. Nobody comes. I am left with the killer lobsters.

As I understood it, the drain symbolized my blood vessels and the lobsters my blood. Thus the dream described what was happening to me—instead of supporting my life, my poisoned blood was taking me towards death. Moreover, being in the grip of Death Mother I wanted to escape through the black door, and disappear into darkness. On waking I knew that had I opened that door and walked through it, I would have died. Fortunately, it didn't open and I'm still here!

Daniela: It seems to me that having internalized Death Mother while growing up, when we find ourselves doing something that we deem to be unacceptable, we silently direct our own Death Mother back on ourselves. At such times we aren't aware of what is happening; all we know is that we have fallen into a self-created and private hell.

Marion: Exactly. If we face Death Mother while growing up, we will inevitably internalize her, and if we have internalized her, then we will either project Death Mother onto others—seeing her in our boss, our lover, or our children, or we will act her out by directing her energy onto others, and/or onto ourselves. Until we begin to examine what we are carrying within own psyches, we risk being possessed by the Death Mother archetype.

Daniela: In terms of our lives, what does it mean to have internalized Death Mother?

Marion: Change is fundamental to being alive—to remain fixed is to rot. If the Death Mother archetype is part of our body-psyche, then profound fear means that we try to destroy anything that might precipitate meaningful change. We will do anything to ensure that our life feels safe and secure, even if it is static, rotten, and dead. Our way of relating to the world is written in stone. Death Mother traps potentially vibrant energy and holds it in a cold, rigid, lifeless form. We are imprisoned by an energy that petrifies and ossifies.

Daniela: Can you give an example of what this might look like?

Marion: When I was five years old I was very quiet, but I had lots of vitality. I was in the kindergarten of Sunday School and found myself being pushed out through garlands of flowers. They were beautiful and I wondered where I was going. People said, "You are leaving kindergarten and you are going to junior school." I replied, "Why would I want to go to junior school? I love kindergarten and I don't want to go to somewhere new!" That has been the story of my life. I did love kindergarten, but my fear of change kicked in whenever I was faced with having to take the next stage in my life.

Daniela: And that trauma was so strong that you lived it time and time again...

Marion: Time and time again! During my training to become a teacher, we were assigned a class to teach. I would be in front of my class speaking, but the room would be filled with a painful silence. I was making the motions with my lips but no sounds emerged. I couldn't understand it at all. After the class our supervisor asked, "Marion, what is happening to you?" All I could reply was, "I don't know. I can't make any sound." At the end of that term I got ninety-eight marks for my lesson plans, and zero for my teaching. The terror was too great.

Daniela: So every time you go into the new there is terror?

Marion: Every time I am overcome with the terror of getting born into a new reality. In every case, I was moving out of an area in which I could perform well into a new area, and I was fairly sure that some terrible disaster would happen, so I wanted to stay put. Being born had taken me into a hostile and dangerous environment, and that seeded a bone-deep ambivalence about change and growth. But if I was going to live my life as fully as possible, I had to discover the buried parts of my personality. I had to risk the expansion that gives life meaning. However, with the archetypal energy of Death Mother permeating the cells of one's body that is incredibly difficult.

Daniela: The paradox is that the anticipated disaster, which for you was manifest in physical illness, occurred because you were fighting against the new, rather than stepping into it.

Marion: Exactly—but there is the trauma. In every one of those situations I was afraid there would not be love. I was certain that I would be found to be unacceptable in the new domain. It was my own terror which permeated my cells and which came to the surface through illness. It was my self-generated fear that stressed my body and created hell.

Daniela: The danger is that when we are overwhelmed by that terror we give in to Death Mother, which can literally mean succumbing to death. I knew an intelligent and vibrant woman who was terrified of being alone. She was married to an older man and had said that when her husband died she would commit suicide. By the time she reached her 60s her husband had severe dementia. Then she was diagnosed with terminal cancer. Her immediate response was, "That's a relief!" Six months later she was dead.

Marion: Relief at the prospect of death comes straight out of trauma. Trauma and fear open the door of the psyche to Death Mother, and once Death Mother has walked through that door we are swamped by unconscious lethargy and paralysis. We are over-come with a desire to sink into comfortable, unconscious womb-like darkness, to give up and end the struggle. That state of existence is more common than we realize, but it's rare for anybody to allow that dynamic into consciousness, let alone to speak it in the way that your friend did.

Daniela: It seems that one of the other things that Death Mother does is to destroy our love for what genuinely moves us. Being fully alive means being able to listen to our hearts, but the Death Mother says "No! You can't love that! Loving that isn't acceptable. You need to love THIS instead."

Marion: That aspect of Death Mother is vividly illustrated in the myth of Medusa. The myth begins when the gorgon makes love to Poseidon in Athena's temple. Athena, born from the head of Zeus, is a father's daughter; her home is in her intellect. By making love to Poseidon in Athena's temple, the gorgon exposes the embodied passion that Athena isn't living. Athena doesn't want her shadow exposed, and so she transforms the beautiful gorgon into the Medusa—a monster with snakes instead of hair, and a look that turns all to stone. Medusa's energy is synonymous with that of Death Mother, and the gorgon was turned into Medusa because she dared to express her love. As you suggest, one of the tragic consequences of repeated encounters with Death Mother is that we are cut off from love.

Daniela: Can you give an example of how that might be manifest?

Marion: When I began working with my first analyst, Dr. Bennet, our work went very well. Then I started turning up for my session and he wasn't there, or worse, he was with another client. I concluded that I wasn't very interesting or important, and that he couldn't be bothered with me. After about four weeks of this I was walking away from yet another session that he hadn't bothered to turn up to, when his wife saw me on the street. She called out, "You better come in," but feeling hurt and abandoned, I replied, "No! I won't!'" and I walked away. I just got in though my front door when the phone rang. It was Dr. Bennet. "I want you to come over here at five o'clock for tea", he said. Ungraciously, I replied, "I'll think about it!" He repeated himself, but with rather more force, "You WILL be here for tea at five o'clock." I gave in. When I arrived he said, "You claim that I missed your sessions. Let me see your diary. It is you that have written them down incorrectly!" I didn't believe him. He challenged me to look at my history saying, "If anybody tries to give you something, you set it up so they can't!" He reminded me of what we had already talked about, "Can you see what you did to that relationship… and to that one… and to that one? As soon as the person truly loved you, you couldn't accept it and found a way to leave. Now you are trying to do that with me. By writing down the times incorrectly your unconscious has set you up to miss your sessions, while being able to blame me for the disintegration of our relationship. You will get rid of me before I get rid of you. You won't take the chance that I'll stay with you, because you are sure that I'll abandon you." He was right. As soon as my deepest love was involved, what came up was my terror of being abandoned. An unconscious and internalized Death Mother was running the show, so I didn't trust my love for others, or the love of others for myself. I was cut off from love in a way that was sabotaging my life.

Daniela: I've heard you say that Death Mother kills the imagination and destroys metaphor through the concretization of that which needs to be explored symbolically. Can you expand on this dynamic?

Marion: Death Mother does indeed kill the imagination through the concretization of metaphors, and the result can be tragic. Metaphors activate a wide array of different brain circuits, so when we are cut off from metaphorical thinking we compromise the process of psychological integration. When we concretize something that needs to be understood metaphorically, we seal it into a dead and isolated world. Additionally, if we cannot relate to metaphors, we are denied access to the archetypal world, whereupon it comes into our lives through warped and toxic routes.

For example, psychological growth is natural; it will happen either creatively or destructively. If our inner Death Mother strangles this process, then the need to grow may be concretized. That could take the form of putting on weight, or, more tragically, it might happen through the development of cancer. In other words, the imperative to grow will find a way to become manifest, and if we don't allow it to happen in its authentic domain, it looks for expression in the concrete world, with potentially tragic consequences.

The confusion between the literal and the metaphorical is symptomatic of addiction, and the results are invariably catastrophic.

We confuse our need for spirit with alcohol. In seeking to live the archetype of union, we get hooked on compulsive and meaningless sexuality. Our unfulfilled desire for nurturance is concretized in an insatiable hunger for chocolate and food. Concretized metaphors destroy our lives. When we turn to the concrete, it poisons us.

More generally, addicts know that something has to die; they know that they need to surrender to something larger than their egos and their fears, but because they aren't able to surrender the defense mechanisms that they developed to survive, they look for seemingly easy alternatives. A binge is driven both by a desire to feel all-powerful, and by a desire to surrender to something bigger than oneself. It is an attempt to go beyond the ego and to connect with the numinous in a way that will instigate a new beginning. A new sexual conquest will bring a fresh start. We finish the bottle of wine in order to forget, and thus wipe the slate clean. We polish off all the chocolate and then throw up, in order to purge ourselves, and so begin anew. But when we succumb to an addictive binge, we are trapped in a vicious circle. There is no change and no learning. We do not connect to the longed-for archetypal energy. We do not uncover our buried self. Instead, we are caught in mindless repetition.

This confusion between metaphorical and literal death runs even deeper in the addict. Addicts who have concretized the psychological edict, "death to the old, life to the new," will be harboring an unconscious belief that it is they that need to die, rather than their behavior. At the deepest level, every addict falls into the insidious clutches of Death Mother. Addictions are ultimately symptoms of an unconscious and concretized death wish.

Daniela: What role does fear play in the concretization of metaphor?

Marion: Whatever we fear we tend to concretize, only to find that what has been written in stone continues to oppress us. My father was a minister and I was very drawn to the world of spirit, however my mother was terrified by that aspect of who I was. She was responsible for the practical side of our family life and she feared for my sanity, and for my ability to cope in the everyday world. In many ways she was right—you have to have your feet on the ground in order to cope with the everyday world. However, in the face of her fear I had to repress the spiritual part of myself. Eventually, it found its way to the surface through the back door of anorexia. Starving oneself is a sure-fire way to get into spirit: the thinner you are, the lighter you are, and the lighter you are, the happier you are. Starvation can take you higher into spirit than alcohol; every anorexic that I've worked with has harbored a yearning to rise into spirit. But because the spiritual yearning has been concretized, the anorexic is on the road to death.

Daniela: Although one side of anorexia is a concretized desire for spirit, would you say that at the opposite pole anorexia can also symbolize the experience of having endured profound emotional hunger during childhood?

Marion: That is fair. Addictions have many layers to them; they are replete with opposites. They are a manifestation of the desire to live what we have been unable to live in any other way; at the same time they may offer us an image of what we have suffered. On yet another level they represent a slow, but relentless, march towards premature death.

Daniela: You've said that insatiability is another of Death Mother's characteristics. Could you talk about that?

Marion: One layer of insatiability derives from the fact that in chasing after concrete goals we can never be satisfied. Chocolate does not provide the nurturance we seek, but we mistakenly believe that if only we can get a little more of it, then maybe we will finally be satiated. The rise into spirit provided by alcohol crashes down to hell when we wake to find ourselves lying in our own vomit, but maybe if we have another drink we can get back up. As Emily Dickinson says in her characteristically concise and poignant way,

> To fill a Gap
> Insert the Thing that caused it —
> Block it up
> With Other — and 'twill yawn the more —
> You cannot solder an Abyss
> With Air.

When we look to the concrete to satisfy the needs of our soul, we are attempting to solder an abyss with air; thus we become trapped in a vicious spiral of insatiability.

Another layer of insatiability comes to the fore within the context of our human relationships. When Death Mother has been internalized, our lack of faith in life constellates a compulsive drive to grasp what we think we need. A child's authentic spark may be petrified into submission by repeated encounters with the Death Mother, but ultimately there is no such thing as triumph by force, even if that force is elegantly disguised. Domination is domination and the body-psyche that has been tyrannized has learned its lessons well. In its desolation, it compensates by becoming possessive, clinging to objects or people, investing them with magical powers. Dependent on these talismans for a sense of vitality, the body becomes ferocious in its demands to possess and control them.

In this fragile and wounded state we cannot allow others to be who they are. We need to manipulate them. What people call love is often an unconscious quest for power. How many children have heard their parents say, "I only want the best for you", when what the parents actually mean is, "I am too scared and insecure to allow you to live your life!" How often are we nice to somebody—burying our anger and disappointment and professing our love for them—when we are actually trying to manipulate them into staying around because we are terrified of abandonment and loneliness? Paradoxically, an overwhelming desire to please turns us into a walking power principle; by pleasing others we are better able to manipulate them, albeit unconsciously.

If we were not wanted, we feel that we need to force our way in. People with nothing hold on very tight, suffocating those who cross their path with a compulsive and insatiable neediness. People who have something to hold onto can relax.

Daniela: In my experience, the archetype of Death Mother is intertwined with that of the victim. When we have Death Mother in our psyche our tendency is to see ourselves as victim, thereby exacerbating the cycle of hopelessness and despair.

Marion: No question! Real suffering burns clean; neurotic suffering creates more and more soot. When we are trapped by Death Mother, we are imprisoned by the neurotic suffering that creates nothing but soot. We are caught in a vicious cycle that is incredibly hard to break out of; Death Mother constellates the victim which then attracts the killer in ourselves.

One way that becomes manifest is through the belief that we are being punished when illness or depression disturbs our nice, cosy lives. The idea of punishment derives from Death Mother and it is rooted in the lifeless perspective of the victim. If we are genuinely trying to work with our wounds, then it looks quite different. In the first part of my adult life I was an English teacher. I taught for twenty-five years, and I loved my students and my life; but during that time I gradually developed oedema. I felt that I was being punished for some unknown crime. I had starved myself in an attempt to remain thin to no avail. In my eyes, my body had become bloated and ugly. However, I was responsible for what was happening because I was making the wrong choices. Unbeknownst to me I was allergic to a myriad of foods, but I was too disconnected from my body to know what it needed. To find my way I had to let go of my vision of myself as a victim, and figure out what was wrong with MY choices. I had to grow up.

But before I did that, my condition slowly deteriorated to the point where I was sleeping for 2-3 days a week. It was only when I became utterly desperate that I was prepared to risk change. My dreams had suggested that I would find the answers to my oedema through the training I would do in Zurich en route to becoming a Jungian analyst, and I was in such agony that I left the teaching job that I loved and took leave of my husband—not knowing if our marriage would survive —and went to Zurich. It was a turning point. In Zurich I finally began to connect to my body and to listen to it. It was a crucial step in my journey towards living my own life, and paradoxically, I wouldn't have taken that step without the oedema. Making the wrong choice ultimately opened the door to life.

It takes courage and perseverance to arrive at this place. We have to be willing to face the darkness that is in us. As von Franz wrote:

> Every dark thing one falls into can be called an initiation. To be initiated into a thing means to go into it. The first step is generally falling into the dark place and usually appears in a dubious or negative form—falling into something, or being possessed by something. The shamans say that being a medicine man begins by falling into the power of the demons; the one who pulls out of the dark place becomes the medicine man, and the one who

stays in is the sick person. You can take every psychological illness as initiation. Even the worst things you fall into are an effort at initiation, for you are in something which belongs to you, and now you must get out of it. "The Feminine in Fairytales", *Spring* 1972, p. 64)

So long as we are blind to our inner tyrant, we blame an outer tyrant when we fall into darkness. The focus of our blame can be a person, a political system, a social system, or it can be our own body. But the moment we turn to blame the initiation fails and we remain buried in the darkness. We sink ever more deeply into the clutches of Death Mother.

Daniela: If we remain buried in the darkness, thinking of ourselves as victims, then we develop a propensity to see Death Mother when she is not there. On occasions somebody will say something with a clean and loving energy, but due to our wounds, shame, and victim-identity, we perceive the comment as coming from Death Mother.

Marion: The point that you make is important. As you say, there are times when a person is directing loving energy at us, but due to what we have internalized we mistakenly feel the action as that of Death Mother. That can happen in a myriad of ways. We may misinterpret somebody's comment or actions; our conditioning means that we hear what is not there. Or we may have a teacher who has opened us to our deeper selves and who has helped us find life, but who for whatever reason can no longer be there for us. Then we can experience that withdrawal of life-energy as Death Mother, when it is nothing of the sort. Either way, if we are to grow, we have to remain awake in order to differentiate what is actually happening, and to own what is ours.

Daniela: Similarly, once we become adults, the degree to which we are petrified by Death Mother's attack depends just as much on our own wounds and vulnerabilities as it does on the energy that is directed at us. At times, somebody will attack us with one of Death Mother's arrows, but because the arrow doesn't target our most wounded and shame-infused spot, it has little effect and we are able to protect ourselves in a healthy and clean way. Other times Death Mother's arrow will lock onto our own particular wounds, and we will collapse. Thus, when we are hit by Death Mother, if we can avoid blame and look inwards to our own response, we have an opportunity to learn about our wounds and defense systems, and that then gives us the chance to take more responsibility for our lives and to grow.

Marion: That is true. The experience of Death Mother will be different for every person, and we are most susceptible where our trauma has left us wounded and vulnerable. As you say, if, when we are hit by Death Mother, we can look inwards instead of getting stuck in the dead-end cycle of blame, then we gain an opportunity to reclaim a little more of our lives.

Daniela: In the myth of Medusa, Perseus—whose task it is to kill Medusa—is warned not to look her in the eye; instead he guides his sword by looking at her reflection in his shield. Similarly, you've said that we can't look Death Mother in the eye. Why?

Marion: It is too dangerous! If we look Death Mother in the eye, we may be overcome by our trauma. We could be turned to stone. We may end up with cancer. So we work with her in reflection. We journal. We work with dreams. We do bodywork. We look at what is happening in our lives. We use a reflective shield because otherwise we are at grave risk. As Emily Dickinson wrote:

> Tell all the Truth but tell it slant —
> Success in Circuit lies
> Too bright for our infirm Delight
> The Truth's superb surprise
>
> As Lightning to the Children eased
> With explanation kind
> The Truth must dazzle gradually
> Or every man be blind —[1]

Facing Death Mother directly leads to blindness—or worse.

Daniela: In the journey of healing, as we work our way towards the heart of our wounds, we eventually arrive at what is darkest in us. Unless we face that ultimate darkness, it is impossible to take responsibility for ourselves. Surely there comes a time when we need to meet Death Mother directly, if we are to reclaim our lives?

Marion: Ultimately we may have to face Death Mother head-on, but NOT before we are ready. I had no consciousness of what I was facing until my second encounter with cancer. In all my years of analysis I never linked my illnesses to the fact that deep in my cells I harbored the knowledge that as a girl, I was an unwanted child, and that consequently a part of me wanted to die. I knew it, but I couldn't open to it at a deep enough level to make a difference. Instead, I spiralled around that reality—each time seeing its reflection from a different angle.

When I was diagnosed with cancer for the second time I was ready to face it head-on, but by then I had developed huge compassion for myself and for my mother and my father. My mother certainly did the very best she could for me, but deep in her heart she was a suffragette, and in marrying a minister of the church she lost her freedom. She couldn't love her own femininity because the consequences of being a woman meant that she had been unable to live her own life and thus she struggled to love a female child. So I had several reflected encounters —spiralling back round and gradually coming closer, until eventually I was ready to face it. It took years and had I tried to speed it up, it would have killed me.

Daniela: But ultimately we have to confront Death Mother if we are going to claim our life!

Marion: Someday perhaps, but it is not a journey to be undertaken lightly. We need to be ready and we need guides. My guides were Jung, my dreams, the images that came through my bodywork, and poetry —especially the poems of Emily Dickinson. Dickinson's images enabled me to understand what was happening, and reading her poems chronologically I saw that it was her compassion for her mother and her sister that got her through her life. I began to see my mother's struggle. I became immensely grateful to her for doing her best for me. I also saw how my father had done his best. I realized that the child I was had also done the best she could.

Daniela: What is it that turns a person into a conduit for Death Mother?

Marion: Death Mother is born out of despair. It is incubated by the crushed hope of an unlived life. Death Mother is the shadow side of disappointment. When you look into the eyes of Death Mother you see that they are glazed over with hopelessness. You see a blank look; there is nobody at home. You see an unconscious, frozen, and profoundly wounded body-psyche devoid of authentic feeling. You see somebody with a desperate need to be in control. You see somebody who is driven by will-power.

A person who acts out the Death Mother archetype will have had to split off much that was vibrant, creative, and unique in herself. In fact, the adults who carry the most ferocious manifestation of Death Mother may have been the most creative of children. Tragically, their intense imaginations collided with the rational, rigid world of their parents and teachers who demanded they "be good", where "being good" meant, "Swallow your anger, initiative, and creativity and reflect me, rather than expose all that I have had to push into the shadow..."

An alternative way to act out the Death Mother is for parents to demand that their children live all that they could not live. In this case, the unconscious message transmitted by the parent is, "I have no life, but you will live what I worked so hard to achieve. You will live what I died for!" When these children try to speak their own truth they find themselves looking into the eyes of Medusa, while hearing the insatiable cries of "More, more, more!" "More of what?" the children ask. "The life I never had," comes the answer. When a parent looks to a child to live his or her unlived live, the actual child is obliterated and goes underground.

Often the development of Death Mother is crystallized when we catch a glimpse of the destruction we have wrought, but are unable to face our deeds. In *Thus Spake Zarathustra*, Nietzsche describes the "Pale Criminal" as one who cannot face what he has done,

> An idea made this pale man pale. Adequate was he for his deed when he did it, but the idea of it, he could not endure when it was done.

Similarly, Macbeth, while contemplating the murder of Duncan, says,

> If th' assassination
> Could trammel up the consequences

…but of course the consequences cannot be trammelled up, and having murdered Duncan, Macbeth rues,

> I am afraid to think what I have done;
> Look on't again, I dare not.

Many parents are unable to look at what they are doing to their children. Many know that they are failing to be "good enough" parents, but because their own wounds prevent them from changing, they can't bear to think about it. Having banished their failures to the basement of the unconscious, they continued to act out Death Mother's energy, thereby handing her ever-more power. Eventually, they may go past the point of no return. Macbeth speaks for them when he says,

> I am in blood
> Stepp'd in so far that should I wade no more,
> Returning were as tedious as go o'er

Daniela: Interestingly, there is an explicit reference to Medusa in Macbeth. On discovering Duncan's body, Macduff cries,

> Approach the chamber and destroy your sight
> With a new Gorgon

And the murdered Duncan did indeed transform into the Medusa in the psyche of both Macbeth and Lady Macbeth, leading to the cold-blooded slaughter of many of their subjects, and ultimately leading the Macbeths to their own deaths.

Marion: Isn't that silencing? The archetypes in Shakespeare are so exact! The lesson from this is that when we have been in contact with Death Mother we *have* to ask where that energy is in ourselves—we have to bring our subterranean death wish to consciousness, and we also have to look out for moments when we are "attacking" others with Death Mother's energy. If we don't own Death Mother we will live it out!

Daniela: One way to sum it up might be to say that when we are wounded during childhood, we become vulnerable to Death Mother, whereupon our lives become ruled by shame and its concurrent fear of exposure. We fear being exposed as inadequate for who we are. We fear being exposed as inadequate for what we have done. We fear being exposed as inadequate for what we have not done. We fear that our supposed inadequacies, if exposed, will lead to our abandonment and annihilation. Once we are ensconced in this toxic and shame-fuelled world, we act out the Death Mother that we have internalized. We develop an embodied, yet unconscious, longing for death and, at the same time, we attack, or abandon, anyone who might expose what we have worked so hard to keep buried. We also try to compensate for our terror of abandonment through the unconscious and insatiable drive for power.

Marion: Exactly! Fear is key. If we have faced Death Mother while growing up, and if we have incorporated the resultant terror, we develop an unconscious, yet profound, fear of life itself. We find it ne'er on impossible to surrender to our lives, believing that the consequences will be fatal. We understand receptivity as capitulation; all we can envision is plummeting through chaotic darkness into an abyss that has no bottom. We do everything in our power to avoid that imagined outcome. Even when the door of our cage opens, we struggle to find the courage to walk through it.

Daniela: You contrast the Death Mother energy, which kills life, with the energy of "Death in the Service of Life". Can you elaborate on the difference?

Marion: The energy of Death in the Service of Life is utterly different to that of Death Mother. The energy of Death in the Service of Life is represented within the Hindu tradition as Kali, the goddess who wears a necklace of skulls that can instantaneously change into blooming flowers and then back to skulls again. She is usually depicted with four hands; one of her right hands says 'Don't be afraid" and the other offers you a bowl of rice. However, one of her left hands holds a sword and in the other is a human head. Kali brings love, ecstasy, and life, but she also brings darkness, terror, and death. She is the natural cycle of life and death. In the European tradition this energy is best represented by the Baba Yaga of Russian fairy stories. The Baba Yaga's hut lies deep in the forest, and her door is always open to the darkest part of that forest. Her hut turns on chicken legs, dizzying our normal perception. In many stories the fence that surrounds her hut is made of human bones, and interspersed along the fence are twelve stakes. There are human heads on eleven of them, leaving one empty for the next victim. Traditionally, the Baba Yaga asks the "difficult" questions. She eats naive people who think life should bring them only happiness. She gobbles up the uninitiated, to whom suffering is unacceptable. She devours those who see life in terms of dualistic categories such as white or black, good or evil, life or death.

Daniela: If we want a generic term for the archetypal energy personified by Kali or Baba Yaga, could we call it "Apocalyptic Mother"? The word "apocalypse" derives from the Greek word meaning "to reveal", or more specifically, "to uncover that which has previously been hidden". We also understand apocalypse to mean the coming of a day of judgment, after which the old will be destroyed and a new order will prevail. It seems to me that this is what a meeting with the Baba Yaga, or Kali, entails; a revelation of what has been hidden, death of the obsolete and birth of the new.

Marion: Yes! You have coined a phrase which does capture that archetypal energy.

Daniela: How do we differentiate between Death Mother and Apocalyptic Mother?

Marion: Death Mother prevents new life coming through. She turns life into stone. She encases us in the mantle of lifelessness. What you have called "Apocalyptic Mother" shatters that stone. All change, all growth, presupposes the death of the old. The death induced by Apocalyptic Mother is excruciating, but it instigates change. Apocalyptic Mother precipitates the death of values which are rooted in fear and power. She creates space for the life we have yet to live. She brings about what Death Mother strives to prevent.

The difference between Death Mother and Apocalyptic Mother is best depicted by the contrast between murder and sacrifice. Both kill energy, but the motives behind them are quite different. Murder, committed by Death Mother, derives from the ego's need for power, control, safety, and domination. It is driven by a need to prevent us from living our reality for fear that we will be found lacking and annihilated. Sacrifice is rooted in the ego's surrender to the guidance of the Self in order to transform destructive, although perhaps comfortable, energy patterns into the creative flow of life. Sacrifice, demands the life-affirming "YES!", which requires all our courage and faith and love to utter.

A life that is being truly lived is constantly burning away the veils of illusion, gradually revealing the essence of who we are. Apocalyptic Mother burns us in her hottest flames to purify us of all that is not authentic. Her energy is impersonal. She doesn't care how painful and terrifying that process is. Her only purpose is to serve life.

How we respond to the Apocalyptic Mother determines whether we experience her as friend or foe. Early in our journey, when Death Mother's strangle-hold is particularly ferocious, and when consciousness is afraid to open itself to the otherness of the unconscious, we experience ourselves as victims of the apocalypse; in time, as we bring Death Mother to consciousness and begin to experience life beyond her clutches, we may gradually come to see ourselves as partners in the apocalyptic process.

Daniela: I once had a dream that spoke to this:

I have given birth to a radiant baby boy, but I am confused and surprised, because I hadn't known that I was pregnant. In fact, I'm not entirely sure when I became pregnant. Then I realize that my son was born nine months after the gardener raped me.

When I had this dream, I was struggling with my inner journey. It was time for me to sacrifice old and toxic ways of being which I no longer needed, however I was fighting against change with all my might. In the end my therapist had to deliver a fierce and painful kick before I would let go of my old ways and allow new life to come in. In this dream my therapist was symbolized by a gardener—somebody who sows new seeds and then protects and nurtures them as they grow. Being raped by the dream-gardener reflected the fact that my therapist was having to be the conduit for the apocalyptic energy, and it also showed that I was not going to open myself to that energy unless I was forced to do so. At times, if Death Mother's energy is to be dissipated, Apocalyptic Mother has to challenge it in an unequivocal way.

Marion: I totally agree. Change means change. Stark honesty, however painful, is needed on this journey toward the Self; the unconscious will not tolerate anything less. One must be willing to face many cruel truths: those we keep hidden from the light of day, and those we keep hidden from ourselves. Not only do we have to die to a false image of ourselves, but we have to change our outer life accordingly. We may have all the insights, but if we do not incarnate them, they are in vain. We may have to die to our job, to particular relationships, to our faith. Death is agonizing and lonely. If we cannot go there willingly, then at times we need to be kicked, and being kicked by somebody who has our best interests as heart is a hell of a lot better than being kicked by illness or loss!

Daniela: What do we have to do when we meet Apocalyptic Mother?

Marion: The key is to stay awake, to listen to what comes into consciousness, and to open to it. If there is to be healing and growth there can be no cover-up in this meeting. Whether we grow or wither in this encounter depends on whether we cling to our ego's rigid standpoint, or whether we choose to trust the Self and leap into the unknown. Change and healing depend on listening with the inner ear. We have to stop the incessant blather and really listen. Fear keeps us chattering—fear that wells up from the past and fear of future repercussions. This is the place where truth can set us free if we can hear it and if we then have the courage to act on it. If, on meeting Apocalyptic Mother, we can stay awake and face our truth despite our pain and terror, we reclaim a little more of our authentic life. If we fail to stay awake, and shut her in the dungeons of our unconscious, we will sink back into the clutches of Death Mother, whereupon we will eat, drink, smoke, or drive ourselves to death.

Sooner or later, we all meet the Apocalyptic Mother. We meet her every day in the parts of us that need to die in order for new life to come in. We meet her in our crumbling job, our disintegrating marriages, our failed projects, our lost loved one and our fading youth. Whether we face her in those meetings, or push her back into the darkness of our unconscious, is our choice. Do we respond as frightened children, and run back to Death Mother in the hope of regaining control and the illusionary security of a static but dead life? Or do we find the courage to ask, "What is going on here? What is my reality? What is my responsibility?" and thus open the door to becoming the vibrant, creative, and unique adult that we were born to be? Eventually, we may be forced to answer the Apocalyptic Mother's ultimate question: "Do I want to live?" If the answer is "Yes!", then it no longer matters what anybody else did to me. If the answer is "Yes!", we have to be prepared to take action.

Daniela: It seems that when Apocalyptic Mother is asking, "Do you want to live, or do you want to die?" we are simultaneously meeting Death Mother head-on. At the deepest level the line between Death Mother and Apocalyptic Mother becomes imperceptibly thin; Death Mother forces us to answer the ultimate question asked by Apocalyptic Mother. Ultimately, whether we meet Death Mother or Apocalyptic Mother is unimportant. Instead what really matters is whether we remain conscious during that meeting. More crucial still is whether, during that meeting, we say "Yes!" or "No!" to life.

Marion: Absolutely! I experienced that during my second encounter with cancer. Initially, I was caught in the despair of Death Mother. I saw the cancer as a death sentence. I wrapped myself in a psychological eiderdown and sunk into that prognosis. Then something flipped. I met Death Mother head-on, which meant linking my childhood wounds to my unconscious death wish. With that understanding I woke up.

Daniela: So, ultimately, cancer was neither Death Mother, nor was it Apocalyptic Mother—instead cancer was just cancer, and it was the energy that was constellated in you which swung between death and apocalypse.

Marion: Yes! It's the attitude with which we respond to that encounter which makes the crucial difference. My first reaction, as always was, "This can't be endured. This is so terrible I will surely die." I was terrified. Yet at the same time there was a spark in my core which declared, "I will not give up! I will not!" When that spark finally ignited into a flame, I opened to what was deeper in my unconscious. I understood the origin of my unconscious death wish, and I could begin working to combat it. I began to believe that I was going to live despite what my doctors were telling me. It was just before Christmas and I was blessed with a precious gift from my unconscious—a truly numinous dream: I was a shepherd on the hillside which overlooked the stable in which Christ was born and I saw a heavenly host flying towards me. A great, big, blond, sexy angel took me in his arms and declared, "Fear not, for I bring you glad tidings of great joy." That encounter was powerful enough to shatter my terror. On waking, I knew that I finally had to trust my own path. I knew that I had to give up the remnants of my desire to control my life. I knew that I had to let go of the last vestiges of my perfectionism.

Daniela: So when we have the strength and compassion to look Death Mother in the eye she transforms into Apocalyptic Mother?

Marion: Despite years of analytical work, I was still living my life as though it were a maze. A maze is a puzzle to be solved. It has dead ends. You may get lost in a maze. You may run into a minotaur and be killed. Before the cancer, the wounded part of me was always looking for the traps, dead ends, and minotaurs. Following that dream, despite being in the midst of a cancer diagnosis, my life opened as a labyrinth. A labyrinth looks superficially like a maze but it is different. There are no dead ends, no traps. There is only one path, and it takes you by a circuitous route to the center. In cancer, in the deepest, darkest recess of Death Mother's domain, was the ultimate gift of trust and joy. I was finally able to surrender to life, because at long last I KNEW there was a center and that if I kept listening, opening, and walking forward, my path would lead me to that center. Life had a different quality after that—there was no more fear. It fell off me like dirty rags. So to return to your question—when I was eventually ready to confront Death Mother head-on, that energy did transform into the Apocalyptic Mother. In the heart of death, I found the gift of life.

NOTES

1. Reprinted by permission of the publishers and the Trustees of Amherst Collect from *The Poems of Emily Dickinson*, Thomas H. Johnson, ed., Cambridge, Mass.: The Belknap Press of Harvard University Press, Copyright © 1951, 1955, 1979, 1983 by the President and Fellows of Harvard College.

Acknowledgements

A deep and soulful "thank you" to Marion Woodman for her generosity of time, spirit, and wisdom and for sharing so much with me. I am richer for having had this opportunity to work with her. I am also extremely grateful to Ross Woodman for all that he has contributed to this interview—his input was precious and made a real difference. While preparing for this interview discussions with Sarida Brown, Barbara Chapman, Judith Harris, Maya Reinau, and Tina Stromsted were invaluable. A heart-felt "thank you" to them all. Bruce Lloyd accompanied me on the internal journey that I travelled while working on this interview. I am deeply grateful for his support.

—Daniela Sieff, May 2009

FACING THE ENEMY

MICHAEL APPLETON
with reflections by
PATRICK MAGEE *and* JOANNA BERRY

[*Editor's Note: In December 2000, British filmmaker Michael Appleton set out to document on film the remarkable journey of healing and reconciliation undertaken by Joanna Berry, daughter of Sir Anthony Berry, a member of the British Parliament, who was killed by an IRA bomb blast sixteen years earlier while attending a Conservative Party conference in Brighton, England in 1984. The result was a 66-minute documentary entitled* Facing the Enemy (2001), *which presented excerpts from a series of meetings that Joanna had with her father's killer, Patrick Magee. Here, Michael Appleton writes about the making of the film, and Patrick Magee and Joanna Berry reflect on their encounters with each other.*]

MICHAEL APPLETON ON THE MAKING OF
FACING THE ENEMY

When interviewed about the consequences of their actions during Northern Ireland's conflict, and about the victims of the bombings and gun attacks they carried out, many paramilitaries tended to fulminate about "British injustice" and the non-jury trial system instead. A version of displacement activity, it helped preserve a demarcation between the perpetrators' deep sense of injustice, and the injustice they left in their wake. More than a decade after the peace process, suppurating memories have deepened rather than diminished in intensity. The collective trauma has barely been addressed. There is no truth and reconciliation process in Northern Ireland as there has been in South Africa and, to a lesser extent, in Rwanda. There would always be a contention about whose truth, and whose process. It was against this backdrop, two years after the Good Friday Agreement, that Joanna Berry and Patrick Magee embarked on a personal truth and reconciliation pact. When Patrick Magee got word that one of his victims, the daughter of a man he had killed, wanted to meet him, he didn't obfuscate. His attitude was (to paraphrase him): If I was prepared to kill for what I believed in, then I should at least be prepared to explain it to a victim. He had just been given an unexpected, newfound freedom. He didn't know the meeting would alter everything.

Patrick Magee was considered one of the most dedicated and dangerous figures in the IRA's inventory, and was convicted of planting the bomb that very nearly wiped out the British government in Brighton. He was given five life sentences. In the US, he would most likely have faced a death sentence. The judge used stentorian terms in describing the crime as being one "of exceptional cruelty and inhumanity," yet, as a beneficiary of the peace dividend under the Good Friday Agreement, he gained early release in 1999. He had obtained a first class degree by correspondence while in prison.

Joanna Berry was born in London on the opposite end of the social spectrum. Her mother, Mary Burke Roche, daughter of Lady Fermoy, was Princess Diana's aunt, and her father, Sir Anthony Berry, a government minister and son of James Gomer Berry, 1st Viscount Lord Kemsley, was of even greater aristocratic lineage. She grew up surrounded by royal household cousins. It was an inheritance she would later disavow for a life in one of the remotest regions of India. But she returned to England for a visit in 1984, and "rediscovered" her father. She and her father forged new bonds, and for the first time since her childhood an intimacy developed between them. Shortly after this reconciliation, the week she was to return to India, Sir Anthony checked into the Grand Hotel, Brighton, where the Conservative Party was having its yearly conference. One month earlier, Patrick Magee had secretly visited the same hotel and primed a complex timing device set to detonate a bomb at precisely the point, many weeks later, when it would do the most damage.

The seeds of this attack were planted three years earlier. The "hunger strikes" in 1981 had altered the battleground of the Northern Ireland troubles: they had scoped the full complexity of the Irish conflict into the interior of Northern Ireland's Maze Prison, but they would have consequences far beyond the prison walls. They encompassed many of the historical psychodramas still unresolved between Ireland and Britain: whether the conflict constituted a war, as the IRA viewed it, or a temporary local emergency, as the British defined it; whether the IRA's actions were political or criminal in nature; and whether IRA prisoners should have special category (POW) status or be treated like other inmates. Prime Minister Margaret Thatcher earned the IRA's lethal enmity following the deaths of ten of the hunger strikers with the argument still unresolved, and the organization vowed to take its revenge to the very heart of the British establishment. Patrick Magee went to England to spearhead the final operation at the Grand Hotel in Brighton.

When the powerful explosion decimated the hotel just before 3 a.m. on October 12, 1984, Sir Anthony Berry was reported missing. Shortly afterwards his body was identified; he was the only member of the government to die in the blast. His death sent Jo into shock. She canceled her return to India. She was 28. When she did begin to recover, she began to formulate a strange thought, that one day she would talk to the man responsible for her father's death. She felt a desperation to understand what motivated the attack. If she could understand it, she felt, she could make some sense of her father's death. It was the only way she could ever imagine coming to terms with what she had lost. She began to visit Ireland and make inquiries. Over a decade later, she was considerably closer to tracking down her quarry.

In late 2000, a woman made contact with me and suggested that we meet. I discovered her name was Anne Gallagher, but her maiden name was a better known one, McGlinchey. Her brother, Dominic McGlinchey, had been one of the most feared figures of the troubles, first as an IRA leader and then as a hardline INLA commander. Much later, he would be gunned down in an INLA feud. Anne had found out that the prosecuting counsel at his trial, Ronald Appleton QC, was my father. She had set up an organization called Seeds of Hope to facilitate meetings between perpetrators and victims—and other encounters "across the divide." She thought our meeting would fall into the spirit of these encounters. She told me that she was trying to facilitate another such encounter, this one with Patrick Magee on behalf of a victim of the Brighton bombing. We talked about how powerful a documented encounter like this could prove. She said that if she succeeded, she would try to arrange for me to meet them. I didn't expect to hear back.

I did hear from Anne, though, in December 2000, and shortly thereafter met Patrick Magee in Dublin, and later the same day, Joanna Berry. After some misgivings, they agreed to be filmed, with the understanding that any decision about broadcasting the film would be made at a later date. I discovered they had already met, secretly, once. I would soon hear more about that first extraordinary meeting. This was only their second encounter, and I had their permission to film it.

"Tell me your story. I want hear everything—the anger, the pain, I want to hear it all." This was one of the things Patrick said to Jo when they first met. It wasn't what she expected. One year earlier, she had seen the chaotic scenes from the Maze Prison on the national news, when Magee, to the outrage of many, had been granted early release. It made her angry—her father would never be able to return home. She had watched Magee closely on the TV screen, surrounded by a noisy phalanx of republican supporters. She had studied his face for evidence of humanity, for some sign of remorse. She hadn't found what she was looking for. Then came the possibility of meeting Magee. When she got the call that the meeting was on, she had just 24 hours to compose herself. She didn't know what to expect as she travelled over. She imagined him closed and unresponsive, defensive. She was nervous and wondered if she'd made an awful mistake.

Waiting in Dublin, Patrick was also anxious. He couldn't know quite what he was walking into, or what state of mind his interlocutor was in. He later told Jo, "It would have been easier if you had been angry." He elaborated in subsequent meetings: "I was prepared for anger. I could have dealt with that. What I wasn't prepared for was someone prepared to listen to me. Or even to forgive me for... for killing your father."

That first meeting played out at a sustained level of emotional intensity. It was different from the subsequent ones. It happened in secret, so neither Jo nor Patrick had to be responsible for anyone but themselves, and therefore in some respects they were freer. So it was only later we learned that Patrick had said to Jo, as they parted on that first occasion, "I'm really sorry I killed your father." In the documentary, this revelation comes at the end. Patrick was protective towards Jo throughout the process, and would object on her behalf if he thought we were making insensitive requests.

One of the hardest things Patrick had to contend with at that first meeting was hearing Jo's seven-year-old daughter's words, "Tell him he's a bad man." For Pat it would preface an intense process of self reexamination without precedent in his life. In my naïveté, I had imagined that prisoners, while in prison, wrestled emotionally with the actions that had put them there. But when I started filming in prisons, I realized that what prisoners are more likely to experience, to a greater or lesser degree, is self pity for the loss of freedom and access to the tiny everyday things that others take for granted—going to a shop, going for a walk, buying a sandwich. Prison and conscience are two separate processes. Patrick, in some ways, sought humanization for himself in the eyes of the enemy through his dialogue with Jo. But it was Jo who humanized the enemy for him instead. He told Jo: "Your father was for us a legitimate target. But meeting you I discovered he was also a father, your children's grandfather, and a human being." The meetings began to take their toll, and Pat mentioned something of the human anguish it was bringing up. "After we talk, for the first time in my life I am being faced with images of the human consequences of my actions."

Joanna's young daughter became both a lightning conductor and a theme for the exchanges between the two participants. In one meeting, Jo told him her daughter had insisted she come along to confront Patrick personally. "I must come and tell him myself," she told her mother. At the next meeting, Pat asked Jo what she had told her daughter afterwards. "Well, she asked me if you were sorry. And I told her, yes, you were sorry." Her daughter's response, as relayed at that moment, became one of the centerpieces of the filming: "Well, does that mean granddad can come home now?" Patrick's unspoken reaction is palpable on film.

The filmed meetings tended to find their own duration. Each one lasted approximately an hour and a half, and they tended to happen at night in remote locations in Britain and Ireland. If we were to do it again, we would probably have a psychotherapist on hand. Whether it would have helped or not is unknowable now, but the aftermath of the encounters was sometimes highly emotional, and a having a psychotherapist present would have provided an expert resource and pressure valve if needed. As it was, we managed without one, partly because the two protagonists and the small crew had become close over the months, and the emotions had their own natural pressure valve.

Sometimes, Pat and Jo hugged after these encounters, and though we caught this on camera, we did not include the footage in the final film.

This was not a made-for-TV construct, a "reality show." Nobody phoned Pat and Jo up and said, "We'd like you to meet so we can make a film." These encounters would have happened whether we had been there or not. Television is a reductionist medium, one that often diminishes publicly the very thing that it purports to convey. Thus, Patrick and Jo were taking a great risk with us and with the cameras. But because of the seriousness of their encounters there was no significant diminution of the content, even though the meetings were heavily abbreviated on film. We were fortunate to have an immensely talented director, Paul McGuigan, and later editor Greg Darby. Filming did of course change the process in subtle ways. It didn't make the process better or worse, just different. Off camera, Jo could have heard Patrick out and chosen whether and to what extent to challenge him. On camera, she didn't have the same luxury—she felt this responsibility strongly. She would, even if disowned by the other victims of Brighton, now visibly be their only representative in the encounter, and Patrick had to be challenged on their behalf at least. Both Patrick and Jo were watched closely by their opposing English and Irish constituencies, and both had much to lose. The IRA and Sinn Fein were probably skeptical about what Pat was embarked upon, but they didn't interfere. Jo was very concerned about how she would be viewed by her family, who knew nothing of the secret meetings, and the other victims of Brighton, one of whom, at least, regarded her as a traitor.

In the end, paradoxically, there was both understanding and impasse. Although his war was over, and that came across, Patrick would not, or could not, disavow violence under all circumstances. This was a sticking point they returned to again and again. They brought it up one final time on September 9, 2001. Two days later, the Twin Towers and over 3,000 people were reduced to dust in the terrorist attacks on New York. Jo was devastated and thought deeply about whether she could continue with the filming. Pat was clearly disturbed by the attack and said so in an interview. Again the issue was unresolved. Jo was also deeply affected when the Oklahoma bomber was executed in the U.S., and she made clear her revulsion on camera at this particular conclusion to McVeigh's life. She felt the media circus around his execution exploited some of his victims, invited to watch the execution and give gruesome live accounts on TV.

Jo chose engagement over revenge, and it redefined her life. Patrick has set up an organization, Causeway, to help former colleagues who are seeking similar encounters with their victims. Pat and Jo still give talks together, and are invited to speak all over the world. Each time they do it's different, because the process is organic, never at rest, sensitive to atmospherics, always adjusting. It's not what most people would choose, and both respect that. But in Northern Ireland there is no parallel process. It is difficult to legislate peace. Politics is certainly working at Stormont, Northern Ireland's parliament, for the first time in existence, even though it often looks like it is one step away from unraveling. But the peace process is a process almost exclusively between the political classes. Dislocation between communities and atomization within them are as deep as ever. Patrick and Jo humanized their broken relationship, and took a personal risk in the process. This has not been replicated on a wider scale, and given the data, it's not surprising. Patrick himself found it easier to feel regret over taking a single human life than to renounce violence towards an undifferentiated and faceless mass.

PATRICK MAGEE REFLECTS ON HIS FIRST ENCOUNTER WITH JOANNA BERRY

I first met Joanna Berry on November 24, 2000. Her father, Sir Anthony Berry MP, was one of the five people killed and over thirty injured in the IRA's bombing of the Grand Hotel, Brighton on October 12, 1984 during the Conservative Party's annual conference. As an IRA volunteer, I was part of the ASU (Active Service Unit) responsible for the bombing and had "served" fourteen years of a multiple life sentence for my role in the operation. Under the terms of the Good Friday Agreement, I was freed on licence in June 1999 as part of the prisoner release program (otherwise, a former Tory Home Secretary, Michael Howard, had determined that I should never be freed). And so, seventeen months after my release, and some sixteen years after the bombing, I sat down and talked with a woman whose father I had killed.

At the time of our first meeting (for, as incredible as it will sound to many people, there *were* subsequent meetings), I'd been laboring on a building site in Dublin. As a recently released republican POW, with Christmas looming, that was the only work I could get (despite having two degrees). Crumbs, as they say, from the Celtic Tiger.

Dublin had changed. The numerous yellow cranes disrupting the capital's low skyline signposted its now insatiable demand for modern office blocks and shopping centers, a testament to Ireland's recently acquired affluence. I had known a different Dublin, having been on the run there in the early '80s, a far from happy period and, in certain regards, one evoking a colder recall than my years in prison. Like many republicans wanted by the British, facing a long prison sentence if captured, I had found it necessary to leave the occupied six counties. Partition had made me an exile in my own country, unable to cross the border for fear of imprisonment or worse. Uprooted because of my circumstances, my then-wife, Eileen, with our year-old son, Padraig, decided to follow me South. We eventually got a council flat in Ballymun, a concrete high-rise wilderness on the edge of Dublin's north side, close to the airport, where many from the North had settled or stayed during the course of the conflict. Harsh days, struggling on the dole with absolutely no prospect of work, and hounded by the southern Special Branch. Some twenty years later, I was back, full circle, but this time working.

The practice in the construction industry is to knock off work early on Fridays. After lugging bags of cement and plasterboards up four flights of concrete stairs since eight that morning, it was a relief to leave before four. Normally I'd feel wasted but with the weekend ahead of me in which to recoup before Monday. This Friday was different. All day I'd been waiting on a call to find out whether tonight I would indeed meet Joanna Berry, mentally gearing up for the moment, but quite calm and settled despite an encroaching sense of the meeting's potential significance. However, I did have misgivings. But I'll add more on that presently.

The day before, Thursday 23, I'd finished work at the more usual time of six, thinking only of a long soak, then early to bed. I got a call from Coiste na nIarchimí, the Irish republican ex-prisoners' support group. I was to meet someone called Anne Gallagher at O'Shea's Merchant, a bar on the south side of the Liffey, a mere stroll along the quays from the arch at Christchurch—she could arrange a meeting between Joanna Berry and me. Sleep could wait. I had been anticipating this hour since the summer. That's when I first heard from Coiste that someone connected with "Brighton" had asked republicans attending a seminar at the Glencree Centre for Reconciliation, County Wicklow, whether they would pass on word that she wanted to meet me. The message did the rounds until a phone call that September informed me of her request. I immediately agreed to the meeting, regardless of already referred to misgivings, certain that this was the right political and moral course. The necessary arrangements had only to be made.

What did I know then about Joanna Berry? Other than the fact that her father was one of the five killed at the Grand Hotel, and therefore that she too must be considered a victim, I scarcely held a perception of her beyond what I had managed to glean from Coiste over the phone two months ago. She had impressed those she met with her openness and sincerity. I had asked, and was reassured to hear that she wasn't seeking to confront me but, rather, to gain an understanding of the conflict that had robbed her of a father and, as I was to learn, her daughters a grandfather. Nothing definite was being proposed at this stage—no venue, no date—but I wanted to be notified the next time she or, indeed, any victim should express a similar wish for contact. I believed then, and still do, that it is incumbent on republicans to avail themselves of any and all opportunities to articulate our perspective, grievances, and objectives, particularly given the backdrop of the decades-long suppression of the republican message. This may strike many as cold and impersonal, perhaps politically calculating and evincing little of the emotional interest one might presume at the prospect of meeting a victim of one's actions. There matters had rested vaguely until Thursday's call from Coiste.

Now I was hours away from meeting her—a daughter of one of the Brighton dead, herself a victim because of *my* actions. An inchoate thought was gathering, bereft of the language then to give it shape and force: the Brighton Bombing was an IRA operation, but I held a personal responsibility; I couldn't hide behind the IRA, however justifiable its actions, and I still do justify them. But the more formed feeling then was of detachment, and I still viewed a possible encounter with her more for its political than its human significance, namely, that a civilian victim of an IRA operation had sought direct contact with the volunteer widely identified with that action.

Only a few years back it would not have occurred to me that one day I might be meeting someone connected with Brighton. Not Brighton. I know that part of any conflict resolution situation involves dealing with the legacy of culpability and pain. But I thought this would at some future date mean meeting with former Loyalist combatants, or ex-British Army squaddies, or Special Branch torturers. But Brighton didn't seem to belong in the same reconciliatory universe. I reasoned that the British political elite would never countenance a face-to-face with someone so intimately identified with such a prestigious attack on them. I thought, "They'll never forgive. I'll always have to look over my shoulder because of Brighton." Joanna, of course, was there representing no one but herself. But still, never for a second had it entered my head that one day I might meet anyone hurt in that operation.

One of my flatmates, Pat, drove me to O'Shea's. Anne Gallagher arrived shortly after us. Because the contact had come through Coiste, I wrongly assumed that Anne herself was either in Sinn Fein or Coiste. Anne clarified that although hailing from a staunchly republican background, she wasn't a republican. Her brother was Dominic McGlinchey, the INLA leader shot dead in February 1994. Other members of the family had also been imprisoned for their involvement in the struggle. Moved by her experiences as a nurse at the Royal Victoria Hospital, Belfast, tending victims from all sides at the height of the Troubles, Anne founded the peace group Seeds of Hope, which aimed to build reconciliation through utilizing the creativity and artwork of former republican and loyalist prisoners. I asked Anne how she knew Joanna Berry. Anne replied that they had been friends since 1986 when they met at a peace conference. Joanna later corresponded with one of Anne's brothers while he was in prison. The upshot of the meeting was that I was to wait on a phone call the next day, Friday, when Anne would give the time and location of the proposed meeting.

Then the call. Again accompanied by Pat, I crossed town from Ballymun to Blanchardstown, a once comparatively prosperous suburb sprawling out of the city to the west, where Joanna was staying at Anne's home before their attendance at a victims' project at Glencree. We got there about seven. I stood at the front door, lacking what now suddenly seemed the stupid confidence that the meeting would be non-confrontational. If roles were reversed and I was the victim waiting to meet the person responsible for my pain, my anguish, my loss, how might I react when face to face with the perpetrator? It is conceivable, regardless of a genuinely expressed desire for rational dialogue, that control over understandable emotions might slip and that I might lash out. Seconds beyond this doorstep was a woman whose father I had killed. Mightn't she be now similarly assailed by doubts, and with thoughts of revenge? The full import of the moment had intruded. This could so easily end disastrously.

I have no idea who rang the bell. Anne opened the door and warmly ushered us down the hallway to her kitchen. The evidence was of a very welcoming house with a steady traffic of visitors. Anne's was, in fact, an open door for many involved in reconciliation and cross-community initiatives. Joanna Berry was clearing up after several departed diners. She was calm, and at least outwardly in control. Anne did the introductions, then Joanna thanked me for agreeing to meet her. What could I say to that? All I managed was to return the thank you. Then Anne offered dessert, all that was left of the meal prepared earlier with Joanna's help. We sat down, Joanna now sitting facing me at an angle. I couldn't eat. There was some polite talk, of which I have no recall, though I am sure I contributed little, Pat and Anne picking up the slack. A threshold had been crossed. I can't say I was relaxed. Surely something of my discomfort was registering with them, if not with Joanna, who seemed serenely in charge over whatever second thoughts I imagined she must be experiencing. Was it so inconceivable that darker emotions might erupt? However, for Joanna there could be no moving forward until she had confronted her demons, that is, come face to face with me; but sitting there seemed inappropriate. Too informal. I couldn't play at being sociable. I felt a need to be on my own with this woman, whose father I had killed. I sensed she felt the same—that we both would prefer not to share before any third party; that we both needed to be rid of the rather forced informality, the stopgap social chatter. To my intuition that Joanna was of a like mind and wanted to talk alone with me, the presence of anyone else would be intrusive and superfluous. What were the rules? Where could we seek a precedent? Whom could either of us have approached for guidance? None of this could have been foreseen. I think I was afraid of Anne and Pat being witness to any outward expression of my inward emotional churning. Additionally, I felt inhibited in front of witnesses, even friendly, sympathetic witnesses, inhibited from being as frank and open as the significance and gravity of the moment demanded. This was a very private moment.

One unalterable factor, intrusive and unsettling, continually asserted itself: I had killed this woman's father. The thought recurred.

How would I react if the circumstances were reversed and I was the victim meeting the perpetrator? I still cannot answer that question. Who can predict how they might react in the aftermath of the violent death of a parent, a child, a spouse? But I would be grateful for one iota of Joanna's demonstrable integrity. Nothing in her demeanor or conduct that evening betrayed any hint of hostility or bitterness. Instead, she epitomized dignity and poise. But could she be completely sincere? Her composure certainly appeared genuine. I sensed then, and it was confirmed in all subsequent meetings, that she was blessed with truly remarkable inner reserves of gentleness and moral courage. The word "grace" kept coming to mind. I was also to learn that her gentle manner masked a steely moral determination, for she held to a deeply personal conviction that her loss, as for all loss, represented a rip in the fabric of humanity that somehow had to be mended, a breach that had to be restored. As for who asked first whether we might talk privately, I cannot recall. Perhaps Anne, socially astute, recognized the signals and inquired whether we preferred privacy. That insight would be in keeping. Anne did suggest that her conservatory was an ideal space. And so it proved to be, for we talked alone for some three hours, sitting on wicker armchairs, the room bedecked in cushions and soft drapes, candle-lit, a perfect setting to put us at some semblance of ease. Except for the distraction of coffee, we were left undisturbed, Anne entering and exiting, only to check whether we needed anything else.

Three hours! With hindsight, I attribute our need to talk alone to our mutual recognition that nothing less than the complete, most profound honesty was demanded and that any third, uninitiated party might corrupt the purity of the occasion. As for what was said, I would stress that it was one of the most intense encounters I have ever experienced. We seemed to inhabit a different temporal order for the duration of our conversation. The time ticked by to a point of unhurried closure. Yet I cannot recount verbatim what was exchanged, what thoughts were shared.

I came with an idea of what was expected of me, of the issues and questions likely to arise: Why? Why her dad? Why Brighton? Despite the forethought, I was tentative. I remember thinking, what would the other Brighton victims make of this? I was all too conscious of the expressions of hostility towards me subsequent to my arrest and public identification with the bombing.

I imagined that she would have expectations about her father's killer. For years I had been demonized as the Brighton Bomber. A certain tabloid had recently dubbed me a "Mad Dog." The only corrective to the misrepresentation open to me was to present myself, for better or worse. I had to begin by stating something about my involvement in the Brighton attack. What else was she here for? Justifying the operation—the targeting, the bombing, the political and personal consequences—to the daughter who had lost her father may seem insensitive, perhaps obscenely crass. It is hard to imagine a more difficult message for a victim to hear. But that is how I began, and there is no way to finesse what I had to say. I believed ultimately that the armed struggle was morally justified, and that the targeting of the Thatcher administration was a legitimate act of war. The moment demanded utter candor. She was there precisely to hear my perspective. What would be the point of anything less than the fullest honesty? Which isn't to say that I could reveal operational detail. Parameters for what was to follow had to be clearly set. But I stated to her that I would be as open about Brighton as possible, that as a republican I felt obliged to explain the republican perspective when asked. As I've said, this was against the backdrop of what I would argue is the gross distortion of the republican cause, the censorship of our viewpoint. I felt a political obligation to explain when a platform was offered or when answers were sought. That obligation underlay my reasons for readily agreeing to the meeting. But it had to be acknowledged that there were aspects to the Brighton operation, again specifically operational details, that I couldn't and wouldn't discuss. She appeared to accept this condition, and demonstrated that she knew and understood my position, and perhaps also preferred to be spared the details of this dimension to her father's death. Within that constraint, we proceeded.

Joanna's questions and comments revealed that she was extremely knowledgeable about the causes of the struggle. Moreover, judging from her informed remarks about people and places and events, she clearly had developed affection for Ireland, having been in recent years a regular visitor. She had come a long way in her personal journey of understanding, having invested years trying to grapple with issues of cause and effect, and to gain answers as to why, as she expressed it, she had so cruelly and suddenly been projected into the conflict as a casualty from the moment the bomb detonated.

There was another reason why she kept returning, one only intimated during that first meeting but which became clearer after subsequent exchanges. I was to learn that as an English victim of the conflict she shared the isolation of other English victims who, geographically dispersed, from Warrington to Bishopsgate, Birmingham to Brighton, and without community support, had little or no opportunity to talk through their loss with others who had been similarly bereaved. Today, Colin Parry's Warrington project is striving to address the need, but back then there simply was no group—and few individuals—that Joanna and other victims could turn to in Britain. Ireland offered the chance to share her pain with others, many others, who had been traumatized, damaged by the conflict. She was certainly not alone in Ireland, where the currency of trauma was readily accepted within communities that had suffered greatly.

At a mid-point—I cannot be more precise—Joanna offered to read a poem she had written in May of the previous year, entitled "Bridges Can Be Built." It was an amazing, almost hypnotic, recital. I asked had she written before. The poem was her first in twenty years, she replied. I still have the typewritten copy she gave me that night. I've read the poem many times since. What struck me most the first time was how accurately the poem seemed to prefigure the spirit of our actual meeting: *and now I stand alone with you who killed my Dad.* How could she so correctly realize my viewpoint and anticipate my response to our encounter? I was simply awestruck, disarmed at her apparent lack of bitterness, her magnanimity and perceptiveness.

At some point, she asked to be called Jo. It would take me a while to become habituated to that, unsure as I was of the degree of familiarity that would be appropriate. She also mentioned having done an interview as far back as 1986 for the *London Standard*, that is, before I was sentenced, in which she had said, "I forgive the man who killed my father." Further, she stated that one day she wanted "to meet her father's killers." She would later also give me a copy of the original edition, dated Wednesday, 22 January 1986. I've wondered since how I might have responded had I read the article at the time of publication. Then I was being held on remand at Brixton Prison, a grim time, perhaps too absorbed in the looming Old Bailey trial. If I possess any degree of insight into my own mind, I am sure I would have been deeply moved and would have also realized that contact might follow someday.

Towards the conclusion of that first meeting, Jo, as I will call her henceforth, said an extraordinary thing: "I'm glad it was you." It was a spontaneous remark, not meant to be provocative. For what could she have meant? Sensing my confusion, she explained that the person who killed her father might not have wanted to meet her, nor be motivated to understand her perspective. The meeting seemed to dispel that fear for her. That was crucial to her and justified the risks she had taken.

Moreover, the breaking down of stereotypes was a two-way street. Over the course of many meetings, I was to learn that Jo's father was a decent man. It had evidently been more comfortable living with the perception that as a Tory he was simply the enemy, without a personal moral code, or rounded background. I, too, was guilty of demonizing the enemy. Now I had learned from the experience of meeting the *other*, and in my former ignorance, delusion, arrogance, I hadn't foreseen how valuable and how liberating that lesson would be in terms of my own humanity and perception of the world. But I must stress, lest there be any misunderstanding, that my core beliefs have not changed, and that to this day I stand by my role. Brighton was more than a revenge attack on the Tory architects of repression in Ireland. The bombing was a wake-up call to Britain's political establishment. As long as their predatory, selfish, undemocratic hold on the six counties was maintained, the Republican Movement would organize to take the war to England.

As we ended the meeting, Jo and I hugged. I told her that I was sorry that I had killed her father. I was to grow towards the knowledge that all I eventually came to admire in Jo—her integrity, kindness, intelligence—were part of her father's gift to her. Such a realization cuts through all the layers of defense and denial, the justifications, reasoning and rationalizing, and you are left in the presence of the human tragedy. We agreed to meet again, both committed to somehow furthering the experience so that others might avail themselves of the then as yet unformulated benefits.

JOANNA BERRY REFLECTS ON HER JOURNEY OF RECONCILIATION
WITH PATRICK MAGEE

My journey begins on October 12, 1984, when my father was killed by an IRA bomb whilst he was attending the Tory conference in Brighton. I remember being overwhelmed with feelings of shock and trauma as well as the awareness that I was now part of a war. Two days later, I made a silent vow to bring something positive out of the destruction, to try to understand those who had killed him. I was without a map and support, but knew I could trust that life would bring me the opportunities that I needed.

Three months later …

I am going home on the subway and I have a sudden strong urge to get off before my destination, so I do. I then wait in a busy area looking for a taxi, but I can't find one. I start talking to someone beside me, and we decide to share a taxi. In the taxi, I ask him where he is from. He says Belfast, and I tell him about my Dad. He says his brother had been in the IRA and had been killed by a British soldier. We could have been enemies, but we share our vision of a world where peace is possible and where no one uses violence. As I get out of the taxi, a phrase comes to me—Ah! This is one way I can help: by building a "bridge across the divide."

A few months later …

I have an opportunity to travel to Northern Ireland and I welcome it. I attend a workshop by Elizabeth Kubler Ross on unfinished business. At the end of the workshop, I share my story about my dad and I am asked to stay on in Belfast and visit reconciliation groups. I write down my thoughts and they are photocopied and circulated around Ireland, with the result that I begin receiving letters from a prisoner who was in the INLA. I also meet a politician in Sinn Fein. I meet many who describe to me what life is like with soldiers living on their streets. I meet those who understand my experience and want to listen. I speak to hundreds of people at a reconciliation meeting and begin to understand the reasons why someone may choose to join a paramilitary. I go back several times to Northern Ireland, but I find it, in the end, too emotionally challenging, as I have yet to deal with my trauma.

It was only after the peace process in 1999 that I got involved again. I found myself reliving Brighton as if it were that very day, and I knew that it was time to look for ways to heal and get support. I had put my trauma in a box and now the box was opened. Miraculously, I heard about a project at the Glencree Reconciliation Centre that was designed to provide support to victims who lived in England as well as to those from Northern Ireland. I knew this was exactly what I needed. I remember walking into the room and looking at the faces of all who were there, mothers and fathers of dead soldiers, people injured by bombs, the father of a dead son. I knew it as safe for me to open up and feel my pain. No one there would be scared of my pain—they would understand. And over the next few months I did grieve, rage, cry, and laugh with the others. I knew how important it was, since I was beginning to trust myself again as I felt and let go of each piece of the pain.

I also met ex-combatants and found that by seeing them as human beings, discovering their humanity, I was discovering my own humanity. After a particularly intense weekend during which I had spent the whole time hanging out with four ex-IRA guys, I woke up overcome with feelings of guilt over my betrayal. These men could have killed my dad, and I had walked in the hills with them. I felt the feelings and discovered a wall of pain and I cried for hours and hours, and afterwards I knew that the saddest thing was that they were my brothers, not my enemies, that in truth there is no us and them, only you and me. I knew then that betrayal—the idea that we cannot be friends with the other side without being disloyal to our own—is a myth that keeps us from realizing that we are all brothers and sisters, and in that moment I knew that the only real betrayal was the betrayal of my heart, which was telling me that we are all connected.

Later that year I met some people who knew Pat Magee, the man who had been charged with and sentenced for planting the bomb that killed my dad. I had first talked about meeting him in 1986, and now the opportunity was there. He had been released from prison as part of the Good Friday Peace Agreement. I received a phone call on Friday November 22nd that Pat would meet me that evening at my friend Anne Gallagher's house. I was going to Ireland anyway, and I would just arrive late at Glencree. My first thought was: "Oh, I'm not in the mood. I'm not ready." Then I thought, "No, I can trust that this is the day I have been working towards for so long." I took the ferry to Ireland, and to take my mind off the enormity of the meeting, I played cards with two businessmen sitting next to me. I lost each time, but it got me to Ireland. I was scared, but then thought he might be more scared than I was. I remember the door opening—and he walked in.

Pat Magee enters the room. I reach out and shake his hand.

"Thank you for coming," I hear myself say.

"No. It's you I should thank." He speaks in a quiet voice.

He sits down at the table and we start talking. After two minutes, we move into the quiet back room. We talk for three hours. Then exhausted, elated, we say goodbye.

Much of what we said at that first meeting I can't remember. For me it was extremely intense, every feeling amplified, every word he spoke important. I felt compelled to listen to his story, to hear his thoughts, to experience his humanity. I remember feeling shocked at myself, unable to believe that I was talking to him.

I am entering madness. I take a few deep breaths and say to myself, "Jo, This is For Your Healing. This Will Be OK."

I remember sharing with him how wonderful my Dad was, how painful it was to lose him, how we had got very close the summer before he was killed. He told me his history leading up to the planting of the bomb and the reasons why he had joined the IRA. He was very clear he couldn't talk about the technical details of the "operation" and that suited me too.

He's giving me the political justification, somewhat detached from the reality of his actions. This is familiar through talking to other men from the IRA and it is what I expected, but it's painful to hear of my Dad's death as a strategy. I look at him and have to remind myself: "He Killed My Father." I want to listen to him, I need to understand what made this man in front of me, a man who seems sensitive and caring and yet chose violence.

After an hour and a half he stops talking, takes off his glasses—there's silence. Then he says: "I have never met anyone with so much dignity and so open. I want to hear your anger. I want to hear your pain. What can I do to help?"

At that moment I sense that this is the beginning of a new journey, one that we will make together. I am scared, out of my depth, wanting to run away and also embracing the opportunity. I know his need to engage with me meets my need to engage with him. I feel like I am being pushed by a huge wave to a new place, where the old ways no longer exist. I thought we would meet just once, but now that Pat has taken off his political hat and opened up, I know it is safe and important for my healing to meet him again.

I have to let go of my expectations and prejudices. I breathe through and let go of my betrayal, my anger, my pain, and my shock. I am left with my heart open. My brain feels like a computer that has been sent so many contradictory messages that it has crashed. I am left with the vulnerability of my heart and driven by my need to understand.

The overall feeling I have is one of recognition. Here is the man whose shadow I have been walking in since 1984. I know him on a very deep level, and yet, paradoxically, I know nothing and want to know everything. I have so many questions to ask him, so much I want to share. There is an emotional intensity between us of a sort I have never experienced before. I need to understand, I need to comprehend how Patrick could have killed my Father.

As he is finally leaving, he says: "I am sorry I killed your Dad."

I find myself saying, "I am glad it was you."

The words pop out even before I have thought them. But they are true, as he could have been someone with a closed mind and with no desire to engage with me. I know that my need to meet him matches his need to meet me. We are starting on a journey together and I have no idea where it will take me. I just know that I want to embark on this voyage with all the challenges it will bring. I am glad it is him, because I know he is prepared to go on the journey too.

After he leaves, Anne and I drive to Glencree. We get lost on the Wicklow mountain roads, arriving very late. At the Glencree Recreation Centre there are always people who stay up late. I find many friends there, other victims whom I had been meeting during the past year. They all hug me and listen as I try to convey a sense of the meeting. I feel elated, and it's hard to describe all I feel. My hands and arms are full of energy and I find myself massaging the shoulders of seven of them at three in the morning! I can hardly sleep and still have so much energy. The facilitators give me time to share with all the participants as I tell my story. I talk gently, aware that most there have had their loved ones killed and this may be distressing for them.

This was the beginning of a complex emotional journey in which there were so many people that could be hurt by what I had done. I had to learn to be with many contradictory feelings and learn which ones to trust and which to let go of.

The next week was strange, I felt disoriented, and nothing seemed the same. I remember walking down the road watching everyone shopping, going about their daily lives and just being normal. I felt so abnormal. I thought, "If only people could see what it is I have done, what would they say?" I felt as if I had broken the taboos of society. I seemed to be totally out of my depth, in the sea without a lifejacket, yet I was just swimming. I yearned to seek others who had walked a similar path.

Now I knew that my fear of reaching the summit of this mountain only to find it to be the end of my journey was a false one. Instead, I had now encountered an even bigger mountain. The feeling of no map, of uncharted territory, was immense. Once again I was alone in my journey, but with many holding my hand as I climbed the mountain, trusting that step by step I would know what to do and that this was the only way to say: "Violence and revenge for me end now—Right Here."

I felt a need to get together with this man again as soon as possible. A part of me was still there with him at that meeting. Our work together was not finished. I had begun to heal the most broken relationship I had ever had. I had taken a big step in healing the wound inside myself caused by the devastation of the bomb. I had glimpsed the humanity inside the man who killed my father and nothing would ever be the same again.

I went back two weeks later to meet Pat again. This time there would be a friend of Anne's, Michael Appleton, there with a video camera. We were just going to film it for reconciliation purposes, for Seeds of Hope to use. I remember meeting Michael and how he soon made me feel relaxed and gave me support. I was filled with a mixture of emotions at meeting Pat again, and to be filmed only added to the tension. As we started talking, I was so compelled to listen and share that I forgot everything else. I gave Pat a message from my middle daughter, then seven years old:

"She wants you to know that you are a very bad man for killing her granddad."

Pat's face expressed shock and pain at this. As he took it in, he was at loss for a reply. He took this comment and the next ones very seriously, and her voice became an important part of our dialogue, helping the opening process even more.

After the meeting, Michael got in touch with me and said he would like to videotape more meetings and he thought it could end up as a documentary. My first thought was: "No! I don't want to go public with this; it is hard enough just doing it for me." Michael listened to my fears and suggested that we start and see how things progressed. He assured me that I could end it at any time if I felt that things were getting too uncomfortable for me.

Over the next nine months, Michael arranged for Pat and me to meet several times, and he filmed our conversations. He also filmed me on my own, in the house I grew up in, visiting Brighton, and Pat back in England. There were many challenges as the filming progressed, and Michael became a great support, both with the challenges of meeting Pat and with the difficulties I faced as my marriage started falling apart. He was always there, being empathic and understanding, never judging me or giving solutions but empowering me to believe more in myself. I needed to carry on meeting Pat, and the filming gave us the opportunities we otherwise wouldn't have had. Michael also has a deep spirituality and a beautiful, open heart, which gave the precarious, demanding documentary the stability that was needed to bring it to completion. I know that without him it would never have happened. As it was, there were many fragile and scary moments that nearly put an end to the filming. The others in the team were also amazing and special, and their friendship also gave me strength.

I grappled with so much that year. I was still learning to trust myself and had fairly low self-esteem, so I was always unsure about what I was doing. Was it going to hurt people more? Would it help the peace process? Would it re-traumatize my family and the other families affected by the bombing? Something else I found difficult was coming to terms with the fact that though Pat regretted that his actions had caused loss and pain, he stood by his role in the bombing. He still saw Brighton as a positive strategy, whilst I was still dealing with the consequences of the bombing. My life was in chaos because of decisions I had made just after the bombing, having experienced secondary trauma. And I could never see violence as an acceptable strategy. I would never want anyone to experience the pain that I had to go through. At different times I would have different fears and doubts, and then I would have a moment of clarity and calmness: Yes, I can trust this; the documentary will be positive.

During the month before it was to be broadcast I met with members of my family and told them what I had done, and this led to close family openings-up and a sharing of things I had not heard before. I also wrote to other families to prepare them for the documentary. As soon as the documentary was aired, the phone began ringing, with calls from other victim families, leading peace builders, and my family. The responses were all positive. I knew then that it was a success and that this would change my life. And it has. Doors have opened, taking me into new areas of work and furthering my peace building.

Since then, Pat and I have been invited to speak at numerous places and at conferences, both national and international—at prisons, schools, universities. Our dialogue has progressed and Pat now sees my Dad as a wonderful man with a soul, and he knows that he could have sat down with him and talked. Pat sees and feels the consequences and ramifications even more. He continues to meet up with me even though it can be difficult for him. His courage touches me deeply, and I have grown close to him—close enough to call him my friend.

I still have difficult moments. Sometime when Pat is talking my feelings become overwhelming. I do always share with Pat what I am feeling, and he takes my feelings very seriously.

I remember after a long hard day at a Basque peace conference, I am listening to men talking about strategies when violence can be used, all in a very detached way. I want to run out of the room and fly home, but instead I take a deep breath and share my feelings through uncontrollable tears. Pat stops talking straight away and turns to the men.

"We must listen to Jo. Her feelings are important. We need to hear this," he says.

And he gives me the space to talk some more. I feel heard, acknowledged, and I start to feel much better. This respect for my feelings makes it safe for me to continue to meet Pat, as I know he will always listen to me, giving me the acknowledgment I need. Without this I would have stopped years ago.

I am not sure how I feel about forgiveness; it is a word that does not capture my experience. I know that after a particularly long, intense sharing with Pat I have reached a place in me that knows that if I had lived Pat's life I may have made the same choices as he did, and in that moment there is so much understanding that there is nothing to forgive.

I know that the words I uttered so naïvely just after the bombing have come true. I have brought something positive out of the tragedy. My Dad will never come back, but I am making the world more peaceful as I am transforming my trauma into action for peace and ending the cycle of violence and revenge in me.

BEYOND FORGIVENESS:
RE-WEAVING THE REMAINS OF WAR

HENDRIKA DE VRIES

What, then, was War? No mere discord
of flags. But an infection of the common sky...
—Robert Graves, "Recalling War"[1]

ON OPPOSITE SIDES

"The oppressed and the oppressor alike are robbed of their humanity", Nelson Mandela wrote in his autobiography, *Long Walk to Freedom*.[2] The deep wisdom in those words came back to me again recently in a memoir written by German-born writer, Karin Finell. The book, entitled *Good-bye to the Mermaids*, tells the personal story of the author's lost childhood in Hitler's Berlin. Her handwritten inscription to me reads: "Strange, but we probably experienced similar scenes and circumstances—though on opposite sides. The good thing is, now we can be friends."

Hendrika de Vries is a licensed depth-oriented Marriage and Family Therapist in private practice in Santa Barbara, California. She has served as adjunct faculty in the Mythological Studies and Counseling Psychology programs at Pacifica Graduate Institute and has presented at Pacifica conferences. Her published articles and public presentations include: "The Chrysalis Experience: A Mythology for Times of Transition," *Depth Psychology: Meditations in the Field,* edited by Dennis P. Slattery and Lionel Corbett (Carpinteria, CA: Daimon Verlag & Pacifica Graduate Institute, 2000), pp. 147-159; "Seeing in the Dark: the Power of Mythic Perception in Troubled Times;" and, "Inviting the 13th Fairy: Embodying Soul in our Personal Myths."

As the inscription implies, both Karin Finell and I lost our childhoods in World War II, and our experiences were indeed on opposite sides of the conflict. For my people, hers were the oppressors, and we were the oppressed; yet both she and I witnessed the same kind of horrors of hunger, destruction, death, and betrayal that war inevitably brings with it.

I grew up in Nazi-occupied Amsterdam. My mother worked for the Dutch Resistance and hid a young Jewish woman in our two-bedroom apartment, while in Germany Karin saw the perversion of her people by the political father figure Hitler, whose monstrosities she would gradually come to recognize. I witnessed my hidden Jewish "sister" being dragged out of our apartment and my mother being interrogated by a Dutch Nazi holding a revolver to her head. Karin, not yet a teenager, witnessed the battle for Berlin and the mass rapes perpetrated on German women by conquering Russian troops.

No matter whose military battle is being fought, children of war share a common bond across borders. They lose their innocence at an early age as they awaken all too quickly into a world where fear, hunger, brutality, and betrayal are everyday experiences out of which many will spend the rest of their lives trying to make sense. And one way they will do this is by telling their stories to those who will listen.

As they tell their stories, they will no doubt be advised by well meaning, deeply caring people that the road to healing is to forgive. My hope is that those who preach forgiveness will first pause and listen to what the story they are being told is trying to convey. The stories told by survivors of mass movements of violence and atrocities contain deep wisdom for the community, for the culture, and for humanity at large. A precipitous push to forgiveness may stifle the depth of the story and prevent the listener from hearing its wisdom. If we can pause and enter into the unspeakable darkness of the stories, we may begin to recognize the capacity for violence within ourselves and perhaps together learn to re-imagine what it means to be "human".

War releases the shadows of fear and deception where the lines between enemy and victim, good and evil can become all too quickly blurred. Its stories reveal a depth of human complexity and contradiction that is not easy to embrace. We prefer the simplicity of thinking in terms of opposites: black versus white, good versus evil, you versus me, or us against them.

Even with the best intentions, we moralize, psychologize, and theologize to divide ourselves into groups of those who need to be punished, rescued, cured, conquered, or forgiven and those who are authorized to do the punishing, the rescuing, the curing, the conquering, and the forgiving. This simplistic splitting has been concretized into a way of life in which large portions of the population live behind bars in prisons and another large segment secure themselves within gated, luxurious, well-guarded communities. The "other" is imagined on the other side of the man-made barrier or border. In the process we have severed ourselves from our shared human connection to the vast and complex archetypal ground of being and have lost sight of the fact that we share a common sky that envelopes one planet.

A reflection on "War and Remembrance" in the *New York Times* some time ago told the story of Dr. Abe, a quiet Japanese/American family doctor who was part of the infamous Nisei generation during World War II.[3] Born in Seattle to Japanese immigrant parents, he had hopes of going to medical school. But when the Japanese attacked Pearl Harbor, he and his family became part of the interned "enemy aliens," stripped of their belongings and forced into prison camps. Eager to prove his loyalty, he enlisted in the all-Japanese-American fighting unit. His Regimental Combat Team fought with distinction and became one of the most highly decorated units in U.S. Army history. Many lost their lives. More than half a century has passed, but Dr. Abe and other veterans of the Nisei generation who are still alive continue to get together to tell their stories.

The United States has apologized and paid reparation to the Nisei victims. But the money and the apology could not replace that which had been lost, nor has it taught us how to change the way we handle our fear of those who are other than ourselves. This was made clear by the precipitous harassment of American Muslims after 9/11.

The ability to apologize and to forgive is an important step in healing the wounds, but it is through listening to the stories that we stay aware of our own participation in the creation of those wounds. "The country owes a debt to those who forgive but do not forget, who live to tell their stories as often as they need to be repeated," because they offer the antidote to our "toxic forgetfulness" about our own brutal treatment of others.[4]

War stories most profoundly challenge our deep desire to believe that the human heart is inherently good and that darkness is an individual thing, an aberration or flaw that can be healed or cured. And in our psychological age survivors' stories are often heard only as attempts at personal healing; but depth psychology challenges this notion.

Both Carl Jung and Joseph Campbell believed that human actions reflect deep mythic patterns through which we determine, shape, and influence the world around us. Groups and cultures are also informed by these mythic or archetypal configurations, the mythic stories that underlie and determine policies and strategies in their relationship to other groups and nations. Carl Jung himself struggled with this realization when he became aware that the collective German psyche was under the influence of the archetypal hero, the blonde Siegfried. He recognized the will-to-power drive that this generated in the German people as well as in himself.[5]

Literature on violence and trauma reveals that a story will continue to be told until it is fully heard. Far beyond personal healing, it seems that the stories themselves insist on being heard into communal awareness. In *A Chorus of Stones: The Private Life of War,* author Susan Griffin reflects on listening in this deeper way to an old Greek warrior who repeatedly retold his stories of the time he fought in the war with the Turks.

> We laughed at his constant telling. But now I am hearing the repetition of the old warrior in a new way. Is there perhaps a silent hope, buried along with inadmissible memories, that perhaps some fragment of what has been censored from the official story will be restored? And the pain and shock of that memory woven thus into a fabric of meaning, shared in the common arena of knowledge?[6]

A Personal War Story

I have also shared my war story at conferences and in my classrooms, and still it seems to have more to reveal.

My memories include lying in bed pretending to be asleep while members of the Resistance secretly met in our darkened living room in Amsterdam to listen to the BBC on a clandestine radio that was normally hidden behind a fake partition in one of our kitchen cupboards, an act that I knew even at age six was punishable by death. Children grow up fast in times of war. Some images remain vivid, as that of the young Jewish woman we hid in our two-bedroom apartment being dragged out by Dutch Nazis, and of myself six years old, clinging to my mother's arm as she sat upright in a dining room chair while three men, one with a revolver pointed at her head, interrogated her. That was long after the day we learned that my dad had been taken away to a German Prisoner of War camp where he would remain for the next two years of my life.

One much earlier memory, less vivid, still haunts me with a dull sad ache from time to time. I was walking with my father through his beloved Jewish neighborhood. He was not Jewish, but he had many Jewish friends with whom he liked to socialize, and he would often take me with him on those visits. He was a story teller as were they, and the visits were filled with laughter and jokes, which as a little girl sitting on his lap made me feel contained in a safe, secure, and happy world.

On this particular day as we walked with my small hand safely clasped in his large one, we saw that a group of people had stopped to watch some activity on a square in front of the familiar apartment buildings. As we approached more closely, I have a vague image of men, women, and children being dragged out of their homes and being loaded roughly into a truck. But I remember clearly that one little girl was crying because she had dropped her rag doll, and I wanted to pull my hand out of my dad's so that I could run over and pick up the doll to give to her. I still recall the shock of my dad hurting my hand as he grabbed it with a rough grip and, grim-faced, pulled me away from the crowd. It was the first and only time that I remember him ever hurting me physically.

My most vivid memory of war's unpredictability, however, holds an eerie mixture of dancing, screams, and laughter, of flag-waving and gunshots, of splattered blood and running to save our lives. The event happened on the day that peace and liberation were declared in Amsterdam.

The day is May 5 of 1945. After months of starvation and deprivation, the people of Amsterdam are awakened by the rare sound of singing and jubilation in the streets outside our bedroom windows.

Excited voices call out that the war is over, peace has been declared and there is to be a celebration and a parade of the Allied Forces on the large square in front of the Queen's Palace. My mother and I dress quickly and join the throng on its way to the celebration.

When we reach the square, crowds of people are already gathered. They are singing and dancing with the joyous abandonment of being free. Suddenly, without warning there are shots, machine-gun shots from somewhere over our heads. Screams and gunshots mingle as people run for safety. Some fall to the ground, dead or wounded. A little boy screams for his mommy who, covered in blood, collapses to the ground in front of us. Someone grabs him as my mother grabs me, and we begin to run for shelter.

I learn, years later, that the Germans on their last desperate killing spree were quickly captured, and after the dead and wounded were gathered up, the orange flag was raised on the palace and the celebration continued. But at that time, my mother and I walk home as if in a dream, enveloped in a strange bubble of silence from which all worldly sound has been sucked out.

THE PUSH TO FORGIVE

As I worked with these and other memories in later years, people whom I respected and admired repeatedly told me that my most important task was to forgive the Nazis. I went to church and subsequently spent three years studying theology in an Episcopal Seminary where it was lovingly stressed that forgiveness was at the core of spiritual healing. I began to study the works of Carl Jung and entered Jungian analysis. A woman analyst whom I deeply admired told me that if I could forgive those Nazi figures from my past it would speed my psychological healing. And while I believed that there was a deep truth to that, it felt to me that something in my stories kept being overlooked. Some truth, some part of the story that I could not yet articulate but could intuit was not being addressed.

The distress was not just within me. It was not all about me as an individual. Something had happened to the fabric of the world around me that my forgiveness of the Nazis did not address. The world, that emotional, cultural, spiritual, and physical fabric into which we are born, had been torn apart. The men, women, and children that had peopled that world had disappeared, had been killed, or were emotionally damaged. Amsterdam, the city of my birth, the city that my parents and their friends had loved, had been violated, trampled on by oppressors' boots, and had its heart ripped out. Reality itself had been altered.

James Hillman, in a conversation with Michael Ventura, expressed his concern that "emphasizing the inner soul and ignoring the outer soul supports the decline of the actual world."[7] He prefers to redefine the idea of self as the "interiorization of community,"[8] and he does not limit his idea of community to other people, but includes buildings, animals, and trees. It is the complex ecological or psychic field in which character is formed in ongoing interaction with its culture and energy. Hillman's perspective moves the trauma experienced by a survivor of an invaded, raided, or bombed city or place beyond the strictly personal and extends it to the trauma perpetrated on the soul of place, of city and land, of community.

Community psychologist Robert Leaver reminds us that cities contain layers of memory, "layers by which one remembers the faces and words of the ghosts and ancestors who have gone before and built what one is now walking through".[9] And we have to ask ourselves how the soul of a city or place holds the memories of its abuse and destruction.

Survivors of war-torn cities and towns will often talk about the times before the war in almost mythological terms. It is as if not yet having found a way to re-imagine a reality that can reconcile their war experience, they cling to a mythic time when the fabric of their communal world was still intact. My parents, their friends, and relatives would nostalgically talk about the Amsterdam they knew before the war as if of a Paradise lost. And peace and forgiveness could not bring it back. It belonged to an old mythology of place that no longer gave meaning.

The loss of place may even be personified as one of its own victimized inhabitants, as it is in the writing of black South African journalist, Bloke Modisane, whose home town Sophiatown was leveled in a White Apartheid slum clearance program:

> Sophiatown was like one of its own many
> victims; a man gored by the knives of Sophiatown,
> lying in the open gutters, a raisin in the smelling
> drains, dying of multiple stab wounds, gaping wells gushing

forth blood; the look of shock and bewilderment, of horror and incredulity, on the face of the dying man.[10]

The bombing or leveling of a city, town, or familiar landscape not only induces shock and trauma, but it also disconnects those who lived there from the stories that continually speak out of the soul of place. In our focus on inner healing we are in danger of overlooking the loss of that external matrix, the nurturing engagement with the familiar psychic field, or soul, of town or city. Perhaps that is why stories of people having to escape homes and cities in times of disaster so often show their grabbing not jewels or other priceless possessions, but objects of comfort and familiarity, things of little value except to the body and soul. Psychology might call them transitional objects.

After my mother's place of birth, Rotterdam, the city in which she and her brothers and sisters grew up, was destroyed by Hitler's bombing raid early on in World War II, the family would often repeat the story of my *Omaatje's* (little grandma's) slippers. My grandmother, known for her feistiness, grabbed not the family bibles or precious heirlooms but her old, comfortable worn-out slippers as she ran for safety. On the opposite side of the war during the bombing of Berlin, Karin Finell and her family also had to flee for their lives. She writes in her memoir that as they ran out of their flame-engulfed apartment, her mother grabbed sunflowers out of a vase and then risked her life to run back to grab her child's toy bear.[11]

Comfortable slippers for an old woman's feet, fresh flowers to bring nature's beauty to a room, a child's doll or toy bear—these images remind us of the imminence of the Sacred within the Ordinary. It calls forth our shared humanity and the universal need for safety, comfort, and natural beauty. They are symbolic of what is willfully destroyed in our acts of war, the safety and ordinary comforts of home, a child's innocence, and the precious beauty of the earth. This is not the place to go into a discussion of the horrific intentional destruction of the earth that our global wars have perpetuated over the past hundred years. Suffice it to say that some landscapes have been so poisoned that they may never fully regain their original fertility, while others may need hundreds of years to recover.

Survivors of violence often shake their heads at the luxury of forgiveness. Forgiveness is a beautiful, healing spiritual act, but the soul that lies forgotten under the rubble of the city and the spirit that wanders through the world looking for its home need stories to reweave the fragments of reality into a new whole, a new mythology to live by. To forgive our own trauma may be a good thing, but the question often asked is, "do we have the right to speak for the landscape that was laid waste, perhaps for centuries?"

In my own story I sensed that to forgive the perpetrators that peopled my memories might give me personal serenity, but I also knew that it could not repair that broken world or bring back that mythical world of safety. There was a bigger story to be discovered.

Pilgrimage

With the help of a caring male Jungian analyst I came to the conclusion that I needed to take myself back to Amsterdam, the place where the violence had happened, to speak the familiar language of that landscape again and to walk the neighborhoods and town square where the unredeemed ghosts of my childhood still roamed. This type of pilgrimage is one many war survivors find themselves compelled to make at some point in their lives. Karin Finell went to revisit Berlin. Vietnam vets have told me that they had to go back to Vietnam before their world took shape again. The analyst in Amsterdam who generously made himself available to work with me was a Rabbi who worked with holocaust survivors. He intimately understood the importance and the challenges of revisiting the places that haunt survivors' memories.

My initial session with him focused on the question of forgiveness: "Doctor, I am here because I cannot forgive the Nazis." It felt like an admission of a terrible flaw in my moral character or an embarrassingly unhealed wound.

Imagine my relief when his response was simply "Did they ask you to be forgiven?" Stunned by his response, I knew that he had hit the mark of my resistance with a precise and careful aim. No one had ever asked me that question before.

As I told my story and also daily explored the old familiar places of my childhood, the torn fragments of my childhood's haunted landscape began to weave together. On the last day of my pilgrimage, I stood weeping on the bridge over the dark canal outside of Anne Frank's house, which stands only a few blocks from where I had lived.

Rain poured down out of a heavy low-slung sky, and as it mingled with my tears, I felt a heavy burden drain away from me into the ancient cobble-stoned ground. Dark or light, good or evil, this was my world, the psychic field in which I had grown up. I was a part of its fabric. My questing spirit had found its way home, and the soul of the old city graciously opened itself up to receive it.

For children who grow up in war-occupied lands, the landscape is a tangled mix of violence and goodness, of those who betray their next-door neighbors and those who risk their lives for strangers, of violent deaths and of great imagination as in the writings of Anne Frank. Here as a child I had been initiated into the dark side of human nature; and, like the young Persephone of Greek mythology who was abducted into the underworld of Hades, I had eaten the pomegranate seeds of the dark god's world. I did not want my experience erased by prematurely airbrushing it with the light brush of forgiveness.

HOLDING THE TENSION

Resisting a premature push towards forgiveness in order to tell their story as often as it wants to be told helps a survivor to hold the tension of opposites in the psyche. It creates the opportunity to listen into that fragile space between the tribal instinct for revenge and the regressive longing for a return to blissful innocence or forgetfulness. It is in that fragile space between rage and forgiveness that we may intuit, but perhaps not yet be able to articulate, the grace and imagination that could heal and make meaning of the fragments of a destroyed world.

Holding an intentional space for the whisperings of the soul creates a link between the unconscious and conscious. This activates what Carl Jung called psyche's transcendent function and starts a process of symbol formation. If the tension between the old reality and the not-yet-known can be held long enough, the images arising from the soul can craft a new myth.

Archetypal psychology makes a distinction between soul and spirit. "Spirit swiftly transcends, soars, and wants to leave the messes behind. It has a quick, ascending tone. Spirit is above, where it is pure and clear."[12] Spirit wants to climb over the debris of history, running the risk of causing history to be repressed and fated to repeat itself. It is spirit that seeks to forgive and move on. The soul, on the other hand, involves us in the messes and the beauty of our personal, ancestral, and cultural histories.[13] "Soul is the layering of experience, the mess, the incompleteness, culturally crafted over time in a mythic sense."[14] Soul thrives in the stories of community.

My pilgrimage back to Amsterdam was for me a re-engagement with soul as lived in the cultural history and stories that I heard from others while I was there. Visiting a weekend market, I found old books about the winter of hunger when thousands of people died of starvation in Amsterdam and my mother and I barely survived. Many of the books included photographs taken by Resistance workers who at the time had risked their lives to preserve the painful images for future generations. The stories of courage and also the stories of betrayal began to weave a new variegated tapestry of reality.

Upon my return home to the United States I had a dream that had a profound impact.

In my dream I am climbing out of a deep dark well. It seems that I have been down in the well for a long time. I can see daylight above my head and silhouetted against the sky behind them I see soldiers in uniform. They hold machine guns in their hands. The guns are pointed down and aimed directly at me. I am very tired, angry and afraid because I realize that I cannot stay in the well any longer. I decide that I must climb out whether I will be killed or not. I keep climbing. The soldiers' faces now become clearer. Their guns are glistening and aimed at my head. As I drag myself wearily over the edge and expect to be shot, they raise their guns to the sky. I stand up. My legs are shaking. The soldiers raise their rifles and align themselves in an honor guard through which I slowly walk towards freedom and safety.

Dreams, especially those revealing the inner world of trauma, can of course be interpreted and worked with in a variety of ways depending on one's psychological and/or spiritual orientation. I was in Jungian analysis at the time of this dream, and for me it heralded a major shift in my life.

After I had the dream, I came to know that in my inner landscape the figures of the soldiers had transformed themselves from menacing killers into true warriors, men who honored courage and gave me a sense of strength, protection, and inner sturdiness. The warrior remained an ambiguous image but it now held possibilities of connection and conversation.

A GLOBAL TRIBE

In the subsequent months and years other people's stories and unexpected synchronicities began to come my way. For example, I had assumed that there were no recorded pictures of the tragedy that occurred on the square in front of the royal palace in Amsterdam. One day a client, who in our work together had named her wounded inner little girl Sky, brought me a book titled *Sky*. It is a true story of Dutch resistance during World War II by Hanneke Ippisch.[15] In the book, written for a young audience, Ms. Ippisch describes the events on the square in Amsterdam from her own perspective as a Resistance worker and illustrates it with photographs taken by a friend. I was touched and humbled by the depth at which the soul connects.

Other war survivors approach me with their stories. I start befriending and working with several Vietnam vets. They are pleased and surprised that I can listen deeply and can be fully present when they share their painful experiences and horrific images.

I meet an old German man who had been sent to the Russian front as a very young soldier during World War II. We share war stories, my halting German reaching out to his deeply accented English. I don't forgive him for having been a German soldier. There is no need. In my new mythology we belong to the same tribe. We are a global tribe of initiates who were abducted or seduced by the god of war.

Who or what needs to be forgiven? I meet an artist in Southern California who was a child in Holland at the same time that I was. He says he never thinks about the war, that it didn't really affect him. We look at his paintings. Many of them show pictures of a Lucifer, a devil-type figure. He notices my interest and remarks with a thoughtful smile: "Well, maybe that's where that guy comes from." We laugh and connect on a deeper level. We recognize each other as part of a tribe that can hold the image with mutual unspoken understanding. Perhaps it is Lucifer that needs to be forgiven?

As we share our stories, the concept of forgiveness becomes more vague, the shape of the enemy, the other, more blurred. We do not see ourselves as victims. The fabric of our cosmos is beginning to reform itself. Its hues are more intense, its shape more complex; and the tribe spans time, place, and language. We could have taken flight into the darkness of revenge or the light of forgiveness, but both would have been a departure from our experience and its cultural and archetypal tapestry. Rather, like the old Greek warrior in Susan Griffin's book, we just tell our stories and we "weave our memories into a fabric of meaning," to be shared "in the common arena of knowledge."

Those who have survived war or mass violence are encouraged to forgive, to heal, and get on with their lives. But across manmade borders and ideologies the stories insist on being told and retold until the fragmented memories of lost childhoods, violated bodies, and ravaged lives and lands are gathered patiently, fragment by fragment, and woven into a new fabric. We deprive the community of its opportunity to see its own nuanced reflection in the multi-hued tapestry of these stories if we hear them only as attempts at personal healing.

IMAGINING A NEW REALITY

Stories of war, with its imagery of intentional violence and mass destruction, are hard to listen to. Those who listen with the ear of soul are challenged to hear below the facts and details into the communal depths of the stories. In that deep empathic engagement we are moved to examine our own deeply held beliefs about the nature of reality.

In Sebastian Faulks' novel of love and war, *Birdsong*, the protagonist is a British soldier who has survived the unthinkable World War I battles in the corpse-filled trenches in France. As he struggles with his memories, a woman who cares about him encourages him to think about being free to resume his earlier life. She doesn't understand that the reality of the life that she remembers and encourages him to look forward to no longer exists for him. He cannot pick up the pieces of his life until he is able to imagine a new reality that can include the horrors he has experienced. "I would do what you say," he tells her. "But it's not the details of a life I've lost. It's the reality itself."[16]

We miss something profound if we limit the loss of that reality to the soldier's loss alone. If we listen with soul we descend into the common darkness of his story where we are all interconnected, and we will hear his despair also as a wake-up call to the greater community. The trench-warfare of that war, in which the earth churned with thousands of wounded and dying young men crawling for their life through corpses of friend and enemy alike, irrevocably altered the nature of reality for every thinking human being.

Since that First World War, the strategies used around the world to defeat and demoralize the enemy have rapidly expanded beyond the battlefield where warrior fought against warrior. Those who have the technology can now obliterate the world, while others have systematized the brutal use of innocent civilians, especially women and children as weapons of war.

An essay entitled "The Weapon of Rape" by Nicholas D. Kristof appeared in the *New York Times* on June 15, 2008. It discusses the increase of the phenomenon of systematized mass rape of women and children as a strategic weapon of war in many countries. Many women are gang-raped, often with pointed sticks and then mutilated. In the Congo a former UN force commander said it is "more dangerous to be a woman than a soldier." And while the international community mostly treats it as "not our problem," the women press forward to tell their stories "despite the stigma and risk of reprisal." Kristof wishes that the world would "begin emulating the courageous outspokenness of those Congolese women."[17]

Their stories confront us not just with their own excruciating victimization, which is horrific, but they challenge the world to look into the true nature of war itself. They remind us of what we have always known—that war and rape are inextricably linked. The bayonet, the gun, and the bomb are also weapons that pierce and destroy soft vulnerable bodies and rape the fertile earth.

If we only hear the women's stories as victims' attempts at personal healing, we diminish their voices. They are risking social shame and attack to address the world and give the global community an opportunity to pause, hear, and listen, possibly even awaken from the illusion of separateness that does not see their plight as our problem.

Those who tell of their violent experiences take us on a journey into the dark side of the human mind. But they also offer the opportunity to recognize that "the part of the mind that is dark to us in this culture, that is sleeping in us," as Susan Griffin states so eloquently, "is the knowledge that we are inseparable from all other beings in the universe".[18]

And if we care to keep on listening it may actually dawn on us that the ways we are alike are more profound than the ways in which we differ. Through empathic engagement with the stories we may finally move through the deeply private grief and trauma of war to the common tragedy of the unbearable capacity for cruelty and self-delusion in the human mind.

The ancient Greeks understood this. They translated personal grief and afflictions into common tragedy in their amphitheatres so that the audience participated emotionally in the timeless human flaws and cruelties. Mythology does not split the psyche into opposites but embraces the contradictions. Myths, those archetypal tales of deep imagination, "penetrate into the great universals of human experience."[19]

In his powerful book, *A Terrible Love of War,* James Hillman reminds us that "there remains the wish at the end of every war that this not happen again, that war must find its stopping point before it ever again begins". But he warns also that it is "only a wish", and that our terrible love of war is at the foundation of being.[20]

Hillman sees war as "a mythical happening" and asserts, "those in the midst of it are removed to a mythical state of being..."[21] To penetrate the meaning of war, therefore, we need the help of mythic imagination. Myth offers a way of re-imagining the unthinkable because it sees through human activities into the timeless forces, the archetypal constellations, the gods and goddesses that impel human behavior.

World Mythology, of course, tells tales of numerous warlike gods and goddesses. The Greeks place the god Ares, who was transformed into the Roman god Mars, at the core of mankind's love affair with war. And Hillman turns to the Homeric "Hymn to Ares" to see if he can "catch a glimpse of ways to 'cure' war", or at least slow its start.[22] One such clue, he believes, may be the warrior's plea to the war god for help in diminishing the "deceptive rush of my spirit" in order to restrain the "shrill voice in my heart that provokes me to enter the chilling din of battle."[23] We may not be able to stop war altogether, but perhaps we may gain the wisdom to "diminish the 'deceptive rush' into war."[24]

The blood of a violent century covers our earth. Forgiveness has without a doubt been proven to be beneficial for emotional and spiritual healing. But for many survivors of mass brutality their suffering and dislocation from reality may be better approached as initiatory experiences.

Mythic initiation stories across the world teach that the experience of the dark side of the gods can bring a deep wisdom that demands to be shared in story, song, and myth in service to the emerging consciousness of the community. We owe those who tell their stories a debt of gratitude because they confront the dangerous naiveté of innocence and the delusion that the blood stains only the hands of the "other." Together, we may have a chance at re-imagining a new vision for the future.

When my mother was asked after World War II why she risked her life and that of her child to reach out and hide a Jewish girl, her answer was "because I would hope that someone would do the same for my daughter one day if it were necessary". She then added, "Remember, not one of us is safe, unless we are all safe."

NOTES

1. Robert Graves, "Recalling War," in *Blooming Through the Ashes: An International Anthology on Violence and the Human Spirit*, edited by Clifford Canin and Aili McConnon (New Jersey: Rutgers University Press, 2008), pp. 140-141.

2. Nelson Mandela, *Long Walk to Freedom: The Autobiography of Nelson Mandela* (Boston: Little Brown, 1994). Also quoted in *Blooming Through the Ashes*, p. xi.

3. Lawrence Downes, "From a Quiet American, A Story of War and Remembrance," *New York Times*, 16 August 2008, A26.

4. *Ibid.*, p. A26.

5. C.G. Jung, *Memories, Dreams, Reflections* (New York: Vintage Books, 1965), p. 180.

6. Susan Griffin, *A Chorus of Stones: The Private Life of War* (New York: Anchor Books, 1993), p. 259.

7. James Hillman and Michael Ventura, *We've Had a Hundred Years of Psychotherapy—and the World's Getting Worse* (San Francisco: HarperCollins Publishers, 1992), p. 5.

8. *Ibid.*, p. 40.

9. Robert Leaver, "The Work of James Hillman: City and Soul, and Providence, RI," in *Archetypal Psychologies: Reflections in Honor of*

James Hillman, ed. Stanton Marlan (New Orleans, Louisiana: Spring Journal Books, 2008), pp. 446-447.

10. Bloke Modisane, Excerpt from "Blame Me on History," in *Blooming Through the Ashes,* p. 132.

11. Karin Finell, *Good-bye to the Mermaids: A Childhood Lost in Hitler's Berlin* (Columbia and London: University of Missouri Press, 2006), pp. 93-94.

12. Leaver, "The Work of James Hillman: City and Soul, and Providence, RI," in *Archetypal Psychologies,* p. 444.

13. James Hillman, "Peaks and Vales: The Soul/Spirit Distinction as Basis for the Differences between Psychotherapy and Spiritual Discipline," in *Puer Papers* (Irving, Texas: Spring Publications, 1979), pp. 61-62.

14. Leaver, "The Work of James Hillman: City and Soul, and Providence, RI," in *Archetypal Psychologies,* p. 444.

15. Hanneke Ippisch, *Sky: A True Story of Resistance during World War II* (New York: Simon & Schuster for Young Readers, 1996), pp. 115-117.

16. Sebastian Faulks, *Birdsong: A Novel of Love and War* (New York: Vintage International, 1997), p. 413.

17. Nicholas D. Kristof, "The Weapon of Rape," *New York Times,* Sunday, 15 June 2008, Sunday Opinion section, 14.

18. Susan Griffin, *Pornography and Silence: Culture's Revenge Against Nature* (New York: Harper & Row, 1981), p. 260.

19. James Hillman, *A Terrible Love of War* (New York: Penguin Books, 2004), p. 8.

20. *Ibid.,* p. 201.

21. *Ibid.,* p. 9.

22. *Ibid.,* p. 202.

23. Lines from the Homeric "Hymn to Ares", translated by Charles Boer, quoted in James Hillman, *A Terrible Love of War,* p. 203.

24. James Hillman, *A Terrible Love of War,* p. 205.

HEALING A WARRIOR WORLD

JULIE A. SGARZI

What She Said:
The only cure
I know
is a good ceremony,
that's what she said.

—Leslie Marmon Silko, *Ceremony*

This is a story about following a thread, and, like Ariadne, finding a way in and hopefully a way out again. The labyrinth of this meander is the consuming cycle of violence and suffering that remains long after war or conflict subsides, miring individual combatants, families, communities, and nations in a complex maze of consequences. What fates befall the returning warriors of the 21st century? How can we as a culture ameliorate their wounds and facilitate healing a generation of young men and women who have experienced such brutality, presumably on our behalf? The stories that follow provide a helpful thread in this exploration.

Julie A. Sgarzi, Ph.D. (Depth Psychology), writes and lectures on contemporary issues. She is Vice-Chairman of the Board of OPUS Archives and Research Center on the campus of Pacifica Graduate Institute and participates with an advisory group for the Philemon Foundation.

In May 2008, I attended a stunning presentation given by Deborah O'Grady at the Art and Psyche Conference in San Francisco. Ms. O'Grady, a landscape photographer, spoke about her part in the creation of an original work, *Enemy Slayer: A Navajo Oratorio,* composed for the 60th anniversary season of the Phoenix Symphony Orchestra. The piece (music by Mark Grey, libretto by Dr. Laura Tohe, visual score by Deborah O'Grady, produced in 2007) is rooted in the Navajo sacred myth of the hero twins, Monster Slayer and Child Born for Water, but is contemporized in the story of Seeker, a Navajo veteran returning from the Iraq War. The oratorio is inspired in part by the traditional Navajo (or *Diné*) "Enemy Slayer Ceremony," which is conducted to assist warriors ritually in returning to life among their people and on their native lands. Rarely has a theme or presentation inspired me to pursue its various threads so wholeheartedly. Deborah O'Grady's evocative photographic images and personal reflections on the creation of this complex project compelled me to attend a performance of *Enemy Slayer* at the Colorado Music Festival in Boulder, Colorado and to listen as the composer and librettist reflected on their unusual collaboration. This uncommon union of a socially charged theme about an emotionally wounded returning veteran, combined with a community-based rite for the restoration of soul conveyed through music, language, and image, awakened a desire for a more textured way to understand our shared cultural wound.

Yellow ribbons, parades, and medals ceremoniously acknowledge our returning heroes, yet often fail to nurture the fragile psyche that returns disoriented and wounded. We have ceremonies and sacred rites for those killed in battle, but unlike the Navajo people, we lack the needed rituals to contain the full impact of the experiences of these surviving warriors. Collectively, we muse that they are the lucky ones, returning without the visible scars of war, and in our yearning for a normality that would deny the darkest shadows of combat, we subtly, unconsciously expect the warrior to resume his or her pre-war persona as quickly as possible, devoid of the ravages of combat, loss, and brutality he or she remembers all too well. The Navajo tradition has long honored the role of the warrior, recognizing that in sending a "brother" off to battle, the community has unleashed the warrior's archetypal power. The community, therefore, bears a responsibility to help contain and transform that archetype so that the warrior may return home proudly, welcomed and assisted in the inevitable struggle to reintegrate heart and mind into life as a mere mortal once again. Seeker, in the *Enemy Slayer* story, suffers a loss of soul that leads him to contemplate suicide as he recalls the horror of his slain warrior-brother, his inability to save him, and the conflicting emotions associated with his heroic welcome home. Seeker sings:

> I'm in a world of pain
> I'm hard core
> I seek and destroy the enemy
> This is my war horse
> I charge the enemy
> I am the home town hero!
> I am child of war!
>
> I am lost
> What's the use
> To go on living
> When I am here
> And want to be there?
> *T'áadoo biniiyéhi'dah'* †[1]

Seeker's is a common experience among returning veterans, many of whom suffer survivor's guilt, have flashbacks of horrific events, or simply feel disoriented as they struggle to re-establish their place in the family or on the job after a prolonged absence.

Enemy Slayer is composed as an oratorio—a musical form that is somewhat difficult to appreciate and a bit foreign to the modern ear. An oratorio is akin to an opera, but performed as a concert piece composed for symphony, chorus, and soloists rather than as a theatrical production. Traditionally, the oratorio addressed sacred themes drawn from the Bible. This unfamiliar form was, however, well chosen to honor the sacred content of this particular story, offering homage to the native healing ceremony that inspired it, while demarcating the realm of a timeless spiritual quest. Mark Grey, the oratorio's composer, sought a collaborator who could weave native traditions into modern social conditions. His choice of Dr. Laura Tohe was fortunate. Tohe, the author

---

† What's the use of my existence?

of *Enemy Slayer's* text, is a *Diné* poet, writer, professor, and daughter of a Navajo Code Talker. Intrigued by the project, she crafted the story to address the noble tradition of the warrior in Navajo society while simultaneously reflecting on the psychic suffering afflicting so many returning veterans. Respecting the guidance of Navajo elders, the team began a collaboration that echoes the sacred ceremony and traditional story without violating its spiritual integrity. Musical themes hint at native sounds without attempting to replicate the rhythms or songs performed during sacred ritual. The libretto recalls recitations and images central to the "Corn Pollen Path" or the "Beauty Way," which lies at the heart of the lost soul's journey home, but it does not attempt to explicitly re-enact any part of the ceremony. Deborah O'Grady contributes a "visual score" that integrates a sense of place integral to Navajo life, grounding the composition in the physical landscapes and images of the story. Her beautiful photographs trace an outer journey among the four mountains sacred to the Navajo people, simultaneously framing the inner, psychic restoration and renewal so desperately needed by Seeker in his struggle to survive after the war. The libretto uses both Navajo and English with lyrics and translation projected on either side of the stage. As required for an oratorio, the production includes a full orchestra, a large chorus intoning the voice of tribal and community wisdom, and a principle soloist performing the role of Seeker. *Enemy Slayer's* added visual dimension provides a compass guiding the viewer along Seeker's journey. These intersecting elements, however, make the production complex and extremely dense, compelling the viewer to absorb the power of a (sometimes) dissonant score, the complex lyrical interactions between chorus and protagonist, and the visual montage that binds the story within its sacred, literal, and metaphorical landscapes. However, if one engages this labyrinthine performance with the curiosity of a seeker, one discovers intimations of potentially curative properties studded throughout that may help in addressing the psychic well-being of our nation's contemporary war veterans.

    Enemy Slayer unfolds as a six-part story, beginning with the Prologue and proceeding through the four cardinal directions, symbolized by the four sacred mountains, strikingly imaged in O'Grady's photographs. Each direction and mountain embodies a transformational stage in Seeker's struggle to survive the transition from archetypal warrior, through the emotional traumas of memory, guilt, and disorientation, returning finally to an accepting sense of self. His journey moves from *Sisnaajini*, Mount Blanca of the East (Spring/Birth) (Fig. 1), to *Tsoodzil*, Mount Taylor of the South (Summer/Youth), to *Dook'ooslid*, Mount Humphreys of the West (Fall/Adulthood), to *Dibé Nitsa*, Mount Hesperus of the North (Winter/Old Age/Death), culminating in his return to the East for rebirth and renewal.[2] This full circuit of the four directions and the return to the East facilitates Seeker's assimilation of wartime memories and reflections on his experiences, his feelings of pride, guilt, worthlessness, shame, and his final recovery of humility and honor. Throughout this story, the Navajo community recognizes that Seeker cannot find his way alone. He must be guided and protected by the voice of his people, the ancestral wisdom of a tradition, and the resonance of a landscape that steadfastly supports him throughout his "dark night of the soul." The oratorio Chorus conveys the loving, unrelenting presence of Seeker's ancestral and contemporary community. They refuse to let him lose his way, constantly reassuring him, reminding him of his real name, his "warrior name," and of the path that can redeem him in wholeness and peace. The members of the Chorus immediately recognize Seeker as part of their community and intuitively appreciate the horrors he has witnessed and participated in. They welcome him in the Prologue, singing:

Fig. 1: Mount Blanca (Photograph courtesy of Deborah O'Grady)

> Seeker returns home
> Earth Surface child returns
> From across the big water
> Traveling lightly on a rainbow
> And leaves the reign of blood
> He calls forth, *'shik'éi,shidiné'é'* †

In the East, Seeker proudly claims his heritage and his honor as a warrior. He is confident in his ability to slay the enemy, but is quickly inundated by a tormenting memory of his slain companion. Images haunt him as he sings: "In my mind, I see the mound of earth/and the plastic flowers baked by the sun that cover you now." Inner demons begin to devour Seeker and the hero's welcome wears thin. As he sinks deeper into despair, the Chorus reminds him of the Navajo "Beauty Way" and the "Path of Corn Pollen," (see Fig. 2) which provide the teachings necessary to sustain a soul in need. Moving south, Seeker admits that he "smoked himself in the mad smoke of war," forgot his brother's warrior name, dropped his turquoise shield, and allowed his brother to be killed. He is bereft and begs forgiveness, surrendering to

> Death, you perfect equalizer, twin brother to
> War, you shiny, beautiful prostitute of the powerful!

Moving west, Seeker no longer feels like the hero society praises. He becomes increasingly despondent and wants only his own death. The Chorus reminds him:

> Your spirit weighs heavily
> And has wandered away
> From your heart and mind;
> War causes imbalance in you and in the world.

He is warned to be careful about wishing for his own death. The Chorus rightly admonishes:

> You are speaking for all of us
> *Nihiyázhi nílí* ††
> You were not born without a reason

---

† my relatives, my people
†† You are our beloved child

You are a miracle
Brought to life,
Given breath.

The Chorus continues imploring Seeker to return to the path of *h0zh=,*
or the "Beauty Way," in order to restore the balance that he needs
personally, and that the community desperately needs as well. They
understand that the fate of one member and the fate of the entire collective
are mutually dependent. As the journey proceeds north, the Chorus
pleads for Seeker to remember his true nature: "remember the stories, /
remember the songs, / remember the prayers, / remember who you are."
They remind him that he embodies the wisdom of his people; this arms
him with the courage and strength he needs to slay his inner demons
and thus become the true Enemy Slayer who will restore his own
psychological balance and that of his people. Seeker realizes that he must
"take myself back/I make the world safe." His survival is intimately
entwined with the well-being of his world. As he apprehends this
interdependence, Seeker slowly regains his footing and participates in a
personal restoration and redemption. From this point forward, Seeker
knows that he has defeated the real enemy, the enemy within, and he
rejoices that he has found the way to recover his lost soul:

Fig. 2: Dinetah Petroglyphs showing symbols associated with healing ceremonies
(Photograph courtesy of Deborah O'Grady)

> By means of sacred prayer
> I am cleansed of war
> am renewed with the four directions
> I am restored in a sacred manner

Upon his final return to the Eastern Mountain, the Chorus sings a greeting to the morning spirits, reminding Seeker of his blessings, borne of love, compassion, and *hOzh*= (peace and spiritual harmony). This cathartic resolution initiates a sense that as a warrior, Seeker has found a framework that blends the wisdom, compassion, and steadfastness of a tradition with the powerful presence of the archetypal energies needed to wean him from the murderous drives of the soldier; his nobility and courage in the face of the inner enemies that would destroy him are restored. In the end, Seeker acknowledges that he is a "child of dawn, daylight, evening twilight, and darkness." He does not deny the shadow side of his experience, but finds the equilibrium that the Chorus spoke of, which permits him to go on living, having restored his balance within his interdependent community of people and natural surroundings.

Would that a single ceremony or the embrace of a deeply held tradition could heal our wounded warriors and restore harmony to our communities. While there is no single magical ritual that can be imported from another time or culture, the Navajo ceremonial tradition points toward an understanding that has much to offer to our time and society. As a collective, we have a duty to extend to our returning warriors our capacity to contain the darkest shadows of war without ignoring their traumas in favor of the facile glorification of the hero. In celebrating the heroic, our community has unwittingly buried the consequences of war that are implicit in the hero's shadow. Contemporary society has pathologized the loss of soul and the psychic wounds that inevitably accompany the struggle to release the grip of the warrior archetype in order to resume a civilian life on a human scale. The struggle of the returning veteran, however, is not pathological. It is the inescapable corollary to the role of warrior. The Navajo understand this and anticipate the need for a sacred ceremony specifically attuned to the warrior soul, fully aware that the archetypal nature of war and the warrior demand a healing process that addresses the deep soul impact implicit in the experience. The "combat fatigue" and "shell shock" of earlier times have morphed into a clinical pathology—Post Traumatic Stress Disorder (PTSD). The physical and psychic exhaustion imaged in the word "fatigue" becomes something quite different when imagined as "stress" associated with a prior unnamed "trauma." The trauma is combat and war itself—a reality conspicuously absent from the description of this state of mind and heart. For many, the trauma is not "post," not in the past, but a living presence that infuses waking and dreaming life. It lives as ongoing combat, rife with the archetypal energies of war and the warrior, long after the departure from the battlefield. True compassion— a suffering *with*—is essential for the returning veteran and our wounded collective psyche. Instead of expressions of compassion, our culture offers its returning warriors a disembodied response; we do not speak of the impact of war and many of us may never personally engage with someone who still bears the physical and emotional scars of battle. As a society, we do not accept responsibility for the consequences of our actions as they affect the returning soldiers or the possibility of post-war healing both here and abroad.

In Seeker's world, there is no need for a diagnosis of pathology. The tradition remembers that all warriors must be held, protected, and supported when they return from an archetypal assignment. Returning veterans are young individuals who have intentionally been transformed into warriors on our behalf. They were trained to act and respond in particular ways. Those skills and afflictions accompany them home and remain part of their physical and psychic structure. Wisdom understands that everyone subjected to such experiences must be embraced as both hero and frail soul simultaneously. We must collectively assume our responsibility to them to facilitate their repatriation to an inner and outer landscape that recognizes them as neighbor, lover, parent, or friend, while they slowly disassemble the archetypal garb of warrior. After the parades pass by and the banners fade, what ceremonies, rituals, or words do we have to assist these veterans? In many ways, therapy groups, online communities, and veterans' associations have become the places where rituals of return are engaged in; the rituals enacted here do not shy away from the unspoken truths and memories, even as they honor the veterans' heroic testimonies. But these are gatherings among the soldiers themselves. We, the perpetrators of the assignment to war and the beneficiaries of their courage, remain isolated from those conversations and do not consciously engage them with compassion and acceptance. Calls to support our troops fail to delve below the surface; they indulge only superficial hero-worship and misplaced sentimentality. Of course we support the troops. Who does not feel compassionate support for the thousands of 20-, 30-, and 40-year-olds who are placed at risk of injury and death every day in Iraq and Afghanistan as a result of choices made by our ruling "elders"? Rather, it is our willingness as individuals and as a community to acknowledge the ugly impact of our decisions on these young men and women that is the real measure of our support. Can we take the steps necessary to preserve and redeem the psychological and spiritual wholeness of each warrior as he or she returns filled with the images, memories, and traumas of service?

While consistent numbers are difficult to secure, sources estimate that over 1.6 million U.S. active duty military personnel and over 416,000 National Guard and Reservists have been deployed to Iraq and Afghanistan since 2001.[3] Each of these returning veterans enters a family and community in a rippling embrace of those personally touched by the realities and memories of these twin wars. Among the MTV generation, the contemporaries of these young warriors, nearly 70% of those surveyed said they knew someone who had served in Iraq.[4] "In some ways we think it's the defining issue of this generation," observed Ian Rowe, Vice President for Public Affairs and Strategic Partnerships at MTV.[5] The defining issue of a generation, yet its consequences remain largely unspoken. Nearly 4,000 soldiers have been killed in Iraq, leaving behind spouses, children, and families grieving, struggling to adapt to a new rhythm of life. Many thousands more—over 24,000 wounded in Iraq alone with more than 10,000 suffering injuries preventing redeployment[6]—return home with disabling physical handicaps that affect their lives and those of families and friends.

Many more veterans return in need of material, medical, and psychological assistance to cope with the legacy of war and the stress of re-engaging in their civilian or non-combat lives. Estimates place the number of Iraq combat veterans suffering from PTSD at between 12-20% with nearly one-third of all returning veterans seeking assistance for mental health disorders; while many in need still do not seek services because of the stigma associated with such afflictions, particularly in the military.[7] Further complicating such a horrific portrait is a relatively new dimension to the story of the returning warrior. The Army's fifth Mental Health Advisory Team survey estimated that about 12% of combat troops in Iraq and 17% of those in Afghanistan were taking prescription antidepressants or sleeping pills to cope while on active duty.[8]

> In some ways, the prescriptions may seem unremarkable. Generals, history shows, have plied their troops with medicinal palliatives at least since George Washington ordered rum rations at Valley Forge. During World War II, the Nazis fueled their blitzkrieg into France and Poland with the help of an amphetamine known as Pervitin. The U.S. Army also used amphetamines during the Vietnam War ....
>
> When it comes to fighting wars, though, troops have historically been barred from using such drugs in combat. And soldiers ... have been prescreened for mental illnesses before enlisting ....
>
> Any drug that keeps a soldier deployed and fighting also saves money on training and deploying replacements. But there is a downside: the number of soldiers requiring long-term mental health services soars with repeated deployments and lengthy combat tours.[9]

The use of psychotropic drugs for combat personnel in Iraq and Afghanistan far exceeds that of any previous U.S. military engagement, and the military has acknowledged an easing of screening standards for new recruits in an attempt to field sufficient troops. These two realities combine with serious and sometimes lethal consequences. The suicide rate among active duty soldiers in Iraq and Afghanistan has increased to the highest level since the keeping of records on suicides in the military was initiated in 1980. Approximately 40% of those suicides were taking prescribed psychotropic drugs like Prozac and Zoloft at the time of their death.[10] Multiple deployments further exacerbate the mental health and well-being of the troops, complicating their re-integration into society at the eventual end of their tour. More than 170,000 U.S. Military and 84,000 National Guard and Reservists have served multiple tours in Iraq.[11] Such practices impact the incidence of PTSD and related mental health conditions, contributing to a radically more intense homecoming experience for the veterans themselves and for the communities they return to.

The ability of American society to empathize with returning veterans or appreciate the extent of the devastation and horror experienced by them is in part hindered by the unofficial policies of the military limiting access to graphic wartime images. While many have noted that television brought the Vietnam War into the living rooms of ordinary Americans, the limitations on reporting from Iraq and Afghanistan have minimized our visual connection to the war. Journalists Michael Kamber and Tim Arango argue, in their article "4000 U.S. Deaths, and a Handful of Images," that "the case of a freelance photographer in Iraq who was barred from covering the Marines after he posted photos on the Internet of several of them dead has underscored what some journalists say is a growing effort by the American military to control graphic images from the war."[12] The number of reporters and photojournalists covering the wars in Iraq and Afghanistan continues to dwindle for various reasons, and the explicit images of the wars that in some small way help prepare the community to welcome the returning soldiers with a compassionate embrace are few and far between.

Over the years, society has recognized that there is a cost attached to consumption and in some places we have begun imposing disposal fees paid at the time of purchase of large appliances and similar items. We have begun to acknowledge future responsibility associated with present decisions, and have learned to integrate unavoidable later costs into our reckoning from the outset. Why not acknowledge the full cost of war, including that associated with the re-entry of returning veterans into society and the restoration of their psychological and physical well-being? We owe this to every returning warrior, not just those diagnosed with a known problem within a medical system. Each warrior suffers and returns in a very personal way, but all merit our compassionate support. If every Pentagon expenditure affecting military personnel anticipated and acknowledged the cost of care and re-assimilation of the warrior into family and community, we would begin collectively to face the full spectrum of consequences implicit in our decisions. Our collective well-being depends on this no less than the health of the individuals who have personally shouldered the burdens of our national political and strategic choices (see Fig. 3).

Finding appropriate rituals and community roles requires an acknowledgement of the necessity for individual and collective healing steeped in truthfulness, candor, and compassion. From that exploration can come a more nuanced understanding of the suffering and the paths to recovery for both the returning soldiers and our nation as a whole in the aftermath of war. *Ceremony*, a novel by Leslie Marmon Silko, explores exquisitely the territory of the returning soldier in the Native American tradition, delving into questions of healing and recovery necessitated by war. Set in the aftermath of World War II, *Ceremony* recounts the struggle of Tayo as he returns from war in the Pacific to his home reservation in the Southwest. The intricacies of language, medicine, and ceremony are explored as this fragile and damaged soul tries to reconcile his experiences of war with an ongoing life. Tayo's story is much like Seeker's and shares the color of experience recognized by veterans of every war. In his haunting affliction Tayo's family recognizes that something beyond traditional medicine is needed because Tayo's wounds are greater than the body and even the mind. They appreciate the need to redeem a lost soul and seek the help of a traditional healer named Ku'oosh. Ku'oosh is sensitive to the intertwining stories revealed in language and begins his conversation with Tayo by recognizing that the world is fragile.

Fig. 3: The Navajo Veteran's Cemetery in Fort Defiance, Arizona. The tattered American flags are a fitting symbol of the war-damaged national psyche that is so desperately in need of healing. (Photograph courtesy of Deborah O'Grady)

> The word he chose to express "fragile" was filled with the
> intricacies of spider webs woven across paths through sand hills
> where in the early morning the sun becomes entangled in each
> filament of web.[13]

Ku'oosh tells Tayo that he has come to hear what had happened in the
war and to listen to Tayo's experience. This is not personal therapy alone,
but a process needed by both of them to initiate healing for the war-
torn world and for the individuals who were engulfed in the immediacy
of the drama. Tayo struggles to express himself, recognizing the
impossibility of describing his experiences to someone who was not a
part of that war; besides, he is even uncertain whether he personally
killed the enemy or not.

> But the old man would not have believed white warfare—killing
> across great distances without knowing who or how many had
> died. It was all too alien to comprehend, the mortars and big
> guns; and even if he could have taken the old man to see the
> target areas, even if he could have led him through the fallen
> jungle trees and muddy craters of torn earth to show him the
> dead, the old man would not have believed anything so
> monstrous. Ku'oosh would have looked at the dismembered
> corpses and the atomic heat-flash outlines, where human bodies
> evaporated, and the old man would have said something close
> and terrible had killed these people. Not even oldtime witches
> killed like that.[14]

All veterans are, like Tayo, part of a war machine, whether or not
they are personally engaged in combat. By far the larger number of
military personnel are employed in support functions, enabling active
combat troops to pursue their mission. Even among non-combat forces,
memories and images of the war remain as living cells encasing the
experience of war. Like Tayo, they too need ceremonial understanding
and ritual assistance in healing and integrating experience into an
ongoing life. Ku'oosh understands that the amorphous agony afflicting
Tayo in body and soul is both personally debilitating but also
dangerous to society. Ku'oosh laments with Tayo,

> "I am afraid of what will happen to all of us if you and the others
> don't get well," ....
>   ... The old man only made him certain of something he had
> feared all along, something in the old stories. It took only one

person to tear away the delicate strands of the web, spilling the rays of sun into the sand, and the fragile world would be injured.[15]

As Tayo continues to struggle with suicidal and destructive thoughts, the family consults another healer, Betonie, recognizing that he has made changes to the traditional ceremonies, daring to engage in a process of evolution. For some, these changes are heresy, but Betonie offers a wise reflection:

> "The people nowadays have an idea about the ceremonies. They think the ceremonies must be performed exactly as they have always been done …."
>
> …
>
> "At one time the ceremonies as they had been performed were enough for the way the world was then. But after the white people came, elements in this world began to shift; and it became necessary to create new ceremonies. I have made changes in the rituals. The people mistrust this greatly, but only this growth keeps the ceremonies strong.
>
> "She taught me this above all else: things which don't shift and grow are dead things. …"[16]

As the novel unfolds, Tayo discovers a unique connection between the land of his people in the vicinity of Los Alamos and the destruction inflicted by the atomic weapon sired in his ancestral landscape. The memories, dreams, and images of his psychic landscape entwine with the realities experienced in the war. Like Seeker, Tayo also must walk the landscape's path to help generate understanding and a reconciling attitude toward his experiences.

> There was no end to it; it knew no boundaries; and he had arrived at the point of convergence where the fate of all living things, and even the earth, had been laid. From the jungles of his dreaming he recognized why the Japanese voices had merged with Laguna voices …; the lines of cultures and worlds were drawn in flat dark lines on fine light sand …. From that time on, human beings were one clan again, united by the fate the destroyers planned for all of them, for all living things; united by a circle of death that devoured people in cities twelve thousand miles away, victims who had never known these mesas, who had never seen the delicate colors of the rocks which boiled up their slaughter.

> ...
> He cried the relief he felt at finally seeing the pattern, the
> way all the stories fit together—the old stories, the war stories,
> their stories—to become the story that was still being told. He
> was not crazy; he had never been crazy. He had only seen and
> heard the world as it always was: no boundaries, only transitions
> through all distances and time.[17]

Silko's novel reminds us that healing evolves with the culture and with
the evolution of the illness. Fundamental understandings remain, but
the implements of restoration continue to expand. For the Navajo as
for us, the nature of war has changed over the decades and so have the
particulars of the physical and psychological afflictions.

Ronald Schenk, in a 1988 journal article "Navajo Healing:
Aesthetics as Healer," discusses "Navajo healing as cultural form at work
and ... [examines] Western healing practices as a reflection of another
world view in the hopes of gaining a new perspective on the larger
question, 'What heals?'"[18] Schenk rightly observes that the shared
reality, values, and beliefs of a culture impact both the characterization
of illness and corresponding treatment methods, requiring an
appreciation of the operative cultural world-view to discern suitable
healing techniques.[19] Based on his personal experience living and
working among the Navajo people, and drawing on the work of other
researchers, Schenk notes that the "Beauty Way" of the Navajo
intimately entwines relationship, health, harmony, and the interplay
between creator and the created as the true essence of beauty. For
example, Schenk notes that "to the Navajo, the sand paintings in
themselves are not beautiful but *they create beauty through their healing.*"[20]
Schenk further elaborates the importance of language in healing. "In
the Navajo view, things *are* because they are first known, then thought,
and finally spoken. ... The magical power inherent in the word itself
has psychological life. *The word is the speaker, the mover, the healer.*"[21]
The word, ritually sung or prayed, is a fundamental ingredient in the
healing process, restoring balance and harmony to the individual and
to the community psyche.

The Native American ceremony for the returning warrior evolves
directly from a view of illness, disequilibrium, and healing at the core of
the Navajo appreciation of life, implicitly weaving the interconnectedness
of community and place with the well-being of the individual.

Additionally, citing anthropologist Gary Witherspoon's work, Schenk reflects on four foundational elements in the Navajo aesthetic: control, containment, order, and creation.[22] The sense of sacred container or *temenos* is beautifully captured in the libretto and visual score of *Enemy Slayer*. As *Enemy Slayer* demonstrates, the "Beauty Way" is intimately bound to the natural surrounding as a necessary companion in the inevitable confrontation with inner monsters that linger as a by-product of the warrior assignment. An appreciation of the cycles of birth, youth, adulthood, old age, death, and renewal helps re-establish a healthy psychic foundation, grounded externally in the presence of the sacred mountains and the symmetry of the cardinal directions. The mountains point the way and embody the mythic stories needed to reassure the fragile being along the journey home.

> To paraphrase a former Indian Health Services psychiatrist, Robert Bergman, Navajo ceremonials could be likened to a Western spectacle in which a lecture, psychoanalysis, High Mass, grand opera, major surgery, and the unveiling of a masterpiece are all going on at once. In the Navajo world, art is not imprisoned in museums, performance not confined to theaters, healing not relegated to hospitals and therapy chambers, intellectual life not imprisoned in academia, and religion not compartmentalized into chapels. For the Navajo, the lecture is the performance, the prayer is the operation, the painting and song are the cure. Aesthetics, religion, biology, medicine, epistemology, and ontology are all one. Beauty is being.[23]

The American worldview privileges science and the medical model in healing, favoring diagnosis and pharmaceutical treatment. Brain physiology and genetic sequencing are today's Holy Grail containing the as-yet-unfathomed secrets of well-being. However, our view of treatment and healing can perhaps continue to evolve, embracing the discoveries of the sister sciences, which explore the quantum realities of our experience. Perhaps healing, like light, can be appreciated as both wave and particle, simultaneously impacted by the observer and the observed. Our century of experience with psychotherapy and the increasing respect for dreams, stories, and images as part of the whole healing story is slowly opening our perceptive field. If we can find a way to incorporate all of these in a ceremonial, reverential stance afforded to every returning soldier and every receiving family and community, we might further open our individual and collective hearts in ways not only healing to veterans, but healing as well to the nation that inflicted war on a land invisible to most Americans, on a people little known to us, and on our own younger generation. Do we ask forgiveness of the returning veterans for the risk we imposed on them? Do we think about the generations it will take to restore well-being among families of veterans in this country and in the Middle East? And do we appreciate the devastation inflicted on the landscape and natural environment as a result of our combat and weapons?

In closing her San Francisco presentation, Deborah O'Grady emphasized that she was not advocating pilgrimage to the Navajo sacred mountains and not suggesting that we imitate Navajo ceremony. She did, however, recognize that the *Enemy Slayer* story offered valuable "universal principles" that might contribute to contemporary healing of psychic wounds.

> Those must include the acceptance of the archetypal nature of war, the recognition of the changes of personality affecting the soldier, validation of the soldier's intentions and experiences, inclusion of family and community in the process of re-integration and healing, and a container, a sacred space within which to create the spiritual connection to the world that allows for a real transaction between the participants and their surroundings. That everything on the earth is sacred is both an awe-inspiring characteristic of the Navajo world-view and also something very humble, something to which we can all aspire. Namely, allowing the natural world to remind us, at every moment, of its connection to that immensity, that transcendent realm we touch through psyche, art, and archetype.[24]

The story of each veteran returning today from Iraq and Afghanistan is part of an ongoing story. The herald in *Agamemnon* laments the horrors experienced in battle in Troy even as he struggles to accept the hero's welcome offered the returning soldiers in this timeless tale retold by Aeschylus in the fifth century B.C.E. Tayo speaks from World War II and Seeker from Iraq. This story continues to unfold, and, sadly, countless warriors return sharing psychic and physical wounds with their predecessors over the centuries. If we appreciate the universality in the wound and undoubtedly in the healing, we begin to move towards an appreciation of the ceremonial rites needed to contain our particular modern chapter of this unfolding saga. If we could glean from the wisdom of the American native peoples an appreciation of the interconnected nature of malady and remedy, the inescapable web between physical world and psychic territory, and the inseverable bond between the collective and the individual, then we might begin to imagine the small and large ceremonies that could support the troops in a meaningful way. Like the individual warrior who does not see or know the actual victim, we are a part of the combat machinery that has created this reality in a land that most of us can barely imagine. We, each of us individually and in community, are a part of the reconciliation needed to end this suffering and shape the ongoing story in a way that does not shy away from the shadow it casts on us all. Ceremony evolves from a root meaning of awe and reverence. To the extent that we bring awe and reverence to our act of receiving home the warriors we have created, to that extent we might further the healing of the warrior world, restoring in some small measure the harmony and balance that is needed when we cast off the warrior archetype in favor of our flawed mortal existence.

> Child of dawn
> Child of daylight
> Child of evening twilight
> Child of darkness ...
>
> May there be beauty all around
> May there be peace all around
> On earth,
> On earth.[25]

ACKNOWLEDGMENT

The author wishes to thank Deborah O'Grady for graciously granting permission to use the photographs included in this article. All photographs reproduced here are copyright Deborah O'Grady, 2007.

NOTES

1. *Enemy Slayer: A Navajo Oratorio,* text by Laura Tohe, in "The Phoenix Symphony World Premier Performance Program Notes", February 2007. (Note: included excerpts from *Enemy Slayer* are all from this source.)

2. Deborah O'Grady, "Following Seeker: Landscape, Music, Myth and Transformation," (presentation at the Art and Psyche Conference, San Francisco, May 2008).

3. Office of the Speaker of the House of Representatives, Hon. Nancy Pelosi, "By The Numbers: The Iraq War and US National Security", Department of Defense Estimate of Jan. 31, 2007, <http://majorityleader.house.gov/docUploads/Iraqbythenumbers 031907.pdf>.

4. Brian Stelter, "Back from the War and On MTV's Radar," *New York Times,* July 28, 2008, Arts section.

5. *Ibid.*

6. Office of the Speaker of the House of Representatives, Hon. Nancy Pelosi, Department of Defense Estimate of March 19, 2007, <http://majorityleader.house.gov/docUploads/Iraqbythenumbers 031907.pdf>.

7. Shankar Vedantam, "Veterans Report Mental Distress: About A Third Returning From Iraq Seek Help," *Washington Post,* March 1, 2006, online edition, <http://www.washingtonpost.com/wp-dyn/content/article/2006/02/28/AR2006022801712_pf.html>.

8. Mark Thompson, "America's Medicated Army," *TIME Magazine,* June 5, 2008, 2, accessed online at <http://www.time.com/time/nation/article/0,8599,1811858,00.html>.

9. *Ibid.,* pp. 2-3.

10. *Ibid.,* p. 4.

11. Office of the Speaker of the House of Representatives, Hon. Nancy Pelosi, "By The Numbers."

12. Michael Kamber and Tim Arango, "4000 Deaths, and a Handful of Images," *New York Times,* July 26, 2008, Front Page, section A.

13. Leslie Marmon Silko, *Ceremony* (New York, Penguin Books, 1977/1986), p. 32.

14. *Ibid.,* pp. 33-34.

15. *Ibid.,* p. 35.

16. *Ibid.*, p. 116.

17. *Ibid.*, pp. 228-229.

18. Ronald Schenk, "Navajo Healing: Aesthetics as Healer," *Psychological Perspectives*, 19, no. 2 (1988): 223-240.

19. *Ibid.*, p. 225.

20. *Ibid.*, p. 226.

21. *Ibid.*, p. 232.

22. *Ibid.*, p. 233.

23. *Ibid.*, p. 237.

24. *Ibid.*

25. Laura Tohe, *Enemy Slayer* libretto, final Chorus.

FOR "A NEW HEAVEN AND A NEW EARTH:"[1]
THE GOSPEL OF JUDAS—AN EMERGING POTENTIAL FOR WORLD PEACE?
A JUNGIAN PERSPECTIVE[2]

GOTTFRIED HEUER

A story told, heard, attended to,
carries with it the possibility of living.
—Lisa Appignanesi, 2008[3]

INTRODUCTION

In the middle of the last century, C. G. Jung interpreted a change in the valuation of Mary in Christian religion by the then-pope as an important indication of a change in the values of the culture at large, understanding the event not from a religious perspective, but rather regarding the Church as an important factor in both expressing as well as shaping attitudes of the collective.

Dr. Gottfried Heuer is a Jungian training psychoanalyst and training supervisor with the Association of Jungian Analysts, London. Initially trained as a neo-Reichian bodypsychotherapist, he has over 35 years of clinical experience and has published and lectured widely on the links between analysis, radical politics, spirituality, and the history of analytic ideas. For the International Otto Gross Society (www.ottogross.org/) which he co-founded and currently chairs, he has (co-)edited five volumes of congress proceedings (www.literaturwissenschaft.de).

which involves a complete reversal of the view hitherto held for the last two millennia about another figure, Judas, who is possibly the most despised figure in Christianity.

In a different context, to describe such a complete volte-face, Jung borrowed the Greek term *enantiodromia* from Heraclitus, who had first used this term to describe how, in his view, everything ultimately turns into its opposite. "It is the opposite which is good for us,"[4] Jung quotes him as saying. In sketching out some of the wider sociopolitical implications of the current *enantiodromia* regarding the Judas figure in Christianity, I am concerned with the role of shadow-projection and power in both personal as well as collective relationships. Touching on the role of forgiveness in the process of reconciliation, my considerations also include the religious realm, thus linking politics with spirituality in such a way that they each dialectically may enliven the other in working for "peace on earth and goodwill towards all."[5]

A JUNGIAN PERSPECTIVE

When the time is fulfilled a new orientation will irresistibly break through.

—C. G. Jung, 1953[6]

One of the many different ways of approaching dreams as well as situations and issues from ordinary life in the clinical practice of Jungian analysis is to understand them in a teleological sense as speaking of a potential that may be ripe to be realized. Events and enactments— also, of course, within the therapeutic relationship—may thus sometimes be seen as indicators of future maturational steps. Some sixty years ago, Jung applied this approach to the then-pope's "attempts at bringing about the official recognition ... that Mary has been taken up to heaven together with her body,"[7] attempts that led two years later to the dogma of the *Assumptio Mariae* that declared the Assumption an article of faith. Jung understood this as "a spiritual fact which can be formulated as the integration of the female principle into the Christian conception of the Godhead."[8] At the time, he felt that "[t]his is certainly the most important religious development for 400 years,"[9] because it constituted an important step towards a revaluation of the feminine which had been devalued, if not outright despised, since the very beginning of the Christian Era, both expressing as well as furthering a negative bias against the feminine in Western culture. As mentioned earlier, Jung voiced these thoughts not from the denominational perspective of the Catholic Church, but understood the church as one of the important cultural forces that shape our worldviews. He assumed that such a reversal of values regarding the feminine within the church would have reverberations in the world at large. Corresponding with the American writer Upton Sinclair, Jung spoke of a "feminist revolt," a term he borrowed from Sinclair.[10] Jung himself did not live long enough to witness the subsequent demonstration of the accuracy of his interpretation—he died in 1961—but I believe that looking back from today's perspective it does make sense to link the proclamation of the Assumption with the powerful upsurge of feminism that occurred in the following decade, and to see it as heralding the great changes in feminine values and the transformation of our world by them since then.

In addition to the Jungian approach briefly outlined above, I will also be following a conceptual framework initiated some one hundred years ago by the psychoanalyst Otto Gross and his anarchist friends Erich Mühsam and Johannes Nohl, in which analysis, revolutionary politics, and spirituality are seen as a trinity in which each of the three constituents is understood as embracing the other two in such a way that each and all dialectically enhance one another.[11]

The Gospel of Judas: "A Revolutionary Point of View"[12]

You must give birth to your images.
They are the future waiting to be born.
Fear not the strangeness you feel
The future must enter into you long before it happens ...
Just wait for the birth, for the hour of new clarity.

—Rainer Maria Rilke[13]

It now seems that today, some fifty years after the Assumption proclamation, right at the very beginning of the new millennium, a shift in consciousness of at least similar proportions is occurring—unnoticed, as far as I can see, by psychologists. The event that I am referring to is the publication, in 2006, of *The Gospel of Judas*. The emergence of the *Judas* manuscript has been hailed as the "'Greatest archaeological discovery of all time' [and a] threat to 2000 years of

Christian teaching."[14] The Cambridge New Testament scholar Simon Gathercole subtitles his book on this gospel, "Rewriting Early Christianity,"[15] echoing the American religious scholar Bart Ehrman's earlier statement that "The discovery of this Gospel marks a turning point in the history of the Christian understanding of Judas."[16]

> Historians already knew about *The Gospel of Judas* from the writing *Against Heresies* by the second century church father Irenaeus, who wrote abut a group of Christians:

>> They declare that Judas the traitor … alone, knowing the truth as no others did, accomplished the mystery of betrayal; by him all things, both earthly and heavenly, were thus thrown into confusion. They produced a fictitious history of this kind, which they style the Gospel of Judas.

The Gospel of Judas must thus date back at least to the time when Irenaeus wrote these words, around 180 C.E.[17]

But since then, nobody had seen the text—until much more recently: "Hidden over eons in the Egyptian desert,"[18] the manuscript was discovered probably around 1978 "during a clandestine outing"[19] in the Al Minya province of Middle Egypt. "In fact, one version of the story goes, next to a shrouded skeleton a limestone box was found containing four codices," among them "the codex of Gnostic works which included *The Gospel of Judas*."[20] With the passage of time, the document disappeared into the underworld of antiquities dealers and ended up hidden away in a bank vault in a strip mall in Hicksville, New York. Sixteen years later, in 2000, Frieda Nussberger-Tchacos, a Zürich-based antiquities dealer, was able to negotiate the purchase that brought the manuscript to the attention of the academic community. She is quoted as having said that she felt "guided by Providence."[21] "Everything is predestined. … I was myself predestined by Judas to rehabilitate him."[22] By the time the papyrus got into the hands of the scholars who would translate it and prepare it for publication, it "was decaying into [nearly 1000[23]] fragments, its message on the verge of being lost forever."[24] Rodolphe Kasser, one of the translators, stated, "I have never seen [a papyrus] as degraded as this one."[25] He later "commented on the survival of the text: 'It's a miracle—this word is not an exaggeration.'"[26] What has survived is "the complete beginning and end of the Gospel, and much of the middle, but some portions have now been lost ...; about 10-15 percent is unrecoverable."[27]

In order to counter doubts as to the gospel's authenticity—doubts not infrequently voiced[28]—it might be worth mentioning that, as Simon Gathercole has pointed out, "[n]ot many manuscripts go through a process of scrutiny as that initiated by the Maecenas Foundation and National Geographic, the two organisations which have been responsible for the restoration and publication of the codex."[29] Carbon-dating gave the origin of the manuscript, generally assumed to be a Coptic translation of a lost Greek original, a date range of 220-340 C.E.[30] When the original text was written is unknown. However, Ehrman makes the confident claim that

> [t]his [is] not a Gospel written many centuries after the days of Jesus. It was written soon after the Gospels of the New Testament. They were all produced in the second half of the first century, from possibly 65 to 95 C.E. This one must have appeared fifty years later, in the mid-second century, if not before.[31]

Ehrman also notes that whereas the common way of designating the canonical gospels is "The Gospel *according* to Matthew," and so on, "[h]ere it is not the Gospel according to Judas—that is, his version of the Gospel story. It is the Gospel *of* Judas, that is, the good news about Judas himself."[32]

What is this "good news" and why is it so uniquely important? In *The Gospel of Judas* we find a complete reversal of how Judas has been traditionally seen: far from being the most despised and condemned of Jesus' disciples—in many European languages his very name is a synonym for "traitor"—here Judas is presented as the disciple Jesus feels closest to, the only one who truly and profoundly understands him. And it is for this reason that Jesus chooses Judas to play the most difficult role in fulfilling his destiny. "In contrast to the New Testament gospels, Judas Iscariot is presented as a thoroughly positive figure in the Gospel of Judas, a role model for all who wish to be disciples of Jesus."[33] But this is not all: religious scholars Elaine Pagels and Karen King of Princeton and Harvard, respectively, write,

> The Gospel of Judas turns upside down what we know about the other disciples—or what we thought we knew. This gospel does more than champion the disciple that all the rest regard as

> the villain; it also sharply condemns "the twelve." ... Here the
> very disciples revered by many Christians as leaders and founders
> of the movement appear as if it is they—not Judas—who are
> betraying Jesus.[34]

The reaction of the established Church seems to have been one of
doubt and reserve, as "[t]he very name of 'Judas' raises among Christians
an instinctive reaction of criticism and condemnation. ... The betrayal
of Judas remains ... a mystery."[35] In the orthodox tradition he continues
to be seen as being beyond redemption.[36] Specifically in response to
The Gospel of Judas, the English bishop Thomas Wright states that it
"tells us nothing about the real Jesus, or for that matter the real
Judas."[37] This is confirmed by the German Biblical scholar Prof. Thomas
Söding, member of the Papal Bible Commission, who "emphasizes that
the [Gospel of Judas] did not contain any words by Jesus that might
be regarded as authentic."[38] Rather cunningly, both authorities imply
that *they* either know "the real Jesus" or have words by him that are
authentic, though this is clearly not the case, as even the earliest gospels
were written many decades after his death.[39]

Of course, literary re-imaginings of the Judas myth preceded the
publication of *The Gospel of Judas*—Thomas De Quincey, Dorothy
Sayers, Luis Borges, Nikos Kazantzakis, and others come to mind. Most
recently, exactly a year after *The Gospel of Judas* was released, Jeffrey
Archer's *Gospel According to Judas*[40] was published, co-authored by the
theologian and papal advisor Father Francis Moloney. Although the
author(s) deny that their text has anything to do with *The Gospel of
Judas*, there are some striking parallels, and British theologian Justin
Thacker writes, "... [T]here is perhaps more of a connection between
the two 'gospels' than Moloney, in particular, would like to admit.
Admittedly, this connection is not so much between the text [*sic*] of
the two books. Rather, it exists, I would suggest, in a certain *gnosticising
tendency* that is evident in the recent work" (emphasis added).[41] The
book was launched at the Vatican and, in England, at Westminster
Cathedral,[42] and no less a person than Archbishop Desmond Tutu lent
his voice to the audio version.

Yet the newly rediscovered actual *Gospel of Judas* speaks with a
different authority, that of being older than all the aforementioned texts
by more than 1,800 years. In the language of the New Testament, this
truly is an instance in which "the stone which the builders rejected

the same is become the head of the corner."[43] In the context of his studies of alchemy, Jung was echoing this idea when he said that "the shadow can contain up to eighty percent pure gold," its essence is "pure gold."[44]

The Gospel of Judas purports, in its Introduction, to be "[t]he secret account of the revelation that Jesus spoke in conversation with Judas Iscariot during a week three days before he celebrated Passover."[45] In contrast to the canonical gospels, it "is not a Gospel about Jesus' entire life or ministry, in the way Matthew, Mark, Luke, and John are. It is about his last days on earth and the conversations he held then,"[46] which were intended to be "secret" and "a revelation" intended exclusively for Judas's ears.[47] At the Last Supper, when Jesus challenges the disciples to "stand before my face," none of them dare to do so except Judas Iscariot. "Judas [said] to him, 'I know who you are and where you have come from. You are from the immortal realm.'"[48] "Jesus [said] to him, 'Step away from the others and I shall tell you the mysteries of the kingdom. It is possible for you to reach it, but you will grieve a great deal.'"[49] And later he continues, "[Come], that I may teach you about [secrets] no person [has] ever seen. For there exists a great and boundless realm, whose extent no generation of angels has seen."[50] Jesus says to Judas, "But you will exceed all of them. For you will sacrifice the man that clothes me."[51] Ehrman interprets this to mean that "Judas is above all other humans. He has received Jesus' mysterious revelation and is about to do Jesus' mysterious will."[52] The gospel concludes with, "Look, you have been told everything. Lift up your eyes and look at the cloud and the light within it and the stars surrounding it. The star that leads the way is your star."[53] Of all the disciples, it is only Judas who, having received and understood these secret revelations, is chosen to be transfigured and glorified—just as Jesus himself was. The text continues with: "Judas lifted up his eyes and saw the luminous cloud, and he entered it."[54] Pagels and King comment, "Just as both Judas and Jesus enter the luminous cloud while living on earth, so those who follow them may ... know God here and now."[55] The text ends with Jesus' capture. From this new perspective, Judas's kissing Jesus to point him out to his captors can no longer be seen as the epitome of vile treachery. It now becomes an act of trust and loving intimacy between Jesus and his most faithful follower— Judas "is doing Jesus the greatest favour possible"[56]—and a fond farewell. From our traditional perspective, it is a moving example of the Jungian concept of "embracing the shadow." The text ends with the words, "The Gospel of Judas." The editors comment at this point:

> It is possible that the title means to suggest that this is the gospel, or good news, about Judas and the place of Judas in the tradition. What he accomplished, the text concludes, is not bad news but good news for Judas and for all who would come after Judas— and Jesus.[57]

Ehrman adds, "Only those who receive this 'secret revelation,' Judas and those like him, will come to realize how we came to be here, who Jesus really is, and how we can return to our heavenly home."[58] In a similar vein, Elaine Pagels is of the opinion that the Gnostic texts found earlier at Nag Hammadi as well as *The Gospel of Judas* "were probably not meant to be publicly read, they were meant to be advanced-level teaching."[59]

It is well worth mentioning that *The Gospel of Judas* on several occasions portrays Jesus as *laughing*—not something he is known to do in any of the canonical gospels, whereas depictions of the laughing Buddha are comparatively common! One is reminded of the German artist Joseph Beuys's rhetorical question, "Can you *really* conceive of a revolution without laughter?"[60] I see this as directly relevant to the theme of my contribution.

Herbert Krosney makes the point that in Judas's *Gospel*,

> Jesus appears to be a less suffering, more joyful figure than in the canonical gospels, and he has the capacity to laugh. ... [He] is not a tormented figure who will die in agony on the cross. Instead, he is a friendly and benevolent teacher with a sense of humor.[61]

A more serene and joyful Jesus is one of the "striking similarities"[62] between *The Gospel of Judas* and some of the Nag Hammadi texts. In one of these, *The Acts of John*, Jesus dances with his disciples and instructs them: "He who does not dance does not know what happens. To the Universe belongs the dancer. Amen."[63] This has been celebrated more recently in Sydney Carter's lyrics for "Lord of the Dance," which end with:

> I am the Life that'll never, never die!
> I'll live in you if you'll live in Me—
> I am the Lord of the Dance, said He![64]

We may well ask ourselves at this point what the history of Christianity might have looked like if the embrace and kiss of friendship from *The Gospel of Judas* had become the emblem of Christianity instead of the cross, an instrument of torturous execution, a symbol of a slow and lonely sacrificial death. With those connotations, the cross is clearly non-relational. But Christ's embracing Judas, who thus far has been perceived as "evil incarnate,"[65] redeems the symbol of the cross. If we were to replace the pre-eminent traditional Christian symbol, the cross, with that of the loving embrace, might we find in *The Gospel of Judas* an image on which to construct a new Christian paradigm for the new millennium, one that is relational—as well as truly healing for the very same reason?[66]

This new paradigm would also call into question the central importance traditionally given to suffering as the *sine qua non* both of redemption, in the Christian religion, and, parallel to this, of individuation in Jungian psychology. Gathercole goes so far as to deplore the "lack of suffering"[67] in *The Gospel of Judas* on the grounds that "closely connected to the New Testament themes of Jesus' embodied incarnation and his love is *the importance of suffering*" (emphasis added).[68] And again: "The New Testament is full of this language *celebrating* the coming of Jesus and *his suffering* ..." (emphasis added)[69;] "... [suffering is] considered to be integral to Christian discipleship."[70] For that kind of understanding of the Christian message, the cross is an apt symbol indeed.

Correspondingly, Frieda Fordham writes of individuation as "a state which cannot be reached without suffering."[71] This echoes the passion of Christ, which in the Jungian paradigm is seen as archetypal. In a similar vein, over-identification with the archetype of the Wounded Healer may easily degenerate into a masochistic romanticization and glorification of one's own suffering and pain.[72] The analyst, who, in identification with the centaur Chiron, has resigned himself or herself to suffering from an incurable wound, will actually no longer be able to bring deep healing to the patient.

Pagels and King write that "many of Jesus' followers would come to believe that suffering was required for salvation, and these understood their own suffering as a sacrifice to God, an imitation of the sacrificial death of Christ."[73] Yet, very explicitly, the Jesus of *The Gospel of Judas*, commands his disciples to "Stop sac[rificing] ...."[74] In a central passage of their commentary, Pagels and King state,

Jesus rebukes the "twelve" for making such a mistake— a fatal one .... What was wrong with "the twelve" was that they ... mistakenly imagined that "their God" required sacrifice .... Even when they worship their God, they "celebrate" their Eucharist by re-enacting a death—the crucifixion seen as sacrifice. When Jesus laughs at their worship, instead of asking him why or considering that they might make a mistake, they angrily blaspheme in his face. Thus their own angry violence mirrors that of "their God." ... They wrongly think that God requires suffering and sacrifice.[75]

And elsewhere they write:

[T]he author of *The Gospel of Judas* not only denies that God desires such sacrifice, he also suggests that the practical effect of such views is hideous. It makes people complicit in murder.[76]

The Gospel of Judas restores to us one of the voices of dissent, a call for religion to renounce violence as God's will and purpose for humanity.[77]

Pagels and King clearly differentiate this kind of sacrifice from the one Jesus speaks of when he asks Judas to "sacrifice the man that clothes me."[78] This sacrifice is to "help him demonstrate to his followers how, when they step beyond the limits of earthly existence, they, like Jesus, may step into the infinite—into God."[79]

Certain Gnostic groups in fact doubted that Jesus actually died on the cross.[80] In her study of the Nag Hammadi texts, Elaine Pagels quotes from various sources that have him say, "I have suffered none of the things which they will say of me."[81] The belief was that someone else was crucified in his place: "He whom you saw being glad and laughing *above* the cross is the Living Jesus" (emphasis added).[82] "I was rejoicing in the height over their error ... And I was laughing at their ignorance."[83]

Jesus' command, "Physician heal thyself,"[84] and the line from the Persian poet Hafez (writing some 700 years ago), "The true kingdom comes to you without any breaking of bones,"[85] may be considered important sobering cautions against an idealization of suffering as both depressive and depressing resistance to healing.

In the traditional paradigms—both Christian and Jungian— suffering and growth are seen as inextricably linked. This coupling results in a mode of being that is centered on pathology and the negative.

However, the centrality of suffering is now being questioned by some post-post-Jungians. Birgit Heuer, for example, writes:

> I wonder what a clinical paradigm might be like that, symbolically speaking, moved from darkness into light, without losing awareness of the darkness.[86]

> Generally speaking, quantum reality suggests a clinical paradigm which would be guided by an underlying fundamentally positive outlook similar to views suggested by faith and particularly by mystical experience or gnosticism.[87]

> … [C]linical change then might also relate to a capacity to unlearn suffering and tolerate and learn reality in the form of innate, but individually specific, goodness.[88]

In the early centuries of the Christian Era ideas like these could not survive: those who propounded them were at best marginalized, at worst persecuted as heretics. But what if, after a peak of destructiveness in the past century (which, significantly, also gave birth to and shaped analysis), the time has indeed come to reconsider these ideas and fill them with new life appropriate to our times? What if we ascribed a synchronistic significance to the fact that these ideas, buried for nearly 2,000 years, are suddenly re-entering our awareness at this turning point on the threshold of the third millennium? In clinical terms, this would usher in a shift in our basic paradigm from a focus on pathology to one on "sanatology,"[89] as Birgit Heuer has been calling the post-postmodern—and post-post-Jungian—paradigm, which focuses on healing and which she has introduced to the Jungian discourse. In religious terms, this could be seen as part of the long-awaited Second Coming of Christ.

The concept of a "Christianity without the Cross," as it were, is actually less wayward than it may seem at first glance. After centuries of a Christendom dominated by the Cross, we may, understandably, find the idea rather unusual today. But this has not always been the case. The earliest Christian communities gathered for safety in the catacombs of Rome, which form a vast labyrinth of underground passageways right underneath the dome of St. Peter's and other areas of the city. Also used as burial places, the catacombs constitute in a very literal sense the foundation of the Christian Church as we know it today. The many miles of underground passages housed the skeletons of thousands of Christians and the walls were covered with a large number of frescoes, which contain the very earliest known representations of Jesus Christ. In a recent television documentary on the catacombs of Rome by Thomas Schaefer, Prof. Fabrizio Bisconti, a member of the Papal Commission for Christian Archaeology in Rome, makes the interesting observation that

> [n]owhere in the catacombs do we have a depiction of the crucifixion, because one thought much more of the moment of resurrection, the final moment, paradise. All frescoes in the catacombs correspond to paradisiacal, serene images full of flowers, people in prayer, shepherds, and fishermen.[90]

"Christ is portrayed as a young man, as healer, as youthful philosopher. The passion is not being illustrated at this time."[91] In the same documentary, Prof. Hugo Brandenburg, who has researched the catacombs for several decades, points out that

> ... the earliest known depictions of the crucifixion are from the early 5th century. ... But even there, Christ, albeit on the cross, seems more to be lying on it. ... He does not appear to be suffering. At that time, that was not seen as being of particular importance.[92]

> It is only since the Middle Ages that the passion of Christ gains center stage. From now on he is mostly depicted in his role as martyr ... in direct contrast to the early beginnings, when Jesus Christ was portrayed as a philosopher filled with the joy of life.[93]

In concluding the documentary, Schaefer asks rhetorically, "Was the Christian faith a very different one then?"[94]

Thus, the central message of this newly discovered *Gospel of Judas*, its truly "good news," is a very explicit condemnation of violence in any form and a rejection of suffering as a means towards salvation. *The Gospel of Judas* can be seen as one that genuinely and unequivocally promotes love and peace. How are we to understand the collective significance and meaning of the rediscovery of this gospel in our time, at the very beginning of the new millennium?

POTENTIAL FOR PEACE?

We can create such a world as the world has never seen before: a world distinguished by no longer knowing of war, nor of going hungry, and that worldwide. That is our historical potential.

—Rudi Dutsche, 1968[95]

After two millennia of keeping Jesus and Judas apart as the polar opposites of light and dark, we are suddenly presented in *The Gospel of Judas* with the mystery of their union, a union that Jung termed *mysterium coniunctionis*. In this union, the opposites form the same wholeness that is, for example, portrayed in the yin/yang symbol of the East in which light and shadow embrace. "Judas was always used to represent evil," says the theologian Aaron Saari. "He is the scapegoat."[96] In what has been called the "Scapegoat Complex,"[97] unwanted shadow aspects of the individual are projected onto a shadow-carrier, originally literally a goat that was then ritually sent into the desert to perish.[98] It is the psychological mechanism whereby we "behold the mote" in our brother's eye, but miss "the beam" in our own.[99] There is no conflict, no war—individually or collectively—without such shadow projection, a process in which the other is demonized in unconscious acting out. As Eckhart Tolle writes, "violence would be impossible without deep unconsciousness."[100] Hitler is reported to have replied, when asked in 1939,

> whether the removal of Jews from Germany would rid the world of his No. 1 enemy, "We would have to invent them; one needs a visible enemy, one in plain sight. The Jew is always within us, but it is simpler to fight him in bodily form than as an invisible evil."[101]

It is almost incredible that Hitler, at least at the moment when he said this, seems to have been aware of an external splitting that reflects an internal one. The solution to such splitting lies in withdrawing the projection and thus retrieving the projected negative content into oneself. I understand this as being clearly implied in the Biblical challenge about beholding the mote in our brother's eye. Splitting and projecting afford us the delusion of superiority, as is seen, for example, in the extreme racism of Nazi Germany and the conviction of belonging to "the Master-Race." I say "delusion" because this way of trying to heal the narcissistic wound of feeling utterly insignificant not only does not work, but, on the contrary, actually constitutes further self-abuse: "Whenever I see someone else as guilty, I am reinforcing my own sense of guilt and unworthiness,"[102] the psychiatrist Gerald Jampolsky writes. As the collective example of Nazi Germany shows, this can become a vicious circle that may well spiral into ever more darkly depraved depths. Jampolsky expands on this theme as follows:

> Attacking always stems from fear and guilt. No one attacks unless he first feels threatened and believes that through attack he can demonstrate his own strength, at the expense of another's vulnerability. ... Instead of seeing others as attacking us, we can see them as fearful.[103]

As the object of Christian projections, "in the Middle Ages Judas became the prototypical 'Jew'— a greedy, thieving, demon-driven Christ-killer."[104] Saari traces one of the roots of anti-Semitism to the linguistic convention of regarding "the name Judas as synonymous with or equal to 'Jewish.'"[105] Pagels corroborates this, noting that "Judas can also mean 'Jew.'"[106] The German word for Jew, *Jude,* is almost identical to Judas. (Actually, the name "Judah" means "praise"!) Gathercole, too, notes the connection between Judas's name and the word "Jew," and devotes a section of his book to the question, "Is Judas the Stereotype of the Evil Jew?"[107] He quotes the Swiss theologian Karl Barth, who wrote in 1957 about Judas: "Obviously he does not bear his name for nothing. Within the apostolic group—and this shows us what is meant by the uncleanness of the feet of all the apostles—he obviously represents the Jews."[108] Saari adds his voice to the chorus with this comment:

> Jesus and the other eleven disciples become Christians, ... and Judas remains the only Jew. When he becomes associated with the Jewish people, we see an unbelievable rise in anti-Jewish violence. Part of this is owed to the idea that Jews are Christ-killers or God-killers.[109]

Thus, "[t] the portrait of Judas in the New Testament may not have directly, but indirectly fed into the poisonous stream that led to the Holocaust."[110]

What is called for, at the current turning point of radical change, is nothing less than a surrendering of that very delusion, a giving up of that "power over others" that, in Tolle's words, "is weakness disguised as strength."[111] I am reminded of a piece of London graffiti from the mid-1970s that declared: "POWER IS LOVE GONE BAD!" What is required in order to reverse this state of affairs is a rediscovery of love. I am speaking here of healing through love—as Freud did over 100 years ago, when he wrote to Jung, "Essentially, one might say, the cure is effected by love."[112] As a further illustration of that mysterious, ineffable turning point of change, we might also imagine, drawing upon another Biblical story, that pivotal moment in which the prodigal son decides to turn around in his wanderings and go back home to bring about a reconciliation with his father by kneeling in humility before him, as in Rembrandt's moving painting.

Jampolsky seems to be aiming for a similar pivotal turning point of inner change when, in his "Mini Course For Healing Relationships And Bringing About Peace of Mind,"[113] he offers the following suggestion for meditation/contemplation:

> *Do I want to experience peace or do I want to experience conflict?*
>
> If I want peace, I will be concerned only about giving; if I want conflict, I will be concerned with trying to get something or evaluating why I am not getting it.
>
> Ask yourself the following question about every communication:
>
> *Is this communication loving to the other person and to myself?*[114]

The aforementioned Otto Gross, the first psychoanalyst to link analysis with spirituality and the radical political transformation of society, spoke of this process in terms of the necessity to replace "the will to power" with "the will to relating."[115] He conceived of this both intrapersonally as well as interpersonally, individually as well as collectively. Gross understood this transformational step from "the will to power" to "the will to relating" as "the highest essential goal of revolutions."[116] For him relationship included a spiritual dimension; he spoke of it in spiritual terms as numinous, as "the holy third."[117] These ideas can be understood as the earliest beginnings of relational analysis, of intersubjectivity.[118] Collectively, in more modern terms, it is the "Make Love, Not War!" of the 1960s, the idea of reconciliation. Important steps in the process of reconciliation are the withdrawing of projections and the act of apologizing, both of which form a basis on which forgiveness can come about. Our neurotic fear—from the perspective of traditional power relationships—tells us that admitting what we have done, implied in asking for forgiveness, may weaken us, seal our fate of defeat, whereas in actual fact it strengthens, raises, even ennobles us: "Through true forgiveness we can stop the endless recycling of guilt, and look upon ourselves and others with love."[119]

Among the examples that come to mind are the kneeling of the then-German Chancellor Willy Brandt at the memorial of the infamous Ghetto in Warsaw in December 1970, and of course the nationwide collective effort of the South African Truth and Reconciliation Commission in the 1990s. In Australia, likewise, after many decades of mutual antagonism, on February 13 last year the Australian Prime Minister "opened a new chapter in Australia's tortured relations with its indigenous peoples ... with a comprehensive and moving apology for past wrongs and a call for bipartisan action to improve the lives of Australia's Aborigines."[120]

At the International Congress for Analytical Psychology in Cape Town in 2007—the triennial gathering of Jungian analysts worldwide —Andrew Samuels suggested in a plenary session that the International Association for Analytical Psychology apologize to Black and colored people for the way they had been treated both theoretically as well as clinically in the past. Sadly, this appeal fell on deaf ears—there was not a single public reaction to it—and yet, I not just hope but trust that eventually it will be heard and will lead to the desired result.

We may be still many years away from a formal apology by the West to Islam for its defamation of Muslims in recent times.[121] And, yes, of course, to return to *The Gospel of Judas*, the publication of the text is not the same thing as a formal recognition of Judas's sainthood by the pope. (Incidentally, there is, as I just learned to my surprise, a St. Jude—a variant spelling of "Judas"—who is identified as either the Apostle Thaddeus, or Jude, the brother of James, or Jesus' brother Jude, the supposed writer of "The Epistle of Jude"; St. Jude is venerated in Catholicism as the patron saint of lost causes.[122]) It may also well be argued that with the *Assumptio,* Mary, on her way to heaven, had a shorter distance to travel, so to speak, since she was already highly venerated within the Church, something that can, as yet, certainly not be said for Judas. Yet, in the spring of 2005, one year before the publication of *The Gospel of Judas*, a work of art entitled "Requiem for a Friend, Judas Iskarioth" went on display at the Ursuline Church in

Linz, Austria (Hitler's hometown), as part of an art exhibition. The exhibit was accompanied by text calling for Judas to be canonized as a saint.[123] And in 2009, at the launch of *The Gospel According to Judas* at the Vatican, when Prof. Francis Moloney, co-author of the book and advisor to both the previous and the present pope, was asked by a reporter whether he believed Judas to be in hell, he responded by saying, "No, I am not saying that at all."[124] Can we understand these events as first steps in the direction of redeeming the evil personified by Judas, even a thawing towards forgiveness? Might the publication of *The Gospel of Judas* thus constitute an important stepping stone towards reconciliation and, ultimately, world peace, as a potential ripening that urgently needs to be realized, since there is "No Future Without Forgiveness"?[125]

CONCLUSION

I have applied a Jungian—as well as a Grossian—perspective to the contemporary event of the publication of the recently discovered *The Gospel of Judas*. I have described how this may be understood as an important milestone in the way we individually and collectively deal with shadow aspects that have hitherto been projected onto an enemy other, leading to separation and, ultimately, persecution and war. Healing this kind of splitting both intrapersonally as well as interpersonally requires a withdrawal of the shadow projection, and possibly a public act of apologizing in order to facilitate forgiveness on the route towards reconciliation and peaceful, loving relating as equals. I have linked this with cutting-edge developments in the area of intersubjectivity that seem to herald a paradigm shift of post-post-Jungian clinical theory and practice, and I have given some examples from the political sphere to illustrate what these steps might imply for the wider collective.

Some 40 years ago, Martin Luther King, Jr. wrote, "Far from being the pious injunction of a Utopian dreamer, the command to love one's enemy is an absolute necessity for our survival. ... [It] is the key to the solution of the problems of the world. Jesus is not an impractical idealist; he is a practical realist."[126] "We have to live together as brothers or perish as fools."[127]

Now, in the words of Nelson Mandela:

The time for healing the wounds has come. The moment to bridge the chasms that divide us has come. The time to build is upon us. … We know it well that none of us acting alone can achieve success. We must therefore act together … for the birth of a new world. … Let each know that for each the body, the mind and the soul have been freed to fulfil themselves.[128]

NOTES

1. Revelation 21:1.

2. Previous versions of this text were presented to the candidates of the Jungian Analytic Training for Qualified Psychotherapists of the Association of Jungian Analysts, London, March 16, 2008, Palm Sunday; to the students of the Training in Jungian Analytical Psychotherapy of the West Midlands Institute of Psychotherapy, Birmingham, June 28, 2008; at the IAAP-IAJS ETH Conference, "Contemporary Symbols of Personal, Cultural and National Identity," Zürich, July 3-5, 2008; to The Cambridge Jungian Circle, Cambridge, October 17, 2008; and to the Analytical Psychology Club, London, March 19, 2009.

3. Lisa Appignanesi, "All in the Mind," review of *Something to Tell You,* by Hanif Kureishi, *The Guardian,* February 16, 2008, p. 4.

4. C. G. Jung, "Psychological Types," *The Collected Works of C. G. Jung,* ed. Herbert Read, Michael Fordham and Gerhard Adler, trans. R. F. C. Hull, vol. 6 (London: Routledge & Kegan Paul, 1981), § 708. (Hereafter referred to as *CW* followed by volume number and page or paragraph number.)

5. Luke 2:14.

6. C. G. Jung, *Letters, Vol. 2: 1951-1961,* ed. Gerhard Adler and Aniela Jaffé, trans. R. F. C. Hull (London: Routledge & Kegan Paul, 1976), p. 137. (Hereafter abbreviated to *Letters 2.*)

7. C. G. Jung, *Letters, Vol. 1: 1906-1950,* ed. Gerhard Adler and Aniela Jaffé, trans. R. F. C. Hull (London: Routledge & Kegan Paul, 1973), p. 499. (Hereafter abbreviated to *Letters 1.*)

8. *Ibid.,* p. 567.

9. *Ibid.*

10. Jung, *Letters 2*, p. 231.

11. Gottfried Heuer, "The Sacral Revolution: The Synthesis of Analysis, Religion, and Radical Politics," *International Journal of Jungian Studies* 1, no. 1 (2009): 68-80.

12. Bart D. Ehrman, *The Lost Gospel of Judas Iscariot: A New Look at Betrayer and Betrayed* (Oxford, UK: Oxford University Press, 2006), p. 52.

13. I am grateful to my colleague Ruth Williams, London, for drawing my attention to this quotation.

14. Headline from *The Mail on Sunday*, March 12, 2006, quoted in Simon Gathercole, *The Gospel of Judas: Rewriting Early Christianity* (Oxford, UK: Oxford University Press, 2007), p. 1.

15. Gathercole.

16. Ehrman, p. 52.

17. Elaine Pagels and Karen L. King, *Reading Judas: The Controversial Message of the Ancient Gospel of Judas* (London: Penguin Books, 2007), p. xii. The quotation from Irenaeus of Lyons is found in *Against Heresies*, I.31.1, and can be accessed online at http://www.gnosis.org/library/advh1.htm.

18. Andrew Cockburn, "The Judas Gospel," *National Geographic Magazine*, May 2006, p. 81.

19. Rodolphe Kasser, "The Story of the Codex Tchacos and the Gospel of Judas," in *The Gospel of Judas—from Codex Tchacos*, ed. Rodolphe Kasser, Marvin Meyer, and Gregor Wurst (Washington, D.C.: National Geographic Society, 2006), p. 50.

20. Gathercole, p. 6.

21. In Herbert Krosney, *The Lost Gospel: The Quest for the Gospel of Judas Iscariot* (Washington, D.C.: National Geographic Society, 2006), p. 175.

22. In Cockburn, p. 95.

23. *The Lost Gospel of Judas*, TV documentary, directed by James Barratt (Washington, D.C.: National Geographic Society, 2006).

24. Cockburn, p. 81.

25. In Krosney, p. 231.

26. Gathercole, p. 17.

27. Ehrman, p. 71.

28. E.g., "'Judas-Evangelium': Verrat als Wille Gottes," n-tv.de, April 6, 2006, http://www.n-tv.de/653179.html (accessed August 25, 2008).

29. Gathercole, p. 8.

30. *Ibid.*

31. Ehrman, p. 65. But also note this further on: "[W]e don't have the original copies of any of these [Gospels of the New Testament], only copies made later—in most instances many centuries later" (p. 97).

32. *Ibid.*, pp. 97-98.

33. Marvin Meyer, "Introduction," in *The Gospel of Judas—from Codex Tchacos*, p. 9.

34. Pagels and King, p. 33.

35. Pope Benedict XVI, October 2006, quoted in Jeffrey Archer, "The Gospel According to Judas," 2009, http://www.jeffreyarcher. co.uk/gospel.htm (accessed April 19, 2009).

36. *The Secrets of the Twelve Disciples,* TV documentary, directed by David Batty (London: Carbon Media/Channel 4, 2008).

37. N. T. Wright, *Judas and the Gospel of Jesus: Have We Missed the Truth about Christianity?* (London: Society for Promoting Christian Knowledge, 2006), p. vi.

38. In "Judas-Evangelium."

39. Cf. n. 31, above.

40. Jeffrey Archer, *The Gospel According to Judas, by Benjamin Iscariot,* with Francis J. Moloney (London: Macmillan, 2007).

41. Justin Thacker, Fulcrum review of *The Gospel According to Judas by Benjamin Iscariot* by Jeffrey Archer, Fulcrum website, 2007, http:/ /www.fulcrum-anglican.org.uk/news/2007/20070508thacker.cfm ?doc=207, para. 6 (accessed April 19, 2009).

42. Catherine Bennett, "Jeffrey Archer Longs for Redemption: Was He Sent to Challenge the Forgiveness of the Church?", *The Guardian,* March 22, 2007, http://www.guardian.co.uk/commentisfree/2007/ mar/22/religion.comment (accessed April 19, 2009).

43. Matthew 21:42.

44. Quoted in Molly Tuby, *The Shadow*, Lecture No. 216 (London: The Guild of Pastoral Psychology, 1984), p. 13.

45. Kasser, Meyer, and Wurst, eds., *The Gospel of Judas—from Codex Tchacos*, p. 19.

46. Ehrman, p. 87.

47. *Gospel of Judas*, p. 19.

48. *Ibid.*, p. 22. Here and in all subsequent quotes from the text of *The Gospel of Judas*, the square brackets are from the translated text and are used by the editors to enclose words that they have inserted, either for clarification or to fill in gaps in the original manuscript.

49. *Ibid.*, p. 23.

50. *Ibid.*, p. 33.

51. *Ibid.*, p. 43.

52. Ehrman, p. 96.

53. *Gospel of Judas*, pp. 43-44.

54. *Ibid.*, p. 44.

55. Pagels and King, p. 90.

56. Ehrman, p. 97.

57. *Gospel of Judas*, p. 45, n. 151.

58. Ehrman, p. 95.

59. In *Lost Gospel of Judas* (TV).

60. Joseph Beuys, in *Beuys & Beuys: Der Jahrhundertkünstler zwischen Fettstuhl und sozialer Skulptur*, TV documentary, written and presented by Peter Schiering (Mainz: 3sat, Zweites Deutsches Fernsehen, 2006).

61. Krosney, pp. 278, 286.

62. Marvin Meyer in *Lost Gospel of Judas* (TV).

63. Quoted in Elaine Pagels, *The Gnostic Gospels* (New York: Vintage Books, 1981), p. 89.

64. Sydney Carter, "Lord of the Dance," 1963, Marc Gunn's Irish-Song-Lyrics.com, 2008, http://www.irish-song-lyrics.com/Lord_Of_The_Dance.shtml (accessed April 27, 2009). In the 1970s I photographed a fragment of a poster on a wall in New York, which proclaimed: "IF I CAN'T DANCE ... YOU CAN KEEP YOUR REVOLUTION."

65. *Lost Gospel of Judas* (TV).

66. I am grateful to my wife and colleague Birgit Heuer for contributing this particular idea in the course of our ongoing and continuing in-depth discussions.

67. Gathercole, p. 170.

68. *Ibid.*, p. 168.

69. *Ibid.*, p. 170.

70. *Ibid.*, p. 168.

71. Frieda Fordham, *An Introduction to Jung's Psychology* (Harmondsworth, UK: Penguin Books, 1953), p. 77.

72. We may consider here that, correspondingly, this attitude has sadly also dominated almost the entire field of the arts throughout the 20th century.

73. Pagels and King, p. 53.

74. *Gospel of Judas*, p. 28.

75. Pagels and King, pp. 65-66.

76. *Ibid.*, p. 74.

77. *Ibid.*, p. xxiii.

78. *Gospel of Judas*, p. 43.

79. Pagels and King, p. 75.

80. *Die Evangelien der Ketzer,* TV documentary, hosted by J. P. Behrendt (Berlin: Atlantis Plus, commissioned by Zweites Deutsches Fernsehen, 2008).

81. "Acts of John," in Pagels, pp. 89-90.

82. "Apocalypse of Peter," in Pagels, p. 87.

83. "Second Treatise of the Great Seth," in Pagels.

84. Luke 4:23.

85. Hafez, *The Angels Knocking on the Tavern Door: Thirty Poems of Hafez*, trans. Robert Bly and Leonard Lewisohn (New York: HarperCollins, 2008), p. 9.

86. Birgit Heuer, "Clinical Paradigm as Analytic Third: Reflections on a Century of Analysis and an Emergent Paradigm for the New Millennium," in *Contemporary Jungian Clinical Practice*, ed. Elphis Christopher and Hester McFarland Solomon (London: Karnac Books, 2003), p. 334.

87. Birgit Heuer, "Discourse of Illness or Discourse of Health: Towards a Paradigm Shift in Post-Jungian Therapy and Thought," in *Dreaming the Myth Onwards: New Directions in Jungian Therapy and Thought*, ed. Lucy Huskinson (Hove: Routledge, 2008), p. 186.

88. *Ibid.*, p. 187.

89. Heuer, "Discourse"; Birgit Heuer, "On Clinical Theory, Zero-Point Field Theory, and Mysticism: Towards Sanatology—A Clinical Theory of Health and Healing." (Ph.D. thesis, University of Essex and the Centre for Psychoanalytic Studies, Colchester, in progress).

90. In *In den Katakomben von Rom: Auf den Spuren der frühen Christen*, TV documentary, written and presented by Thomas Schaefer (Hamburg: Spiegel TV, 2008).

91. *Ibid.*

92. *Ibid.*

93. *Ibid.*

94. *Ibid.*

95. In *1968—Aus dem Bilderbuch einer Revolte: Eine Zeitcollage*, TV documentary, written and presented by Joachin Faulstich and Georg M. Hafner (Frankfurt am Main: Hessischer Runkdunk, 1993).

96. In *Secrets of the Twelve.*

97. Sylvia Brinton Perera, *The Scapegoat Complex: Toward a Mythology of Shadow and Guilt* (Toronto, Canada: Inner City Books, 1986).

98. Leviticus 16:21-22.

99. Matthew 7:3.

100. Eckhart Tolle, *The Power of Now: A Guide to Spiritual Enlightenment* (Novato, CA: New World Library, 1999), p. 61.

101. Gertrud Hardtmann, "The Shadows of the Past," in *Generations of the Holocaust*, ed. Martin S. Bergmann and Milton E. Jucovy (New York: Basic Books, 1982), p. 244.

102. Gerald G. Jampolsky, *Mini Course for Healing Relationships and Bringing about Peace of Mind* (Tiburon, CA: Foundation for Inner Peace, 1979), n.p.

103. *Ibid.*

104. Ehrman, p. 10. Jung also speaks of "Judas who must have been a very interesting object of hatred to the Christians". See C.G. Jung, *Collected Works 18*, § 1561. I am grateful to Evangeline Rand for pointing out this quote to me.

105. In *Secrets of the Twelve*.

106. Pagels in *Lost Gospel of Judas* (TV).

107. Gathercole, p. 41.

108. Quoted in Gathercole, p. 42.

109. In *Secrets of the Twelve*.

110. *Lost Gospel of Judas* (TV).

111. Tolle, p. 36.

112. Sigmund Freud and C. G. Jung, *The Freud/Jung Letters*, ed. William McGuire, trans. Raph Manheim and R. F. C. Hull (London: Hogarth Press and Routledge & Kegan Paul, 1974), pp. 12-13.

113. Jampolsky.

114. *Ibid.*, n.p.

115. Otto Gross, "Zur funktionellen Geistesbilduing des Revolutionärs," *Räte-Zeitung: Erste Zeitung der Hand-und Kopfarbeiterräte Deutschlands* 1, no. 52 suppl. (1919); cf. Gottfried Heuer, "Jung's Twin Brother: Otto Gross and Carl Gustav Jung," *The Journal of Analytical Psychology* 46, no. 4 (2001): 662-663.

116. *Ibid.*

117. Otto Gross, "Notiz über Beziehung," *Die Aktion* 3, no. 51 (1913): 1118; cf. Gottfried Heuer, "'The Sacredness of Love,' or

'Relationship as Third, as Religion': Otto Gross's Concept of Relating Today," talk given at the "Sexual Revolutions" symposium, Freud Museum, London, January 30-31, 2009.

118. Gottfried Heuer, "The Birth of Intersubjectivity: Otto Gross—Life, Work, and Impact on the Development of Psychoanalytic Theory and Clinical Practice," talk given at the Freud Museum, London, January 13, 2009.

119. Jampolsky.

120. Tim Johnston, "Australia Says 'Sorry' to Aborigines for Mistreatment," *The New York Times*, February 13, 2008, http://www.nytimes.com/2008/02/13/world/asia/13aborigine.html (accessed March 2, 2008).

121. Nevertheless, at the time of this contribution being finalized for publication, President Obama is to deliver "his anticipated appeal for reconciliation between the Muslim world and the west early next month [in Cairo], after more than 10 years of escalating tension and violence" (Ewen McAskill, "Obama's Plea for Reconciliation," *The Guardian,* May 9, 2009, p. 15).

122. I am grateful to my friend and colleague Evangeline Rand, Edmonton, Alberta, Canada for mentioning this saint to mc. (Rand, personal communication, email April 30, 2009, IAJS Discussion List, iajsdiscussion@iajsdiscussionlist.org), and also to Michael Mendis at *Spring* not only for additional information but also for his congenial, sensitive, and understanding copyediting of my text.

123. Catholic Church Conservation Blog, "Shrine to Judas in the Town of Linz, Austria," posted March 22, 2005, http://cathcon.blogspot.com/2005/03/shrine-to-judas-in-town-of-linz.html (accessed April 21, 2009).

124. John Hooper, "Guilty or Not Guilty? Jeffrey Archer's Book about Judas Raises a Serious Theological Issue," *The Guardian*, March 23, 2007, http://www.guardian.co.uk/commentisfree/2007/mar/23/theiscariotenigma (accessed April 19, 2009).

125. Desmond Tutu, *No Future Without Forgiveness* (London: Rider Books, 1999).

126. Martin Luther King, Jr., *Strength to Love* (London: Fontana, 1969), p. 47-48.

127. Martin Luther King, Jr., Handwritten draft of "Remaining Awake Through a Great Revolution," in *The Papers of Martin Luther*

King, Jr., Volume II: Rediscovering Precious Values, July 1951 - November 1955 (Berkeley, CA: University of California Press, 1994), p. 224.

128. Nelson Mandela, "Statement of the President of the African National Congress Nelson Rolihlahla Mandela at His Inauguration as President of the Democratic Republic of South Africa," Union Buildings, Pretoria, May 10, 1994, http://www.anc.org.za/ancdocs/history/mandela/1994/inaugpta.html (accessed 2006).

AN END TO EVIL*

Gottfried Heuer

Apparently,
there'd been a scandal
in the media before:
Madame Tussaud's, Berlin,
was to put on show

a waxen Adolf Hitler:
him
back in his bunker
—albeit just a replica—
right in *Berlin*?!

This was to be presented,
first time,
to the public
on the very day, and
the very time of day,
that I, in Zürich,
some 5 / 600 miles southwest,
—as the crow flies—
was to present a talk

on Judas's Gospel,
newly published,
where he, the "vile traitor,"
"epitome of evil,"
is shown as the disciple
who—so Jesus says—
has best understood
the teachings of our Lord
and hence is chosen by Him
to help fulfill His destiny:
an altogether
new perspective,
an embracing
of the shadow
that here proves to be
the carrier of light.

Whilst I begin to speak in Zürich,
at Madame Tussaud's, Berlin,
just minutes after
opening time,

---

* From "Pilgrimage to Non-violence: We Must Live Together as Brothers or Perish as Fools!"—A Cycle of Poems in Celebration of the 80th Anniversary of the Birth of Martin Luther King, Jr. (1929 - 1968)

a man,
pushing aside two guards,
storms into
the reconstructed bunker,
and, calling out,
"Nie wieder Krieg!"
—Never again war!—
knocks the head
off Hitler's effigy!—
Even the police report,
so the papers quote,
speaks of
"Attentat geglückt!"
—Assassination complete—but
not only that,
the German verb
contains the word
for luck: "*Glück*"!

Now, why
does that delight me
deeply—
so that I,
in fact,
feel close to tears?

The whole point
of my talk
was Judas's redemption
in this newly found
yet ancient text,
that moves me
just as deeply.
Am I just glad

to have found Hitler
as a welcome substitute,
exchanging one
scapegoat for another?

Or is it possible
that *both* events,
my talk and
the "assassination,"
aimed to put
an end to evil,
each in its own way?

Judas's elevation
from the stone
rejected by the builders
to become
the cornerstone
ends his existence
as a scapegoat.

Might Hitler's "assassination"
be a way that one of us
in *symbolic* form,
for all Germans,
is finally saying
a clear "No!"
to what Hitler stood for,
as bloody scapegoater
par excellence—
thus, too,
yet in a diff'rent way,
proclaiming publicly
an end to evil?

Obama and Icarus: Political Heroism, "Newspaper Mythology," and the Economic Crisis of 2008

MICHAEL VANNOY ADAMS

From Journalism to Jungian Analysis

A lthough I am now a Jungian analyst, I once aspired to become a journalist. So, too, did another Jungian analyst, James Hillman. Hillman says that as a young man he "thought the way to take on wrongs was through politics and journalism." That, he says, was "where my ambition was."[1] Those were exactly my thoughts at that time in my life. My ambition was to become a political journalist and to right wrongs by writing about them.

If I were to write a memoir of that period, the title might be *A Portrait of the Young Man as a Journalist*. I was the editor of my high school newspaper, and then I was the editor of my university newspaper. As an undergraduate student, I majored in journalism. In the summer of 1968, I was an intern on the *Washington Post*. That was before Watergate and Deep Throat but just after the assassinations of Martin

Michael Vannoy Adams is a Jungian analyst in New York City. He is a clinical associate professor at the New York University Postdoctoral Program in Psychotherapy and Psychoanalysis. He is also a faculty member at the Jungian Psychoanalytic Association and the New School, where he was previously associate provost. He is the author of three books: *The Fantasy Principle: Psychoanalysis of the Imagination*, *The Mythological Unconscious*, and *The Multicultural Imagination: "Race," Color, and the Unconscious*.

Luther King, Jr., and Robert Kennedy. With the other interns, I covered
the Poor People's Campaign of Ralph David Abernathy and the Southern
Christian Leadership Conference. I also covered a racial murder trial (a
white man had shot a black boy to death). Larry L. King—the magazine
writer, novelist, and playwright (the Broadway musical *The Best Little
Whorehouse in Texas*)—took me for a "nine-hour lunch" of Scotch, Bloody
Marys, and beer at four different bars on Capitol Hill. King describes
me as eventually getting "real silent" and then, after the usual catharsis,
becoming "pale but lucid."[2] For me, that was a memorable initiation
into one of the most venerable traditions of journalism. In New York,
I visited Willie Morris, the editor of *Harper's,* who on a previous occasion
had presented me with a copy of *North Toward Home* and had inscribed
it, "From one editor to another." That was the period of the "New
Journalism" and Tom Wolfe, when journalists were not only reporters
of events but also participants in those events—and when Morris
published such writers as Norman Mailer. In the summer of 1969, I
was an intern on the *Atlanta Constitution.* I covered the Atlanta Pop
Festival (not quite Woodstock but still quite a sex, drugs, and rock-and-
roll experience) and civil rights protests against the anti-integration
tactics of Lester Maddox. In 1970, I was a reporter on the *Texas Observer.*
I covered the case of a black political activist in prison for the ostensible
sale of a single marijuana cigarette, and I covered the provision of legal
aid to conscientious objectors against the Vietnam War.[3]

Soon, however, I realized that journalism was not for me. Events,
especially current events, felt superficial. What appealed to me were
ideas, which felt deep. Hillman says that he eventually realized that,
for him, journalistic life was unsatisfying and that he "was dying for
intellectual life."[4] That was precisely what I, too, realized. As a graduate
student, I pursued an interdisciplinary education in the humanities
and social sciences. I studied intellectual and cultural history, political
and economic history, the history of ideas, literature, the philosophy
of science, and psychology. The very first course that I took as a graduate
student was "Freud in America," a seminar on the intellectual and
cultural history of psychoanalysis in America.

I became a professor, which I continue to be, and eventually I
became a Jungian analyst. Psychoanalysis is a "depth psychology," or
psychology of the unconscious, and the ideas of Freud and Jung felt
(and still feel) deep to me. What feels most profound to me about

psychoanalysis—and especially Jungian analysis—is the idea that the deepest dimension of the unconscious is mythological.

As a Jungian analyst, I now feel that events, even current events, need not be superficial but can be just as profound as any ideas. From a psychoanalytic perspective, what is decisive is the experience of an event. Ultimately, what most deepens an event is an experience of the unconscious mythological dimension of that event. In this respect, an important recent event was the 2008 American presidential election. The election of Barack Obama was, in the experience of all Americans, an event of mythological proportions.

POLITICIANS AS HEROES

Most journalists do not appreciate the relevance of mythology for current events. Maureen Dowd of the *New York Times* is one of the few who do. In a sense, Dowd is a "Jungian" journalist. For several years, she has written articles and columns on political heroism. They are examples of what Jung calls "newspaper mythology."[5]

Betty Sue Flowers says that "we must to learn to read the news mythologically."[6] Dowd writes the news mythologically. In effect, she applies to politicians the Jungian method of "amplification," which is a comparative method. When Jungian analysts amplify an image from the unconscious (for example, from a dream), they compare it to the same or similar images from other sources (for example, from myths). When Dowd practices newspaper mythology, she compares modern politicians to ancient heroes in order to identify similarities between them. (She also contrasts them in order to identify differences, often for satirical purposes.)

In an article during the 1992 American presidential election between Bill Clinton and George H. W. Bush, Dowd mentioned *The Hero with a Thousand Faces*. "The arc of a political campaign," she said, "traces the standard pattern of mythological adventure, as described by Joseph Campbell." (This standard pattern is, of course, an example of what Jung means by an archetype. In this instance, the archetype is what Jung calls the "hero myth.") The politician, Dowd said, has to become a dragon-slaying or giant-slaying hero. "One important campaign ritual," she said, "comes when the candidate assures the voters that he has completed the 'hero-task,' as it is called by myth experts, that he has slain the dragon or the giant."[7]

In a column in 2001, Dowd noted that "Jackie Kennedy understood the power of myth." The allusion was to the television series "Joseph Campbell and The Power of Myth." (Jacqueline Kennedy Onassis was the editor who persuaded Doubleday to publish the book *The Power of Myth*.) Dowd recounted that after the assassination of John Kennedy, Jackie Kennedy encouraged Robert Kennedy to read *The Greek Way* by Edith Hamilton. Dowd said that "the great families of Greek mythology" transfixed Robert Kennedy. "He recognized the hubris of the house of Atreus," she said, "with doom seeping down through the generations." In effect, the Kennedy family was a contemporary house of Atreus, which Hamilton described as "an ill-fated house." Dowd quoted Hamilton: "A curse seemed to hang over the family, making men sin in spite of themselves and bringing suffering and death down upon the innocent as well as the guilty." She also quoted Evan Thomas, author of a biography of Robert Kennedy. Thomas applied another myth to the Kennedy family—the myth of Icarus. "The Kennedys," he said, "flew too close to the sun."[8]

During the 2008 American presidential election, Dowd criticized Obama from a mythological perspective. Dowd implied that he needed a new, mythological name—Barack "Jason" Obama. Seeking the Oval Office, she said, was tantamount to seeking the golden fleece. (Previously, William Proxmire employed the myth of Jason for political purposes. Annually, from 1975 to 1988, Proxmire bestowed the "Golden Fleece Awards" on federal agencies that funded grants with tax money, or "gold," for frivolous research projects that "fleeced" the American public.) Obama was not, Dowd declared, sufficiently attentive to the mythological dimension of politics:

> The Illinois senator doesn't pay attention to the mythic nature of campaigns, but if he did, he would recognize the narrative of the classic hero myth: The young hero ventures out on an adventure to seek a golden fleece or an Oval Office; he has to kill monsters and face hurdles before he returns home, knocks off his father and assumes the throne.

The immediate context for this criticism was the controversial comments of Jeremiah Wright, the African-American minister of the church that Obama attended in Chicago. Obama denounced those remarks and ultimately renounced Wright. This denunciation and renunciation, Dowd said, was for Obama "a painful form of political patricide."[9] In effect, as I have previously noted, Obama became a monster-slaying hero, or at least a minister-slaying hero[10]—or, as Dowd emphasized, a father-slaying hero.

In another column, Dowd said that Obama needed to become a Herculean hero. She said that "he has to swiftly and convincingly perform the political equivalent of the Labors of Hercules." In contrast to Hercules, who had to perform twelve labors, Dowd said that Obama had to perform four labors. The first labor was the most formidable. Dowd implied that George W. Bush had left such a pile of political manure (the euphemism that Harry Truman famously employed) that even a flood would not immediately wash away the mess. "Cleaning the Augean stables in a single day," she said, "seems like a cinch compared with navigating the complexities of Afghanistan, Iraq, Israel, Palestine and Jordan." The second labor that Obama had to perform was to handle Hillary Clinton. "Instead of obtaining the girdle of the Amazon warrior queen Hippolyte," Dowd said, "Obama has to overcome the hurdle of the Amazon warrior queen Hillary." The third labor that Obama had to perform was to handle Bill Clinton, that Arkansas razorback who, Dowd implied, was a real swine. "Obama must capture his own equivalent of the Erymanthian Boar," she said, and decide whether he "will be help or hindrance, or both," and "how to use him, if at all." The fourth and final labor that Obama had to perform, Dowd said, "should be the simplest for him, nailing his Denver convention speech." It would be, she said: "Not half as hard as getting past that 100-headed dragon to steal the Apples of the Hesperides."[11]

In yet another column, Dowd mentioned a comedy sketch that Jon Stewart presented on "The Daily Show." She noted that Stewart combined allusions to Jason and the Argonauts, the dragon-slaying hero, and Odysseus. "Jon Stewart was poking fun at the grandiosity of the 'Obama Quest' and the 'Obamanauts,'" she said. "He showed film clips of 'our hero' in chain mail fighting off dragons and a Cyclops in his crusade to come home and rule over Dreamerica." She then mentioned a conversation that she had with Obama as he returned to America from a trip to Europe:

> By happenstance, on O-Force One I raised the matter of quests and Cyclops with the candidate. Having read that he had left the trail in early June to go back to Chicago and see his daughter Malia perform in "The Odyssey" for theater class, I wondered if

that rang any bells on this trip? The hero on a foreign journey, battling through obstacles to get back home, where more trouble would wait?

"The whole sort of siren thing, the Cyclops, that's interesting," he said.[12]

What, exactly, was interesting to Obama about the siren thing and the Cyclops (and whether Obama identified himself in any respect with Odysseus) Dowd did not say.

"Obama," Dowd declared, "does not see himself in terms of Greek myth." She did, however, acknowledge that Obama informed Jeff Zeleny, a reporter for the *New York Times*, that "he knew the risks of 'flying too close to the sun.'" The allusion, of course, was to the myth of Icarus. When Obama returned to America from the trip to Europe, more trouble did wait—the economic crisis of 2008. "Sure enough," Dowd said, "'our hero' came home to a passel of economic troubles in Dreamerica, rushing to talk to Bernanke & Paulson" (Ben S. Bernanke, Chairman of the Federal Reserve Board, and Henry M. Paulson, Jr., Secretary of the Treasury). To deal effectively with the economic crisis, she implied, Obama should see himself in terms of the myth of Odysseus rather than the myth of Icarus. "Odysseus's heroic trait," Dowd emphasized, "is his cunning intelligence." In contrast, Icarus's heroic trait (if, in fact, it is heroic at all) is his soaring ambition—his aspiration to fly close to the sun. Much more than soaring ambition, cunning intelligence is a trait that it will be necessary for Obama to possess in abundance, Dowd said, if he is to become a political hero. She said that "even flying close to the sun Obama will need all that he can muster."[13]

THE ICARUS MYTH

Obama is one president who has had personal exposure to the myths of various cultures. In an article that describes how Obama became a Christian, Lisa Miller and Richard Wolffe note that Obama's mother, Ann, although an agnostic, had a special interest in mythology. "One of Ann's favorite spiritual texts," they say, "was 'Joseph Campbell and the Power of Myth,'" which they describe as a television series about "common themes" in mythology.[14] Obama also recounts how he grew up among books of mythology. "In our household," he says, "the Bible, the Koran, and the Bhagavad Gita sat on the shelf alongside books of Greek and Norse and African mythology."[15]

In spite of what Dowd said, Obama does see himself in terms of Greek myth—or at least in terms of one quite specific Greek myth. More than once, he has invoked the myth of Icarus. For example, on "Charlie Rose," David Axelrod, who was chief campaign strategist and is now senior advisor to Obama, recounted how Obama mentioned the myth of Icarus the day after he lost the New Hampshire primary, with only three hours of sleep and with no notes, before a speech in Boston. According to Axelrod, this is what Obama said:

> "I know this sounds like spin, but I think it was meant to be that we didn't win the primary. It would have been far too easy." And he said: "Change is never easy. Change is something you have to fight for. And this would have come too easily." He said: "I think we were a little bit like Icarus, flying too close to the sun." And he said: "We're going to have to work for every vote from this point on. And let me tell you why it's worth the struggle, why it's worth the fight."[16]

In this anecdote, Obama sees himself not in terms of Jason, Hercules, or Odysseus but in terms of Icarus.

In mythology, there is not just one hero—there are many heroes. (As Campbell says, the hero has a thousand faces.) As an archetype, the hero is a general, abstract concept, of which there are many particular, concrete images. An archetype is a theme, and there are many variations on that theme. All heroes have to perform tasks, but the specific tasks and the specific styles in which specific heroes perform them vary considerably. Different heroes have very different styles.

For example, not all heroes are monster-slaying heroes, or at least they are not always monster-slaying heroes. Even Hercules is only occasionally a monster-slaying hero. Most famously, he slays the Nemean lion and the Lernaean Hydra, but most frequently he is a monster-capturing hero. Similarly, in only some versions of the myth of the golden fleece is Jason a monster-slaying hero. In most versions, he does not slay the dragon that guards the golden fleece but enlists the aid of Medea, who, with a magic spell and potion, charms the dragon to sleep so that Jason can steal the golden fleece. Odysseus is not a monster-slaying hero. He does not slay the Cyclops. He blinds the Cyclops with a fiery stake in the eye so that he can escape the cave. With the assistance of Medea, Jason is a monster-charming hero. Odysseus is a monster-blinding hero.

Icarus is also not a monster-slaying hero. He does not slay—he flies. He is a high-flying hero (if he is, by any definition, a hero). The expressions to "fly high" and "flying high" are idioms. To "fly high" means to be "ambitious,"[17] or it means to be "elated."[18] "Flying high" means "very successful" either "in one's ambitions" or "in an important or powerful position," frequently "with the implication that this is not the usual situation or will change,"[19] or it means "doing well" or "very excited or happy."[20]

What does the myth of Icarus actually say? It is a myth about a father and son, Daedalus and Icarus. Some heroes go on what Jung calls the "night sea journey." In contrast, Daedalus and Icarus go on a "day sky journey." Daedalus is artisan and architect to Minos and Pasiphae, king and queen of the island of Crete. Pasiphae orders Daedalus to create a model of a cow that enables her to have sexual intercourse with the bull of Poseidon. The result of this bestial perversion is a monstrous birth, the Minotaur. Minos then orders Daedalus to create the labyrinth, in which he confines the Minotaur. (There is a monster-slaying hero, but it is Theseus, not Icarus, who enters the labyrinth, slays the Minotaur, and then, with the assistance of Ariadne, exits the labyrinth.) Minos also confines Daedalus and Icarus in the labyrinth, but Pasiphae releases them. Then, to escape the island of Crete, Daedalus creates two pairs of wings. He sews the larger feathers with thread and glues the smaller feathers with wax. Daedalus warns Icarus not to fly too high. He also warns him not to fly too low. If Icarus soars too high, the sun will melt the wax, and he will fall from the sky and drown. If he swoops too low, the sea will wet the feathers, and he will fall from the sky and drown. Daedalus then warns Icarus to fly close behind and not to fly off. Icarus, however, flies up, up, and away, flies too high, flies too close to the sun, burns and crashes, and then drowns.

The myth of Icarus is what I would call an "admonitory" myth. Although the myth includes an admonition not to fly too low, what it emphasizes is the admonition not to fly too high—and, more specifically, not to fly too close to the sun. As a myth of excessive ambition, the myth of Icarus is also what I would call a "transgressive" myth. In this transgression, exuberance carries Icarus away—carries him way beyond the upper limit of endurance. In the index that Stith Thompson provides of typical (or archetypal) motifs, the high-flying

hero is type "F 1021.2 *Extraordinary effect of high flight*," and Icarus is
an image of subtype "F1021.2.1 *Flight so high that sun melts glue of
artificial wings*."[21] The myth of Icarus graphically illustrates the
catastrophic consequence of flying too high, too close to the sun. The
hero who does so suffers a "meltdown."

In terms of physical energy, the sun is radiantly, radioactively hot.
From a Jungian perspective, the sun is a quite specific image of the
archetype of libido, or psychic energy. In 1992, at the "Festival of
Archetypal Psychology in Honor of James Hillman" at Notre Dame
University, I delivered a presentation on several of my dreams of
Hillman.[22] After the presentation, a Jungian analyst recounted to me
one of her dreams of Hillman. In the dream, she was at Versailles, and
Hillman was in the palace of Louis XIV, the "Sun King." As the Jungian
analyst interpreted the dream, it cautioned her not to get too close to
Hillman, for, among Jungian analysts, he was a "sun hero" who radiated
such hot psychic energy that he could incinerate her. To her, the dream
implied that if Jungian analysts could not stand the heat of Hillman,
they should get out of the palace.

THE ICARUS COMPLEX (AND THE PHAETHON COMPLEX)

The *DSM-IV,* the fourth edition of the *Diagnostic and Statistical
Manual of Mental Disorders*, includes only one mythological diagnosis
—"Narcissistic Personality Disorder." The allusion, of course, is to the
myth of Narcissus. If there were a "Jungian" manual of mental disorders,
it would include many more mythological diagnoses—among them,
"Icarian Personality Disorder." Although currently there is no Icarian
Personality Disorder, there is an "Icarus complex." Henry A. Murray,
who directed the Psychological Clinical at Harvard University and, with
the assistance of Christiana Morgan, developed the Thematic
Apperception Test, or "TAT," originally proposed the diagnosis. As
Murray defines the Icarus complex, it comprises an "ascension-
descension sequence."[23] The individual with an Icarus complex rises
(or flies) and then falls—calamitously.

Although Murray calls this diagnosis the Icarus complex, he might
just as well have called it the "Phaethon complex." When Murray
discusses the myth of Icarus, he also mentions the myth of Phaethon.
That myth is also about a father and son, Phoebus and Phaethon.
Phoebus is Apollo, the sun god who drives the chariot of the sun across

the sky. In the myth, Phaethon persuades Phoebus to permit him to drive the chariot. Phaethon is a teenager who, in effect, drives a "hot rod" across the sky, loses control, careens across the sky, flies too fast, flies both too high and too low. When he scorches the earth, Zeus strikes him with a lightning bolt, and Phaethon burns and crashes. Phaethon is what Jung calls a *puer aeternus*, an eternal youth. Michael Perlman observes that the tragedy of Phaethon is similar to "that of other high-flying pueri such as Icarus."[24] Just as Daedalus warns Icarus not to fly too high or too low, Phoebus warns Phaethon, Perlman emphasizes, "to keep a safe, middle course."[25]

As I have previously noted, the tendency of modern corporations to advertise products by an appeal to ancient gods or heroes is cogent evidence that the mythological unconscious remains just as relevant as ever.[26] For example, in 2002, Volkswagen introduced a new luxury sedan and named it after Phaethon (although the corporation spelled it "Phaeton"). As Diana Winstanley remarks, there was a certain irony in the decision to name the vehicle after the victim of the first car crash in history. A representative of Volkswagen attempted to justify the decision. He argued, Winstanley says, that it was perfectly appropriate to name the vehicle after Phaethon, for, although the driver had died, "the car had survived without damage"—as if this would reassure customers! The death of Phaethon, Winstanley says, did not imply to Volkswagen any "failure of the vehicle."[27]

The myths of Icarus and Phaethon are both myths of a father and son. Both myths involve the sun. Both Icarus and Phaethon are sun heroes. Icarus flies too close to the sun, and Phaethon flies out of control in the chariot of the sun. Both Icarus and Phaethon are adolescents who fly and then burn and crash. They both experience exhilaration. Icarus flies too high, and Phaethon flies too fast and both too high and too low. Murray says that the individual with an Icarus complex (or a Phaethon complex) "belongs with the adolescent, overreaching, would-be solar heroes, Icarus and Phaethon—father-superseding enthusiasts with unstructured ego systems."[28]

Although the adage says that if we had been meant to fly, we would have been given wings, flying is not intrinsically an impossible, inappropriate, or psychopathological activity. (I do not mean literal, physical flying, like Orville and Wilbur Wright or Charles Lindbergh. I mean metaphorical, psychic flying—imaginal flying: the flight of

the imagination.) When Hillman discusses the *puer aeternus*, he notes
that there is a "winged godlike imago in us each." (An imago is a
psychic, or intrapsychic, image.) As examples, Hillman cites "Icarus
on the way to the sun, then plummeting with waxen wings," and
"Phaethon driving the sun's chariot out of control, burning up the
world."[29] Each and every individual has what I might call an "inner
Icarus" or an "inner Phaethon."

ICARIAN FLIGHT VERSUS DAEDALIAN FLIGHT

Both Icarus and Phaethon are examples of the high-flying hero as
the *puer aeternus*. "The *puer* flies because he has to," Peter H. Tatham
says. "It is, inescapably, his way of going through the world: of
transcension." Tatham also notes, however, that "the dream of flight
brings with it a fear of falling that easily and often prevents take-off."
Some heroes never even get off the ground, he says, "for, to anyone but
puer, falling is seen only as death and extinction." What goes up must
come down. Some heroes land safely, but other heroes fall. The
consequence of transcension (or the ascension-descension sequence)
may be a downfall that is, ironically, a comeuppance (as in the myths
of Icarus and Phaethon), but this need not be the case. Tatham says
that "since the vertical dimension works both ways, a 'coming-down'
is inevitable, whether that be seen as a fall or as safe landing." What
distinguishes the *puer aeternus* is a risky attitude that defies and denies
death. "The fall," Tatham says, "is something he is dying to risk: a risking
to die, because for him there is also 'life in death.'"[30]

Tatham says that Icarus "lives, it seems, but to fly and to fall, which
is the sum of his whole existence."[31] What is problematic is not flying
as such but flying too high and then falling. "It often seems," Tatham
says, "as if it is only young men aspiring to flight in general and
approaching the overbright sun in particular who come to a fiery end
(Icarus, Phaethon)." In this respect, he notes that Daedalus "flew on
to safety." He says that "it is only Icarian flight that falls and kills."[32]
Daedalian flight has a very different trajectory and a very different
conclusion. In contrast to Icarus, who flies and dies, Daedalus flies and
lives. Daedalus, Tatham emphasizes, epitomizes the capacity for "flying-
without-falling."[33]

Dreams of Flying (and Falling) and the
Dream of Flight

Among what Freud calls "typical dreams" are dreams of flying and falling. He says that these are dreams "in which the dreamer finds himself flying through the air to the accompaniment of agreeable feelings or falling with feelings of anxiety." Freud notes that one interpretation of such dreams is purely physical—dreams of flying and falling ostensibly derive from the sensation of the rising and falling of the lungs during sleep. He rejects that interpretation and, as an alternative, proposes that such dreams derive from games that adults play with children. "There cannot be a single uncle," Freud says, "who has not shown a child how to fly by rushing across the room with him in his outstretched arms, or who has not played at letting him fall by riding him on his knee and then suddenly stretching out his leg, or by holding him up high and then suddenly pretending to drop him."[34]

Subsequently, however, Freud offers a different interpretation of dreams of flying. He wonders why "so many people dream of being able to fly." From a psychoanalytic perspective, he says, the wish to fly is "only a disguise for another wish"—quite predictably, a sexual wish.[35] Freud asserts that "in dreams the wish to be able to fly is to be understood as nothing else than a longing to be capable of sexual performance." Finally, he also contends that "aviation, which in our day is at last achieving its aim," also derives from sexual wishes.[36]

Jung also notes that there are typical dreams, "such as of flying."[37] As examples, he mentions dreams in which the dreamer is "flying through space" or is actually "the sun."[38] Jung does not, as Freud does, interpret these dreams in sexual terms. Nor does Jung interpret them in mythological terms. He does not amplify them—that is, compare dreams of flying to myths of flying. It is not Jung but G.S. Kirk, a specialist in Greek mythology, who relates dreams of flying to the myth of Icarus. Kirk observes that modern studies have established that "dreams about flying are surprisingly common." He says that although the implication of such dreams is "arguable," they do demonstrate why the myth of Icarus "flying towards the sun" is so evocative.[39]

If Jung does not relate dreams of flying to the myth of Icarus, at least one Jungian analyst does. Stanton Marlan recounts the following dream of a woman:

> I am standing on the Earth. I think: "Why should I do this when I can fly?" As I am flying I think I would like to find my spiritual guide. Then I notice, clinging to my waist, a person. I think this may be my guide. I reach behind me and pull the figure to the front so I can look it in the face. It is a young, borderline schizophrenic girl. I know this is not my guide. I put her aside and continue on my journey to the sun. Just before I get there, a wind comes and carries me back to Earth.[40]

Like Icarus, the woman flies toward the sun, but, unlike him, she does not fly too close to the sun and then fall. She does not burn and crash. Just before she gets to the sun, a wind comes and carries her back to the earth—where, apparently, she lands safely.

Just as there are dreams of flying, there is also what Gaston Bachelard calls "the dream of flight."[41] Bachelard relates the myth of Icarus to the history of aviation and recounts an anecdote about flying and falling:

> If we read the history of efforts to imitate Icarus, we will find many examples of materialistic thinkers who believe that participating in the nature of feathers is the same thing as participating in flight. For example, Father Damian, an Italian living at court in Scotland, tried to fly in 1507 using wings made out of feathers. He took off from the top of a tower, but fell and broke his legs. He attributed his fall to the fact that some rooster feathers had been used to make the wings.[42]

Unlike Icarus, Father Damian does not fly too close to the sun. In fact, he does not fly at all—he just falls. In an effort to imitate Icarus, he tries to fly, but the feathers fail him, and he suffers fractures in a painfully funny pratfall.

Not all dreams of flying are about flying to the sun. Some are about flying to the moon. Some are simply about flying in the sky. Some are about flying through space. For example, Lauren Lawrence quotes a dream that occupies a quite special position in the history of aviation—it is a dream of Wally Schirra, commander of Apollo 7 in 1968:

> During my youth my best dream recurred frequently, where I would just lift off from the ground and start flying in the sky. I would fly higher and faster and farther than could be imagined. It was a wonderful dream of mine that was accomplished in reality by the NASA space program. Once I became an astronaut these dreams stopped.[43]

This dream of flying is not only a recurrent dream but also what Jung calls a "prospective dream"—a dream that is "an anticipation in the unconscious of future conscious achievements."[44] In this example of the prospective function of the unconscious, imagination coincides with reality, and a dream of flying coincides with the dream of flight. For Schirra, becoming an astronaut and flying through space is quite literally a dream come true.

Mania and Depression in Psychology and Economics

Jungian analysts caution against what they call an "inflation" of the ego, but an "elation" of the ego is equally problematic. Only one psychoanalyst, Bertram D. Lewin, not a Jungian but a Freudian, has specifically studied elation. One explanation for this dearth of studies, Lewin says, is that "mild forms" of elation are not "apt to bring persons into analysis, or once they are there to provoke much desire for change or therapeutic effort."[45] It is not happy individuals but sad individuals who tend to enter analysis. In extreme, or psychopathological, forms of elation, Lewin mentions "the illusory sense of reality that attaches to the mood."[46] In such instances, there is, he notes, a disparity, or incongruity, between the sense of elation and the sense of reality. The manic ego is a radically unrealistic ego.

In the diagnosis of "Bipolar Disorder," mania is a "high" and depression is a "low." In terms of mood, a manic individual is "up" and a depressive individual is "down." As the *DSM-IV* says, in a manic episode, the elated individual experiences a mood that is "persistently elevated" and may experience a "flight of ideas." The mood of the manic individual is "euphoric," or "high."[47] In this respect, the myth of Icarus is about elation and elevation, attitude and altitude—and psychoanalysis is not only a depth psychology but also a "height psychology."

The word "depression" is not only a psychological term but also an economic term, as in the phrase "Great Depression." Hillman notes that "this one word 'depression' combines both economics and psychology, suggesting that any downward trend in economics points toward disease and any melancholic phase in personal psychology could herald economic disaster."[48]

So, too, are the words "mania" and "panic" both psychological and economic terms. As Charles P. Kindleberger says, "Speculative excess, referred to concisely as a mania, and revulsion from such excess in the form of a crisis, crash, or panic can be shown to be, if not inevitable, at least historically common."[49] Although Kindleberger does not mention the myth of Icarus, he does employ an idiom about flight. After a mania that ends in a crisis, he says, "some time must elapse" before investors are "willing to take a flyer again."[50] The expression to "take a flyer" is an idiom that means to "take an ambitious gamble; take a risky chance or chancy risk," especially "financially."[51]

Hyman P. Minsky and John Kenneth Galbraith also discuss the relation between economics and psychology (or between economics and psychopathology). Both cite euphoria as a factor in economic crises. Minsky says that "the fundamental instability of a capitalist economy" is a tendency to enter a "'euphoric' state."[52] He says that "euphoria is a necessary prelude to a financial crisis" and that "euphoria is almost an inevitable result of the successful functioning of an enterprise economy."[53] Galbraith emphasizes the "speculative mood" and the concomitant "retreat from reality or, more precisely, perhaps, from sanity." The economy, he says, is historically episodic. Periodically, it becomes so euphoric as to be psychotic. "Euphoria leading on to extreme mental aberration is a recurring phenomenon," Galbraith says, "and one that puts the affected individual, the particular enterprise, and the larger economic community at risk."[54] He calls these episodes "flights into what must conservatively be described as mass insanity."[55] The implication is that, diagnostically, capitalism is intrinsically bipolar, a recurrent cycle of manias and depressions, or economic mood swings.

THE RATIONAL AND THE IRRATIONAL

Economists assume that the allocation of resources in the production, distribution, and consumption of goods and services is a rational function of supply and demand. This model arbitrarily excludes from consideration any factor that is putatively irrational. In this respect, Jung says that the irrational is an "existential factor" that "may be pushed out of sight by an increasingly rational explanation." He notes that science (which presumably would include economics as a social science) "posits objects that are confined within rational bounds, because by deliberately excluding the accidental it does not consider the actual object as a whole, but only that part of it which has been singled out for rational observation."[56] When economists arbitrarily exclude irrational factors from consideration, on the assumption that such factors are merely accidental (not necessary to the model), they comprehend only a part, not the whole, of the object (which, in this instance, is the economy). Only occasionally—when some event that does not strictly conform to this model occurs—do economists momentarily ponder the implications and, even then, they tend to dismiss such an event as an anomaly that does not oblige them permanently to revise the model. If there is a psychology of economics, it is a psychology of rational motives (for example, the profit motive).

Psychoanalysis is what I call an *affective-attitudinal psychology*. It is a psychology that comprises both rational and irrational factors. In contrast, the psychology of economics is a "cognitive-behavioral psychology" that omits irrational factors. (A psychology adequate to economics would be one that scrutinizes affects and attitudes—among them, irrational ones—not just cognitions and behaviors.) What is problematic about the psychology of economics is not just that the exclusion of irrational motives is arbitrary. It is also that what economists regard as rational may, in fact, be irrational.

Epistemologically, what is rational and what is irrational is no simple matter. For example, Jung observes that apparent rationality may be mere rationalization, or bias:

> The very rationality of the judgment may even be the worst
> prejudice, since we call reasonable what appears reasonable to
> us. What appears to us unreasonable is therefore doomed to be
> excluded because of its irrational character. It may really be
> irrational, but may equally well merely appear irrational without
> actually being so when seen from another standpoint.[57]

Similarly, Max Weber says that "what is rational from one point of view may well be irrational from another."[58]

It is an exceptional economist who is enough of a psychologist to include any consideration of irrational motives. Robert J. Shiller is one such economist. He employs the term "irrational exuberance," which he derives from remarks by Alan Greenspan, Chairman of the Federal Reserve Board, in 1996. Shiller defines the term as "wishful thinking on the part of investors."[59] (This is similar to the Freudian notion that all dreams are wish-fulfillments.) Shiller says that irrational exuberance is a "useful name" for those historically recurrent instances when the economy rises "up to unusually high and unsustainable levels under the influence of market psychology."[60] Not all economic excesses are a function of economic crazes. For example, the irrational exuberance of the 1990s, Shiller says, is "not the kind of investor euphoria or madness" that economists have ascribed to previous "speculative excesses." Investors who are irrationally exuberant are not insane. "Irrational exuberance," Shiller emphasizes, "is not *that* crazy." It is merely, he says, "the kind of bad judgment we all remember having made at some point in our lives when our enthusiasm got the best of us."[61] Irrational exuberance is a recurrent factor in what Shiller calls the "ups and downs" of the economy.[62]

THE ICARUS PARADOX AND THE ICARUS EFFECT

It is not just individuals who may fly too high and then crash. So may institutions—for example, the stock market, as in the "Wall Street Crash" of 1929. So, too, may corporations fly too high and then crash. In this respect, two recent books by economists explicity invoke the myth of Icarus.

In *The Icarus Paradox*, Danny Miller notes that it was the wings of Icarus that "gave rise to the abandon that so doomed him." Paradoxically, Miller says, "his greatest asset led to his demise." As Miller defines the "Icarus paradox," corporations frequently experience a crash when success leads to excess and then to failure. Miller says that "their victories and their strengths often seduce them into the excesses that cause their downfall." This tendency, he says, leads to "falling sales, plummeting profits, even bankruptcy."[63] Miller says that "overconfident, complacent executives extend the very factors that contributed to success to the point where they cause decline." He says that "Icarus flew so well that he got cocky and overambitious"—and so do corporations.[64]

In *Icarus in the Boardroom*, David Skeel describes Icarus as a "risk-taker."[65] In this respect, Icarus is not only a high-flying hero but also a risk-taking hero. Skeel calls this tendency the "Icarus effect." He says that when an entrepreneur emulates Icarus and risks everything—for example, "puts every dollar he or she has or can borrow into an Internet innovation"—and then "loses everything," the effect may not extend "much further than a few family and friends." When, however, an executive risks all the assets of a corporation and then loses them all, the effect extends much, much further. "Put Icarus in the boardroom and everything changes," Skeel says. "The ability to tap huge amounts of capital in enterprises that adopt the corporate form, together with the large number of people whose livelihood depends in one way or another on the business, means that the stakes are extraordinarily high if Icarus is running a major corporation." The executive who emulates Icarus and "who takes excessive or fraudulent risks with a large corporation," he notes, "may jeopardize the financial lives of thousands of employees, investors, and suppliers of the business."[66] Skeel says that not only "excessive and sometimes fraudulent risks" but also "competition" and "size and complexity" are the three factors that lead to the failure of corporations.[67] He refers to "crashes that fit this pattern as Icarus Effect failures."[68]

As a scandalous instance of corporate excess, Skeel mentions Enron and Kenneth L. Lay. He cites Lay as a notorious example of an executive with Icarian tendencies. After the bankruptcy of Enron, Lay was convicted of fraud but died before he could be sentenced. In an obituary, Vikas Bajaj and Kurt Eichenwald say that Bill Burton, an attorney who had known Lay for over a decade, "compared Mr. Lay to Icarus, the figure in Greek mythology who was given wings made of feather and wax but fell into the sea when he flew too close to the sun." In the mythological narratives of Enron and Lay, Burton said, the tragic flaw was pride. "'The Enron and Ken Lay stories are best told in an English literature class, or a classics class,' Mr. Burton told an interviewer in 2002, 'where you are trying to explain what hubris is all about.'"[69]

THE ICARUS ALLUSION AND THE ECONOMIC CRISIS OF 2008

A politician who is "high on himself" (or, if he is an ideologue, so high on ideas that he experiences a flight of ideas) is susceptible to flying too close to the sun. In this respect, Obama aspires to become a hero stylistically different not only from politicians who slay monsters, giants, dragons, and fathers but also from politicians who fly too high and then burn and crash.

Icarus is an example of what Michael Balint calls a "philobat." A philobat is a thrill-seeker. In this respect, Icarus is not only a high-flying hero but also a thrill-seeking hero. What thrills the philobat is danger. As Balint says, "We understand now why the thrill is the greater the farther we dare get away from safety—in distance, in speed, or in exposure; that is to say, the more we can prove our independence."[70]

In just this way, Icarus is a son who distances himself from his father in order to prove his independence. As a philobat, Icarus also assumes that he possesses the necessary skill to experience the thrill and not to suffer any disastrous consequences. "The philobat apparently firmly believes," Balint says, "that his skill will be sufficient to cope with all hazards and dangers, and that everything will turn out all right in the end."[71]

Although Obama sees himself in terms of Icarus, he does not identify himself with Icarus. In fact, he disidentifies himself from Icarus —quite consciously. To Obama, Icarus is no hero to emulate. For him, the myth of Icarus is a cautionary tale about the exercise of restraint. It is about moderation, not extremism. As a politician, Obama does not appear to be either a risk-taking hero or a thrill-seeking hero. He does not believe that "the sky's the limit"—an idiom that means there is "no upper limit,"[72] or "no limit (to ambition, aspirations, expense, or the like)."[73]

Obama does not aspire to become an Icarus, and it is improbable that he will get carried away on the wings of ambition, fly too close to the sun, and then burn and crash. He is ambitious, but not excessively so. In what I might call the "Icarus allusion," Obama is quite conscious that "Icarus can be alluded to as someone who fails because of excessive ambition."[74]

The myth of Icarus does not say not to fly—it says not to fly too high (or too low). The moral of the story is to fly just high enough and not fall. The myth emphasizes what Hillman calls "the inherent difficulties of flying."[75] In this respect, it remains to be seen whether Obama will be a too-high-flying hero, a too-low-flying hero, or a high-enough-flying hero.

When Obama assumed the office of president on January 20, 2009, he immediately addressed the economic crisis of 2008. He tried to get off to a "flying start"—an idiom that means an "initial advantage" or a "good beginning" that "takes one some way towards the completion of a race, journey, or any other enterprise."[76]

A month and a half later, however, on March 5, 2009, the Dow Jones Industrial Average fell 281.40 points to close at 6,594.44—53% lower than the record high of 14,164.53 on October 9, 2007. The *New York Times* described the situation as "A Continuing Free Fall."[77]

To address the economic crisis, Obama authorized the expenditure of $787 billion and proposed an additional expenditure of $275 billion. The total was over $1 trillion—a very high figure but a figure that, even so, some economists worried might be too low. Paul Krugman, recipient of the 2008 Nobel Prize in economics, wondered whether Obama would be, in effect, "up" to what was necessary under the circumstances. The situation was so extreme, he argued, that moderate measures simply would not suffice. In such dire circumstances, he said, only a radical intervention would be effective. Krugman worried that the program that Obama advocated to address the economic crisis "isn't going to fly."[78]

Obama obviously wants the program to succeed, or to "fly." In this respect, there are two political "wings" in America, the "right wing" of conservative Republicans and the "left wing" of liberal Democrats. Obama wants the program to fly not on one wing but on two wings, on both political wings. He wants the effort to address the economic crisis to be bipartisan. He does not want just to "wing it" with liberal Democrats. What Obama prefers is pragmatic consensus, not ideological conflict. (In spite of this preference, it is a fact that, at least so far, no conservative Republicans have supported the effort by Obama to address the economic crisis. Not one Republican in the House of Representatives and only three moderate or liberal Republicans in the Senate voted to approve the $787 billion expenditure.)

REGULATION AND RESTRAINT

Half a century ago, Daniel Bell proclaimed the "end of ideology." He declared that "there is today a rough consensus among intellectuals on political issues." For example, Bell said, few conservatives still insisted that the government "should play no role in the economy." He said that both conservatives and liberals now concurred that "a system of mixed economy" was necessary.[79] Since then, however, there has been a resurgence of radical (or reactionary) ideology among conservatives.

Since Ronald Reagan, Republicans have tried to abolish the system of mixed economy that Franklin Roosevelt introduced to address the economic crisis of the Great Depression. They have advocated privatization of the economy, on the assumption that there is no public interest that the private sector cannot serve (and serve much more efficiently than the public sector). The notion is that the government should play no role in the economy—that, at least in terms of the economy, the best government is not just the least government but no government at all, that business is no business of government. The most radical version of this position is not just conservative but libertarian or even anarchistic.

Republicans have also advocated deregulation of the economy, on the supposition that any intervention by the government in the economy is, by definition, interference—an intrusion that is not only utterly unnecessary, superfluous, and gratuitous but also invariably detrimental. Democrats—among them, liberal Democrats—have colluded with conservative Republicans in this effort. (An especially egregious example of this collusion was the repeal, in 1999, of the Glass-Steagall Act of 1933, which had separated commercial banks from investment banks.) In this deregulation of the economy, both Republicans and Democrats have been negligently permissive. (In recent years, the Securities and Exchange Commission, the most important agency accountable for regulation of the stock market, has also been irresponsibly lenient. For example, it did not properly investigate complaints about Bernard L. Madoff, who for twenty years operated a $50-65 billion Ponzi scheme and finally pleaded guilty to committing fraud, theft, and perjury and laundering money. Madoff, of course, opposed regulation.)

The definition of "regulation" is "restraint." Republicans (with the complicity of Democrats) have systematically tried to remove every restraint on the economy. The consequence has been a high-flying economy—one that has flown too high, flown too close to the sun, and that, if it has not yet burned and crashed, has now fallen perilously low.

Galbraith says that intrinsic to "the speculative episode is the euphoria, the mass escape from reality, that excludes any serious contemplation of the true nature of what is taking place." He identifies two factors that contribute to euphoria. The first factor, he says, is "the extreme brevity of the financial memory." Galbraith says that "financial disaster is quickly forgotten," with the result that the errors of the past tend to be repeated in the present. "There can be few fields of human endeavor," he says, "in which history counts for so little as in the world of finance." The second factor, Galbraith says, is "the specious association of money and intelligence."[80] The fallacy is, the more money, the more intelligence. The assumption, Galbraith says, is that the mere possession of money necessarily implies "some special genius."[81] In combination, these two factors tend recurrently to render an economy unconscious—or, as Galbraith says, euphoric and insane. "Recurrent descent into insanity is not," he sardonically remarks, "a wholly attractive feature of capitalism."[82]

Merely to state, as Galbraith does, that the financial memory is extremely brief is not to analyze the problem psychologically. I would emphasize that, from a psychoanalytic perspective, when financial disaster is not remembered, it may not just be "forgotten"—it may be *repressed*. Financially, there is no apparent profit in remembering economic crises. In fact, there is every incentive to repress that history —to relegate it to the unconscious, to consign it to oblivion.

The solution, Galbraith says, is not regulation. "Regulation outlawing financial incredulity or mass euphoria is not a practical possibility," he says. "If applied generally to such human condition, the result would be an impressive, perhaps oppressive, and certainly ineffective body of law." Ultimately, Galbraith says, the only practical solution is "skepticism that would resolutely associate too evident optimism with probable foolishness."[83]

Although a vigilantly skeptical attitude as a deterrent against folly is a splendid notion, it does not seem to me to be a viable alternative to regulation. Just as it is not feasible to legislate morality, it is not feasible to legislate mood (for example, to outlaw euphoria). As Galbraith says, any such attempt would be an exercise in futility. That, however, is not the issue. Rather, the issue is whether and, if so, how to regulate (or restrain) certain economic activities so as to mitigate the cyclical highs and lows of what W. W. Rostow (who famously employs an image of flight, the "take-off," to describe the dynamics of economic growth) calls "the upswing and the downswing."[84] Regulation is simply a moderation of economic extremism by the imposition of restraint on the conduct of individuals (as well as institutions and corporations) who episodically experience such exhilaration that they exhibit radically Icarian tendencies. The purpose of regulation is not to "clip the wings" of the economy but to curtail moody excesses.

THE APOLLONIAN MAXIMS: "KNOW THYSELF" AND
"NOTHING IN EXCESS"

In this respect, it is fortuitous that in the current economic crisis America has a president who does not identify himself with the archetype of the high-flying hero but who quite consciously disidentifies himself from it. Obama appears to have an ego that is more Apollonian than Icarian (or Phaethonian).

The maxims of Apollo are "Know thyself" and "Nothing in excess." Obama seems to know himself (or, from a psychoanalytic perspective, to be quite conscious of himself). He also seems not to be especially prone, even under stress, to anything in excess. Jung notes that the Apollonian style entails an appreciation "of measure, of controlled and proportioned feelings."[85] In this respect, Obama appears to be prudent rather than impulsive or compulsive. Temperamentally, he seems to have a disposition (and the discipline) to explore practical solutions to actual problems. He seems to have an ego that is more pragmatic than ideological—more heuristic than hubristic. (Perhaps Obama has a tragic flaw, but, if so, pride does not seem to be it.) Obama exudes poise. He appears to possess the equanimity necessary to address a crisis. Of course, composure is no substitute for competence—and it remains to be seen just how capable as a president Obama will ultimately be.

In the pantheon of what Hillman aptly calls "polytheistic psychology,"[86] Apollo is neither the only god nor the god for every occasion. (Different gods have different specializations and different proficiencies. The expertise of one god may be very different from that of another god. From a Jungian perspective, a god is not a literal, metaphysical entity in a supernatural dimension but a "god," a metaphorical, psychic factor—an archetypal image in what I call the "mythological unconscious."[87]) In the current economic crisis, however, Apollo may be the most apposite god (or archetypal image) for Obama to invoke as he attempts to perform a political task of truly heroic proportions. As Phoebus, Apollo does, after all, know how to drive the chariot of the sun across the sky.

"The road of excess," William Blake says, "leads to the palace of wisdom."[88] Perhaps, in this instance, it also leads, ironically, from Wall Street and the New York Stock Exchange to Pennsylvania Avenue and the White House. In contrast to the high-flying heroes who indulged in such speculative excess in recent years, Obama now has an opportunity to be wise—to deal with the current situation in ways that, not only in style but also in substance, differ radically from the unwise practices that led to what is, by many accounts, the most serious economic crisis since the Great Depression.

NOTES

1. James Hillman [with Laura Pozzo], *Inter Views: Conversations with Laura Pozzo on Psychotherapy, Biography, Love, Soul, Dreams, Work, Imagination, and the State of the Culture* (New York: Harper & Row, 1983), p. 9.

2. Larry L. King, *Larry L. King: A Writer's Life in Letters, Or, Reflections in a Bloodshot Eye*, ed. Richard A. Holland (Fort Worth, TX: TCU Press, 1999), p. 134.

3. Michael Vannoy Adams, "An Interview with Maury Maverick Jr.," in *Fifty Years of the Texas Observer*, ed. Char Miller (San Antonio, TX: Trinity University Press, 2004), pp. 54-61.

4. Hillman, *Inter Views*, p. 98.

5. C. G. Jung, "Does the World Stand on the Verge of a Spiritual Rebirth?" in *C. G. Jung Speaking: Interviews and Encounters*, ed. William McGuire and R. F. C. Hull (Princeton, NJ: Princeton University Press, 1977), p. 75.

6. Betty Sue Flowers, "Practicing Politics in the Economic Myth," in *The Vision Thing: Myth, Politics and Psyche in the World*, ed. Thomas Singer (London and New York: Routledge, 2000), p. 209.

7. Maureen Dowd, "Of Knights and Presidents: Race of Mythic Proportions," *New York Times*, October 10, 1992, p. A9.

8. Maureen Dowd, "Pappy and Poppy," *New York Times*, January 7, 2001, Week in Review Section, p. 17.

9. Maureen Dowd, "Praying and Preying," *New York Times*, April 30, 2008, p. A19.

10. Michael Vannoy Adams, "Imaginology: The Jungian Study of the Imagination," in *Archetypal Psychologies: Reflections in Honor of James Hillman*, ed. Stanton Marlan (New Orleans, LA: Spring Journal Books, 2008), pp. 237-238.

11. Maureen Dowd, "Ich Bin Ein Jet-Setter," *New York Times*, Week in Review Section, p.13.

12. Maureen Dowd, "Cyclops and Cunning," *New York Times*, July 30, 2008, p. A17.

13. *Ibid.*

14. Lisa Miller and Richard Wolffe, "Finding His Faith," *Newsweek*, July 21, 2008, p. 28.

15. Barack Obama, *The Audacity of Hope: Thoughts on Reclaiming the American Dream* (New York: Crown Publishers, 2006), pp. 203-204.

16. David Axelrod, "Charlie Rose," PBS/WNET, January 26, 2009.

17. A. P. Cowie, R. Mackin, and I. R. McCaig, eds., *Oxford Dictionary of Current Idiomatic English: Volume 2: Phrase, Clause, and Sentence Idioms* (Oxford, UK: Oxford University Press, 1983), p. 193.

18. Christine Ammer, ed., *The American Heritage Dictionary of Idioms* (Boston and New York: Houghton Mifflin, 1997), p. 215.

19. Richard A. Spears, ed., *McGraw Hill's Dictionary of American Idioms and Phrasal Verbs* (New York: McGraw-Hill, 2004), p. 223.

20. Paul Heacock, ed., *Cambridge Dictionary of American Idioms* (Cambridge, UK: Cambridge University Press, 2003), p. 135.

21. Stith Thompson, *Motif-Index of Folk Literature,* vol. 3 (Bloomington, IN, and London: Indiana University Press), p. 260.

22. Michael Vannoy Adams, "My Imaginal Hillman; or, James, I'll See You in My Dreams" (Boulder, CO: Sounds True Recordings, 1992), audiotape.

23. Henry A. Murray, "American Icarus," in *Puer Papers,* ed. James Hillman (Irving, TX: Spring Publications, 1979), p. 95.

24. Mike Perlman, "Phaethon and the Thermonuclear Chariot," *Spring* (1983): 91.

25. *Ibid.,* p. 96.

26. Michael Vannoy Adams, *The Fantasy Principle: Psychoanalysis of the Imagination* (Hove and New York: Brunner-Routledge, 2004), p. 60.

27. Diana Winstanley, "Phaethon: Seizing the Reigns of Myth," in *Myths, Stories, and Organizations: Premodern Narratives for Our Times,* ed. Yiannis Gabriel (Oxford, UK: Oxford University Press, 2004), p. 183.

28. Murray, p. 95.

29. James Hillman, *The Dream and the Underworld* (New York: Harper & Row, 1979), p. 65.

30. Peter H. Tatham, *The Making of Maleness: Men, Women, and the Flight of Daedalus* (New York: New York University Press, 1992), p. 27.

31. *Ibid.,* p. 43.

32. *Ibid.,* p. 44.

33. *Ibid.,* p. 131.

34. Sigmund Freud, *The Interpretation of Dreams, SE* 4, p. 271.

35. Sigmund Freud, *Leonardo da Vinci and a Memory of His Childhood, SE* 11, p. 125.

36. *Ibid.*, p. 126.

37. C. G. Jung, "On the Nature of Dreams," *CW* 8, § 535.

38. C. G. Jung, *The Relations between the Ego and the Unconscious, CW* 7, § 250.

39. G. S. Kirk, *The Nature of Greek Myths* (Harmondsworth, UK: Penguin Books, 1974), p. 87.

40. Stanton Marlan, *The Black Sun: The Alchemy and Art of Darkness* (College Station, TX: Texas A&M University Press, 2005), p. 30.

41. Gaston Bachelard, *Air and Dreams: An Essay on the Imagination of Movement*, trans. Edith R. Farrell and C. Frederick Farrell (Dallas, TX: Dallas Institute Publications, 1988), pp. 26-27.

42. *Ibid.*, p. 37.

43. Lauren Lawrence, *Private Dreams of Public People* (New York: Assouline, 2002), p. 52.

44. C. G. Jung, "General Aspects of Dream Psychology," *CW* 8, § 493.

45. Bertram D. Lewin, *The Psychology of Elation* (New York: W. W. Norton, 1950), p. 15.

46. *Ibid.*, p. 171.

47. American Psychiatric Association, *The Diagnostic and Statistical Manual of Mental Disorders: Fourth Edition* (Washington, DC: American Psychiatric Association, 1994), p. 328.

48. James Hillman, *Farewell Welfare* (Buffalo, NY: Analytical Psychology Club of Western New York, 2001), pp. 13-14.

49. Charles P. Kindleberger, *Manias, Panics, and Crises: A History of Financial Crises* (New York: Basic Books, 1989), p. 4.

50. *Ibid.*, p. 17.

51. Robert L. Chapman, ed., *Dictionary of American Slang* (New York: HarperCollins, 1995), p. 547.

52. Hyman P. Minsky, "Financial Instability Revisited: The Economics of Disaster," in *Can "It" Happen Again? Essays on Instability and Finance* (Armonk, NY: M. E. Sharpe, 1982), p. 118.

53. *Ibid.*, p. 145.

54. John Kenneth Galbraith, *A Short History of Financial Euphoria* (Knoxville, TN: Whittle Direct Books, 1990), p. 1.

55. *Ibid.*, p. 3.

56. C. G. Jung, *Psychological Types, CW* 6, § 775.

57. C. G. Jung, "The Transcendent Function," *CW* 8, § 137.

58. Max Weber, *The Protestant Ethic and the Spirit of Capitalism*, trans. Talcott Parsons (London: Routledge, 1992), p. 26.

59. Robert J. Shiller, *Irrational Exuberance* (Princeton, NJ, and Oxford, UK: Princeton University Press, 2006), p. xvii.

60. *Ibid.*, p. 1.

61. *Ibid.*, p. 2.

62. *Ibid.*, p. 172.

63. Danny Miller, *The Icarus Paradox: How Exceptional Companies Bring about Their Own Downfall* (New York: Harper Business, 1990), p. 3.

64. *Ibid.*, p. 18.

65. David Skeel, *Icarus in the Boardroom: The Fundamental Flaws in Corporate America and Where They Came From* (New York: Oxford University Press, 2005), p. 4.

66. *Ibid.*, p. 5.

67. *Ibid.*, p. 6.

68. *Ibid.*, p. 7.

69. Vikas Bajaj and Kurt Eichenwald, "Kenneth L. Lay, 64, Enron Founder and Symbol of Corporate Excess, Dies," *New York Times*, July 6, 2006, p. C7.

70. Michael Balint, *Thrills and Regressions* (New York: International Universities Press, 1959), p. 29.

71. *Ibid.*, p. 83.

72. Adam Makkai, M. T. Boatner, and J. E. Gates, eds., *A Dictionary of American Idioms* (Hauppauge, NY: Barron's, 2004), p. 324.

73. Ammer, p. 589.

74. Andrew Delahunty, Sheila Dignen, and Penny Stock, eds., *The Oxford Dictionary of Allusions* (Oxford, UK: Oxford University Press, 2001), p. 11.

75. James Hillman, "Oedipus Revisited," in Karl Kerenyi and James Hillman, *Oedipus Variations: Studies in Literature and Psychoanalysis* (Dallas, TX: Spring Publications, 1989), p. 141.

76. Cowie, Mackin, and McCaig, p. 193.

77. "A Continuing Free Fall," *New York Times*, March 6, 2009, p. B7.

78. Paul Krugman, "The Big Dither," *New York Times*, March 6, 2009, p. A27.

79. Daniel Bell, *The End of Ideology: On the Exhaustion of Political Ideas in the Fifties* (Glencoe, IL: The Free Press, 1960), p. 373.

80. Galbraith, p. 12.

81. *Ibid.*, p. 13.

82. *Ibid.*, p. 79.

83. *Ibid.*, p. 80.

84. W. W. Rostow, *The Process of Economic Growth* (New York: W. W. Norton, 1962), p. 19.

85. Jung, *CW* 6, § 236.

86. James Hillman, "Psychology: Monotheistic or Polytheistic," in David L. Miller, *The New Polytheism: Rebirth of the Gods and Goddesses* (Dallas, TX: Spring Publications, 1981), pp. 109-137.

87. Michael Vannoy Adams, *The Mythological Unconscious* (New York and London: Karnac, 2001).

88. William Blake, *The Marriage of Heaven and Hell,* in *Complete Writings,* ed. Geoffrey Keynes (London: Oxford University Press, 1976), p. 150.

FILM REVIEWS

No Country for Old Men. Screenplay by Joel and Ethan Coen, based on the novel by Cormac McCarthy. Tommy Lee Jones, Javier Bardem, Josh Brolin, Woody Harrelson, Kelly Mcdonald. Directed by Joel and Ethan Coen.

REVIEWED BY VICTORIA C. DRAKE

In the Shadow of Eros:
Double Agent of Archetypal Fate and Destiny

*N*o *Country For Old Men* (2007), based on the riveting 2005 novel of the same name by Cormac McCarthy, opens onto a vast, arid, deserted xeriscape, a wasteland for body and soul where the Darwinian "survival of the fittest" has taken its toll. Sheriff Ed Tom Bell (Tommy Lee Jones) surveys this bleak view (ostensibly somewhere in the American Southwest, but which might as well be the Asphodel Fields) with us on the lookout, serving as our metaphorical guide and raconteur. He is an aged man, too old and weary for this country now. We intuitively

Victoria C. Drake is currently working on her Ph.D. in Depth Psychology at Pacifica Graduate Institute. After attending Harvard University (B.A. 1983), she followed her passion to become a life-long international wildlife conservationist and environmental community justice advocate. Victoria lives in Chicago with her husband, James Evan-Cook (from Kent, UK), their three daughters, Angelica, Isabella, and Lily, and assorted animal companions.

sense that something is coming just over the horizon, bearing down—out of sight, but always in motion. It has been coming for a while. His dreams portend as much, that mortal fate is nearing soon enough. Though his eyes may be weak from a life viewing dissolution and decay, his will to attend his duty-bound conscience and resolve to honor the badge he wears still beats strong with every breath.

It is 1978. Enter Anton Chigurh (brilliantly portrayed by Javier Bardem), the enigmatic, emotionless antithesis of Bell and pathological Houdini howitzer of a serial killer, ostensibly enlisted to recover a grubby valise of stolen drug money. Chigurh is undeniably one of the most chilling, affecting, unforgettable characters ever to successfully forge the gap from the static pages of literature to flickering celluloid. With his inimitable Beatles' moptop and dead-pan, monosyllabic delivery, Chigurh is larger than life. He is a hybrid agent of fate and destiny intertwined as embodied by his ironic, signature coin toss, which he hauntingly initiates by demanding: "Call it, Friend-O? Heads or Tails?" Inevitably the toss proves to be a mere formality, a brief warm-up ritual designed to lull his spellbound victim into a momentary, false sense of free will while their fate and inevitable outcome are already sealed. Our anxiety could not be more potent as the illusion of any potential chance for choice in the matter or option for revoking the misfortune of being caught in Chigurh's cross hairs is symbolically revealed. Only one thing is certain: Chigurh is reliably faithful to his personal code and, true to form, executes whomever he pleases and whoever displeases him. Like death and the river Styx, no one can ultimately delay or even contain Chigurh's death drive for long. Nothing ever will. As von Franz writes:

> The Styx symbolizes the frightening aspect of the mother archetype and in a certain sense also of the collective unconscious. The fact that we cannot "hold" it in a vessel seems to me to be very meaningful. We cannot indeed entirely grasp or manipulate the collective unconscious. It resembles a wild river of psychic energy which we cannot regulate ....
>
> ... [O]nly the principle of creativeness in the human soul can hold its own against the destructiveness of the water of Styx.
>
> ... Styx has also to do with the goddess of Nemesis, the mysterious, revengeful "justice of nature." ... [But] from it stems Nikè ("victory"), this mysterious power of fate, which

> dooms ... or promotes ... life. If we look at the dust of history ... Then we realize the meaning of the water of the Styx. It seems to be an inescapable destiny, the cruel justice of nature which we cannot halt.[1]

The pivotal choicepoint that yokes Sheriff Bell with Chigurh is the unfortunate decision of a young opportunist grifter named Llewelyn Moss (Josh Brolin) to steal a valise of two million dollars cash he finds in the desert shortly after a grisly massacre between warring drug dealers, which leaves no survivors. Thereafter, Moss is on the run to protect his ill-gotten bounty with Chigurh closing in on his tainted scent. None of these three men really knows the others (though they know of one another) or even appear in the same frame together during the course of the film, and yet each is intimately and irrevocably affected by the others' actions. They form an archetypal male triad in contraposition to the three (invisible) female Fates. The few women who do feature in the film are tolerated as little more than passive witnesses to the unfolding drama, watching from the edge of the frame like us, the viewers, inert vessels, powerless to intercede. McCarthy is first and foremost a quintessential man's writer, and this is a man's story after all, to which the film is doggedly loyal.

Moss' hapless impulse of selfish greed catapults his loom of fate into premature overdrive, ensuring that it will veer head on into Chigurh's relentless path. This, in turn, triggers Bell's life-worn contract to engage in tracking both hunted and hunter—with violent, tragic consequences. But, it is also not without a few messy unforeseen lapses and detours, especially by Chigurh's swift, tidy standards. Still, Bell plods across the denuded landscape adding up the trail of bodies in Chigurh's wake, all too aware he is no match for this unstoppable force.

It is comforting to objectify Chigurh as a mere mythic phantasm, but he may be rooted in a reality too close for comfort. Chigurh evokes a Titan, one of those twelve or thirteen dark, powerful elder gods who reigned before being overthrown by a tribe of younger gods, the Olympians. Reflecting such Titanic impulses, Chigurh, in his rapacious tyranny, takes the form of a violent psychopath, an archetypal "Invalid of Eros"—one who cannot love or relate. As Guggenbühl-Craig so poignantly writes:

> The warrior without Eros is a brutal mercenary, a senseless mass
> murderer, a demonic exterminator. ...
>   The Archetype of the Invalid is no different than any other
> archetype. ... Invalids without Eros are nasty, tyrannical, boring,
> and parasitic. They compensate for their invalidity by dominating
> others. ... Whether the incarnation of the Archetype of the
> Invalid be a blessing or a curse depends upon Eros. How an
> archetype, any archetype, is experienced depends upon Eros'
> presence or absence.[2]

Seeing Chigurh here as an invalid of Eros exposes a glimmer of his own
carefully concealed wounds and mirrors the traumatic "psychic
invalidism" called "psychopathy"[3] in all of us. He forces us to consider
why we are not amoral in spite of the fact that we have tendencies to
amorality in us. We consider our feelings, asking ourselves about the
nature of ethics and love. Psychopathy can be "a tool with which we
can better understand ourselves."[4] Perhaps this is what makes Chigurh
as compelling as he is repulsive.

So, what does Chigurh and his eclipsed Eros ask of us as viewers
and as a society, and what are the costs for not individuating and
integrating those parts of Chigurh that are in us? Can the threatening
possibility of his mythological presence in and out of our midst
illuminate anything about our personal and collective fears in a neutral
versus negative light? Hillman writes about how this horrifying side of
the instinctual life is personified by the god Pan; how "if Pan is
suppressed ... nature and instinct will go astray no matter how we
strain on rational levels to set things right." "Respect for life is not
enough ...." So, "[t]he re-education of the citizen in relation to nature
means nothing less than a wholly new relationship with the 'horrors'
and 'moral depravations' and madness which are part of the instinctual
life of the citizen's soul."[5]

Chigurh's relentless on-screen presence may reflect the
psychological necessity of facing these horrors and depravities. If he
sees you: tag, you're it. As long as he can't see you, time is on your
side. But, sooner or later, mere mortals have to stop running. They
have to sleep. Not Chigurh. He doesn't sleep and therefore doesn't
dream, in stark contrast to Bell. Chigurh instills a 360-degree state of
palpable panic wherever he goes, preying not just on the literal lives of
others, but also slaking his archetypal thirst on whatever remaining

reservoirs of shriveling, stricken psyche he can consume. Even his name is irritating and ungraspable, like a parasitic chigger that gets under your skin. His power is fearlessness, and an effective, mechanical, unquestioning commitment to propelling deterministic chaos. Another way to consider the problem of Chigurh (i.e., evil) is that he personifies the archetypal shadow of society in stasis seeking to resolve into a new order. In this paradigm, "country" could mean society or culture.

The archetypal shadow can lead to behavior that is clearly destructive. The archetypal shadow is also a creative force within the unconscious that alternately destabilizes and balances consciousness in order for psychological growth to occur. As a conspicuous purveyor of this shadow, is Chigurh working on behalf of deepening into Mother country/Gaia consciousness, in which we are but temporary visitors, effectively slamming us with the darkest of psyche's depths? As Jung reminds us: "One of the toughest roots of all evil is unconsciousness."[6] Or is Chigurh's depravity simply a stunted archetypal response to the godless, "Venus-deprived society"[7] in which we live? Not only does Chigurh represent fate, death, and karmic Cronus (?) time, but he also carries those parts of a culture (or "country") and a species that has become irreparably disconnected, removed, or uprooted from Mother Earth ethics and the Divine Feminine; a society that values and rewards materialism (the root word of matter is *mater* or mother) and personal gain over balance and harmony with the world at large. Are we not all also, in part, an opportunistic Llewelyn Moss setting an Anton Chigurh in motion?

As a verb and as an inheritable dynamic, Chigurh viscerally represents a manic phase of what we could become in miniature, if we continue to blindly violate and rupture the laws of nature, from which we are not exempt. Similar to Dexter (the kinder, gentler vigilante serial killer from the Showtime series "Dexter"), Chigurh shows up like clockwork when something has gone awry with the natural order and inherent morality of things in his sphere. Both characters are deadly assassins who need to kill to assimilate and assert their identity and actualize their true nature. Both clear the ground for a new order of consciousness, a new pantheon of gods, goddesses, and renovated myth, such as the myth of Eternal Return. This is no country for old men or old gods, beliefs, or practices, for that matter. The old patriarchal, tribal order is dying out. Change is on the horizon. Indeed, we are on the edge of seismic, transformative shifts no matter which way you turn.

It is bigger, more terrifying, and ultimately more consciousness-cultivating than anything before.

Chigurh is just hastening this cosmological transit with frightening precision. When was death evil or unnatural in itself? Aren't we all implicated in the same dog-eat-dog cycle by archetypal extension; capable and culpable of ingesting animal flesh, using animal products, or carving out carbon footprints, desiccating the Earth beyond imbalance? What is the carrying capacity of global excess and national self-indulgence? As Robert Sardello writes:

> The heart of the dramatic imagination of the world is this violent reforming of the cosmos and when it is possible to really feel the soul of the world, meeting it with soul, a restructuring of soul results. ... M. Foucault points to this most important aspect of transgression when he describes violence as profanation in a world that no longer recognizes the presence of a sacred element.[8]

Archetypal (*nigredo*) armageddon is here, and Chigurh is our self-reflecting mirror of longing and soullessness. There is a little bit of Chigurh participating in all of us, if we agree with Robert Segal's view that for Jung myth was a map of the mind not place.[9] We co-create Chigurh just as surely as death will come for each of us one day. Chigurh's initiatory violence is a paradoxical sign and a prescient reminder to live each moment in all its affirmative, expendable fullness. Recall that evil/live/devil/lived are forever entwined as poles of human experience. Thomas Aquinas defined evil as the absence of good, which ought to be present. Another view is that evil is not just the absence of good; it is matter without spirit. The time has come not only to reconsider evil for ourselves, our culture, and our society, but to begin to discern the newly emergent forms of evil in a terrified and terrorized PTSD world, which never sleeps and thus spares no time to dream.

The film ultimately serves as Bell's memory, which becomes our own as well. It is now for us to continue in his footsteps and consciously create new landscapes, new horizons, new relationships with Gaia's body and soul. Individuation is, after all, concerned with transforming the suffering and trauma of existence. As Casey writes:

> Soul, like time itself, "is always at a beginning *and at an end.*" Which is to say that it is also always dying. ... This underworld has its own temporality, which is neither eternal time nor now-

time nor non-time. We can only imagine what it is like, though
just in doing so, we enter it and participate in it as if we had known
it all along. As perhaps we have: in the soul and of it, subtending
it, and being at once its sameness and its difference. ... If soul is
made, time is made, and ... time and soul themselves merge in a
dis-soluteness in which being in and out of time become one: in
the kind of imagining which soul does and, doing, dies.[10]

Bell peacefully surrenders the chase as he recounts an elliptical dream
featuring his long-dead father waiting for him, portending a natural
close. Finally, having secured the tainted cash, Chigurh crashes his car
and stumbles away from what should have been an instant fatality
while two teenage boys look on, stunned in disbelief. "You never saw
me," cautions the survivor, too disoriented to even toy with a
coin toss this time. They hastily nod their heads in agreement, averting
their gaze, luckier than they will ever know. This cautionary tale lingers
on hauntingly, long after Chigurh removes to his mythic horizon,
having briefly closed the gap between *kairos* and *chronos*, stop-lossed
from whence he came. For the time being.

"Sailing to Byzantium"[11]
W. B. Yeats

That is no country for old men. The young
In one another's arms, birds in the trees
—Those dying generations—at their song,
The salmon-falls, the mackerel-crowded seas,
Fish, flesh, or fowl, commend all summer long
Whatever is begotten, born, and dies.
Caught in that sensual music all neglect
Monuments of unageing intellect.

An aged man is but a paltry thing,
A tattered coat upon a stick, unless
Soul clap its hands and sing, and louder sing
For every tatter in its mortal dress,
Nor is there singing school but studying
Monuments of its own magnificence;
And therefore I have sailed the seas and come
To the holy city of Byzantium.

O sages standing in God's holy fire
As in the gold mosaic of a wall,
Come from the holy fire, perne in a gyre,
And be the singing-masters of my soul.
Consume my heart away; sick with desire
And fastened to a dying animal
It knows not what it is; and gather me
Into the artifice of eternity.

Once out of nature I shall never take
My bodily form from any natural thing,
But such a form as Grecian goldsmiths make
Of hammered gold and gold enamelling
To keep a drowsy Emperor awake;
Or set upon a golden bough to sing
To lords and ladies of Byzantium
Of what is past, or passing, or to come.

NOTES

1. Marie-Louise von Franz, *The Golden Ass of Apuleius: The Liberation of the Feminine in Man* (Boston, MA: Shambhala Publications, 1992), pp. 123-124.

2. Adolf Guggenbuhl-Craig, *The Emptied Soul: On the Nature of the Psychopath* (Woodstock, CT: Spring Publications, 1980/1999), p. 26.

3. *Ibid.*, p. 39.

4. *Ibid.*, p. 52.

5. James Hillman, *Pan and the Nightmare: Two Essays* (Putnam, CT: Spring Publications, 1972).

6. C. G. Jung, *The Collected Works of C. G. Jung*, ed. Herbert Read, Michael Fordham, Gerhard Adler and Michael McGuire, trans. R. F. C. Hull, vol.11 (Princeton, NJ: Princeton University Press, 1969), § 291.

7. James Hillman, *A Terrible Love of War* (New York: Penguin Books, 2004), p. 176.

8. Robert Sardello, *Facing the World with Soul* (Hudson, NY: Lindisfarne, 1992), pp. 143, 152.

9. Cited in Raya A. Jones, *Jung, Psychology, Postmodernity* (East Sussex, UK: Routledge, 2007), p. 63.

10. Edward Casey, *Spirit and Soul: Essays in Philosophical Psychology* (Putnam,CT: Spring Publications, 1991/2004), p. 286.

11. In *The Classic Hundred Poems: All-Time Favorites,* ed. William Harmon (New York: Columbia University Press, 1998), pp. 212-213.

BOOK REVIEWS

Edith Hall. *The Return of Ulysses: A Cultural History of Homer's Odyssey*. Baltimore: The John Hopkins University Press, 2008.

REVIEWED BY DENNIS PATRICK SLATTERY

One of the many delights that attends teaching a classic epic like Homer's *Odyssey* year after year, is that the same plot never enters the classroom in quite the same way. It continually, like Proteus himself, shape-shifts, reveals new angles of vision, inflects some scenes more than others, and mirrors in many ways the attitude, temper, and demeanor of the reader for this reading only. Next reading may very well illumine other passageways in the caverns of the deep text.

Edith Hall's stunning new work on cultural history reveals with thick and engaging scholarship just how informing and powerful

Dennis Patrick Slattery, Ph.D., is currently Core Faculty member in the Mythological Studies Program at Pacifica Graduate Institute. He is the author or coeditor of twelve books, among them: *The Idiot: Dostoevsky's Fantastic Prince* (1984); *The Wounded Body: Remembering the Markings of Flesh* (2000); and *Grace in the Desert: Awakening to the Gifts of Monastic Life* (2003). With Lionel Corbett, he coedited *Depth Psychology: Meditations in the Field* (2001) and *Psychology at the Threshold* (2002); with Glen Slater, he coedited *Varieties of Mythic Experience: Essays on Religion, Psyche and Culture* (2008); with Jennifer Leigh Selig, he coedited *Reimagining Education: Essays on Reviving the Soul of Learning* (2009). He has composed three volumes of poetry: *Casting the Shadows: Selected Poems* (2001); *Just Below the Water Line: Selected Poems* (2004); and *Twisted Sky: Selected Poems* (2007).

Homer's classic has been on operas, operettas, film, poetry, other epics, novels, autobiography, painting, social shifts in values, and memoir. After finishing her exhaustive study, I felt exhausted, having traversed centuries of iterations of this magnificent poem; I was more than persuaded that it may be the text of all literary texts, so many children has it spawned in its persuasive poetics over millennia.

In addition, her Bibliography, with over 525 entries, is more than sufficient to keep people reading about the myriad permutations of this one work for the rest of their lives. Bibliographies, I would add, are their own story, tucked in the caboose of the major story of a text. What it suggests to me, in a plot that is more alphabetical than chronological, is that the mythos undergirding and supporting the poetic logos of Homer's language is not only ubiquitous in space but in time. The range of writers from dozens of countries has been pulled into the vortex of this poem and see in it, through its glazed contours, attributes of their own time, circumstance, and social upheavals.

For that reason I begin this review at the back of Hall's elegant achievement. She ends her study by quoting Arthur Machen, who in a work entitled *Hieroglyphics* (1902) claimed that "it is impossible to discuss literature without acknowledging the numinous and indefinable qualities underlying the extraordinary," and he believed that "the *Odyssey* was the yardstick by which all other great literature is to be judged." (p. 215) She follows this assertion with the words of Henry Alford, Dean of Canterbury, who ended his own study of the *Odyssey* by writing in 1841: READER—THIS IS THE GREATEST WORK OF HUMAN GENIUS (p. 216). Hall concurs with both of these encomia by confessing that "after having just expended thousands of words analyzing what has made the *Odyssey* able to surpass the bounds of its own age...Anglican Alford and the Mystic Machen really had quite a point" (p. 216).

Hall divides her study into three sections: Part I: Generic Mutations; Part II: World and Society; Part III: Mind and Psyche. Perhaps the title of the third section will attract most readers of this review, but I assure you the other two sections, giving the *Odyssey* a local habitation in history and a name in its offshoots, is also well worth one's time. The theme of *nostos,* or homecoming, is a dominant force and a compelling action that drives Homer's epic through history. But leaning on etymology a bit more, Hall reveals "that *nostos* is not only related to the name Nestor," but it also has deeper significance; it is related to other Homeric words in the epic, like *neomai* (come, go, arrive) and *noein* (to have an accurate mental perception of a person or situation" (p. 163).

She suggests from this connection that Homer wants us to see that one can never truly go home until one has used one's mental capacities of knowing; homecoming therefore has an epistemological grounding in thought. Perhaps then, thinking does indeed make home so.

Homer's epic has also spawned a particular form of the heroic, asserts Hall, as well as understandings of animals, divinity, women's role in the heroic quest, and the heroism of women themselves.

Being shipwrecked on an island has been in the psyche of civilizations since Homer's story gave it such shape as well. Confronting monsters, showing cunning display as a substitute for power or might, being seduced by figures and forces on one's journey, suffering forgetfulness, being fatigued as a leader and letting one's guard down, seducing and being seduced, telling one's story as part truth, part fabrication, visiting the underworld and conversing with the dead, suffering the trauma of war and heading home disoriented, scarred, shattered, reestablishing one as a leader in one's community, witnessing the grieving wife and mother sustaining the household through cunning by weaving her way into more time, the whining son who comes of age and is guided by a divinity in disguise to seek out his own life, magically turning men into pigs—indeed all the magical situations that fairy tales and stories of the supernatural offer our imaginations— these are a sampling of incidents and conditions that Hall explores through cultural historical metamorphoses of this one epic, at once episodic and particular. It serves as a large and fathomless reservoir of so many tales of the psyche that seem to be, in one format or another, part of our heritage, if not our destiny.

Proteus himself Hall regards as "emblematic of the whole *Odyssey* because of the central position it gives to transformation and disguise— indeed acting of parts" (p. 35) in a chapter entitled "Shapeshifting." Assuming disguises, acting parts that are fictional, antedate the invention of theater in Athens centuries later. In this regard, the divine Athena is the power of disguise, cunning, fabrication, fictionalizing the self, as she transforms Odysseus after he has been washed ashore on the island of the Phaecians. She "made him look taller and stronger,

and made his locks hang in curls from his head, like Hyacinth petals"
(p. 36). Now he reenters the civilized world and the space where he
will tell his story and, through his dramatic achievement, find his way
home. The truth or falsity of the story, the epic reveals, is less important
than a story well-told with consummate craft and well received by an
appreciative audience starved for narratives.

Hall stays with this quality of the epic by suggesting that "the
Odyssey's status as the archetype of all fiction—the mother of all stories
as well as the mother of tall stories...stresses the plurality of tales
echoing the master theme of wandering and return" (p. 46).

On a broader range of her study, one of the most fascinating threads
that Hall weaves through her entire sleuthing of Homer's text through
history is the manner and intensity in which each age, culture, and
national propensity slices into the *Odyssey* with particular alacrity, at
times full of vitriol, and at others as model and as guide. What surfaces
for me in reading this thread is the power of history's association with
myth and the prescience of myth as the inner fabric, its inner lining,
of history. To settle on one version of Odysseus' encounter with Calypso,
Circe, the young daughter of the King and queen of Phaecia, the Sirens,
and other feminine presences of varying powers, for instance, is to miss
perhaps the central purpose of this and other works of the poetic
imagination.

Hall's subtext, in this regard, is to track and document the ways
that the *Odyssey* inspires new thought, is clubbed by oppositional
readings of the action, is used to support and colonize a point of view,
is torqued to fit a sociological inflection, can serve as the foundation of
a political cause, is subsumed into a grander scheme, belief, or fashion
or is used to break into taboos of a cultural period. I find this aspect of
the study as fascinating as the hundreds of permutations in a range of
disciplines and conduits, most energetically in film. There are enough
film titles mentioned that spin from the soil of Ithaca that one could
keep Blockbusters and Netflix busy handling one's single account.
Adding the categories of Travelogues and Science Fiction writing to one's
queue would add yet another lifetime.

In chapter 9, "Women's Work," Hall focuses on perhaps the
strongest symbol next to the scar that Odysseus carries from boyhood:
the loom. Her reading here is worth noting, for "the weaving Penelope
has reappeared in countless paintings, sculptures and tapestries over

the centuries" (p. 115). Since weaving is "a symbol of technology, of taming the natural world until it becomes serviceable to humans" (p. 115), it has connections to the oral quality of epic poetry. The loom and weaving may also be an image of the "oral poet's endless recreation of his song" (p. 115).

Hall goes on to cite one critic, Carolyn Heilbrun (and here is a good example of the way the *Odyssey* may be opened to new ways of seeing), who observes that Penelope "wove the same pattern anew, as emblematic of the feminine project of rewriting the literary canon. Penelope is author of a text, but also the object of new texts which women write as they put male interests under the feminist spotlight" (p. 216). Penelope's weaving is a metaphor for the possibility of "forming new fictions for themselves, but women must 'transform old tales,' and recognize how [they] have transformed old tales in the past" (p. 216).

One last area that might be of most interest to the audience of this review is the Jungian associations and keener interest today in the *Odyssey:* "The journey homeward is the permutation of the quest myth that has attracted attention from Jungian psychoanalytical theorists" (p.164). Hall cites the work of Jean Houston, *The Hero and the Goddess,* as one example of using the work for a therapeutics of self (p. 165). Moreover, "some Jungian critics fuse their concept of the evolution of consciousness as instantiated in mythical archetypes with other notions, developed in Perennial Philosophy" (p.165). Reading, in the fashion and manner of mythologist Joseph Campbell, that metaphor is the native tongue of myth, it is not surprising that Hall cites Jungians interested in the metaphorical and symbolic levels of the epic: "The Jungian Ithaca is a positive destination to be sought assiduously" (p. 166).

Closer to medicine than to myth is the work of Jonathan Shay, whose two books, *Achilles in Vietnam* (1994) and more recently, *Odysseus in America* (2002), use Homer's epics to work with the traumas of Vietnam vets at the Department of Veterans Affairs in Boston and then with wounded soldiers from the Gulf war and the present battles in Iraq and Afghanistan. He uses the poems as ways into the interior world of soldiers by adapting their viewpoint in his therapy. Each episode in each epic serves as an analogy of a psychological or physical locus of woundedness and potential prescriptions for healing. Shay's work is a remarkable recognition of the healing potential of poetry. Hall does not focus on Shay's work in order to preach how "useful" studying classical works of literature can be, but rather to show the polysemous opportunities imbedded in poetic insights into human behavior and human suffering.

I end this review where Edith Hall begins her book: the *Odyssey* is a text that mutates to reflect and absorb the prevailing ethos of the reader couched within a particular mythos, or its absence. The epic ebbs and flows, depending on what psychological state or condition a people is in when they come to it: "the Renaissance, seeing it as a charter text of colonial expansion, emphasized the maritime wanderings; the eighteenth century found the teachable Telemachus more appealing than his father; Modernists were obsessed with the trip to the Underworld" (p. 5). So it goes, and so goes the prevailing attractions of psyche's multivariate barometer.

But both the *Iliad* and the *Odyssey* are poems first and last. In any discussion of what they reveal and conceal, that should not be lost on the reader. Hall's ending affirms this quality of the stories. Poems expand and deepen our orbit of awareness and our conscious level of participation. They should not be used to set agendas or create public policy. Letting them be poems is perhaps finally the greatest gift we can bestow on these and other works of perduring and penetrating fiction.

BOOK REVIEWS

Kathryn Wood Madden. *Dark Light of the Soul.* Great Barrington: Lindisfarne Books, 2008.

REVIEWED BY PAUL W. ASHTON

What a pleasure it has been to review this excellent book on a subject close to my heart, the *ungrund,* the abyss, the void, but the positive aspects of that subject, the idea that the abyss may contain all the good too, and not just the blackness of the bad. For Madden's leitmotif is that the "ground of being ... contains all opposites in potentiality" and this "ground of being" she calls "unitary reality." (p. x). For her, unitary reality underlies both spiritual and psychological experiences, and it is "the culmination of an encounter with the deepest layer of the collective unconscious, the psychoid, archetypal layer, in which we meet all forms of otherness." (p. 1)

Madden uses material from two individuals who have had a profound effect on modern thought: Carl Jung and Jacob Boehme. These

Paul W. Ashton is a psychiatrist and Jungian analyst in private practice in Cape Town where he lives with his wife and youngest daughter. He is the author of the monograph, *From the Brink: Experiences of the Void from a Depth Psychology Perspective* (2007), published by Karnac, and he is the editor of, and contributor to, *Evocations of Absence: Multidisciplinary Perspectives on Void States* (2007), published by Spring Journal Books. He also has published various reviews and lectured on topics such as art, literature, and the Void. He is a member of South African Association of Jungian Analysts (SAAJA) and is at present secretary of the organization.

two men had different experiences of unitary reality, Jung's *nekyia* lasted six years although he wrote his penetrating *Septem Sermones ad Mortuos (Seven Sermons to the Dead)* after three of them, whereas Jacob Boehme's experience occurred in more of a "flash" as he gazed on a pewter bowl bathed in sunlight. For both men their experience led to a profound change in the way they understood the world and became the impetus that led to their later writings and explications. Madden suggests that each man had an experience of "radical otherness" out of which the sense of unitary reality arose and that this reality was interpreted by them in their own way; Jung developing the idea of the Self and Boehme calling that reality Christ.

It is the ego that suffers as it loses its position of feeling that it is the center of psychological life. And it is particularly the fragile ego that suffers as it may become "totally overwhelmed" by what Jung referred to as the chaos of the unconscious. The clinician should watch for that overwhelming as well as for inflation, or a deflation that may result in depression. Jung's image of unitary reality was the Pleroma, an undifferentiated totality that preceded any manifestation, whereas Boehme imagined it as the *Ungrund* or abyss. In Madden's 2007 essay[1] she quotes Waterfield as saying that the "Byss" is "the ground or original foundation", and hence the "Abyss" is "that which is without ground or bottomless and fathomless." This makes sense of the idea that the *Ungrund* or Abyss is the state of formlessness beneath or anterior to all form.[2]

What makes Madden's views so pertinent is that she bridges the gap between Psychology and Spirituality. In writing of "transcendent ultimacy" (which is not unlike Bion's "O"[3]) versus "surface immediacy" she suggests that "our previous notions and images of God, the transcendent, the ultimate—whatever we call it—are shattered and redefined" through our experience of unitary reality. (p. 5) Jung made that a psychic reality whereas Boehme saw it as a direct experience of the divine essence, as spirit, an emanation from God but also from "a primal preexistent freedom that is before God." (p. 8) Thus there is a connection between Jung's Pleroma, before its first differentiation into Effective Fullness (or God) and Effective Emptiness (or Devil), and the idea of the primal void or state of formlessness. Madden calls this a "pre-differentiated state of being" and suggests that it "reaches all the way back in time, to the mother of our developmental years, and *before time*, to that moment of severance from our creator, the moment in which we became incarnate." (p. 14, my italics) Here she moves unashamedly from the psychological to the spiritual. (It makes me think, too, that Developmental Jungians and Archetypal Jungians should combine their areas of expertise.)

In Chapter 2, Madden addresses the "Distinctions between Psychology and Religion." She begins by stating that "the boundaries between psychology and religion are humanly forged [by the ego perhaps] but the membrane between them is a permeable one." (p. 19, my brackets) Later she writes: "I am interested in inner experience that leads into dimensions of the unconscious that point beyond us." (p. 24) In fact she feels that Jung's grounding of the "transcending principle in the psyche ... is important, but, ... incomplete." (p. 21) For her there is something more outside of the psyche. I like the following quotation: "A part of the self, which Cousins[4] calls the 'abyss of the self, plunges into the divine abyss, or better, finds itself undifferentiated from the divine abyss. There in that divine abyss questions of differentiation cannot arise.'" (pp. 26-27)

Some analogies that she draws in this chapter I found unhelpful. However her description of different types of abyss and their effects, ranging from the terrifying to the ecstatic, is excellent, and gives one a useful sense of what one could call the "intermittent bipolarity" of the experience of unitary reality, as one of a pair of contained opposites enters consciousness. It is this reality, symbolized by the abyss, that "may help us to understand how our dealing with contrast and otherness from the inside view informs how we deal with otherness outside ... in the course of the individuation process." (p. 46)

Chapter 3, "Radical Otherness", extends Maddens exploration of the theme of unitary reality, which implies "diving beyond what we know ... and letting what is found there inform us." (p. 49) John Dourley in his exploration of the Beguine mystics calls this "the mystical anamnesis of the nothing."[5] Dourley makes the point that it is not only the descent that is important, but the return with new information or insight. Madden relates an example of a patient of Frances Wickes where figures wove "threads of blackness" into "a great void that had no form nor boundaries." (p. 51) She then describes in more detail the context of Boehme's life and his visions and writings that seemed to spring from a period of deep melancholy. Initially he understood that the "true ground of God" was an "un-ground or *Ungrund*", but later he equated "the *nothing* with the *all*. The *emptiness* is also the *fullness;* both beyond space and time, the *abyss* is also the "Pleroma."(p. 58) This paradox is an apophatic realization that explores the fact that any definition of God limits God, unless the definition is phrased in a negative way. God is not the ground, God is not-ground.

Chapter 4 is titled "Jung and the Pleroma", and in this chapter Madden successfully differentiates Jung's experience and writings about the abyss from those of Boehme. She focuses on Jung's direct encounter with the abyss through his years of "breakdown and breakthrough" from 1913 to 1916 and beyond, and suggests that Jung was one of the prophets who "are summoned as vessels through which new insights are made manifest of a consciousness higher or more satisfactory than the one that previously existed." (p. 71) She writes convincingly of Jung's near overwhelming by the currents of the unconscious as well as of his spiritual guide in the form of Philemon and the transformation of his understanding of the abyss from the negative view of Christianity to that of the Pleroma in which all the opposites co-exist but in an occult form. "The Pleroma, for Jung, describes an uncreated potentiality beyond time and space from which all being emerges." (p. 79) Jung wrote down his ideas in the short work *Septem Sermones ad Mortuos,* and it was only later that he came across similar ideas in his reading of Gnostic texts. Madden gives one an invigorating tour of the "new" ideas that poured out from Jung during this time.

In her next chapter, "When Deep calls unto Deep", Madden first identifies five characteristic features of the (healthy) experience of unitary reality. She suggests that it is a dynamic process, follows "a period of confusion, melancholy, and/or psychic suffering", involves entering "an extraordinary 'inner space'", and "leads to further integration of the personality" and feelings of "awe and gratitude." (p. 88) She fearlessly enters the debate about whether mystical experiences are spiritual or psychotic and draws on the 1992 work by T. Agosin whose paper was titled "Psychosis, Dreams, and Mysticism in the Clinical Domain." Using Agosin's criteria she analyses both Jung's and Boehme's experiences, saying about Jung: "In the end (his) 'breakdown' was a 'breakthrough', a creative illness from which emerged a new man." (p. 106) It seems likely "that there is one unitary reality that is encountered in mystical and psychotic experience alike" and that experiencing that may have different outcomes depending on the particular ego's capacity to integrate the encounter or be disintegrated by it. (p. 107)

In chapter 6, Madden discusses "The Self: Uniting Opposites", and the way that the Self orders or centers the personality but also seems to be the container for the *coniunctio oppositorum* through fostering an experience of unitary reality. She quotes from Neumann and discusses Jung's assertion that "(f)or lack of empirical data I have neither knowledge nor understanding of such forms of being, which are commonly called spiritual." (p. 112) This is in spite of his experiences of the Pleroma and journey into the depths of the unconscious. Yet she also quotes Jung writing about the "veil" that may be hiding "the uncomprehended absolute object". (p. 112) Clearly, for Madden, this "object" is real despite being unknowable; it is not just a psychological theory, or truth even, but exists outside of the psyche, it is "preexistent".

It has often seemed to me problematic that individuals with a religious or spiritual bent seem to lose that connection with the "radically other" during their analysis. A few of my clients have been able to separate out the "church" and its dogma, which they have experienced as a collective or social "man-made" organization, from their "relationship with God" which, for them, is an entirely private affair. In the following three chapters, "Meeting Clinical Otherness", "Trauma, Dreams and Resistance to Otherness", and "Soul Retrieval: The Lonely One", Madden describes and amplifies case material in a modest and helpful way, using the concepts, such as unitary reality, the transcendent function, spirit, soul, etc., that she has elaborated in the early chapters of the book. These chapters are very useful in that they keep alive the idea of something outside the psyche itself, contact with which has been transformative for individual patients.

Although her last chapter is called "Through the Air Hole", it takes one deeper still while giving a tour of some of what has gone before. Here are Madden's words again:

> In the end, we are not left with a nameless, meaningless chaos, some kind of grand 'cosmic joke.' In the experience of the abyss or of 'the divine as eternity, truth and goodness,' we come to see that we reflect a far deeper reality than our ego consciousness could possibly know. We may see through the 'air hole' into the dark, pre-existent void, but our longing gaze is met and returned by the light of a star. (p. 255)

I wish that this fine book had been around when I wrote my monograph on the void.[6] *From the Brink* would have been the richer for it.

NOTES

1. Kathryn Madden, "Images of the Abyss", *Quadrant* XXXVll:l Winter 2007, 51ff.

2. See John Dourley, "Jung, Some Mystics and the Void", in Paul W. Ashton (ed.) *Evocations of Absence: Multidisciplinary Perspectives on Void States* (New Orleans: Spring Journal Books, 2007), p. 72.

3. James S. Grotstein, *"Bion's Transformation in 'O' and the Concept of the 'Transcendent Position'"*. (1997). Obtained from the Internet in 2004.

4. E.H. Cousins, "The Self and Not-Self in Christian Mysticism", in R. Carter (ed.), *God, the Self and Nothingness* (New York: Paragon, 1990).

5. John Dourley, "Memory And Emergence: Jung And The Mystical Anamnesis Of The Nothing", from the CD of the *Proceedings of the 16ᵗʰ IAAP Congress in Barcelona*, Lyn Cowan (Ed.). (2003).

6. Paul W. Ashton, *From the Brink: Experiences of the Void from a Depth Psychology Perspective* (London: Karnac, 2007).

BOOK REVIEWS

Janet O. Dallett. *Listening to the Rhino: Violence and Healing in a Scientific Age.* Aequitas Books, 2008.

REVIEWED BY CRAIG CHALQUIST

Although many books have been written about the psychology of violence (as I learned during my days directing a program for court-referred perpetrators), Dr. Dallett's clearly and concisely written book offers thoughtful and sometimes surprising reflections, case anecdotes, and scholarly musings on violence as a *spiritual* problem.

One of the most refreshing aspects of the book is that instead of filing away discussion of aggression and violence in a handy "archetypal evil" pigeonhole (the Jungian "daimon made me do it" counterpart to Freud's unfruitful hypothesis of a death drive), Dallett uncovers the actually lived relationship between repressed archetypal potentials and the conscious mind that does the repressing. "To the extent we are … torn between perfectionist ideals and the reality of what a person can be or achieve … a rage-filled counter-personality builds up energy in

Craig Chalquist, Ph.D., is a core faculty member of the School of Holistic Studies at John F. Kennedy University, where he teaches depth psychology, ecopsychology, and social science research. He is the author of *Terrapsychology: Re-engaging the Soul of Place* (Spring Journal Books, 2007) and co-editor with Linda Buzzell of *Ecotherapy: Healing with Nature in Mind* (Sierra Club Books, 2009). He lives and works in California's Bay Area.

the unconscious" (p. 82). In my men's groups, we always knew which men were at greatest risk for another violent incident: those who maintained that their anger was an aberration they had now overcome with penance and good intentions.

The same dynamic of denial applies to entire nations—and goes far toward explaining why the "nicest" and most restrained people sometimes pick up a gun. Here is a sentence that should be framed in every courtroom instead of the Ten Commandments: "... Violence is the human spirit's protest against the enforcement of more goodness than it can stomach" (p. 92). An overemphasis on decency and virtue not only darkens the personal and collective shadow, it unconsciously identifies with divine goodness and thereby falls into inflation and self-righteousness. In light of this observation, the missionary and the terrorist stand revealed as brothers-in-arms.

Listening to the Rhino deals not just with outwardly expressed violence, however, but with confronting and transforming archetypal violence (as imaged by the dream figure of the Rhino) manifesting from within the psyche. The chapter headings reflect this depth-psychological emphasis:

1. Freeing the Spirit Trapped in Sickness
2. The Rhino
3. How to Listen to The Rhino
4. Teresa [a case example]
5. The Paradoxical God of Violence
6. Sedating the Savage
7. The End and the Beginning

Following up on Jung's advice to translate emotions into images, Dallett writes about how a symptom or an illness, whether somatic or psychogenic (or both), represents an attempt at incarnation imparted by a spiritual force badly in need of translation from a literal source of suffering into an actively lived symbolic work. "Your symptoms are a potential friend, not an enemy to be destroyed, for they speak with the voice of a vital spirit that is asking for attention" (p. 64). Healing requires finding what this force wants and needs for its own realization. Making a work of art, breaking a therapeutic impasse, or modifying a relationship are three of many possibilities for new forms of expression that liberate the archetypal power from remaining trapped "in matter" (in symptom or illness).

Active imagination furnishes a primary Jungian tool for this kind of deep work, but as Dallett reminds the reader, Marie-Louise von Franz always insisted on the importance of completing at least these four steps: setting the ego aside, tending the images, reacting to the images, and *putting the results to work in life* (italics added). It is easy for introverts in particular to skip the final step, but doing so severs inner from outer, contemplation from action. (I once inadvertently offended an analyst who was boasting that her male patients were adept at writing love poems to the anima and painting passionate pictures of her by wondering out loud, "Do these guys ever go out on a date?") As an introvert I know that we will seize any excuse to hide, especially when the outer world feels dangerous; one of our best strategies for staying under cover is the omnipotent but largely unquestioned belief that inner change somehow magically transforms outer reality.

This belief may well be a candidate for what Dallett identifies in another context as a pathological identification with spirit: what Jung identified as inflation. An example discussed in the book is the New Age canard that we cause all our problems. Also criticized is the widespread habit of using meditation to get rid of (repress) the emotionally charged images flowing from the unconscious. These and other New Age maneuvers are enlisted in the service of propping up the happy persona that conceals the darker dimensions of conflictual psychic life. One can almost hear in popular "thinking positive" propaganda the voice of the family cheerleader castigating brothers and sisters for being so "depressing" as to discuss Dad's alcoholic violence— or on a national level, the violence inflicted by the precarious rule of empire—out in the open.

In the chapter "Sedating the Savage," Dallett presents many examples of how psychotropic medication represses unpleasant emotions while supporting artificial idealized states of happiness and surface contentment. James Hillman has presented a similar critique, which can be summed up by the dictum: Silence the symptom and lose the soul. Furthermore, all forms of repression ultimately strengthen that which they repress. Yet Dallett goes farther: Psychiatric medication should be used only to contain severe symptoms, she argues, preferably in small doses and even then only temporarily. Although the alarm should be raised about overmedication—psychotropics are even being found in public water supplies—I have known people with major psychiatric disorders for whom the advice to go off meds to do "psychological work" has been disastrous. I am thinking of people legitimately diagnosed with bipolar disorder who took similar advice from their gurus and ended up psychotic; one, a former student, is still homeless and ranting in the streets. I have also known people with schizophrenia who could never hold down jobs or attend school without some kind of long-term antipsychotic medication. What's important in such cases is to prescribe a correct and accurate dosage not only to contain extreme symptoms but to make psychological work possible—work that includes dealing with the psyche's responses to the need for medication.

"Some—maybe all—destructively violent actions spring from the ego's inability to respect, confront, and wrestle with the Self's enraged response to galling levels of powerlessness" (p. 104). I would like to see this insightfully expressed logic extended more often to the state of the oppressed struggling on every side and in all corners of the world. Most of the examples of violence in this book break forth from the uptight middle class, where swings are removed from parks to prevent lawsuits. What about the poor who live in the parks? As fantastic amounts of money continue to be funneled upward, the number of Americans living below the poverty line soars higher than ever before. Racism and sexism continue to be major American sources of suffering. If the Self in such sufferers is enraged, social constraints and injustices give it excellent reason to be, for as Martin Luther King, Jr. pointed out long ago, a riot [like a symptom] is the language of the unheard.

BOOK REVIEWS

Nathan Schwartz-Salant. *The Black Nightgown: The Fusional Complex and the Unlived Life*. Wilmette, Illinois: Chiron, 2007.

REVIEWED BY AUGUST J. CWIK

At first glance, the dynamics discussed by Nathan Schwartz-Salant in his new book, *The Black Nightgown*—fusion and separation—might seem familiar to clinicians as merger/attachment/identification and separation/avoidance/disconnection. We generally tend to think of them as alternating in a patient's life, i.e., approach/attachment to a love object, followed by fears of merger, leading to withdrawal and separation. But as one reads further you begin to realize that Schwartz-Salant is attempting to describe a much more nuanced clinical state/field in which these opposing tendencies are experienced simultaneously. He has always been a keen tracker of mad parts in otherwise sane people as evidenced in his previous books.[1] The "madness" of the fusional dynamic under discussion is clearly identified in his statement, "When the Fusional Complex is activated, separation from an accustomed 'safe territory' of established patterns—or, in an interaction, separation from another person's spoken or unspoken

August J. Cwik, Psy.D. is a clinical psychologist, hypnotherapist, and Jungian analyst in private practice in the Chicago area. He is a member of the Chicago Society of Jungian Analysts and the Inter-Regional Society of Jungian Analysts. He is an Assistant Editor of the *Journal of Analytical Psychology* and has published articles on the structure of analysis, alchemy, supervision, dreams, and active imagination as well as numerous reviews.

desires or demands—can lead to extreme and destabilizing anxiety, a compensatory rage, and temporarily impaired capacity for reflection and clear thinking" (pp. 5-6).

The concept of the Fusional Complex, just by its nature of being comprised of opposite and conflicting tendencies, tends to be difficult to grasp, both intellectually and clinically. At one moment one feels a depth of understanding for it only to fade into confusion the next. Schwartz-Salant does his best to explicate the experience of the dynamic both through comprehension and therapeutic examples. As an aid to understanding, the very first chapter clearly delineates both the purpose of identifying the presence of the Fusional Complex and gives a detailed summary of its features. According to Schwartz-Salant, the reasons for identifying and understanding the nature of the Fusional Complex include: being better able to appreciate the power of the psychotic anxieties that are disrupting the patient's sense of existence while becoming more aware of the activities that trigger these anxieties; acquiring a deeper understanding of "stuck" analyses in conditions such as borderline, narcissistic, or dissociative states, as here-and-now awareness is caught and relayed to the patient; the analyst's conscious awareness of the existence of fusional states can have a positive unconscious impact on the patient's defensive system (although mutual experience and awareness is preferred); and, the concept itself helps us to see what hides from ordinary perception which is rarely revealed in history taking, dream interpretation, or even traditional forms of transference interpretation. This last notion is one of Schwartz-Salant's longstanding clinical arguments: one has to have some conceptual idea of a dynamic before it can be brought to light in a clinical encounter. The theory provides a lens through which interactive experiences can be seen and made conscious.

The main features of the Fusional Complex are the simultaneity of fusional drives and impulses with a tendency towards distance and non-communication, and the chaotic, disorganizing energy at the archetypal core of the complex which can threaten a patient's sense of coherence and identity. A number of auxiliary features are noted by Schwartz-Salant: attempts at separation lead to extreme anxiety and loss of energy; there is often a hidden and extreme fantasy life; containing space is precluded by the complex, so projective identifications that usually invoke the analyst's imagination are not available for interpretation; the patient has a damaged relationship to his/her own inner life replaced by substitute "skins", such as self-hatred, anomalous body experiences, and passive fantasizing; the field can be permeated by extreme fear and anger while there is a need to blame someone for being at fault; there can be sudden jumps in emotion or discontinuity of experience that is bewildering or frightening; there can be a powerful feeling of abjection with fears of contagion; there is often much unlived potential and life leading to humiliation; the analyst tends to dissociate from the field because of the confusion or experience of extreme physical symptoms; the analyst may feel blank or deadened; the psychotic nature of the field can cause a sense of strangeness that things said are often taken in some bizarre manner; the analyst tends to think in traditional diagnostic categories, i.e., schizoid, borderline, but the underlying complex leads to "anti-therapeutic reactions" and severe resistance; and finally, and more hopefully, as the analyst learns to "see" into the field and name what is happening, the opposites of fusion and distance may become more conscious as a sequence of states.

Schwartz-Salant has always emphasized a kind of "seeing" by using "non-ordinary perception or vision" in which statements to the patient about what is perceived take precedence over developmental interpretations. This book, similar to his previous books, provides numerous clinical vignettes. Activation of the Fusional Complex causes the analyst to be unable to distinguish his/her own feelings or "innerness" from that derived from the patient. Traditional techniques tend to cause extreme anxiety as they force a premature subject-object separation. Following Gebser, Schwartz-Salant encourages "aperspectival awareness." This way of seeing is achieved through "ego contracting, loosening its hold, and joining the felt processes of the unconscious field between people" (p. 23). The analyst must "lean into the field" in order to become more interested in the confusion and contradictory nature of the field that he/she would tend to avoid. Schwartz-Salant is one of those analysts who talks directly to the patient "about" what he envisions as opposed to Ogden[2] who makes a point of speaking "from" inner awareness. Schwartz-Salant emphasizes that the Fusional Complex is not the thing that he first looks for; it is only after other explanations have been exhausted does he go to this dynamic for understanding. It tends, like a mercurial element, to escape detection. He states that naming the complex with a patient and reflecting upon the "impossible" mixture of opposites, often is enough to free the analysand from a sense of possession. Patients suffering under the Fusional Complex often feel a lack of having an inner sense of self. Similar to Kalsched's[3] description of trauma patients who have developed a "self-care system" to protect the latent self, Schwartz-Salant thinks of these patients as never having embodied or activated the self into space-time existence. He makes the powerful statement that, "Uncovering the Fusional Complex is the beginning of the energizing of an individuation process that urges the integration of previously unconscious material, or engages a long-denied creativity issue or conflicts in relationship, or the fear of embodiment, or a phase of work in the transference relationship" (p. 52).

After establishing that the Fusional Complex is often difficult to detect, perhaps appearing only after years of analysis (an example is given of uncovering one in an analysand after 25 years of analysis), Schwartz-Salant goes on to describe that it is ubiquitous and found everywhere. He states, "...the Fusional Complex is like the despised alchemical *prima materia*, said to be vile and worthless, ubiquitous and easily discarded, and yet essential for the creation of that most highly goal of the alchemical *opus*: the *lapis*, a symbol of the self" (p. 69). He makes a convincing argument that the Fusional Complex is behind many humiliating incidents of everyday life in which something or somebody cannot be left due to the resulting anxieties, i.e., addictions, codependency, procrastination, lateness, and even losing things. Indeed while reading this book I was working on another paper. I was so obsessed about not losing it from the computer (an experience I am sure nearly everyone has had), I set-up an additional back-up system, even though I already had a quite suitable back-up in place. Through a technological fluke, read unconscious disconnection, I managed to lose newly written material three times, before I discovered the problem! It appears, *a la* the Fusional Complex, I was so fused with, yet wanting separation from, the paper that I managed to generate considerable amounts of anxiety and anger for myself.

Schwartz-Salant coins the word "skins" to denote a type of defense against experience of this impossible fusion-distance dilemma. A skin is a protective garment of inner life or the subtle body as he prefers to think of it. The "Black Nightgown" of the book's title is a reference to one such skin used by a particular patient. It is symbolic of the rigid containment of her subtle body as it protects against the dread of separation. In this book Schwartz-Salant moves away from using traditional psychoanalytic jargon to express his points. Integration of other analytic perspectives was a hallmark of his earlier works. This can be seen as a senior theorist attempting to discuss clinical insights in a new way without the encumbrance of old paradigms. The psychopathology he describes is being a kind of "hollow man" with an un-embodied self due to the workings of the Fusional Complex. He discusses case material in which a hidden fantasy life functions as a substitute skin. Often these passive fantasies reveal underlying rage and fear. For individuation to occur one must consciously embrace the suffering of the Fusional Complex rather than take refuge in passive fantasy. Schwartz-Salant astutely describes the utter feelings of abjection and the need to blame others in working with those caught in a severe Fusional Complex and how these feelings are transmitted to the analyst in a type of contagion. The analyst's own Fusional Complex can get constellated and disrupt his/her ability to function analytically.

The archetypal core of the Fusional Complex, the inability to either separate from an object or stay connected, is best expressed in the myth of Cybele and Attis. This myth has provided Schwartz-Salant with many clinical insights over the years. The final chapter is broadsweeping in scope, and this myth becomes the primal myth underlying all myth while the Fusional Complex becomes the core of all psychopathology. The Attis-Cybele myth receives a kind of centrality comparable to the Oedipus myth in Freudian psychoanalysis. This chapter is eloquently written as it describes the collective pathology of modern culture caught in a fusional state that does not allow individuals to see and appreciate otherness. In a strange sense, these claims actually tend to undermine the beautiful simplicity of his clinical acumen. The sharp clinical lens that he provides throughout the book becomes somewhat obscured by his hopes that he has indeed found the Philosopher's Stone of analysis.

NOTES

1. Nathan Schwartz-Salant, *The Mystery of Human Relationship: Alchemy and the Transformation of Self* (London: Routledge, 1998); *The Borderline Personality: Vision and Healing* (Wilmette, Illinois: Chiron,

1989); *Narcissism and Character Transformation: The Psychology of Narcissistic Character Disorders* (Toronto: Inner City, 1982).

2. T.H. Ogden, "Reverie and Interpretation," *Psychoanalytic Quarterly, LXVI,* 567-595, 1997.

3. Donald Kalsched, *The Inner World of Trauma: Archetypal Defenses of the Personal Spirit* (London and New York: Routledge, 1996).

Marion Woodman Foundation

Photo credit: Cheryl Van Scoy

The Marion Woodman Foundation is a non-profit organization founded to ensure the work initiated in BodySoul Rhythms® Intensives, created by Marion Woodman, Mary Hamilton, and Ann Skinner, continues and flourishes. This work is based on the belief that psyche and soma are inseparable, and must be worked on together to become more conscious. The unique integration incorporates working with dreams and imagery together with body and voice in a powerful way while honoring the uniqueness of each individual.

The roots of this work grow out of C.G. Jung's understanding of the psyche, a deep respect for dreams, the wisdom of the body, and Marion Woodman's passionate commitment to articulating the Sacred Feminine and the embodied Soul.

The Marion Woodman Foundation offers a variety of seminars, workshops, and intensives throughout the world. Space is available in the following programs:

Wellsprings of Feminine Renewal VI: Stars Beneath the Sea
July 3-9, 2009, in Santa Barbara, California

Psyche/Body Connection: A BodySoul Intensive in Switzerland
September 6-13, 2009

In the Realms of Coatlicue: A BodySoul Intensive in Mexico
January 29-February 5, 2010

The Soul's Journey in Dream and Body: A BodySoul Intensive in Ireland, *June 8-15, 2010*

Contact the Marion Woodman Foundation:

address: 492 Corralitos Road, Corralitos, CA 95076
email: office@mwoodmanfoundation.org
phone: 831-724-4040   **fax:** 831-724-4044

www.mwoodmanfoundation.org

University of Essex

Centre for Psychoanalytic Studies

MA in Jungian and Post-Jungian Studies

Yearly intake in October. Early applications recommended.

A unique and internationally acclaimed MA designed for a wide range of students from both clinical and non-clinical backgrounds.

- Examines in depth the texts, contexts and concepts of Jungian psychology, as well as its applications both clinically and in areas such as cultural and gender studies, social and political theory, philosophy, myth, and religion

- Full-time and part-time provision

- Taught by internationally renowned academics and analysts

Also of interest: **MA in Myth, Literature and the Unconscious** (taught jointly with the Department of Literature, Film and Theatre Studies)

For further information, visit:
http://www.essex.ac.uk/centres/psycho/programmes/ma/ma-schemes.htm
Or contact: Senior Student Administrator, Centre for Psychoanalytic Studies, University of Essex, Wivenhoe Park, Colchester CO4 3SQ UK; email: cpsgrad@essex.ac.uk; telephone: +44 (0)1206 873745

quadrant

Journal of the C. G. Jung Foundation for Analytical Psychology

Quadrant is the C. G. Jung Foundation's journal of interesting and accessible articles and reviews on analytical psychology and related subjects. It is devoted to the full spectrum of Jungian psychology.

Quadrant offers essays grounded in personal and professional experience, which focus on issues of matter and body, psyche and spirit. Major themes of Jung's work are explored through mythological, archetypal and alchemical motifs and images, as well as through historical, scientific, clinical, and cultural observation.

quadrant is published twice annually, two issues to a volume.

Subscribe to quadrant.

Subscription Rates: *Take advantage of our multiple-year subscription discounts!*

- 1 year (2 issues): $32
- 2 years (4 issues): $58
- 3 years (6 issues): $87

Add $12.00 per year postage and handling for international subscriptions.

**To subscribe or to order back issues, please visit our website at:
www.cgjungny.org.**

Quadrant: Journal of the C.G. Jung Foundation for Analytical Psychology

28 East 39th Street, New York, NY 10016
Tel: (212) 697-6430.

UNIVERSITY OF CALIFORNIA PRESS

JOURNALS + DIGITAL PUBLISHING

JUNG JOURNAL
Culture & Psyche

JUNG
JOURNAL
Culture & Psyche

WINTER 2009   VOLUME 3, NUMBER 1

Jung Journal: Culture & Psyche
is an international journal
offering readers a Jungian
perspective on contempo-
rary culture–including film,
literature, art, poetry, music,
and multimedia.

PUBLISHED QUARTERLY
ONLINE AND IN PRINT

"for those seeking thoughtfulness and depth on the night-sea journey"
—CLARISSA PINKOLA-ESTÈS, Ph.D.
Author of *Women Who Run with the Wolves*

"it seems to embody the emerging creative spirit itself"
—JOAN CHODOROW, Ph.D.
Editor, *Jung on Active Imagination*

"a prime source for anyone wanting to keep up with thoughtful developments in the Jungian world"
—JOE CAMBRAY, Ph.D.
President-Elect, International Association for Analytical Psychology

www.ucpressjournals.com

where depth psychology is happening

M.A. & Ph.D. Programs in Depth Psychology, the Humanities and Mythological Studies

Interdisciplinary Coursework
Our programs expand the study of the science of psychology to include the study of literature, religion, art, and mythology.

Talented and Dedicated Faculty
Our faculty includes many of the world s leading scholars and practitioners of depth psychology. They bring true passion and a wealth of experience into the classroom.

Three-Day Learning Sessions
Psychology and mythological studies students attend monthly three-day learning sessions during fall, winter, and spring.

Pacifica Online
Humanities students learn in their home environments, and gather on campus twice each year for a week in residence.

PACIFICA
GRADUATE INSTITUTE

For additional information
call 805.969.3626, ext. 103
or visit www.pacifica.edu
249 Lambert Rd., Carpinteria, CA 93013

Pacifica Graduate Institute is an accredited graduate school with two beautiful campuses a few miles south of Santa Barbara, California. Students come to Pacifica to pursue a variety of personal and professional goals within a challenging and diverse academic community of like-minded colleagues. The Institute s degree programs are informed by the traditions of depth psychology, and presented in an innovative format sensitive to the needs of adult graduate students.

New from

Spring Journal Books

(THE BOOK PUBLISHING IMPRINT OF SPRING: A JOURNAL OF ARCHETYPE AND CULTURE, THE OLDEST JUNGIAN PSYCHOLOGY JOURNAL IN THE WORLD)

Reimagining Education
Essays on Reviving the Soul of Learning

EDITORS: **Dennis Patrick Slattery and Jennifer Leigh Selig**

ISBN 978-1-882670-63-5 | 212 pgs | Price $25.95

In this collection of essays, Dennis Patrick Slattery and Jennifer Leigh Selig bring together eighteen master teachers—from elementary, high school, undergraduate, graduate, and adult education and across many disciplines—to share their reflections on reviving, revisioning, and renewing the soul of learning.

What timeless and perennial qualities of excellence are germane to teaching and learning both of which serve the life of imagination and the further cultivation of the soul? The answers rest in these essays themselves, which contain repositories of wisdom by teachers with decades of experience in the classroom, whose only mandate in contributing to this volume was to speak their own truths that have informed thousands of learners young and old.

Contributors include James Hillman, Thomas Moore, David L. Miller, Christine Downing, an interview with Stephen Aizenstat by Nancy Galindo, and much more.

JENNIFER LEIGH SELIG, PH.D., was a high school teacher for sixteen years before moving into "higher" education for the last five years. She has taught literature, composition, psychology, mythology, drama, and educational theory to students between the ages of 12 and 78. She currently serves as department chair in the Depth Psychology program at Pacifica Graduate Institute.

DENNIS PATRICK SLATTERY, PH.D., has been teaching for 40 years in classrooms that include special education in elementary grades, secondary, undergraduate, graduate, and adult education programs. He believes the soul never ceases its craving to know and to know with the entirety of one's being. He is the author or co-editor of 13 books and dozens of articles on literature, psychology, mythology, popular culture, and spirituality.

To order, please visit our online bookstore at:
www.springjournalandbooks.com

Spring Journal Books
(504) 524-5117
627 Ursulines Street, #7 New Orleans, LA 70116

New from

Spring Journal Books

(THE BOOK PUBLISHING IMPRINT OF SPRING: A JOURNAL OF ARCHETYPE AND CULTURE,
THE OLDEST JUNGIAN PSYCHOLOGY JOURNAL IN THE WORLD)

Imagination & Medicine
The Future of Healing in an Age of Neuroscience

EDITORS: **Stephen Aizenstat and Robert Bosnak**

ISBN 978-1-882670-62-8 | 212 pgs | Price $24.95

In this groundbreaking collection of essays, medical scientists from the fields of psychoneuroimmunology, neuroscience, and the placebo effect join with practitioners from the fields of non-Western medicine—the Asklepieia, body/soul therapies, and dreamwork—to explore the intimate relationship between imagination and physical health. By looking at medical science, present and past, native and modern, these scholars, physicians, and healers offer their vision of what medical treatment and psychotherapy might look like in the future. Artists and architects with expertise in health care also describe and present new designs for healing centers that bring together current scientific knowledge and age-old healing practices. This collection will be of great interest to those looking to the future in the fields of therapy, medicine, and the healing professions.

STEPHEN AIZENSTAT, PH.D., is a clinical psychologist, marriage and family therapist, and the founding president of Pacifica Graduate Institute. He has conducted hundreds of dreamwork seminars through the United State, Europe, and Asia. He is the author of the book *Dream Tending* (Spring Journal Books, 2009).

ROBERT BOSNAK, PSYA, is a Zürich-trained Jungian analyst who has developed a method of working with dreams called Embodied Imagination. He is the author of *Embodiment: Creative Imagination in Medicine, Art and Travel, A Little Course in Dreams, Dreaming with an Aids Patient,* and *Tracks in the Wilderness of Dreaming.*

Contributors include: Stephen Aizenstat, Marion Woodman, Robert Bosnak, Kimberley Patton, Michael Kearney, Michael Ortiz Hill, Judith R. Harris, Esther M. Sternberg, Lauren Y. Atlas and Tor D. Wager, Ernest Lawrence Rossi and Kathryn Lane Rossi, Bessel A. van der Kolk, Richard Kradin, and Anthony Lawlor.

To order, please visit our online bookstore at:
www.springjournalandbooks.com

Spring Journal Books
(504) 524-5117
627 Ursulines Street, #7 New Orleans, LA 70116

New from

Spring Journal Books

(THE BOOK PUBLISHING IMPRINT OF SPRING: A JOURNAL OF ARCHETYPE AND CULTURE,
THE OLDEST JUNGIAN PSYCHOLOGY JOURNAL IN THE WORLD)

MICHAEL KEARNEY

A Place of Healing
Working with Nature & Soul at the End of Life

AUTHOR: **Michael Kearney, M.D.**

ISBN 978-1-228670-58-1 | 292 pgs | Price $23.95

Dr. Michael Kearney demonstrates in this book that while the medical model has undoubted strengths in easing pain, it is limited in its ability to alleviate the psychological and spiritual suffering that often accompanies terminal illness. Complementing physical treatment with such depth approaches as dreamwork, poetry, divination, and a revitalized connection with nature, Kearney, a palliative care specialist, allows us to begin to integrate scientific and psychological metaphors. We may thereby forge a more comprehensive and holistic response to the greatest challenges we all have to face: suffering and dying.

Through imaginative re-envisionings of the mythology and rites of ancient Greek Asklepian healing, Kearney helps us discover a way of recognizing and caring for the soul in its most critical moments and proposes a new model for the healing of suffering which draws on the best practices of both the medical and Asklepian traditions.

MICHAEL KEARNEY, M.D., has spent over 25 years working as a physician in end-of-life care. He trained and worked at St. Christopher's Hospice in London with Dame Cicely Saunders, the founder of the modern hospice movement, and subsequently worked for many years as Medical Director of Our Lady's Hospice in Dublin, and later with Professor Balfour Mount at McGill University in Montreal. He is currently a Medical Director of the Palliative Care Service at Santa Barbara Cottage Hospital and an Associate Medical Director at Visiting Nurse and Hospice Care, also in Santa Barbara. He also acts as medical director to the Anam Cara Project for Compassionate Companionship in Life and Death in Bend, Oregon.

To order, please visit our online bookstore at:
www.springjournalandbooks.com

Spring Journal Books
(504) 524-5117
627 Ursulines Street, #7 New Orleans, LA 70116

New from

Spring Journal Books

(THE BOOK PUBLISHING IMPRINT OF SPRING: A JOURNAL OF ARCHETYPE AND CULTURE, THE OLDEST JUNGIAN PSYCHOLOGY JOURNAL IN THE WORLD)

STEPHEN AIZENSTAT, PH.D., is a clinical psychologist, marriage and family therapist, and the founding president of Pacifica Graduate Institute. For more than 35 years he has explored the power of dreams through the study of depth psychology and the pursuit of his own research. He has collaborated with many masters in the field, including Joseph Campbell, Marion Woodman, Robert Johnson, and James Hillman; as well as native elders worldwide. Dr. Aizenstat has conducted hundreds of dreamwork seminars throughout the United States, Europe, and Asia. He lives with his wife and three children in Santa Barbara, California.

Dream Tending
Hardback Edition

AUTHOR: **Stephen Aizenstat**

ISBN 978-1-882670-55-0 | 287 pgs | Price $38.00

You had the most amazing dream last night. It spoke to your highest aspiration, your most secret wish, presenting a vision of a future that was right for you. But now, in the cold light of day, that inspiring dream is gone forever...or is it? According to Dr. Stephen Aizenstat, a psycho-therapist, university professor, and dream specialist, dreams are not just phantoms that pass in the night, but a present living reality that you can engage with and learn from in your daily life. In *Dream Tending* Dr. Aizenstat shows how to access the power of your dreams to:

- Transform nightmare figures into profound and helpful mentors
- Bring fresh warmth and intimacy into your relationships
- Overcome obsessions, compulsions, and addictions
- Engage healing forces of your dreams through imaginal "medicines"
- Re-imagine your career and cope with difficulties in the workplace
- Discover the potential of your untapped creativity
- See the world around you with a new and dynamic perspective.

Rooted in Stephen Aizenstat's 35 years of work with the greatest dream masters of the West, as well as respected traditional shamans and healers worldwide, *Dream Tending* is packed with revolutionary insights and practical methods that will help you to experience the powerful, mutually beneficial interaction of dreams and reality.

To order, please visit our online bookstore at:

www.springjournalandbooks.com

Spring Journal Books

(504) 524-5117

627 Ursulines Street, #7 New Orleans, LA 70116

New from
Spring Journal Books

(THE BOOK PUBLISHING IMPRINT OF SPRING: A JOURNAL OF ARCHETYPE AND CULTURE,
THE OLDEST JUNGIAN PSYCHOLOGY JOURNAL IN THE WORLD)

VINE DELORIA, JR., (1933-2005) was born and raised in South Dakota, the son and grandson of Dakota Sioux Indian leaders. In 1965, he began serving as the Executive Director of the National Congress of American Indians, and worked tirelessly to mobilize Indian people toward effective participation in the American political process. A noted scholar of American Indian legal, political, and religious studies, he is the author of numerous works, including the 1969 bestseller *Custer Died for Your Sins: An Indian Manifesto, God is Red* (1973), and *The Metaphysics of Modern Existence* (1979).

C.G. Jung and the Sioux Traditions
Dreams, Visions, Nature and the Primitive

AUTHOR: **Vine Deloria, Jr.**
EDITED BY: **Philip J. Deloria & Jerome S. Bernstein**

ISBN 978-1-882670-61-1 | 292 pgs | Price $25.95

In the winter of 1924-25 while visiting the U.S., C.G. Jung visited the Taos Pueblo in New Mexico where he spent several hours with Ochwiay Biano, Mountain Lake, an elder at the Pueblo. This was a seminal encounter in Jung's life. It impacted him psychologically, emotionally, and intellectually and had a sustained influence on his theories and understanding of psyche.

Dakota Sioux intellectual and political leader, Vine Deloria, Jr., began a close study of the writings of C.G. Jung over two decades ago, but had long been struck by certain affinities and disjunctures between Jungian and Sioux Indian thought. This book, the result of Deloria's investigation of these affinities, is written as a measured comparison between the psychology of C.G. Jung and the philosophical and cultural traditions of his own Sioux people. Moving between Jung's writings and Sioux tradition, Deloria constructs a fascinating dialogue between the two systems that touches on cosmology, the family, relations with animals, visions, voices, and individuation. He does not shy away from addressing the differences between the two and the colonial mindset that characterized Jung's own cultural legacy. In this sense, Deloria offers a direct "speaking back" from the cultural position that Jung so often characterized as "primitive" in his writings.

To order, please visit our online bookstore at:
www.springjournalandbooks.com

Spring Journal Books
(504) 524-5117
627 Ursulines Street, #7 New Orleans, LA 70116

New from
Spring Journal Books

(THE BOOK PUBLISHING IMPRINT OF SPRING: A JOURNAL OF ARCHETYPE AND CULTURE, THE OLDEST JUNGIAN PSYCHOLOGY JOURNAL IN THE WORLD)

Intimacy: Venturing the Uncertainties of the Heart
Jungian Odyssey Series 1, 2008

EDITORS: **Isabelle Meier, Stacy Wirth & John Hill**
PREFACE: **Nancy Cater**
FOREWORD: **Murray Stein**

ISBN 978-1-882670-84-0 | 225 pgs | Price $24.95

This collection of essays is the first publication to ensue from the Jungian Odyssey, which began in 2006 and developed into an annual conference and retreat in Switzerland. The authors are Jungian training analysts and faculty members at ISAPZURICH, joined by guest scholars, all of whom lectured at the Jungian Odyssey 2008.

Addressing a broad audience and adopting a variety of approaches, the authors link intimacy to love and hate, home and homesickness, belonging and yearning to belong, Eros and transcendence, the known and unknown—and even to the encounter with the divine. Rather than seeking definitive answers or cures, the authors circumambulate the many guises of the heart and ways in which intimacy and uncertainty enter our lives.

Authors include: Nóirín Ní Riain, Paul Brutsche, John Hill, Raffaella Colombo, Kathrin Asper, Ursula Wirtz, Mario Jacoby, Allan Guggenbühl, Urs Mehlin, Deborah Egger-Biniores, Murray Stein, Thomas Kapacinskas, Dariane Pictet, and Bernard Sartorius.

The Jungian Odyssey, open to the general public, is offered each year by the International School of Analytical Psychology Zurich (ISAPZURICH). ISAP was founded in 2004 by the Association of Graduate Analytical Psychologists (AGAP) for the purpose of conducting post-graduate Jungian training. AGAP itself, domiciled in Zurich, was founded in 1954 by Mary Briner, a graduate of the C.G. Jung Institute Zurich. AGAP is a founding member and the largest member society of the International Association for Analytical Psychology (IAAP).

ISAPZURICH
www.jungianodyssey.ch

To order, please visit our online bookstore at:
www.springjournalandbooks.com

Spring Journal Books
(504) 524-5117
627 Ursulines Street, #7 New Orleans, LA 70116